T0215290

Online Activism in Latin America

"Chacón's volume on the Internet as a tool for community building and political advocacy in Latin American social movements will be a welcome contribution to a burgeoning interdisciplinary field. This collection builds on media communications' and literary studies' work on the aesthetic and consumer implications of the Internet to uncover the geopolitical, economic, environmental, and cultural potential of new electronic media for participatory, citizen-based activism. From music to migration, favelas to bloggers, border activism to performative memory work, these scholars capture the power of digital citizenship."
— *Marcy Schwartz, Rutgers University*

Online Activism in Latin America examines the innovative ways in which Latin American citizens, and Latin@s in the U.S., use the Internet to advocate for causes that they consider just. The contributions to the volume analyze citizen-launched websites, interactive platforms, postings, and group initiatives that support a wide variety of causes, ranging from human rights to disability issues, indigenous groups' struggles, environmental protection, art, poetry and activism, migrancy, and citizen participation in electoral and political processes. This collection bears witness to the early stages of a very unique and groundbreaking form of civil activism culture now growing in Latin America.

Hilda Chacón is Professor of Spanish and Latin American Literatures and Cultures, Nazareth College, USA.

Routledge Studies in New Media and Cyberculture

For a full list of titles in this series, please visit www.routledge.com.

Online Activism in Latin America

Edited by Hilda Chacón

Routledge
Taylor & Francis Group

NEW YORK AND LONDON

First published 2019
by Routledge
52 Vanderbilt Avenue, New York, NY 10017

and by Routledge
2 Park Square, Milton Park, Abingdon, Oxon OX14 4RN

First issued in paperback 2020

Routledge is an imprint of the Taylor & Francis Group, an informa business

Library of Congress Cataloging-in-Publication Data
CIP data has been applied for.

ISBN 13: 978-0-367-58827-4 (pbk)
ISBN 13: 978-1-138-70517-3 (hbk)

Typeset in Sabon
by codeMantra

A Nadia, Jeremy y Elianita.
A Pedro, siempre.

Contents

Introduction

Hilda Chacón

> The modern world is this essential power of connection, and it implies
> the fact that it is clearly necessary for the individual to enter into these
> relations of external existence...
>
> Hegel
> *Hegel's Lectures on the History of Philosophy*, vol. 3 (169)

Online Activism in Latin America is a collection of sixteen chapters
written by scholars who have conducted cutting-edge research in the
fields of Internet Studies, social movements, and cultural studies—based
in the U.S., the United Kingdom, and Latin America. The contributors
were carefully selected due to the scope and impact of their scholarship.
The volume also includes the analysis of similar initiatives undertaken
by Latin@s in the U.S.

This publication constitutes the first book for English-speaking audiences about online activism in Latin America and it has a four-part
goal. First, it aims to contribute to the vibrant and emerging field of
Latin American cybercultural studies, which was pioneered by Claire
Taylor, Thea Pitman, Luis Correa-Díaz, and Scott Weintraub, among
others, for English readers.[1] Second, this publication seeks to add to
the existing debates on mass *media* culture generated in Latin America
(Jesús Martín-Barbero, Ariel Dorfman, Armand Mattelart). Third, it
contributes to the ongoing discussions on modernity *vis-à-vis* the impact
of the globalization process in Latin America, as undertaken by Walter
Mignolo, Néstor García-Canclini, Raquel Olea, Nelly Richard, Mabel
Moraña, Herman Herlinghaus, Enrique Dussel, John Beverley, Francine
Masiello, and Mary Louise Pratt, to mention a few scholars. Finally, the
volume endeavors to contribute to the incipient and lively scholarship
on consumer culture studies of Latin America, a field led by Steven B.
Bunker and Sergio Delgado.

The book also explores specific debates that have not yet been addressed by critics in the context of citizen-driven online advocacy and
focuses on a few key inquiries: (1) the question of how art, technology, and advocacy are intimately intertwined in the culture of online

production and consumption in Latin America (as well as in the U.S.), (2) the question of how citizens reappropriate the discursive forms of the Internet to advocate for what they consider just, and (3) the question of which practices citizens have come to employ in order to define themselves in the process of creating new communities and forms of civilian activism—hence, constructing an "elsewhere" (Berry et al.) as new senses of belonging (Morley) emerge beyond national, governmental, geographical, and linguistic boundaries. In some of the case studies analyzed here, the outcomes are quite remarkable. In others, citizens' advocacy is still a work in progress. What is transparent in all of the cases examined in this volume is that cyberspace constitutes an innovative *medium* with an endless array of possibilities to access massive audiences almost instantaneously.

Without a doubt, at the core of this project lies a basic concern regarding the interdependence of economic development and technology with a focus on citizens' access to *media*. The volume brings to the forefront discussions on citizen-lead activism online in the context of a consolidated network of multinational forms of production (and consumption) that seems to prevail worldwide—a new culture trend that includes the production and consumption of cultural goods as well. By no means does this publication attempt to exhaust the discussion on the aforementioned fields. Nevertheless, what is indeed innovative about this volume is the exploration undertaken from a new angle: citizens-in-action advocacy in Latin America and the U.S. in cyberspace—the online activism or cyberactivism, as the contributors in the volume elaborate in their chapters. What we do seek here is to deepen a cross-disciplinary dialogue that may help scholars and citizens to better understand the complexities and possibilities of this *medium* that contains seemingly infinite ways to create meaning and sense.

I consider the Internet to be *the medium* that is the hallmark of the culture of the global era in which we live, as I have elaborated in other publications,[2] and I would argue that cyberspace is the exemplary *locus par excellence* of the cultural logic of late capitalism (Jameson). Hence, the massive use of the Internet for instantaneous communications is intimately connected to the latest developments and advances of the most sophisticated stage of capitalism that human kind has ever known: multinational entrepreneurship, or what I also refer to as the global era.[3] Consequently, at the base of this incredibly large-scale and (very nearly) instant communication *medium* that we employ today lies an intimate connection to, and an undeniable dependence on, the logic of the stock market and its electronic financial transactions; this is a paradox that accompanies (or haunts) the present collection of chapters. Nevertheless, in spite of the admitted paradox, all of the chapters in this volume attest to a new citizen-led era of advocacy online, an unstoppable new wave of political associations that often challenge the effects of globalization in peripheral societies, such as those in Latin America and within the Latin@ community in the U.S. (which is still a marginal group). As this publication shows, both of these opposite forces coexist in tension within the same dynamics and *medium*.

On Modernity and Its Culture

In one of his lectures in *Lectures on the History of Philosophy*, published in 1892, German philosopher Georg Wilhelm Friedrich Hegel elaborated on "the essential power of connection" that characterized the modern world in which he lived (169). In this lecture, Hegel highlights the need for citizens of his time to reach out to others in order to enter into what he identifies as the "relations of external existence" (169) that were at the core of modern societies; for Hegel, failure to establish such "essential power of connection" would impede full immersion in—and thus, proper understanding of—modernity. On the other hand, Karl Marx, another great thinker of modernity in the 19th century, stated that capitalism, in its continuous search for new markets, had the capacity to constantly transform itself into something new and distinct each time—in such a rapid fashion that it might seem that "all that is solid melts into air" (Manifesto). Marx continues to elaborate on his idea of capitalism's ability to expand and transform, and to a point, he foresees what would eventually become the greater planetary trend of our day: "The need for a constantly expanding market for its products... over the entire surface of the globe. It must nestle everywhere, settle everywhere, establish connections everywhere" (Manifesto). The modern-day cyber-navigator of the global era can confirm Hegel's and Marx's intuitions concerning the interdependence of modernity and capitalism as very tangible realities that acquire corporeality in concrete practices of production and consumption of cultural goods online.

In spite of their visionary predictions, none of the great thinkers of modernity could have imagined the magnitude that such an "essential power of connection" (Hegel) and its need to "establish connections everywhere" (Marx) would attain at the end of the 20th century and the beginning of the 21st century. We are without a doubt witnessing the greatest paradigm shift that humanity has ever observed in the field of communications and global interconnectedness.

The increase in financial transactions in cyberspace and the massive use of the Internet that peaked in the last decade of the 20th century attest to unthought-of new forms of communication that, in turn, have deeply impacted all aspects of our everyday life. The Internet has altered our daily behavior, our attention span, our learning patterns, our expectations when interacting with others, as well as our consumption and production habits; furthermore, cyberspace has made it possible for regular citizens to become producers of meaning and instantaneous communicators who can reach massive audiences without the mediation of any form of censorship—this premise is at the center of this volume. All of these transformations are evidence of a brand-new culture that is capable of reaching beyond geographic, linguistic, national, and cultural barriers among countries and continents. Such a wide-reaching cultural shift has allowed the creation of new niches and dynamics that have, in turn, made possible new forms of interactions among human beings— all of which have no comparable precedent in the history of humanity.

For those of us who come from the Gutenberg culture of books and print media, who remember large tabletop radios with huge vacuum tubes, and who recall when the first televisions arrived—among other "antique" memories, as perceived by our students—the instantaneous, worldwide communication options facilitated by the Internet are certainly among the most amazing phenomena in the "modern world's essential power of connection" (Hegel).

In today's cyber-world, citizens from different identities, languages, localities, affinities, nationalities, and diverse ethnic, gender, and cultural backgrounds depend almost entirely on web-supported devices such as mobile phones, GPS, computer-based interactive platforms, and social media,[4] to name just a few possibilities presently available to almost anyone in the Western world. It is through all of these devices that today's citizens around the world exercise the "essential power of connection" (Hegel) and make a reality of the need of "establishing connections everywhere" (Marx) that the 19th-century philosophers on modernity identified as hallmarks of modern societies.

It is also apparent to us cyber-navigators that the Internet testifies to the predominance of the visual (Jameson 6, 13, 37, 38) and the aural (Jameson 38) as key identifiable features that evolve and mutate continuously, like capitalism itself. Furthermore, as the chapters in this volume attest, there is much more to the Internet than what the foremost theoreticians on Latin American modernity predicted as recently as the 1990s; I refer to Néstor García-Canclini, Enrique Dussel, John Beverley, and Fredric Jameson. Indeed, the common practices (*usos y costumbres*) of the Internet have evolved beyond the mere predominance of the visual and the aural (Jameson) to give way to extremely complex forms of connecting (Hegel, Marx) with others, as well as to vastly sophisticated ways of creating meaning and a sense of community/ies woven together from the threads of widely diverse identities worldwide—this time, online.

Instantaneous Connectedness

Cyberspace has also transformed the way in which societies and individuals in the new millennium have come to define themselves. Today, almost anyone can have easy access to a mobile phone connected to a

Wi-Fi source, and in doing so, the cyber-navigators can be linked to the rest of the world *ipso facto*. As British theorist David Morley affirms, "the networks of electronic communication in which we live are transforming our senses of locality and community" (3). In Morley's view, "new modalities of belonging... are emerging around us" (3). The chapters in *Online Activism in Latin America* underscore the establishment of new communities beyond the geographical location of cyber-navigators, adding different levels of intricacy to the multifarious concept of being Latin American and/or Latin@—complexities that were unimaginable before "the advent of the Internet" (Penix-Tadsen). On the other hand, and as the chapters in this volume reveal, it is also undeniable that the notion of being Latin American and/or Latin@ resiliently prevails (see Taylor's concept of "resistant practice" in *Place and Politics in Latin American Digital Culture*, 170–176). Nevertheless, in my view, those markers of national and regional identity are deeply impacted by countless other forms of belonging that are facilitated by the Internet worldwide in a process that is at times contradictory and vague.

As Taylor and Pitman argue, with reference to Latin(o) American artists:

> the vibrant online cultural practice... play[s] with the existing tools of digital technologies in an ambivalent fashion, at times playing along with the accepted use of such tools, and at others, reformulating them in tactical and partially resistant ways in the interstices of the (global, capitalist) system.
>
> (*Latin American Identity* 200)

Online Activism in Latin America is devoted to analyzing examples of cyberspace-based advocacy that unfold precisely in the interstices of the current multinational capitalist infrastructure *per* the initiative of regular citizens who have perceived the Internet to be a new *medium* through which to exercise civil democracy in a way that was not previously possible. As readers will confirm, the case studies analyzed here "interpellate (often critically) preexisting discourses of the region and beyond" (Taylor and Pitman, *Latin American Identity* 198).

As *Online Activism in Latin America* reveals, the Internet has also given us a different sense of our own temporality by subjecting us to a continuous, nonstop rewriting/restating/redoing/self-transforming-by-interacting-with-others *medium* whose compelling contents may very well disappear overnight—"melting into thin air" (Marx), as it may happen as well with electronic transactions in the stock market. Because of the Internet and its associated cultural practices, the human brain now functions very differently than before. What Jameson calls "new forms of practice and social and mental habits" (xiv), I argue, have become concrete actual practices in the generalized uses of cyberspace by virtually any person with a mobile phone and a service provider.

My interest in cyberspace developed out of my scholarly research on the impact of communications in Latin America in the context of the implementation of globalization. As numerous researchers have established thoroughly (Martín-Barbero, García-Canclini, Dussel), societies in the margins of the main economic trend centers have been able to reappropriate the language and the communication means of those centers of power, which has been the case in Latin America. Right now, that process of reappropriation manifests itself through imaginative ways of using cyberspace to contest the implications and repercussions of expansion *vis-à-vis* globalization; by reappropriating the languages of the Internet, citizens have also been able to expose the underside of "blood, torture, death, and terror" that Jameson recognizes as part of the multinational capitalist advance (5).

From the private space of our homes, citizens of the global era can advocate in effective ways for the causes that they consider just. Consequently, as Morley affirms, the traditional barriers between the private and the public have become blurry, and private matters have become public issues through social media. In turn, public causes enter into the intimacy of private homes with the possibility of becoming part of citizens' intimate lives and senses of communities. As Morley asserts, "Now the home is less and less a self-enclosed space, and more and more [....] a 'phantasmagoric' place—as electronic means of communication allow the radical intrusion of 'the realm of the far' into the 'realm of the near'" (3). Ergo, "the 'domestication of elsewhere'" (3) is a process in which the global becomes familiar (3).

The contributions to *Online Activism in Latin America* analyze citizen-launched websites, interactive platforms, postings, and group initiatives that advocate for diverse causes, ranging from human rights to disability issues, indigenous groups' struggles, environmental protection, art, poetry and activism, migrancy, and citizen participation in electoral and political processes. Some seek to formulate, in a new language, the enduring demand for the reappearance of the disappeared—whether posted in social media, live stream, online video games, or even in applications for cellular phones. Although the wide-ranging analysis confirms the fact that even the "postmodern, or the cultural logic" of our era is a manifestation of a dominant culture imposed and led by the U.S. (Jameson 4), regular citizens with access to the Internet now have the possibility of making their voices and causes heard—including the questioning of U.S. policies toward Latin America in a global context. Consequently, the present book explores the relation between activism and art, authorship and authority, globalization and citizenship, the global expansion of capital and local violence, and the private and the public; it also reveals alternative forms of civil authority and authorship that are now accessible in cyberspace.

Premises

This volume departs from the premise that cyberspace is the *locus par excellence* where citizens can directly access public audiences without passing through the screening of media owners, as occurred in the past. This publication follows Jameson's early notion of culture as commodity (x). However, the readers will indeed detect significant divergences from Jameson's premises when analyzing online activism initiatives in Latin America in this volume. For example, it is evident that, through the Internet, citizens in/from Latin America practice effective activism (*telos*) to contest the societal impacts of the implementation of "transnational business" (Jameson, xix); therefore, regular citizens prove to be empowered to interrogate global business' concomitant consequences. Therefore, Jameson's prediction regarding "the apocalyptic suddenly turn[ing] into the decorative" (xvii) and his pessimistic assertion that our era would lack of any discussion of agency (xviii) are both proven deficient by the collection of chapters gathered here.[5]

The present study also argues that, in spite of the loss of connection with the past that postmodernist theorists point out, the "experiential breaks" (Jameson xiii) that consumers of culture in the global era experience, on the contrary, allow citizens to create a *different* sense of historicity, although perhaps a historicity that is nonlinear and is connected to the historical past in fragmentary ways, with an inapprehensible mobile pattern within a rather global sense of time and space. We can, at the present moment, identify advocating narratives online that consistently and irreverently disarticulate, dislocate, decenter, and interrogate the consequences of the expansion of multinational business enterprises without necessarily missing a sense of historicity. Overall, such displacements, disarticulations, and decenterings all highlight a new sense of relating to historicity—a new cultural trend that is perhaps able to rescue unknown voices and integrate them into a mosaic of mainly unstable (but collective) memories, a choir that lives for as long as other humans may reach out to them in cyberspace. Admittedly, this varied mosaic of voices on the Internet is certainly fragmented, itinerant, but its presence and impact are undeniable. We might be in the presence of a cultural paradigm shift that makes us realize that the ephemeral is the hallmark of historicity in the global era; however, this does not necessarily make that sense of historicity oblivious to a sense of belonging to a historical memory. The grand narratives of social change could be at present obsolete, but as these chapters demonstrate, the "small voices of History" (Ranajit Guha) can start speaking in an electronic, worldwide conglomerate of towers of Babel in quite effective manners.

The new cultural shift allows the emergence of particular modalities of recalling the past, and new forms of belonging (Morley) emerge in the present, reaching far away from the place of enunciation/production of meaning. To a point, the chapters collected in this book prove that the "fun... prodigious exhilaration" (Jameson x), the "delirium" (Jameson xii) and "euphoria" (Jameson xii) of the culture of our time, in spite of its "uncertainty" (Jameson xi)—and volatility, I would add—is still capable of producing ruptures in the very system that created the Internet, in order to give voice to the voiceless and give presence to the systematically invisible ones. This premise is at the very core of the present publication.

We should not lose sight of the fact that the making of the Internet had an instantaneous and profound impact on the stock market.[6] As soon as it was created, brokers immediately adopted the new *medium* that was able to expedite and complete financial transactions from one bank to another located across the planet in seconds, eliminating the need for the physical movement of currency, or goods in general, from overseas. This shift took place in the 1990s in the context of an emergent financial-based, international economy—known as neoliberal initiatives or globalization. In this context, the Internet first facilitated quick communications among bank officers across the planet. Soon enough, it diffused to use by the general public. As this publication strives to demonstrate, citizens' access to Internet-based technologies and platforms (mobile phones, tablets, laptops, satellite-driven maps, etc.) has opened new avenues, secondary roads, and super-fast highways (metaphorically speaking) for citizens to question "the darker side of modernity" (Mignolo).[7]

The cases analyzed in this publication present one or more of the following characteristics: (1) the initiative emerged in response to specific political events or particular economic projects, (2) the website has brought to the forefront causes launched by traditionally marginalized groups, (3) the web-based project impacted (and/or continues to impact) public opinion both locally and internationally, (4) the initiative has forced the government and/or private companies to embrace citizens' claims and halt their projects, and (5) the initiative has demonstrated a sustained presence in cyberspace for a period of time.

In sum, *Online Activism in Latin America* considers citizen-led uses of cyberspace across Latin America and by Latin@s in the U.S., who seek public acknowledgement and validation of their cause. In such new cultural practices, everyday citizens reassert their right to dissent. All the cases analyzed here use the Internet to bring to the attention of worldwide audiences the marginal experiences that are also part of the global project, including failed revolution projects.

The Emergence of this Project

To a certain degree, this project is a result of a lifetime of interest on my part in mass communications in Latin America, an interest that began in my native country, during my years as a college student at the University of Costa Rica. At the time, Central America was immersed in a convoluted political environment that impacted all neighboring countries, including mine. Guatemala, El Salvador, Honduras, and Nicaragua were ruled by military governments whose armies had occupied university campuses in violation of constitutional principles and academic freedom. Nicaraguans were involved in the Sandinista armed struggle to put an end to the Somozas' 30-year dictatorship in their country, while Salvadorans confronted in arms "the 14" coffee-producing families' merciless ruling of their country. Costa Rica, due to its relative political and economic stability, was the land of asylum for political refugees from the area; therefore, students and intellectuals who had been displaced by the political turmoil in their countries ended up residing in Costa Rica at different times.

Like most of the college students of my time, I was part of different solidarity groups with the people of Nicaragua, Guatemala, El Salvador, and Honduras—and we were also connected to homologous student-led organizations from Chile, Argentina, and Uruguay. All of these Latin American countries, and their student-led movements, demanded the return of democracy, the achievement of social justice, and the reappearance of the disappeared (*los desaparecidos*), who were by and large college students like ourselves. We demonstrated against dictatorships and publically rejected all forms of violence; we advocated for peace and solidarity with students and people in the Latin American countries that were enduring violations of basic human rights.

Thus, at the forefront of the student-led movement was the concern about access to, and communication with, the people in neighboring countries. The main objective was to construct a sense of belonging to a struggling international community and, in doing so, to support the internal campaigns for human rights in those countries. Soon enough, student-led movements identified the key role of communications across nations and people in eventually generating that sense of community that students were seeking to create. Consequently, I decided to pursue a degree in journalism and mass media studies in the midst of a complex war environment that involved my home country as well.[8]

I voraciously read a number of intellectuals who reflected on the impact of mass media on any eventual social change and the advancement of democracy in Latin America—a region where the escalating presence of military governments went hand in hand with the increasing installation of transnational companies (Gonzalez 308). Marshall McLuhan's notion of "the medium is the message," presented in his famous treatises *Understanding Media: The Extension of Man* (1964) and the subsequent *The Medium is The Message* (1967), generated an immediate response in the Latin American context.[9] A significant number of Latin American thinkers produced an impressive body of scholarship on the subject, conceived with a local lens. I specifically recall seminal works by Ariel Dorfman, Armand Mattelart, and Jesús Martín-Barbero, which captivated our interest as young thinkers in college.[10]

In response to these debates on mass communications and democracy, and in the middle of generalized movements for peace and democracy in the region, local initiatives related to communication emerged in different Latin American countries at the community level. Overall, these were timid initiatives that sought peace, justice, and the inclusion of marginal groups in the national debates on the future of the nation (mainly with respect to women, indigenous groups, and Afro-descendants). The leading idea behind these projects was the notion of "alternative communication" ("comunicación alternativa" or "comunicación y educación popular") (Martín-Barbero, *Aventuras*), which called for the development of community-based TV and radio stations run by local citizens who were neighborhood leaders embedded in their communities and knowledgeable about their own problems. These community-based communication projects had a wholehearted interest in reaching out to the most remote and forgotten areas of Latin America, in order to include their voices and concerns in the "unfinished project of modernity" (Habermas).[11] Nevertheless, these community-based initiatives struggled to survive financially and were overall technologically weak; consequently, they were unable to compete with the mainstream mass media infrastructure that promptly boycotted such divergent initiatives.[12] Without a doubt, private media owners (of newspapers, radio, and TV stations) in Latin America at the time screened and limited citizens' participation in public *fora* and boycotted most civilian attempts to question national politics and/or current economic trends. Indeed, the access of massive audiences to print and electronic media was practically out of reach, especially for those who were not part of the governing elites.

That said, the emergence of the Internet as a mass *medium* in the 1990s inaugurated a new era in the history of mass communication, while it also unlocked a unique opportunity for citizens' participation to a degree unthinkable in previous decades in Latin America.

Modernity in Latin America

We can easily confirm that the attainment of modernity has been an obsession throughout Latin America's history and that this recurrent debate has been tangible in the region's cultural productions in *genres* such as journalism, essays, painting, political cartoons, art, and literature, at least since the early 19th-century independence movements. In the 20th century, this debate permeated to regional theater and cinematic productions, as well. Latin American countries have shaped their cultural identities with respect to a persistent tension between the social changes brought by modernity-oriented agendas (led by local elites with strong ties to Europe first and to the U.S. after) and the colonial-inherited traditions that marginalized women, indigenous, Afro-descendants, and *mestizo* groups. The unequal levels of modernity reached by Latin America have been defined as "peripheral" (Sarlo), Eurocentric (Mignolo, *The Darker*; Dussel), "modernidad en crisis" (Herlinghaus, Moraña), or un "espejo trizado" [a broken mirror] (Brunner).[13] Argentine scholar Walter Mignolo defines modernity in Latin America as "a complex narrative" that originated in Europe; "a narrative that builds Western civilization by celebrating its achievements while hiding at the same time its darker side, 'coloniality'" (*The Darker*, 2–3). The colonial experience bequeathed a legacy of racism associated with a class structure that still prevails in the social tissue of today's Latin America, while it yet coexists with the region's full immersion in the global project. Still, indigenous groups and Afro-descendants in Latin America continue to be the poorest among the poor, which speaks clearly to the prevailing impact of the colonial legacy.

It is important to highlight the difficulties in mass communications that the Spanish-American colonies had to face when the independence movements began in the early 19th century. The extension of their territories was vast and there were significant geographical obstacles, which made it extremely difficult for the leaders to agree on a given place and time to strategize about the independence war fronts—in comparison to what occurred in the 13 British colonies in the northern hemisphere.[14] Such a unique situation gave birth to independence movements that were notably disperse and, thus, scattered in terms of their political agendas. Due to these conditions of geographical and strategic isolation, what could be identified at the time as "mass communication" manifested itself in the production of letters and newspapers; thus, the printing press became a crucial means for the success of the independence movements all over Latin America (Anderson 204). When independence was finally attained, the link between nationhood and mass communication proved to be a fundamental pillar for the implementation of modernity in the new nations, a project that went ahead in spite of the prevailing deep inequalities and ethnic and class divisions among their citizenry (Chacón, *Poética*).

On the unequal and contradictory implementation of modernity in Latin America, U.S.-based scholar Mary Louise Pratt affirms that the idea of Latin America as a left-behind or underdeveloped region (*atraso*) with respect to the developed northern hemisphere (*adelanto*) is not necessarily accurate. Furthermore, she qualifies this assumption as "fictional" (*La modernidad* 832). Pratt writes, "este *telos* de atraso-adelanto se ha revelado como una ficción, dejando ver la relación entre el mundo atrasado y el mundo adelantado como una relación estructural de subordinación que, lejos de ser eliminada por el sistema, lo constituye" (*La modernidad* 832).[15] Therefore, in a sense, the very assumption of modernity as a straight-line process led by the northern hemisphere, as a path that the southern hemisphere will eventually reach, is not essentially correct. On the contrary, this assumption only demonstrates a biased, subalternizing premise about the south that is issued from the centers of power—usually located in the north.

Brazilian thinker Silviano Santiago states that Latin America's alleged being-behind-progress-and-modernity position, besides being inaccurate, gives Latin American peripheral societies a sort of privileged positionality: that of functioning like a mirror capable of reflecting back to the center those images of itself that the center does not see or does not want to acknowledge (cited in Pratt, *La modernidad* 833). I believe that the chapters included in this edited volume attest to Santiago's and Pratt's respective arguments.[16]

By the beginning of the 20th century, the now-independent countries of Latin America were still considerably weakened by post-independence wars, territorial invasions (led by the U.S. and Europe), internal wars, and the subsequent crash of local economies. Nevertheless, it would be erroneous to consider this abatement to be a generalized situation throughout all of Latin America, which would impede the region from reaching significant progress. The advance of technology in South America was a continuously ongoing process that went hand in hand with technologies developed and implemented in England and the U.S.— in fact, some of these avant-garde technologies were developed in Latin America. With respect to the topic that guides this publication, it would be fair to point out that technological advances, in terms of mass media, have never been a foreign subject in Latin America: let's keep in mind that the first printing press in the Americas arrived in Mexico as early as the 16th century.[17] The printing press, which in the beginning was exclusively in the hands of the Catholic Church, was used for instructing (indoctrinating) Catholicism during the colonization process of the Spanish territories in the Americas, and then its access was extended to the ownership of private hands—media owners who were mainly leaders of the independence movements.[18] It was precisely this ownership shift in the context of an emergent capitalism in the 19th century that made possible the independence processes in Latin America (Anderson 26–65).

Electronic Media in Latin America

Similar to what occurred with the printing press, the introduction and development of electronic media in Latin America occurred simultaneously to its implementation in Europe and North America. The first transmission using radio waves took place in the maritime waters of England in 1899, undertaken by Italian inventor Guglielmo Marconi.[19] However, it was not until 1902 that Marconi produced the first transatlantic radio message in Nova Scotia, Canada. A year later, Marconi facilitated the broadcasting of the first radio transmission to originate in the U.S. (from Massachusetts) when President Theodore Roosevelt sent a greeting to King Eduard VII in the United Kingdom.[20] In 1920, the United Kingdom broadcast the first entertainment radio program (an opera program), which marked the beginning of entertainment broadcasting in that country in 1922.[21]

The radio was introduced in Latin America in the early 1920s in a moment that coincided with what was occurring in the northern hemisphere.[22] On the other side of the Atlantic, Radio Argentina began regularly scheduled transmissions from the Teatro Coliseo in Buenos Aires on August 27, 1920.[23] The role of the radio in integrating masses of individuals, who were geographically dispersed and isolated from urban centers in Latin America, was crucial. In fact, some young Latin American writers even turned their attention to the new *medium* of radio and got enthusiastic about participating in its innovative ways of conveying and producing meaning for massive audiences, as was the case of Cuban writer Alejo Carpentier (Bethell 519). In my view, that moment marked the beginning of the culture of consumption of electronic media products in Latin America. As Bethell argues,

> The introduction of radio in the 1920 was a turning point in the cultural history of Latin America. It would be a mistake, however, to think that Latin America had no communication media before the advent of radio broadcasting. Argentina for example where 345 newspapers where published in 1885, had a large urban audience for popular weekly magazines like *Consejero del hogar* (1903), *Mundo argentino* (1911) and *Atlántida* (1918). Other Latin American countries had well-developed domestic newspapers and magazines (as well as, in some cases, nascent film industries) by the turn of the century.
>
> (Bethell 519)

Therefore, considering Latin America as a region that had been left behind in media-related technology and electronic media developments would be inaccurate. The concomitant interest in, and research on, electronic developments for mass communication definitely marked Latin American scientists. The color TV, for example, was invented by Mexican engineer Guillermo González Camarena in the 1940s as a product of his own research project that started in the mid-1930s in Mexico City, to mention one of the diverse technological discoveries that originated in Latin America.[24] Furthermore, several of Latin America's advancements in scientific research and technology development have been acknowledged by the prestigious scientific journal *Nature*, for example.[25]

Description of Chapters

Part I. Art and Activism in Cyberspace comprises chapters (1) "A Theater of Displacement: Staging Activism, Poetry, and Migration through a Transborder Immigrant Tool" by Sergio Delgado Moya, (2) "Decolonizing Youth Culture: Guatemalan Hip Hop Dissidents in Cyberspace" by Esteban Loustaunau, (3) "*Narcocorridos* and Internet: Demonopolizing Mexico's Narco History in Cyberspace" by Juan Carlos Ramírez-Pimienta, and (4) "Belén Gache's Aleatory Politics: *Radikal Karaoke* and (Robo)Poetics Hacking Politics" by Scott Weintraub.

Delgado Moya's chapter focuses on the performative and the theatrical operations at work in the act of activism, conceived both in its political and its aesthetic dimensions. He analyzes the conceptual framing and the functionality of the Transborder Immigrant Tool (TBT), a cellular phone application created by the members of the artist/activist collective known as the Electronic Disturbance Theater. This cell phone app was designed for use by undocumented migrants crossing the U.S.-Mexican border, with the intention of helping them find water, refuge, and other sites of sustenance. As an act of activism and as poetic device, the TBT works as a form of contestation. It is a response and a retort to reductive, resurgent ways of thinking about the migrant experience.

Loustaunau's critique examines the digital production and broadcasting of hip hop music by marginalized adolescents in Guatemala as a form of contestatory activism. These are youngsters that feel excluded from the dynamics of late capitalism and who endure discrimination because of their age, class, and mixed ethnicity in a globalized Guatemala. They self-organize in horizontal structures to dance, sing, and produce hip hop music that brings to the forefront their pride in their ethnic identity as young "Mayans," and in doing so, they challenge the prevailing racism that is a persistent colonial legacy.

Ramírez-Pimienta's work analyzes the contestatory facets of *narcocorrido* music (drug trafficking ballads) in Mexican border towns and cities. *Narcocorridos* are a citizen-produced cultural expression that challenge the official narratives on what actually occurs in the borderlands of Mexico post-NAFTA—or, Mexico immersed in global economic dynamics. The production of these *canciones*, their massive reproduction, their collective singing in gathering places, and the massive uploading and downloading of *narcocorrido* videos on the Internet all attest to forms of citizen-based activism that question the Mexican government's ambivalent policies toward drug trafficking and exposes its lack of interest in protecting Mexican citizens. *Narcocorridos* have been banned by the government and media owners from being broadcast in the public realm, since, in their view, this cultural expression encourages drug trafficking-related (illicit) activities in these areas. However, as Ramírez-Pimienta demonstrates, within a very complex dynamic, citizens acknowledge certain political agency in the deviant behavior of drug traffickers, who represent the possibility of successful dissention from state-driven corruption.

Weintraub's chapter analyzes the interactive work *Radikal karaoke* by Argentine-Spanish digital artist, Belén Gache, in which the artist makes use of an aleatory poetic procedure online to critique the creation and proliferation of linguistic clichés by political rhetoric. Gache trivializes political language by turning it into a karaoke setting in which the cyber-navigators can participate in, and become aware of, the silliness of such vacuous rhetoric.

Part II. Blogging as Online Activism includes chapters (5) "On Pirates and Tourists: Ambivalent Approaches to *El Blog del Narco*" by Emily Hind, (6) "Blogging and Disability Activism in Mexico: Katia D'Artigues's 'Mundo D'" by Beth Jörgensen, (7) "*Revolución.com?* Resemanticizing the Discourse of Revolution in Yoani Sánchez's *Generation Y Blog*" by Thea Pitman, and (8) "The Uses and Limits of Ethnic Humor and New Media in *¡Ask A Mexican!*" by Amber Workman.

Hind's chapter scrutinizes the controversial and contradictory aspects of a blog of unknown authorship, although highly visited by cyber-navigators—*El Blog del Narco*, produced somewhere in northern Mexico. On the one hand, the blog claims to convey the actual truth of what occurs in areas controlled by drug traffickers; the bloggers identify themselves as "pirates" of the truth, invoking (and somehow thereby redeeming) the illicit endeavor of those who invade rich foreign territories to steal booty—and in this case, the booty seems to be the truth—and while doing this, the blog displays repetitive, bleak images and videos of assassinations and decapitations that somehow invite viewers to be tourists of horror and violence.

Jörgensen's chapter analyzes the interactive power of blogging as a way of building community and advocating for the rights of persons with disabilities in contemporary Mexico. In spite of the country's leadership role in calling for the creation of the United Nations' Convention on the Rights of Persons with Disabilities, this section of the population continues to be a marginalized and largely invisible group, constructed as society's radical other. In this study of the blog "Mundo D" by the Mexico City journalist Katia D'Artigues, the realms of the personal, the ideological, and the political encounter each other in what becomes a public participative online forum to promote and achieve a deeper respect for human rights, human diversity, and inclusive citizenship.

Pitman's work examines the use of multiple discourses of revolution in the work of famous Cuban blogger Yoani Sánchez, whose reputation has transcended national frontiers and has even obtained a secure place in key international newspapers, such as *El País Online* (Spain), for her blog. Pitman starts by observing that specifically contestatory Internet-based practices, such as political blogging, are often referred to as "revolutionary," conflating the fact that new media is seen to "revolutionize" our means of communication with the political content of the blogs themselves. She argues, however, that the use of such an epithet is more problematic when it is applied to a contestatory blog written in the shadow of a consecrated "Revolution." Pitman goes on to examine the sustained focus on the discourse of "the Cuban Revolution" in Sánchez's blog—a rhetoric that Sánchez questions in her posts and interactions with cyber-navigators. Pitman's chapter ultimately questions whether Sánchez can truly escape the centripetal force of the centralized discourse of government and whether she can succeed in proposing an alternative discourse through her references to the blogging "revolution."

Workman's chapter analyzes another blogging case study in which satire and political incorrectness become the *modus operandi* of an interactive media initiative that aims to dispel stereotypes (it incorporates common places and insulting assumptions against the ethnicity of the blogger, strategies for which the blog has been both praised and criticized). Workman elaborates on the uses and limits of ethnic humor and new media as a means of seeking dialogue and a better understanding of cultural differences among U.S. mainstream culture and minority cultures. The blog strongly encourages cyber-navigators to interact, and it incorporates the use of social media and YouTube to do so; hence, the blog creates a dynamic of collective participation that nurtures its sustained criticism of U.S. mainstream culture. In this chapter, Workman analyzes the effectiveness and limitations of such blogging strategies against the blog's aims to promote diversity and respect.

Part III. Enduring Struggles, Now Online, consists of chapters (9) "Five Hundred Years of Struggle Enter Cyberspace. Neo-Zapatism and the (Old) New Insurgency" by Carolina Gaínza Cortés, (10) "*Voces Cubanas*: Cyberactivism, Civic Engagement and Cubanía in Contemporary Cuba" by Omar Granados, (11) "From Wounds to Healing: Transborder Testimonios Through Cyberspace Post-September 11, 2001" by Claire Joysmith, and (12) "Cyberspace as a Tool for Political and Social Awareness: The Killings of Juárez" by María R. Matz.

Gaínza Cortés's chapter analyzes a necessary case study in this volume about online activism in Latin America: the Mayan Zapatista uprising that began on January 1, 1994—the same date the North American Free Trade Agreement (NAFTA) that included Mexico, Canada, and the U.S. was enacted. The Mayan-Zapatista movement constituted the first struggle led by indigenous people from the Americas that transcended geographic, linguistic, and cultural frontiers to become an issue of global interest and solidarity. Furthermore, this was also the first time that a group of human beings (not totally integrated into the category of "citizens") claimed their right to be fully incorporated into Mexican citizenry and into the project of the nation in a virtual *medium*. Gaínza Cortés identifies this pioneering communicational strategy online as "Neo-Zapatismo": an innovative mass communication phenomenon in which the use of digital networks created a new avenue for advocacy both locally and globally, giving digital networks new meanings that were later on emulated by other contestatory social movements around the world.

Granados's work elaborates on cyberactivism and civic engagement in contemporary Cuba, where technology and access to the Internet are rigorously restricted by the government. As Granados's work proposes, the Internet has proven to be the *medium* that younger generations of Cubans have utilized in order to instantly voice their criticism and discontent with a revolution that they consider has failed them. Since early 2007, a significant network of young bloggers has emerged on the island and consolidated their role as dissenting Cuba-based cyberactivists, both internally and internationally. In response, the Cuban government labeled their activism as "ciber-guerra" (cyber-war) and declared this activity as illegal and as a threat to national security, punishable by jail time. In spite of the restrictions, the network of young cyberactivists seems to consolidate itself more strongly each time, in a role that Granados identifies as central to reinforce the cultural heterogeneity of contemporary Cuba and as the seed for new forms of imagining the Cuban civil society in the new millennium.

Joysmith's chapter analyzes the creation of a transnational, or what she calls a "transborder," collective memory online regarding the tragic events of 9/11 in New York City on both sides of the border between Mexico and the U.S. In her view, a sense of collective community was generated when citizens in both countries immediately turned to the Internet with the goal of instantly reconnecting with the survivors, in order to express and execute acts of solidarity and support, thereby constructing a transborder community that immediately created a polyphonic narrative of collective memory beyond languages and across geographical distances. This immediate reaction spawned a transnational cultural trend that captured Joysmith's attention and scholarly interest. As a result of her work and research, these reactions and narratives were collected as *testimonios* in two book publications that eventually gave rise to online updated versions that currently also include more recent reflections on the aftermath of 9/11 to the present moment.

Matz's chapter, in turn, analyzes the interactions of the local and the global in cyberactivism in Ciudad Juárez, Mexico, where citizens have self-organized to denounce online the ongoing systematic disappearance and femicide of hundreds of young women since 1993. Relatives of the disappeared women, mostly families from a working-class background, have found in cyberspace a way of making their cause known beyond geographical, linguistic, and national limits and have also gained the attention and support of human rights activists throughout the world. This support has challenged the indifference of the Mexican government to the disappearances and massive mutilation of female bodies found in mass graves by international human rights officers. As Matz proposes, cyberspace has helped these families create communities of support, and in doing so, citizens in different parts of the planet have intertwined the struggles of the local and the global.

Part IV. Cyberspace and New Citizenry Representations gathers chapters (13) "Digital *favelas*: New Visibilities and Self-Representation" by Tori Holmes, (14) "Online Activist Eco-Poetry: Techno-Cannibalism, Digital Indigeneity and Ecological Resistance in Brazil" by Eduardo Ledesma, (15) "'Yo soy:' Public Protest, Private Expression: Contestatory Uses of Social Media by Contemporary Mexican Youth" by Mary K. Long, and (16) "Interactive Projects from Colombia: Rethinking the Geopolitics of Territory" by Claire Taylor.

Holmes's contribution discusses the implications of greater access to the Internet by residents of Brazilian *favelas* (shantytowns) for the visibility of those urban areas and outlines ongoing representational challenges facing *favelas,* as well as some ways in which these challenges are being overcome. It provides an overview of key projects producing and circulating self-representational digital content about *favelas*, from the established to more recent, and presents data from research into blogging by residents of one Rio de Janeiro *favela*, arguing that the contestatory nature of such content lies in explicitly positioning *favelas* as part of the city, countering dominant discourses that have long posited the opposite. As the chapter shows, however, the growth and diversification of content about and from *favelas* on the Internet and elsewhere has not completely overturned entrenched hierarchies and inequalities in Brazil.

Ledesma's chapter analyzes the multiple and innovative aspects of grassroots cyberactivism focused on protecting the environment in Brazil, especially when it comes to preserving biodiversity in the Amazon River basin. The construction of the Belo Monte hydroelectric dam has brought together indigenous groups and local community members, as well as national and international environmental organizations, among other supporters, all of whom have criticized the construction of this project in cyberspace. Their activism has taken shape mainly in social media and blog formats. Ledesma's work concentrates on a very unique aspect of this project: the use of poetry as an active component of this particular initiative of cyberactivism, which Ledesma defines as "online activist eco-poetry." In the process of questioning the building of the hydroelectric dam, some indigenous poets are posting their work online, reflecting critically on ecological issues. In doing so, their poetry becomes a unique form of political mobilization that challenges the corporate and political structures responsible for environmental abuses.

Long's chapter analyzes the negotiations of the public and the private in the uses of social media by contemporary Mexican youth in the movement "Yo soy 132" (I am 132) that sprung up as a reaction to a controversial visit to the Universidad Iberoamericana campus by the then-presidential candidate Enrique Peña Nieto on May 12, 2012. The movement united university and college students from state-funded and private institutions and brought thousands of protesters to the streets. It also gained the sympathy and support of individuals and groups across Mexico and throughout the world from that moment up to the elections and throughout the following year. Students used YouTube, Twitter, Flickr, Facebook, websites, and other interactive online platforms to successfully organize public demonstrations and contest the power of official media and the electoral process per se, thus bringing their concerns about democracy and citizens' rights to the attention of national and international audiences.

Taylor's chapter analyzes three digital interactive works produced in the last decade by young Colombian e-artists: Juan Ospina González, Clemencia Echeverri, Bárbara Santos, Santiago Ortiz, Andrés Burbano, and Martha Patricia Niño. The artists propose alternative mappings to the cyber-navigators and, therefore, envision alternative ways of experiencing Colombia's territory. In doing so, the digital artists perpetuate a critical reflection on the country's contemporary sociopolitical situation.

Privacy and Security

At first glance, it might seem naïve to put forth an edited volume on *Online Activism in Latin America,* in light of contemporary developments that attest to the worldwide networks of government-driven espionage on citizens via cyberspace, revealed, for example, by the Edward Snowden scandal in the U.S. on May 2013[26]—especially because such events also exposed the associated existence of international espionage systems at the highest levels via the Internet.[27] Furthermore, the scope of such espionage networks extended into Latin America, as well.[28] Such revelations have advanced a global discussion on citizen privacy and cyberspace, a debate that is far from being resolved. Nevertheless, the Wikileaks scandal has eviscerated the assumption of privacy and free-of-vigilance *fora* that the Internet seemed to guarantee for most cyber-navigators. In fact, while Snowden's disclosures brought into the public eye an unthinkable reality regarding governmental uses of citizens' private information, it also revealed the connection between specific massive practices of online consumption and the creation of databases that still are susceptible to being divulged without the consumer's knowledge or consent. Thus, the link between online practices of consumption and the involuntary surrender of privacy was irremediably exposed, leaving behind, in my view, a generalized feeling that in spite of the abhorred abuse against civilians' right to privacy, today's Internet consumers tend to prefer the massive, instantaneous access to cyberspace over the preservation of their privacy. The scandal revealed that all users of mobile phones, computers (with access to Wi-Fi), GPS devices, social media (Facebook, Twitter, Instagram, Second Life, Flickr, Tumblr), and YouTube have inadvertently contributed to the creation of secret databases and unexpected vigilance mechanisms that have been created by our providing of private information when we buy items via the Internet, sign in support of causes, or "like" certain issues in social media. In fact, the Snowden scandal made it known that Google granted the NSA access to individual customer databases without notifying them.[29]

Far from justifying the subsequent trends of data mining, it is noteworthy to highlight that citizens around the world, although infuriated by US governmental intromissions exposed by Snowden, have not stopped their customary practices and uses of cyberspace after the revelation. This reticence to withdraw from current online practices speaks strongly to the overwhelming power of the Internet and to the engrained endurance of users' daily practices. Consequently, the prevalence of current Internet practices justifies the pertinent timing of the edited volume that the readers hold in their hands (or are reading on their screens) right now. Contemporary cyber-navigators are aware that privacy, understood as a closed, secure system, is now a myth of the past. To a point, I believe that we have all chosen to relinquish our privacy rights in favor of rapid access to multiple audiences "elsewhere" (Berry et al.). Even in the face of such clear evidence, we seem to systematically favor the new consumption and production practices that the Internet has opened for us. Let's highlight here that citizens' capacity to question, denounce, and advocate is also part of the wide range of possibilities provided by cyberspace.

As Brazilian political caricaturist Carlos Latuff proposes in one of his cartoons, citizens can use their mobile phones as a means of instantaneous advocacy. In the cartoon, we see a police officer beating up a citizen, and at the edge of the cartoon's frame, we see the hands of eight persons taking pictures with their mobile phones. We can assume that the pictures taken by passers-by will be posted online to make the abuse known at once (see Figure I.1).

The chapters in *Online Activism in Latin America* demonstrate that civilian access and uses of cyberspace as currently practiced can in fact serve to successfully advocate for social justice, denounce governmental abuses, and, to a certain degree, diminish the voracity and speed of the advancement of global capital. By using the Internet, citizens can model and promote "deviant" consumption habits (such as not buying certain products due to their social or environmental cost) and, in doing so, cyber-navigators can invite others locally and globally to reconsider their habits of consumption and associated practices online, and thus contest mainstream projects and initiatives.

Part of the contestatory capacity of the Internet resides in its very nature: it is a system of systems that is not located in one single, or even easily identifiable, location or time. On the contrary, one of its hallmarks is precisely its concealed multilayered and multi-*loci* networks of production of meaning. It is specifically in the cracks of these multiple systems that

Figure I.1 Untitled, by Carlos Latuff (Brazil).

citizens can actually subvert mainstream narratives and advocate for their causes. The current volume is constructed around the key premise that the Internet as a *medium* entails an unprecedented power: the possibility of immediate global contact by almost anyone in such a rapid way that it is near to impossible to deter. It is precisely the Internet's instantaneous reach that inevitably opens interstices and cracks in the system, and these cracks attest to the unfeasibility of the Internet, in our current times, to become a perfectly closed, secure system. It is through those cracks and small ruptures that citizens' voices, homemade videos, and audio recordings produced with cellular phones (to name just a couple of possibilities) open into instant access by millions of human beings without any form of censorship. This is where the Internet's contestatory power resides.

In spite of all the controversy associated with multinational capitalist expansion (some of which has been addressed in this Introduction), it is evident that the globalization of worldwide economies has displaced

the traditional colonial locations of power, creating a slippery and inapprehensible network of local powers. There are many norths and many
souths in the northern and the southern hemispheres, so to speak, online. What does the future hold? It is hard to predict. However, as *Online
Activism in Latin America* attests, it is clear that when united, citizens
can contest and boycott the advancement of a globalization process that
overall does not give much power of decision on dominant economic
trends to millions of individuals on a planetary scale. It is also true that
those millions of individuals can still be proactive, insofar as they can instantaneously create communities beyond the frontiers of language and
geography, this time online.

Notes

1 I refer here to *Latin American Cyberculture and Cyberliterature* (2007) and
Latin American Identity in Online Cultural Production (2012), edited by
Claire Taylor and Thea Pitman, as well as to the *Arizona Journal of Hispanic
Cultural Studies* issue 14 under the topic, "Literatura latinoamericana, española, portuguesa en la era digital (nuevas tecnologías y lo literario)" (2010),
edited by Luis Correa-Díaz and Scott Weintraub. There are other more recent
publications in English that, to some degree, dovetail with the theme of this
publication; I refer to Eduardo Ledesma's *Radical Poetry: Aesthetics, Politics,
Technology and the Ibero-American Avant-Gardes, 1900–2015* (SUNY P
2017), John Burns's *Contemporary Hispanic Poets: Cultural Production in the
Global, Digital Age* (Cambria P 2015), *Digital Technologies for Democratic
Governance in Latin America*, ed. Anita Breuer and Yanina Welp (Routledge
2014), *Technology, Literature, and Digital Culture in Latin America: Medi-
atized Sensibilities in a Global Era* (Routledge 2015) by Matthew Bush and
Tania Gentic, *Beyond Imported Magic: Essays on Science, Technology, and
Society in Latin America* (MIT P 2014) by Eden Medina et al., *Cybernetic
Revolutionaries: Technology and Politics in Allende's Chile* by Eden Medina
(MIT P 2011), and even Phillip Penix-Tadsen's *Cultural Code. Video Games
and Latin America* (MIT P 2016). I must clarify that these publications approach the digital in Latin America from the angle of electronic poetry, sociology, and literary and game studies. *Online Activism in Latin America* is woven
around a unique combined approach informed by the fields of cultural studies,
cyberstudies of Latin America, mass media studies, (post)modernity of Latin
America studies, and consumer culture studies, as I state in this Introduction.
2 See: Chacón, Hilda: "¿Puede Internet (ó la lógica cultural del capitalismo
avanzado) subvertir el proyecto de la globalización? [Can the Internet (or
the Logic of Late Capitalism) Subvert the Globalization Project?]," also "Political Cartoons in Cyberspace. Rearticulating Mexican and U.S. Cultural
Identity in the Global Era" (219), and "Poética y (post)modernidad en usos
contestatarios del ciberespacio en América Latina."
3 I use interchangeably the terms "multinational capitalism," "transnational
capitalism," and "late capitalism," as employed by Jameson in *Postmodernism, or the Cultural Logic of Late Capitalism* (1991). I also use "the
global" or "global era" in reference to what other scholars refer to as "neoliberalism" and/or "globalization." I consider all these terms exchangeable,
since they all aim to grasp and define the same economic-cultural shift and
époque.

4 Here, I am following the notion of social media proposed by Kaplan and Haenlein; "a group of Internet-based applications that... allow the creation and exchange of user-generated content" (61), applications that, in my view, engender new social practices that are at the very core of the concept of "virtual communities," which lies at the very center of this publication.

5 In all fairness, Jameson's first elucidations on the cultural drive of late capitalism were published as early as 1991. See *Postmodernism, Or the Cultural Logic of Late Capitalism.*

6 See Eric Clemons and Lori M. Hitt. "The Internet and the Future of Financial Services...," as well as Franklin Allen, James McAndrews, and Philip Strahan. "E-Finance: An Introduction." Also, "Financial Services: Background," Global Edge, Michigan State University, http://globaledge.msu.edu/industries/financial-services/background.

7 See Walter Mignolo's *The Darker Side of Western Modernity. Global Futures, Decolonial Options.* Durham: Duke UP, 2011.

8 Costa Rica signed the Neutrality Proclamation on Central American conflicts on September 15, 1983, arguing to protect Costa Rica's non-aligned image internationally (Honey, 301). See Martha Honey. *Hostile Acts; US Policy in Costa Rica in the 1980s.*

9 McLuhan's earliest works, such as *The Gutenberg Galaxy: The Making of Typographic Man* (1962), propose for the first time terms such as "communication technology" and "electronic age." He envisioned the medium of the future including television and computers, three decades before the creation of the Internet.

10 See these authors' contributions in Works Cited section.

11 See Habermas, Jürgen. *Habermas and The Unfinished Project of Modernity. Critical Essays on the Philosophical Discourse of Modernity.* Maurizio Passerin d' Entrèves y Seila Benhabib, editors. Massachusetts: MIT P, 1997.

12 In many Latin American countries, like Costa Rica, one newspaper often had an exclusive monopoly over the purchase and distribution of printing paper, and thus, they had the power to decide what other newspapers they would sell paper to. In this way, the owners of the most powerful newspaper business in the country, usually coming from the elites, controlled the voicing of other alternative media. To add to this panorama of centralized control on print media, I must mention that also mainstream TV and radio companies, due to their technical superiority, could easily trace and interrupt alternative communication projects' wave signals, making intended massive access nearly impossible.

13 As several scholars have demonstrated, the reach for modernity in Latin America is at the very core of national and regional identities. See Walter Mignolo, García-Canclini, Carlos Monsiváis, Mabel Moraña, etc.

14 Benedict Anderson asserts that: "The original Thirteen Colonies comprised an area smaller than Venezuela and one third the size of Argentina. Bunched geographically together, their market-centers in Boston, New York, and Philadelphia were really accessible to one another, and their populations were relatively tightly linked by print as well as commerce" (Imagined 63–64).

15 My translation: "This telos of the [linear] relation underdevelopment-development has revealed itself as a fiction; this fictional telos, though, allows us also to see the underdeveloped world and its developed counterpart as a structural relation of subordination that, far from being eliminated by the system, constitutes the system" (Original: "este telos de atraso-adelanto se ha revelado como una ficción, dejando ver la relación entre el mundo atrasado y el mundo adelantado como una relación estructural de subordinación que, lejos de ser eliminada por el sistema, lo constituye").

16 In the present context of globalization, Latin America is so immersed in North's global production processes that the richest man on earth for the last few years has been a Mexican, Carlos Slim, a title that he disputes each year with U.S. millionaire Bill Gates (Dolan, Forbes).

17 Johannes Gutenberg invented the first printing press in 1440, and the first printing press in the New World arrived in New Spain, today's Mexico, as early as 1539. On the other hand, the first printing press to arrive to the British North Americas arrived in 1638 (MacDonald; also see Lienhard, and "Harvard College Sponsored First Printing Press Set Up in the U.S.A.").

18 The creation of the steam engine in Europe allowed the accumulation of capital in the hands of the owners of the means of production; this dynamic increased the assets of those in the production realm, which in turn put some money in the hands of regular workers, thus encouraging the spread of capitalism. This dynamic definitely included Latin America; it is therefore not surprising that the first national romance ever written in the European colonies in the Americas was written in Mexico by José Joaquín Fernández de Lizardi (Anderson 29), the same country where the first printing press in the Americas arrived in the 16th century.

19 German physicist Heinrich Hertz demonstrated the existence of radio waves in 1887.

20 On December 17, 1902, a transmission from the Marconi station in Glace Bay, Nova Scotia, Canada, became the world's first radio message to cross the Atlantic from North America. In 1901, Marconi built a station near South Wellfleet, Massachusetts, which on January 18, 1903 sent a message of greetings from Theodore Roosevelt, the President of the U.S., to King Edward VII of the United Kingdom, marking the first transatlantic radio transmission originating in the U.S. See: https://en.wikipedia.org/wiki/Guglielmo_Marconi. Hertz's demonstrated the existence of radio waves in 1887, proving a concept that until that moment was only a mathematical idea: https://en.wikipedia.org/wiki/Radio_wave.

21 Employing a vacuum tube transmitter, the New Street Works factory in Chelmsford was the location for the first entertainment radio broadcasts in the United Kingdom. A famous broadcast from Marconi's New Street Works factory in Chelmsford was made by the famous soprano Dame Nellie Melba on June 15, 1920, where she sang two arias and her famous trill. She was the first artist of international renown to participate in direct radio broadcasts. The 2MT station began to broadcast regular entertainment in 1922. The BBC was amalgamated in 1922 and received a Royal Charter in 1926, making it the first national broadcaster in the world. (Source: https://en.wikipedia.org/wiki/Guglielmo_Marconi).

22 Brazilian inventor Roberto Landell de Moura broadcasted the first message using human voice and electromagnetic waves in São Paulo in January 1900, even before Marconi; in 1904, Landell de Moura traveled to the U.S. in order to register the patent for three of his inventions: the wireless transmitter, wireless telegraph, and a wireless telephone that could transmit voice via radio waves ("Padre", see www.epochtimes.com.br/padre-roberto-landell-de-moura-o-brasileiro-que-inventou-o-radio/#.VcExbbdl-y0).

23 Argentina, Mexico, Brazil, and Cuba were among the pioneering radio production countries at the very beginning of the 20th century (Bethell, note 15, 519). Also, Radio Argentina continued regular broadcasting of entertainment and cultural fare for several decades. (See source History of Radio: https://en.wikipedia.org/wiki/History_of_radio).

24 González Camarena invented a chromoscopic adapter for television equipment in 1934 when he was 17 years old; this was a device designed to

easily adapt to the regular black-and-white television. He applied for the patent of his invention in 1941 and obtained it a year later. Camarena also applied for additional patents for color television systems in 1960 and 1962. Nevertheless, it was in August 1946 that González Camarena sent his first color transmission from his lab in the offices of The Mexican League of Radio Experiments, in Mexico City. He obtained authorization to make the first publicly announced color broadcast in Mexico, on February 8, 1963, on Mexico City's TV channel XHGC-TV, a station that he established in 1952. Among other remarkable technological developments in Latin America include those undertaken by Mexican engineer Víctor Ochoa, who designed an airship with wings and a glider, to which later on he added an engine in 1904; he invented (and sold the patents on) the adjustable wrench, or clincher wrench, and patented the electric brake for street cars, which he sold to the American Brake Co. In 1907, he invented a fountain pen (and sold the patent to Waterman Co. in 1900) and patented a pen and pencil clip for holding them in one's pocket. He sold that patent to the American Pen and Pencil Co. in 1907 (source: "Inventor and Revolutionary Víctor Ochoa, The Smithsonian Education Organization online, at http://smithsonianeducation.org/scitech/impacto/Text2/victor/man. html). Mexican engineer, Juan Guillermo Villasana, designed the first aircraft ever produced in Mexico in 1912 and in 1915 designed the Anahuac helix that was exported worldwide and made him receive awards worldwide (see www.elministerio.org.mx/blog/2012/01/juan-guillermo-villasana-padre-aviacion-mexicana). Víctor Celorio invented the Instabook, a digital printing technology supporting e-book distribution (Bellis, "Top"). Armando M. Fernández designed the mousepad in 1979 (see All About, http://allaboutmousepads.blogspot.com/2014/12/All-About-Mousepads-History-Benefits-and-Types.html). See also Rubén Gallo's *Mexican Modernity: The Avant-Garde and the Technological Revolution* in Works Cited.

25 *Nature* acknowledges that "there are many bright spots in the world of science" in Latin America and the scientific journal recognizes, for example, the significant contributions of Chile in astrophysics research (their findings supported the project that discovered the accelerating expansion of the Universe though observations of distant supernovae, which obtained the 2011 Nobel Prize in Physics (www.nobelprize.org/nobel_prizes/physics/laureates/2011). Also, *Nature* highlights the leading role of Brazil in developing the Long Latin American Millimeter Array Radio Relescope, a joint project between Brazil and Argentina. It also mentions The International Agriculture Research Center in Colombia that has led to collaborative projects with neighboring countries on research about genetic improvement of crops. In addition, *Nature* underlines the pioneering investigation in alternative RNA splicing in Argentina, which has demonstrated that Latin America "can do world-class research despite tight government budgets and three-month delivery times for reagents that can cost three times as much as they would in the United States or Europe" (Cantazaro et al., *Nature online*; see: www.nature.com/news/south-american-science-big-players-1.15394#auth-1).

26 See "Edward Snowden Biography," MacAskill, Ewen, and "Edward Snowden: Leaks that exposed...".

27 See German Chancellor Angela Merkel's protests due to US vigilance of Germany in Thomas, Andrea. The Wall Street Journal.

28 See Borger, Julian on Dilma Rousseff's reaction to U.S. espionage on Brazil.

29 See Harris, Shane and "Google Hands Data...".

Works Cited

Allen, Franklin, James McAndrews, and Philip Strahan. "E-Finance: An Introduction." *The Wharton Financial Institutions Center.* U of Pennsylvania P, 2001.

Anderson, Benedict. *Imagined Communities. Reflections on the Origin and Spread of Nationalism.* Verso, 1983.

Bellis, Mary. "Top List of Mexican Inventors." *ThoughtCo.* 19 Apr. 2017. http://inventors.about.com/od/famousinventors/tp/mexican.htm. Accessed 13 June 2017.

Berry, Chris, Soyoung Kim, and Lynn Spigel, eds. *Electronic Elsewheres; Media, Technology, and the Experience of Social Space.* Minnesota UP, 2010.

Bethell, Leslie, ed. *The Cambridge History of Latin America; Latin America since 1930: Ideas, Culture, and Society,* Vol. X. Cambridge UP, 1995.

Beverley, John et al., eds. *The Postmodernism Debate in Latin America.* Duke UP, 1995.

Borger, Julian. "Brazilian president: US Surveillance a 'Breach of International Law.'" *The Guardian.* 24 Sept. 2013. www.theguardian.com/world/2013/sep/24/brazil-president-un-speech-nsa-surveillance. Accessed 13 June 2017.

Breuer, Anita, and Yanina Welp, eds. *Digital Technologies for Democratic Governance in Latin America.* Routledge Explorations in Development Studies Series. New York: Routledge, 2014.

Brunner, José Joaquín. *Un espejo trizado. Ensayos sobre cultura y políticas culturales.* Santiago: FLACSO, 1988.

Bunker, Steven B. *Creating Mexican Consumer Culture in the Age of Porfirio Díaz.* U New Mexico P, 2012.

Burns, John. *Contemporary Hispanic Poets: Cultural Production in the Global, Digital Age.* Cambria Latin American Literatures and Cultures Series. Ed. Román de la Campa. Amherts, New York: Cambria P, 2015.

Bush, Matthew, and Tania Gentic, editors. *Technology, Literature, and Digital Culture in Latin America: Mediatized Sensibilities in a Global Era.* Routledge Interdisciplinary Perspectives on Literature Series. New York: Routledge, 2016.

Cantazaro, Michele, et al. "South American Science: Big Players." *Nature* 510, I 7504, 27 June 2014. www.nature.com/news/south-american-science-big-players-1.15394#auth-1. Accessed 13 June 2017.

Chacón, Hilda. "¿Puede Internet (ó la lógica del capitalismo avanzado) subvertir el proyecto de la globalización?" *CiberLetras. Revista de crítica literaria y de cultura/Journal of Literary Criticism and Culture* 4 (Jan. 2001). www.lehman.cuny.edu/ciberletras/v04.html.

———. "Poética y (post)modernidad en usos contestatarios del ciberespacio en América Latina." *Poesía y poéticas digitales/electrónicas/tecnos/New-Media en América Latina: definiciones y exploraciones.* Ed. Luis Correa-Díaz and Scott Weintraub. Bogota, Colombia: Universidad Central Publisher, 23 May 2016. ISBN: 978-958-26-0228-4. www.ucentral.edu.co/editorial/catalogo/poesia-poeticas-digitales.

———. "Political Cartoons in Cyberspace. Rearticulating Mexican and U.S. Cultural Identity in the Global Era." *Mexico Reading the United States.* Ed. Linda Egan and Mary K. Long. Vanderbilt UP, 2009.

Clemons, Eric, and Lorin M. Hitt. "The Internet and the Future of Financial Services: Transparency, Differential Pricing, and Disintermediation." *The Wharton Financial Institutions Center*. U of Pennsylvania, 2001.

Correa-Díaz, Luis, and Scott E. Weintraub, editors. "Literatura latinoamericana, española, portuguesa en la era digital (nuevas tecnologías y lo literario)." *Arizona Journal of Hispanic Cultural Studies* 14 (2010): 149–155.

Delgado Moya, Sergio. *Delirious Consumption. Aesthetics and Consumer Capitalism in Mexico and Brazil*. Austin: U of Texas P, 2017.

Dolan, Kerry A. "Inside the 2015 Forbes Billionaires List: Facts and Figures." *Forbes*, 2 Mar. 2015. www.forbes.com/sites/kerryadolan/2015/03/02/inside-the-2015-forbes-billionaires-list-facts-and-figures/#55c347fa6cec. Accessed 13 June 2017.

Dorfman, Ariel, and Armand Mattelart. *Para leer al Pato Donald. Comunicación de masa y colonialismo*. Mexico: Siglo XXI 2001 [1971].

Dussel, Enrique. "Eurocentrism and Modernity (Introduction to the Frankfurt Lectures)." JSTOR. *boundary 2* 20.3, *The Postmodernism Debate in Latin America* (Autumn 1993), pp. 65–76.

"Financial Services. Background." *Global Edge*. Michigan State University 1994–2016, n.d. http://globaledge.msu.edu/industries/financial-services/background. Accessed 13 June 2017.

"Grandes mexicanos: Juan Guillermo Villasana, padre de la aviación mexicana." *Revista Digital Disidencia*. Blog, Ministerio de Propaganda, Gobierno de México, n.d. www.elministerio.org.mx/blog/2012/01/juan-guillermo-villasana-padre-aviacion-mexicana. Accessed 13 June 2017.

"Edward Snowden Biography." TheBiography.com Website. Bio. By *Biography.com Editors*. 22 Nov. 2016. www.biography.com/people/edward-snowden-21262897. Accessed 13 June 2017.

"Edward Snowden: Leaks that Exposed US Spy Programme." *BBC News*. 17 Jan. 2014. www.bbc.com/news/world-us-canada-23123964. Accessed 13 June 2017.

Gallo, Rubén. *Mexican Modernity: The Avant-Garde and the Technological Revolution*. Cambridge, MA: MIT P, 2005.

García-Canclini, Néstor. *Culturas híbridas. Estrategias para entrar y salir de la modernidad*. Mexico: Grijalbo, 1989.

———. *La globalización imaginada*. Mexico: Paidós, 1999.

Gonzalez, Juan. *Harvest of Empire. A History of Latinos in America*. Penguin, 2011.

"Google Hands Data to US Government in WikiLeaks Espionage Case." *WikiLeaks*. 26 Jan. 2015. https://wikileaks.org/google-warrant/press.html. Accessed 13 June 2017.

"Google Hands Data to US government in WikiLeaks Espionage Case. Letter from WikiLeaks Lawyer to Google." *WikiLeaks*. 25 Jan. 2015. https://wikileaks.org/google-warrant/Letter-to-Google.html. Accessed 13 June 2017.

Guha, Ranajit. "The Small Voices of History." *The Subaltern Studies; Writings on South Asian History and Society*. New Delhi: Oxford UP, 1997.

Habermas, Jürgen. *Habermas and the Unfinished Project of Modernity. Critical Essays on the Philosophical Discourse of Modernity*. Ed. Maurizio Passerin d' Entrèves y Seila Benhabib. Massachusetts: MIT P, 1997.

Harris, Shane. "Google's Secret NSA Alliance: The Terrifying Deals between Silicon Valley and the Security State." *Salon.* 16 Nov. 2014. www.salon.com/ 2014/11/16/googles_secret_nsa_alliance_the_terrifying_deals_between_silicon_ valley_and_the_security_state. Accessed 13 June 2017.

"Harvard College Sponsored First Printing Press Set Up in the U.S.A." 30 Nov. 1928. www.thecrimson.com/article/1928/11/30/harvard-college-sponsored-first-printing-press/. Accessed 13 June 2017.

Hegel, Georg Wilhelm Friedrich. *Lectures on the History of Philosophy: Medieval and Modern Philosophy,* vol. 3. U Nebraska P, 1995 [1840].

Herlinghaus, Hermann, and Mabel Moraña, editors. *Fronteras de la modernidad en América Latina.* Pittsburgh: Instituto Nacional de Literatura Iberoamericana, 2003.

"History of Radio." *Wikipedia.* n.d. https://en.wikipedia.org/wiki/History_of_ radio. Accessed 13 June 2017.

Honey, Martha. *Hostile Acts. U.S. Policy in Costa Rica in the 1980s.* Gainsville: UP of Florida, 1994.

"Inventor and Revolutionary Víctor Ochoa." The Smithsonian Organization. http://smithsonianeducation.org/scitech/impacto/Text2/victor/man.html. Accessed 4 Aug. 2015.

Jameson, Fredric. *Postmodernism. Or, the Cultural Logic of Late Capitalism.* Durham: Duke UP, 1994 [1991].

Kaplan, Andreas M., and Michael Haenlein. "Users of the World, Unite! The Challenges and Opportunities of Social Media". *Business Horizons* 53.1 (2010): 61.

Ledesma, Eduardo. "Ciencia-ficción digital iberoamericana (mutantes, ciborgs y entes virtuales): La Red y la literatura electrónica del siglo XXI." *Revista Iberoamericana* 83 (Apr.–Sept. 2017): 259–260; 305–326.

———. *Radical Poetry. Aesthetics, Politics, Technology, and the Ibero-American Avant Gardes, 1900–2015.* SUNY Series in Latin American and Iberian Thought and Culture. Ed. Jorge J. E. Gracia and Rosemary Feal. Albany: SUNY P, 2017.

———. "The Poetics and Politics of Computer Code in Latin America: Codework, Code Art, and Live Coding." *Revista de Estudios Hispánicos* 49 (Mar. 2015): 91–120.

Lienhard, John. "First U.S. Press. Episode 733." *Engines of Our Ingenuity.* College of Engineering, University of Houston. Radio. Transcript. n.d. www. uh.edu/engines/epi733.htm. Accessed 13 June 2017.

MacAskill, Ewen. "Edward Snowden: How the Spy Story of the Age Leaked Out." *The Guardian.* 12 June 2013. www.theguardian.com/world/2013/ jun/11/edward-snowden-nsa-whistleblower-profile. Accessed 13 June 2017.

MacDonald, Katie. "Innovation in Cambridge. American Printing." *Cambridge Historical Society* (2012). n.d. http://cambridgehistory.org/innovation/ American%20Printing.html. Accessed 13 June 2017.

Martín-Barbero, Jesús. "Aventuras de un cartógrafo mestizo en el campo de la comunicación." *Revista Latina de Comunicación Social* 19 (1999): n. pag. www.revistalatinacs.org/a1999fjl/64jmb.htm. Accessed 13 June 2017.

———. *Comunicación educativa y didáctica audiovisual.* Cali: Sena, 1979.

———. *Comunicación masiva, discurso y poder.* Quito: CIESPAL, 1978.

————. *De los medios a las mediaciones. Comunicación, cultura y hegemonía*, 5th edition. Bogotá: Unidad Editorial del Convenio Andrés Bello, 2003 (1987).

Marx, Karl. Manifesto of the Comunist Party. Chapter 1: "Bourgeois and Proletarians." MIA: Marx and Engels Library. www.marxists.org/archive/marx/works/1848/communist-manifesto/ch01.htm. Accessed 13 June 2017.

Masiello, Francine, et al., editors. *The Art of Transition: Latin American Culture and Neoliberal Crisis.* Latin America Otherwise Series. Durham: Duke UP, 2001.

McLuhan, Marshall, and Bruce R. Powers. *The Global Village: Transformations in World Life and Media in the 21st Century.* Oxford: Oxford U P; Reprint edition (1989, 1992).

————. *The Gutenberg Galaxy: The Making of Typographic Man.* Toronto: U of Toronto P, Scholarly Publishing Division; Centennial edition (1962, 2011).

————. *The Medium is The Message.* Berkeley: Gingko P; 9th ed. (1967, 2001).

————. *Understanding Media: The Extensions of Man.* London: The MIT P; Reprint edition (1964, 1994).

Medina, Eden. *Cybernetic Revolutionaries: Technology and Politics in Allende's Chile.* Cambridge: MIT P 2011.

Medina, Eden, et al. *Beyond Imported Magic: Essays on Science, Technology, and Society in Latin America.* Cambridge: MIT P, 2014.

Mignolo, Walter. *The Darker Side of Western Modernity. Global Futures, Decolonial Options.* Durham: Duke UP, 2011.

Morley, David. "Domesticating Dislocation in a World of 'New' Technology." *Electronic Elsewheres; Media, Technology, and the Experience of Social Space.* Ed. Chris Berry, et al. Minneapolis: Minnesota UP, 2010.

"Mousepad: History, Benefits and Types." *All About Mousepads Blog* 10 Dec. 2014. http://allaboutmousepads.blogspot.com/2014/12/All-About-Mousepads-History-Benefits-and-Types.html. Accessed 13 June 2017.

Olea, Raquel. "Feminism: Modern or Postmodern?" *The Postmodernism Debate in Latin America.* Ed. John Beverely, Michael Arona, and José Oviedo. Durham: Duke UP, 1995.

"Padre Roberto Landell de Moura, o brasileiro que inventou o rádio." *Epoch Times.* 9 Apr. 2014. www.epochtimes.com.br/padre-roberto-landell-de-moura-o-brasileiro-que-inventou-o-radio/#.VcExbbdl-y0. Accessed 13 June 2017.

Passerin d' Entrèves, Maurizio, and Seila Benhabib, editors. *Habermas and The Unfinished Project of Modernity. Critical Essays on the Philosophical Discourse of Modernity.* MIT P, 1997.

Penix-Tadsen, Phillip. *Cultural Code. Video Games and Latin America.* Cambridge: MIT P, 2016.

Penix-Tadsen, Phillip. "Letters, Text, and Dialogue in Contemporary Latin American Video Game Design." *Letras Hispanas, Special Issue: Digital Storytelling in Latin America and Spain (1983–2013).* Ed. Osvaldo Cleger and Phillip Penix-Tadsen. 2015. 11. www.modlang.txstate.edu/letrashispanas/currentvolume.html.

Pratt, Mary Louise. "La modernidad desde las Américas". *Revista Iberoamericana* LXVI, 193 (2000): 831–840.

————. "The Anticolonialist Past". *Modern Language Quarterly* 65.3 (2004): 443–456.

Richard, Nelly. *Masculine/Feminine. Practices of Difference(s)*. Translation by Silvia R. Tandeciarz and Alice A. Nelson. Durham: Duke UP, 2004.

Sarlo, Beatriz. *Una modernidad periférica: Buenos Aires, 1920 y 1930*. Buenos Aires: Nueva Visión, 1996.

Taylor, Claire. *Place and Politics in Latin American Digital Culture: Location and Latin American Net Art*. Routledge Studies in New Media and Cyberculture Series. New York: Routledge, 2014.

Taylor, Claire, and Thea Pitman. *Latin American Cyberculture and Cyberliterature*. Liverpool: Liverpool UP, 2008.

———. *Latin American Identity in Online Cultural Production*. New York: Routledge, 2012.

Thomas, Andrea. "U.S. Spying on Germany Unacceptable, Says Merkel." *The Wall Street Journal*. 12 July 2014. www.wsj.com/articles/u-s-spying-on-germany-unacceptable-says-merkel-1405174452. Accessed 13 June 2017.

Part I

Art and Activism in Cyberspace

1 A Theater of Displacement

Staging Activism, Poetry, and Migration through a Transborder Immigrant Tool

Sergio Delgado Moya

> to drive, to come, go, to cause to move, to push, to set in motion, stir up, to emit, to make, construct, produce, to lead, bring, to drive back or away, to urge, incite, to do, perform, achieve, accomplish, to take action, to do something, to work at, to be busy at, to be busy, to work, to stage (a play), to take a part in (a play), to perform (a part) in a play, to perform (in a play), to play the part of, to behave as, to pretend to be, to strive for, to carry out, execute, discharge, to manage, administer, to celebrate, observe, to spend (time), to experience, enjoy, to live, to proceed, behave, to transact, to discuss, argue, debate, to arrange, agree on, to decree, enact, to press, urge, plead, to deliver (a speech)
>
> ("Act, *v.*", *Oxford English Dictionary*)

It reads like a poem, the list of verbs unfurled in the Oxford English Dictionary to drive home the meanings of "act," root word at the heart of *activism*. Voiced out loud, it rings exalting, a constellation of all that can be done, all that is to be done, when performing acts of activism. Most striking for someone like me, who happened on this string of words while seeking a better grasp of the meaning (the import, the substance, and significance) of activism, is the cluster of references to the world of theater, resting smack in the middle of this verbal assemblage. Striking but not surprising, given all the *acting* and given the high degree of *staging* it takes for activism to take place. Indeed, it seems like the more we embrace these two aspects of activism—the strategic and the theatrical—the more meaningfully consequent activism is. But, for reasons that are easy to rehearse (a perennial distrust of the aesthetic in general, and the poetic and the theatrical in particular; a more recently entrenched "tradition of revolutionary puritanism"[1]), the more playful, the more artistic, and the more beautiful aspects of activism are usually eclipsed—closeted, one might say—in order to foreground the "serious" forces at play in activist praxis and ideology.

This tension between the various dimensions of activism plays out differently in the Transborder Immigrant Tool (TBT). Developed collaboratively from 2009 to 2012, a cell phone-based "code-switch" between computer code and poetry, between activism and aesthetics, the TBT is, fundamentally, an affirmation of the rights (right of passage, right to sustenance) of migrants crossing into the U.S. on foot by way of the treacherous Sonoran Desert. It is also a gesture of contestation, not just of the structures of oppression (physical, legal, technological) standing against migration, but also, and critically, against the terms under which social and political contestation have been historically registered. Not that the TBT foregrounds the theatrical or the poetic over and above the social or the political, nor that it seeks to strike a balance between them. Rather, along with the very real gesture of activism at its core, we find in the TBT a will to disturb the dividing lines that keep what is aesthetic (art, poetry) distinct from and often incompatible with what is political (social intervention, activism). We find, then, a contesting of contestation itself, articulated as an inquiry into the idea of place, staging, and framing: the place of aesthetics at large and poetry in particular and their displacement from direct actions that seek to attain a specific political or social goal; the staging of the figure of the migrant in the political imaginaries that give shape to it within a repertoire of social actors and socialized figures; and the staging of the Sonoran Desert as landscape.[2] Place, stage, and landscape are here envisioned in theatrical and historical terms, through a constant play on the meaning (the sense, the substance, the import) of the notions of stage and staging.

Transbordering by Design

Developed under the auspices of two major North American research institutions,[3] the TBT is a design project conceived around the idea of distributing inexpensive, GPS-enabled cell phones among migrants planning to walk across the desert that straddles the U.S. and Mexico. The cell phones have been shown in academic settings and in art exhibitions. They have been widely discussed in the media and in a wave of recent scholarly articles,[4] but they have not been actually distributed among migrants.[5] The phones come loaded with poems, a key feature of their design discussed at length later in this essay. They are also outfitted with locative software that can guide migrants to water posts, rescue sites, and other resources critical for survival in the trek across the desert. On a more conceptual and political level, the phones disturb the categories (the illegal, the outlaw, the undocumented, the criminal, and, increasingly, the terrorist) that have been historically used to frame images of immigrants in the U.S. The power invested in these categories goes far beyond the rhetorical. They form the basis for a series of policies[6] that seek to turn migrants into social outcasts by placing them beneath the threshold of humanity we uphold when we extend humanitarian aid and other such basic provisions of human welfare (Figure 1.1).[7]

The TBT was conceived in 2007, against a background of increasing hostility in the U.S. toward migrants, undocumented immigrants, and

Figure 1.1 The TBT in operation, showing a cell phone with the Tool's software installed and a screenshot, bottom right, from the same Nokia e71, directing the user to a Water Station Inc. water cache in the Anza Borrego Desert. Photograph and description by Brett Stalbaum.

what Mae M. Ngai conceptualizes as "alien citizens," U.S. born and naturalized persons rendered "permanently foreign and unassimilable to the nation" by immigration policies that racialize national, regional, and (increasingly) religious markers of certain ethnic groups (Ngai 7–8).[8] The latest wave of antagonism peaked intermittently in recent decades,[9] tethered as it is to the mix of social and economic indicators (economic hardship, high unemployment, spikes in inflation, stagnated wages, rising inequality) that Marcela Cerrutti and Douglas S. Massey list as conditions that "make immigration a salient political issue with the public" (Cerrutti and Massey 19). This latest wave dates back to the institution of two concerted, operational plans to quell undocumented migration at the busiest entry points of the U.S.-Mexico border: Ciudad Juárez/El Paso and Tijuana/San Diego. These widely touted plans, Operation Hold-the-Line (1993) and Operation Gatekeeper (1994), effectively militarized the borderlands extending across the urban corridors listed above. In line with other U.S. war zones established after Operation Desert Shield (1990–1991), otherwise known as the Gulf War, these plans mounted a theater of operations both visible and invisible. Visibly, U.S. border patrol agents and their motorized vehicles were positioned in prominent parts of the landscape, becoming a fixture of sorts of the borderlands as seen from either side of the border. Invisibly (or at least less visibly), an infrastructure of electronic surveillance (movement sensors, seismic sensors, low-light cameras, heat-seeking cameras,[10] infrared night scopes, aircraft, etc.) of unprecedented sophistication was put in place at the border.

The objective of Operations Hold-the-Line and Gatekeeper was simple, announced to much fanfare: deter[11] undocumented migration in the major entry ports (Tijuana/San Diego, Ciudad Juárez/El Paso) and move it outside urban areas, to the desert, where the border patrol believes it enjoys a "strategic advantage over would-be crossers."[12] The nature of this "strategic advantage" is grim. It rests squarely on the border patrol's ability to force migrants onto the most dangerous, most treacherous route into the U.S.: the desert. Deterrence is the presumed effect of this "advantage," but as Cerrutti and Massey argue on the grounds of compelling statistical evidence, Operation Hold-the-Line and Operation Gatekeeper, like every other U.S. border enforcement effort implemented since the end of the Bracero Program in 1964,[13] "have had relatively small effects on the likelihood of undocumented migration between Mexico and the United States" (Cerrutti and Massey 40).[14]

While they fail to deter undocumented migration and while they also fail in their efforts to apprehend undocumented border crossers,[15] the concerted government efforts to drive migration out of city limits and into the desert, coupled with dispersed but not entirely unrelated initiatives to dehumanize migrants by criminalizing attempts to provide them basic sustenance, do result in what Ngai theorizes as "impossible subjects," persons outside the polis and outside the law, a "caste, unambiguously situated outside the boundaries of formal membership and social legitimacy" (Ngai 2). In short, the militarization of the U.S.–Mexico border has decimated undocumented migrants attempting to enter the U.S. on foot. And it does so with unspeakable violence. Since Operations Hold-the-Line and Gatekeeper were implemented, anywhere from a few thousand to ten thousand migrants have died in grueling desert conditions as they attempt to cross into the U.S. by foot.[16] Migrants have always risked death as they make their way from Mexico into the U.S., but the number of migrants who have died after Operation Gatekeeper went into effect is appalling, without true precedent.

The rising rate of death among migrants is "strategic," deployed from above.[17] As the borderline cutting across the major urban corridors was further militarized, the path taken by a significantly large group of migrants (the most impoverished and the most vulnerable, those with little to nil financial resources or social capital) was pushed out of the urban grid and into the Sonoran Desert. And thus took shape another form of punishment, another decimation, another "removal" befallen on migrants, one that works physically as well as symbolically. Physically, because it spells death: dead bodies pile up on the grounds of the Sonoran Desert as a direct and strategic result of changes in U.S. immigration law. Symbolically, because the migrant's death, like a path drawn on sand under the desert wind, is blurred away beyond recognition, forced out of memory and into political erasure. Briefly put, to die in the desert is, politically speaking, to die nowhere. A death unseen, unspoken,[18] and un-staged is a death that never quite takes place.[19] To die in the desert, then, amounts to both more and less than death: under the conditions of erasure and anonymity that so many fallen migrants have faced, death becomes more like disappearance. Without place, without background, there is no figure, there is no event, nor is there an act. Without a stage in which to set it, not even death registers. Indeed, four to ten thousand deaths have occurred in the Sonoran Desert since Operation Gatekeeper was begun, and barely a ripple has formed in the imagination of the cities and communities on either side of the border. "*Quién hablaría de la soledad del desierto*," "Who would speak of the desert's loneliness," asks Amy Sara Carroll, citing the Chilean poet Raúl Zurita, in "Of Ecopoetics and Dislocative Media," her introduction to the volume that prints the TBT's working computer code alongside the project's poetry (Carroll et al., *The Transborder Immigrant Tool/ La herramienta transfronteriza*, 2014). Carroll's "Desert Survival Series" poems are, in large part, a response to the silence shrouding the countless deaths in the Sonoran Desert, in much the same way that Zurita writes his own "El Desierto de Atacama"[20] as a way to render the vast Chilean desert "no longer conceivable except if the voices and the deaths in the desert are made part of that desert" (Leonard Schwartz, cited in Carroll, "Of Ecopoetics and Dislocative Media" 1) (Figure 1.2).

Key to understanding the kind of intervention that the TBT and the "Desert Survival Series" seek to make is the way each straddles the

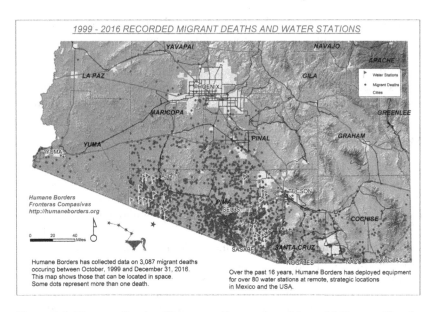

Figure 1.2 Humane Borders/Fronteras Compasivas, Map of Migrants Deaths and Humane Borders Water Stations (1999–2016). Courtesy of Humane Borders.

different senses of "acting"—the way they touch upon the realm of activism and the realm of poetry, the field of politics, and the field of the aesthetic. This movement, this transit, is a tactic willfully practiced by the people behind the TBT: Amy Sara Carroll, Ricardo Dominguez, Brett Stalbaum, Micha Cárdenas, and Elle Mehrmand, members of the Electronic Disturbance Theater (EDT 2.0)/b.a.n.g. lab[21]—a self-described "artivist-based research group."[22] The tactic dates back to the early years of the EDT and its virtual, online sit-ins organized in 1998 in solidarity with the Zapatistas in Chiapas, sit-ins defined theatrically by Ricardo Dominguez as "acts" in a narrative arc. It is a tactic elaborated in the series of remarkable programmatic and theoretical writings produced and published by the tactical media collective Critical Art Ensemble, of which Dominguez was a member. In these writings, "tactical media artists" are described in terms of what they are not:

> [t]hey aren't artists in any traditional sense and don't want to be caught in the web of metaphysical, historical, and romantic signage that accompanies that designation. Nor are they political activists in any traditional sense, because they refuse to solely take the reactive position of anti-logos, and are just as willing to flow through fields of nomos in defiance.
>
> (Critical Art Ensemble, *Digital Resistance* 6)

There is explicit disavowal here of the categories of the artist and the activist and, more pointedly, disavowal of the ideas of discipline and territory subtending these categories. Crucial here is the gesture of displacement (displacement of definition, displacement of discipline and disciplinary categories, and, of course, displacement of human bodies across a desert), as well as the room made by means of this displacement: room for movements between, and slippages within, art and activism.

Mapping and Making Visible

Two distinct and related measures of meaning are weaved into the work of the EDT 2.0/b.a.n.g lab and into the TBT in particular: one spatial (fields, territories), the other temporal (flows, movements). These same measures confront each other in mapping, particularly in that way of producing and relating to maps that materialized with the advent of both GPS locative technologies and the handheld devices used to access these technologies. Mapping, a tool for territory and state formation, imposes an imagined, abstract order over lived space, revealing something about the spatial categories inherent to the social order. In an essay about maps and borders, the Chilean critic Nelly Richard argues that "[b]oth the geometric models and the visual categories employed by map-makers to formulate specific images of spatiality reflect the structures of knowledge which define the philosophical and cultural thinking of a tradition" (Richard, "The Cultural Periphery and Postmodern Decentring" 71).

Recent GPS-based technologies of location and the platforms that have popularized their use—handheld devices and the software that directs these devices' functions—compel us to revisit the models and categories of mapmaking singled out by Richard to account for the link between cartography and structures of knowledge. A series of questions arises *vis-à-vis* the emergence of GPS mapping: What forms of knowledge organization take shape in the cartography of GPS-generated maps? What organs of knowledge break down with the rise of GPS technologies? What are the visual and conceptual categories present and operant in the making of GPS maps, and how do they relate to each other? How is space visualized by means of these categories, and how are our relationships to space and our forms of spatialization reconceived through them? Who has access to these ways of imagining space? Who are the subjects, the figures, taking shape against this way of mapping? And who's gaining, or lacking, consciousness of these forms of spatial knowledge?[23]

One distinctive shift in our structures of knowledge revealed in the move from static, two-dimensional maps to GPS-based maps is the transition from thinking about space primarily in terms of geographic constants to conceiving it as a function of the relationships (the purpose, destination, and movement) singular users have relative to the space around them. In contrast to static, two-dimensional maps, where space is organized as a function of geometric and geographic coordinates rendered from a single, abstract, vertical perspective, GPS maps generate a sense of space based on the location of singularly located users, their purpose or destination, and their mode of transport. Space in the cartographic surface of most GPS-generated maps radiates from the user, its vectors produced as a function of both location (of the user, their destination, and the satellites used to convey and triangulate spatial information) and also, crucially, as a function of purpose and projected movement. Under the terms of this configuration, the center of the map drops down from the elevated, bird's-eye view from which two-dimensional maps order space, landing in the horizontal point of view of a user who relates to space as terrain to be traversed. With this shift to relational space,[24] an integrated sense of place and displacement emerges. Being out in the world, GPS-enabled device in hand, we begin to envision place relationally, not just or not primarily as static, modeled space, but also as a matrix to plot displacement.

As a navigation instrument, the TBT rests primarily on relational categories of space. It does not, strictly speaking, produce a representation of space in the way that two-dimensional maps or GPS-based maps do. It is rather like a cursor, pointing migrants in the direction of water and sustenance without providing them a totalizing image of the space to be traversed. The TBT is geared, in this way, to what Alice Schmidt Camacho terms "migrant imaginaries,"[25] inasmuch as it proceeds primarily from intended or necessary movement and not from static ideas of vision and territory (the terms of engagement of the nation-state). And insofar as it moves through circuits beyond the physical space of the U.S.-Mexico borderlands, the TBT primes the social imaginary (the imagination of the polis) for migrant, transnational conditions of life, making migrants visible and making headways on what Jacques Rancière has theorized as shifts in the distributions of the sensible.[26]

How does the migrant experience, the way migrants occupy space (the space of the desert between the U.S. and Mexico) become visible, recognizable in the community's imagination, through the TBT? How does it enter into the language of the community via the operations, the staging, of the TBT? How can a cultural practice, an aesthetic intervention, a poem, or a work of art orient our attention, putting into focus people and phenomena previously unseen? How, in short, can art be activism? How can the aesthetic as embodied in the TBT shape the measures and categories we use to map the U.S.-Mexico border? Beginning in 2009, reports of the TBT project in several art blogs and websites created a surge of media coverage, culminating in news stories by the major media outlets in the U.S.[27] "With twenty-twenty hindsight," the producers of the TBT note, "we identify the viral reportage on TBT as the first instance of the latter's deployment (a contagion)" (*Sustenance: A Play for All Trans [ ] Borders*).

The language of information transmission as contagion and the correlate image of mass media audiences as body politic are telling. They speak of the feat accomplished by the act of drawing the attention of national media outlets to the humanitarian crisis unraveling along the U.S.-Mexico border. On its own, the gesture of drawing media coverage to the thousands of deaths that have taken place in the Sonoran Desert is significant but hardly stable. By screening death (the deaths of migrants on the U.S.-Mexico borderlands), it makes death visible. This affects the public imagination into action as much as it inoculates it against the violence seen. The producers of the TBT, though, go a step further, bringing the attention of other artists and scholars and of the public of mass media outlets like Fox News to the plight of migrants perishing in the Sonoran Desert in a way that changes the nature of the conversation about migration and displacement. They do so by insisting on the aesthetic grounding of the TBT, its status as a work of art. They write: "For us—EDT 2.0/ b.a.n.g. lab—the post-contemporary moment calls for artwork that can construct gestures of visibility that haunt the fictions of market, of the state, and of institutions" (Electronic Disturbance Theater 2.0/b.a.n.g. lab, *OPERATION FAUST Y FURIOSO*, 31).

Insisting on the aesthetic dimension of the TBT, on its status as artwork, is in itself a complex "gesture of visibility." On the one hand, it has allowed those behind the TBT to disturb highly charged political waters (to wit, policy debates on migration, national security, border militarization, etc.) all the while avoiding—barely, and not without costs for those involved—the legal consequences often leveled against these kinds of gestures. On the other hand—and directly related to this first, more visibly "pragmatic" reason to assert the aesthetic dimension of the TBT—there is a self-reflexive motion, a critique of the aesthetic conceived as the institution of art and the way it features or fails to feature the overtly politicized sights and subjects framed by the TBT. Visibility here aspires to both clarity and ambiguity: clarity in terms of the humanitarian crisis at the U.S.-Mexico border being perceived *as* a humanitarian crisis and ambiguity regarding the role that artists, activists, and artivists can take *vis-à-vis* this crisis. "Artivism," the term used by the producers of the TBT to designate their work, signals an ambiguous disposition toward the institutions, in reference to which the figure of the migrant and the phenomenon of migration become visible, recognizable. The way the poet—an actor in the small and ever-morphing cast of cultural agents that form EDT 2.0—positions herself in the circuit of interventions and disturbances constructed around the TBT provides us with a more detailed picture of how this ambiguity works itself out in practice.

Restaging the Landscape, Reframing the Migrant

As mapped by the TBT, the Sonoran Desert is restaged—or rather, rescreened—from appearing as entryway of furtive migrants to being the site of excruciating deaths numbering in the thousands. Two books describe the gruesome conditions faced by migrants as they trek north through the desert: John Annerino's *Dead in Their Tracks: Crossing America's Desert Borderlands* (1999) and Luis Alberto Urrea's *The Devil's Highway: A True Story* (2004). Each offers a graphic, often ghastly, and at times sensationalist image of the conditions faced by immigrants. The poems encoded in the TBT also manage to impress upon the reader a vivid sense of what the trek across the Devil's Highway entails for most migrants, but they do so differently. In their respective books, Annerino and Urrea expose and denounce, setting the ground for the kind of work the TBT sets out to do. On her part, Amy Sara Carroll, author of the series of poems encoded in the TBT, extends something different: a word of sustenance.

The "Desert Survival Series" is a series of 24 poems ("one poem for every hour of the day") written by Carroll and included in *The Transborder Immigrant Tool/La herramienta transfronteriza para inmigrantes* (2014), a volume that brings together both the poetry and the working computer code of the TBT.[28] Carroll appeals to at least two senses of sustenance in her "Desert Survival Series." The first one is lyrical, Romantic: poetry as landscape, as natural environment. The second one is literal: "sustenance" as physical nourishment, as provisions that keep the body alive. In the *Transborder Immigrant Tool*, Carroll's poems are printed using a carefully thought-out layout that reverberates the TBT's contrasting structures of meaning: division and union, territory and crossing, landscape and history, beauty and function, and so forth. The poems are presented in English and Spanish,[29] with each version printed sometimes separately (the first one places English "north" on the top of the page and Spanish on the bottom of the page), sometimes intermingled, suggesting alternation and crossing between languages. The imperative is the verbal form that most resonates in the poems ("Orient yourself"; "Climb or walk in the morning. Rest midday beneath creosote bush or mesquite, insulating yourself"), and this form instills in them a sense of urgency. These poems are survival poems, and Carroll never loses sight of this feature of her work.

Quickly, by the third poem (Figure 1.3), survival becomes a matter of knowing not only the natural features of the desert landscape, but its history as it incarnates in this and other deserts. The reference to the Bedouins and to "indigenous travelers in the Mexican-U.S. corridor" is part and parcel of a larger discursive strategy, the outline of which is traced out by Carroll herself in "Of Ecopoetics and Dislocative Media," the brief introductory text she writes as an opening for *The Transborder Immigrant Tool*. Carroll begins this text with an epigraph by Raúl Zurita, immediately aligning her work for the TBT as part of a larger hemispheric tradition that subverts picturesque notions of landscape in favor of more nuanced, historically

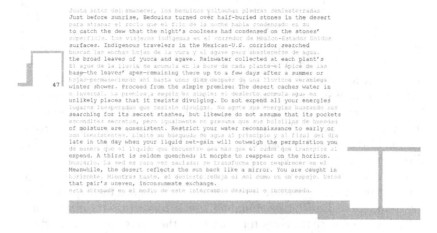

Figure 1.3 Poem from Amy Sara Carroll's "Desert Survival Series" (Carroll et al., *The Transborder Immigrant Tool/La herramienta transfronteriza para inmigrantes*, 47). Courtesy of Amy Sara Carroll.

informed, and politically incisive renditions of the natural environment. Chilean artists and writers have been at the forefront of this politicized understanding of landscape, their national landscape marked as it is by an overbearing presence of natural features (the Andes to the east, the Pacific Ocean to the West, the Atacama Desert to the north, Patagonia to the South) and scarred brutally by a dictatorial regime that used every one of these features as sites for the inscription of violence and death. A layered notion of landscape is present from the very first works by Zurita, "Un matrimonio en el campo," epigrammatic and somberly visual poems printed on plaster slates resembling tombstones and photographed for publication in the groundbreaking *Manuscritos* (1975), a hybrid art/literary/critical magazine published under conditions of great adversity at the height of dictatorial oppression. Lotty Rosenfeld brought this understanding of landscape to new complexities with her intervention on pavement roads, where she used the broken lines typically used as dividing marks between traffic lanes as the basis for her extraordinarily powerful *A Thousand Crosses on the Road* (1979). Catalina Parra, the visual programmer of *Manuscritos* responsible for the publication's complex graphic design, went on to produce a rich body of montages made of newspapers, anticipating the kind of art/activist media intervention that the TBT enacts. More recently, the filmmaker Patricio Guzmán took on the vast expanse and tremendous beauty of the Atacama desert—home to some of the most sophisticated telescopes in the world—in *Nostalgia for the Light* (2010), which screens side by side the work of astronomers and the labor of family members of *desaparecidos*, tireless in their search for human remains, tiny bone fragments left scattered in the desert by the most brutal of state-sponsored political decimations: erasure by explosion, bodies literally blown up by operatives of the repressive state.

Research by the progressive social movement "Patagonia Sin Represas,"[30] which successfully deployed manipulated images of Chilean natural environments to campaign against the construction of hydroelectric dams in Patagonia, suggests that landscape is held by most Chileans as the most distinctive trait of national identity. For decades, artists and poets have appealed to this feature of the Chilean imagination, reinscribing it in ways that make apparent the traces of conflict and violence so often erased from the more idealized, more pastoral renditions of landscape, the ones that function dialectically to suggest both reserves of untouched nature and strata of land upon which the idea of civilization is erected (Figure 1.4).

The TBT takes up the work of recovering a richer, historically nuanced, politicized notion of the U.S.-Mexico borderlands from the very outset. Its computer code is repurposed from software originally designed for recreational purposes, for planning hikes around the kind of picturesque landscapes mined by the TBT creators and by the Chilean

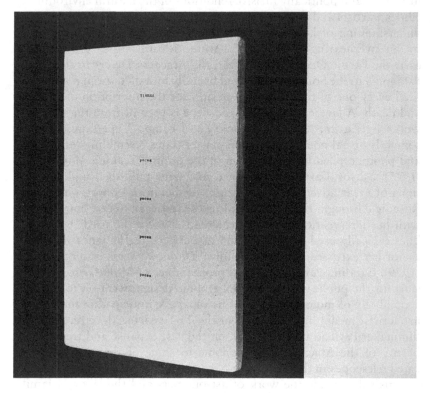

Figure 1.4 Photograph of a poem from "Un matrimonio en el campo" by Raúl Zurita, published in *Manuscritos* (Santiago de Chile, 1975). Printed on a plaster slab. Courtesy of Raúl Zurita.

artists and poets mentioned before. In reference to the introduction Camille Dungy wrote for the anthology *Black Nature: Four Centuries of African-American Nature Poetry*, Carroll writes:

> [i]n Dungy's formulation, a tree can never just be a tree, but also functions as a rememory of lynching. Ecology holds trauma and promise simultaneously, is neither beautiful nor sublime per se, but becomes part of a larger built environment that regulates the policing and disciplining of ungrammatical bodies.
>
> (Carroll, "Of Ecopoetics and Dislocative Media" 1–2)

Carroll builds on this long tradition of poetry, on the tradition embodied by Zurita, and on Chantal Akerman's documentary film *De l'autre côté/From the Other Side* to work against what she theorizes, echoing Eve Sedgwick, as the "privilege unknowing"[31] produced by the staging of the desert as mere landscape, the erasure of migrant deaths from its grounds and from the political imagination.

Carroll's "Desert Survival Series" poems make a vivid impression in this reader's mind. They paint a picture of the desert as a place that can be survived, but hardly. We relate to that picture and place ourselves in it thanks to the images the poems conjure about plants that feed and plants that poison; about birds, snakes, bees, their ways of finding nourishment in the desert, their ways of fending off and confronting perceived dangers; about the drastic shifts in desert weather, dry and searing hot one hour, drenched in rain and freezing cold the next. Rhythmically, methodically, the poems work through the landscape of the Sonoran Desert, fleshing out its rugged features with references and allusions that ballast a vision of the desert and foster our understanding of it. They stay anchored to the bottom line of survival: the landscape they envision is a place that is to be, first and foremost, lived through.

As such, the poems hold the power to transform the image of the migrant in the readers' minds, and they do so without pretending to represent migrants. What the poems do, instead, is to redress and reset the desert as landscape. Undocumented immigrants placed in the context of Carroll's poems are not outlaws; they are migrants and they are survivors. This is what I mean when I point out the ways in which the TBT presents a stage where we can recognize and reimagine the figure of the migrant. With a new stage for undocumented immigration, a new map of the continent emerges, one where tracks of death and stories of survival take precedence over the abstract borders marking national territories. As Carroll writes, "the project as a whole functions as a poem-to-be-rehearsed to remap the continent, to interrupt discourses which, ensconced in their own aesthetic of market-oriented 'transparency' meets military-industrial-complex, reduce the would-be crosser to debris or felon" (Carroll, "FIVE POEMS"). The stage, then, the background, changes, modified by the TBT. This has an impact on the way that migrants are perceived, recognized, imagined: the background changes and so does the figure of the migrant.

One important aspect of this shift rests on the way the TBT and Carroll's poems, in particular, present undocumented migrants as readers of poetry. The poems in the "Desert Survival Series" are, after all, written with undocumented immigrants in mind, and in this respect, they are written in good faith, with utmost consideration. In times of increasing slander leveled against migrants seeking refuge—social, political, economic refuge—in the U.S., against the liberal, patronizing, condescending ethos that often animates progressive dispositions toward undocumented immigration ("Give me your tired, your poor, your huddled masses yearning to breathe free" is the verse by Emma Lazarus famously displayed in the Statue of Liberty on Ellis Island, that border point of yore), Carroll and the makers of the TBT dare to imagine the migrant as someone who reads poetry. In doing so, they force us to reckon with entrenched stereotypes about who migrants are, the objectives they seek, the things they like, and the abilities they nurture.[32] There is a long and hardly disingenuous tradition of imagining undocumented immigrants coming into the U.S. as poor, simple people with little culture and no skills. While it is certainly true that a significant portion of those seeking unlawful entry into the U.S. is economically destitute, to infer from this that undocumented immigrants to the U.S. lack culture is unfounded and misleading. Kelly Lytle Hernandez, the author of a thoroughly researched history of the U.S. border patrol (*Migra! A History of the U.S. Border Patrol*, 2010), sheds lights on how this image of the undocumented immigrant congealed and what purposes it serves. Establishing racial superiority over and above undocumented immigrants is one such purpose, as is, from a perspective more favorable to migration, the notion that immigrants come into the U.S. as blank-slated workers effaced from anything that could threaten the racialized hegemony of citizens with European ancestry. Citing statements made by S. Parker Friselle of the California Farm Bureau Federation in 1926, in reference to Mexican immigrants but following a line of interpretation that well describes the situation of undocumented immigrants from every national origin, Hernandez writes:

> Mexicans, according to Friselle, were nothing more than a source of cheap and disposable labor whose impact upon America would only be measured in dollars and sweat. 'He is not a man that comes into this country for anything except our dollars and our work'.
>
> (Hernández 31)

Most interesting and most egregious is the fact that Friselle made such claim not against migration, but in support of it, to appease nativist concerns about the impact border crossers could have on U.S. culture.

In Carroll's poems, sustenance is elaborated as more than a matter of physical subsistence. By implication, potential users of the TBT are recognized as beings nourished by more than just physical sustenance. Carroll frames her role in the project in reference to "the question of what constitutes sustenance in the quotidian of the conceptual, on the varied musical scales of the micro- and macro."[33] Carroll's answer is poetry, the series of poems screened in the TBT. Carroll writes:

> I wrote pared down prose poems, ideologically neutral (Is any writing 'ideologically neutral'?), procedural, if you will—a poem about locating the North Star, a poem about what to do if you are bitten by a rattlesnake or tarantula, poems that contained details about how to weather a sandstorm or a flash flood.
>
> (Caroll et al. 4)

But how does poetry sustain? How does it "guide" in situations where survival is at stake? Carroll proceeds cautiously as she answers this question, for good reason. In a short text, the title of which announces a cleverly suggested polyvalence of "GPS" as both a poetic and a positioning system, she writes:

> often—rightly enough—conversations about crossing the Mexico-U.S. border refer to disorientation, sun exposure, lack of water. The Transborder Immigrant Tool attempts to address those vicissitudes, but also to remember that the aesthetic—freighted with the unbearable weight of 'love'—too, sustains.
>
> ("A Global Poetic/Positioning System")

The wider, more expansive sense of the aesthetic—the aesthetic as that which is perceptible by feeling—comes to mind upon reading Carroll's avowal. The aesthetic, in all its manifold expressions, sustains through nourishment: the eye, the ear, the sense of touch, the range of channels of perception are fed with new sensibilities, new ways of perceiving the world, new starting points to understand it. The TBT is well designed to direct users to sites of basic physical sustenance, but the kind of world that the TBT imagines is larger, more complex, and the more nourishing for it. The world shown, the sensibility at once teased out and attuned in Carroll's survival poems, is measurable, subject to survey, survivable, but it is also filled with beauty and mystery. It is the desert—its lurking dangers and unlikely sites of sustenance, its historic peopling, the creatures that inhabit it, the plants that grow there, its different forms of death and life—it is the desert that must be revealed, as if from darkness or from a photographic negative. Drawing richly from concrete poetry and land art,[34] the poems written by Carroll carry out this revelation in a way that compels us to take into account the poems' material support in order to gather their measures of meaning. The digital screen on the handheld device where migrants would read the poems is an integral element of this material support, but it is only part of it. The materiality of the poems extends to the level of the environmental, such that the desert landscape so often referenced in the poems gains ground and thickness in the act of reading the poems. The desert, then—that deadly, mesmerizing place against which the poems gain in urgency—and the cell phone—the handheld device where the migrant is so often screened in the everyday reality of digital media and digital life—both function as infrastructures that ballast the form and language of these poems, contributing to their overall construction with an import more obvious and perhaps more substantial than that which we tend to assign to loosely conceived "contexts" of reading and writing.

—

In reference to his work and that of his collaborators on the TBT, Dominguez writes:

> All the members of EDT 2.0/b.a.n.g. anchor their being and becoming as artists and every gesture that we make as an aesthetic gesture. And for us the frame of our work can be traced as an aesthetics of code switching between the Greek etymology of the word 'aesthetic' (*aisthitikos*, that which is 'perceptive by feeling') and the effective poetry of code that functions, that 'works.' Thus we are constantly and concurrently affective and effective.
>
> ("Poetry, Immigration and the FBI:
> The Transborder Immigrant Tool")

The wider sense of aesthetics put forward by Dominguez—aesthetics as all that is "perceptive by feeling" (a sense turned up by Terry Eagleton in his *Ideology of the Aesthetic* and more recently elaborated by Susan Buck-Morss in an essay on "Aesthetics and Anaesthetics")—is crucial in understanding how the TBT operates. In a nutshell, it makes migrants and the experience of the migrant apparent, recognizable, "perceptive by feeling." And it does so in virtue of an "effective poetry of code that functions," a code that places migrants on the map, on a range of maps: aesthetic, political, and, of course, cartographical. This idea of poetry as something that works, something aesthetic ("perceptive by feeling" and so rationally indeterminate), and the correlate notion of aesthetic autonomy that this vision of poetry underscores are among the most lasting effects of the TBT.

Two senses of staging, two senses of making space, come to mind in the context of the acts (political, aesthetic, discursive) staged in and around the TBT. There is, first, the sense of making space for undocumented immigrants: the sense of the desert—so often imagined as no place, as contrast to the life that thrives beyond its arid expanse—being transformed into a place of passage for immigrants and also the sense of making place for undocumented immigrant in the imagination of the city, of the polis, in the central and centered (and increasingly handheld) screens where sense and sensibility (that which makes sense, that which is perceptible by feeling) is parsed and constructed. There is also a will to make way for the aesthetic and for poetry, in particular in the space of the political, in the sphere of activism, a push against the skepticism about, or fear against, embracing play as an integral component of activism. Thus regarded, the TBT acts materially and symbolically, without privileging one aspect over the other. As Rita Raley writes, in reference to the "interventionist tactics" of groups akin to the EDT 2.0/b.a.n.g. lab, "[t]heir battle is at once material and symbolic, fought on the very 'political stage' where power is exercised." Indeed, the "political stage" where the acts of EDT 2.0/b.a.n.g. lab and the TBT, in particular, take place is a stage like any other stage, constituted as such by its material infrastructure (bricks and mortar; sand and heat; platforms, smoke, and screens) as much as it is constituted by the symbolic exchanges that take place on it, within it, bringing it to life.

Notes

1 Roberto Jacoby puts forward the idea of a "tradition of revolutionary puritanism" (which so aptly captures the contempt shown by both liberal and reactionary ideologues in the face of political and aesthetic actions grounded in pleasure and play) in the sprawling retrospective of his work titled *El deseo nace del derrumbe* (2011). He arrives at this idea in reference to what he calls a "strategy of joy" (*"estrategia de la alegría"*), one of the two courses of embodied action he identifies as paradigmatic responses to the violent repression of dissident bodies and dissident voices during the military dictatorship in Argentina (the other course of action being the one enacted by the Madres de Plaza de Mayo). Parallel to the tactics of transit and transition articulated in the TBT, the strategies of joy elaborated by Jacoby are put forward in reference to stages and to theatrical performance—concert stages and the slew of late 70s and early 80s rock acts singled out by Jacoby. See the entry on "La alegría como estrategia" in *El deseo nace del derrumbe* (410–411).

2 Departing from a reading of the TBT that situates it as an object of design (a reading suggested by the producers of the TBT themselves, who often write of their project as a design project), Cynthia Weber analyzes the disciplinary displacing feature of the TBT as part of a larger series of "designs that doubly reposition themselves with respect to borders: both the borders of sovereign nation-states and the presumed border between design and politics" (Weber, "Design, translation, citizenship" 487).

3 The University of California and the University of Michigan.

4 Janez Strehovec, "E-Literature, New Media Art, and E-Literary Criticism" (December 2014); Robert Latham, "The Governance of Visibility: Bodies, Information, and the Politics of Anonymity across the US-Mexico Borderlands" (2014); James Walsh, "Remapping the Border: Geospatial Technologies and Border Activism" (2013); Tamara Vukov and Mimi Sheller, "Border Work: Surveillant Assemblages, Virtual Fences, and Tactical Counter-Media" (2013); David Pinder, "Dis-Locative Arts: Mobile Media and the Politics of Global Positioning" (2013); Elise Morrison, "User-*Unfriendly*: Surveillance Art as Participatory Performance" (2013); Caren Kaplan et al., "Precision Targets: GPS and the Militarization of Everyday Life" (2013); Cynthia Weber, "Design, Translation, Citizenship: Reflections on the Virtual (De)Territorialization of the US-Mexico Border" (2012); Louise Amoore and Alexandra Hall, "Border Theatre: on the arts of security and resistance" (2010).

5 What to make of this "failure" to distribute TBT-enabled cell phones among migrants? A "failure" typical of the avant-garde, characteristic of a kind of will in avant-garde art and in experimentalism in general: the will to propose, to put forward propositions that are consequential with or without being realized. The proposition as plan, as method, and as mode of intervention is what I'm drawing attention to here. Speaking of a different although not entirely unrelated matter, the Brazilian poet João Cabral de Melo Neto wisely

remarked that it is "better to do something that is useless that to do nothing that is useless." The producers of the TBT, on their part, write extensively in "Faust y Furioso" about the reasons behind their decision not to distribute the Tool among migrants, citing as their main concern the possibility of unwittingly abetting violent drug-trafficking operations. They write:

> It quickly became apparent to us that the problem is one of distribution. It wasn't a question as some suspected that we were hesitant to commit a federal felony (although the consequences of such a designation should give any wise person pause) [...] No, the question was regional in a global sense, part and parcel of a yet another hybrid state of emergency. Since 2006, by some estimates more than 100,000 have lost their lives to narco-related violence in Mexico. And, narco-trafficking, which allegedly accounts for 78% of the Republic's economy, does not stop with the movement of illegal substances. Narc@s control the flows of human beings in the borderlands and beyond. Meanwhile, the narc@s are the key suppliers for a U.S. need as surely as U.S.-based distributors supply arms to the narc@s. Again and again, we've asked ourselves, 'What would it mean to insert our project into the complications of this transnational vortex?'.

> (Faust y Furioso 31)

6 To name but one example of this kind of policy: HR 4437, the Border Protection, Anti-Terrorism, and Illegal Immigration Control Act, a bill the U.S. House of Representatives voted in favor of in December 2005. Provisions of the bill would have outlawed charitable and humanitarian assistance to undocumented migrants crossing into and residing in the U.S. See Cynthia Weber, "Design, Translation, Citizenship" for details and a discussion on the U.S. "legal regime that translates humanitarian assistance into criminal activity" (Weber 486).

7 See James Walsh, "Remapping the Border: Geospatial Technologies and Border Activism" (975–977), for an account of the efforts of Humane Borders, one of several humanitarian organizations that was active in the U.S.-Mexico border region in the face of the migrant death crisis.

8 Ngai formulates the notion of "alien citizens" in reference to the Johnson-Reed Act and other immigration laws from the 1920s that declared Asians "racially ineligible for naturalized citizenship" and made Mexicans "the single, largest group of illegal aliens by the late 1920s" (7). A revision of the term "alien citizens" responsive to both the current political situation in the U.S. as well as to immigration policies either enforced or publicly discussed as desirable by elected government officials would need to include religion as another basis (together with national and regional origin) of the "racial formations" responsible for the production of an alien citizenry.

9 The most recent peak being all too immediate at the time of writing, directly related to the election of a mendacious xenophobe, Donald Trump, as president of the U.S.

10 Heat-seeking cameras as instruments of surveillance play a central role in Jordan Crandall's *Heat-Seeking* (2000–2001), a digital media art work where surveillance technology used by the U.S. border patrol gets redeployed in the making of rarified, erotic short videos displayed using personal digital assistant (PDA) devices, popular among business people before the rise of the smartphone. See the catalog to the inSITE 2000–2001 art triennial for which the work was commissioned, *inSITE 2000–2001: parajes fugitivos*, ed. Osvaldo Sánchez and Cecilia Garza (San Diego, 2002).

11 James Walsh points out that the strategy of deterrence was conceived by a corporately managed and corporately operated military research facility, Sandia National Labs, in 1993. See Walsh, "Remapping the Border: Geospatial Technologies and Border Activism" (972).

12 As stated in the "Background" section of an investigation by the Office of the Inspector General of the U.S. Department of Justice in the face of mounting allegations of fraud and misconduct related to Operation Gatekeeper. See "Operation Gatekeeper: An Investigation Into Allegations of Fraud and Misconduct."

13 Cerrutti and Massey periodize modern Mexico-U.S. migration with reference to the end of the Bracero Program in 1964, and, most interestingly, they situate this start point in the context of the 1960s civil rights movements. They write:

> [t]he modern era of Mexico-U.S. migration began with the end of the Bracero program in 1964 [...] As the United States moved into the civil rights era of the 1960s, the Bracero program increasingly came to be seen as an exploitative labor relations system that undermined the well-being of Mexican Americans, discouraged the unionization of farmworkers, and subordinated laborers on the basis of ethnicity.
>
> (Cerrutti and Massey 17)

The modern era of Mexico-U.S. migration is thus embroiled from the outset in the same dynamic of affirmation and contradiction, of progress and concurrent (though not always evident) erasure, that weighs down on the legacy of other civil rights-era movements such as the women's movement and the gay rights movement. The rights and social entitlements claimed under the umbrella banners of women and gay groups constituted a progressive affirmation of wider social groups but did so at the cost of further oppressing racialized constituents of these same groups, who were charged, often explicitly, with the task of effacing their racial difference as a condition of inclusion in the larger groups successfully battling for recognition in the larger social arena. On the immigration front, this dynamic of simultaneous affirmation and oppression was heralded by the Hart-Celler Act of 1965, which lifted some restrictions on previously excluded groups (Africans and Asians) while imposing more restrictions on migration from countries in the Western Hemisphere (Latin American countries included), thus sparking the beginning of the most recent phase of the U.S. history of undocumented immigration. This give-and-take in the social contract, with the state always doing much more taking than it does giving, is a hallmark of the resolution of social conflicts in liberalized, capitalist societies.

14 For an analysis of the failures of Operation Gatekeeper, of the political background against which Operation Gatekeeper was deployed (Bill Clinton's administration's efforts to wrestle from the Republican party control over the immigration debate in the wake of California's Proposition 187), and of the larger, transnational realities that stand in direct contradiction to current U.S. immigration enforcement, see Joseph Nevins, *Operation Gatekeeper: The Rise of the 'Illegal Alien' and the Making of the U.S.-Mexico Boundary* (2002).

15 "As other studies have already shown [...] the probability of getting caught while attempting an undocumented entry has generally trended downward since 1970, and by the early 1990s was at historical lows. Whereas the odds of capture were about one in five through 1980, since the apprehension probabilities have steadily fallen, reaching levels below 10% by the early

1990s. It thus appears that U.S. border enforcement policies have had only a limited effect on the likelihood of undocumented migration or the odds of apprehension at the border" (Cerrutti and Massey 31–32). The failure of U.S. border enforcement and border militarization policies becomes even starker after the 1980s move toward a globalized, neoliberal integration of the North American region:

> The pursuit of restrictive policies in the context of ongoing economic integration between Mexico and the United States under NAFTA have been counterproductive. The likelihood of undocumented migration has not been affected, and the probability of apprehension at the border declined as migrants shifted from fortified segments of the border to more remote and less-patrolled sectors. Meanwhile, the probability of return migration has fallen, yielding an increase in the number of long-term undocumented residents.
>
> (Cerrutti and Massey 22–23)

Regarding the failures of U.S. border enforcement, one thing should be stressed. To the extent that the U.S.'s economy is fundamentally dependent on the cheap labor provided by undocumented immigrants, failure of its border enforcement efforts should be read as a built-in design feature. A "working" border enforcement policy, one that could actually deter and ultimately prevent undocumented migration, would jeopardize U.S. economic and social interests beyond the actual threat that undocumented migration presents to the interests and the security of the U.S. This is what Cynthia Weber argues when she writes:

> These three lines of defence [walls and fences, border patrol operations, vigilante groups] do not stop illegal immigration; nor are they meant to. For the undocumented are a necessary source of cheap labor in the US. Instead, this security system is a means to practically and performatively deny undocumented migrants the right to safe passage into and through the US. It often functions by directing these migrants through a brutal gauntlet of US defensive designs that attacks them from all sides: physically, economically, and legally.
>
> (Weber, "Design, Translation, Citizenship: Reflections on the Virtual (de)territorialization of the US-Mexico Border," 486)

16 In "Sustenance: A Play on All Trans [ ] Borders," the producers of the TBT compare the different sources to have reported on the number of migrant deaths since Operation Gatekeeper was implemented, all the while contextualizing (in reference to the Berlin Wall) the magnitude of the humanitarian crisis unraveling at the U.S.-Mexico border. They write

> It is difficult to procure accurate body counts, but the Customs and Border Protection Agency's 2009 fiscal year report documents 416 border-crossing related deaths from January to October 2009 (add that to 390 in all of 2008, 398 in 2007...). When the Berlin Wall fell, official reports claimed that ninety-eight people died trying to cross from East to West Berlin, while advocacy groups registered the number as exceeding 200. In contrast, humanitarian aid organizations like the Border Angels of San Diego/Tijuana estimate that 10,000 people to date have perished attempting to cross the Mexico-U.S. border (never mind those who've died crossing Mexico).
>
> (*Sustenance: A Play for All Trans [ ] Borders*)

17 Michel de Certeau's theorization of the strategic is what I have in mind here, as is the verticality, the "view from above" (afforded physically or technologically) that Certeau links directly with strategic modes of operation as against tactical ones, which are, by contrast, horizontal, envisioned relationally with reference to movements and variables operational at ground level. See Certeau, *The Practice of Everyday Life* (1984).

18 For an account of the social and symbolic processes that go into the general effacement of racial, sexual, and gender violence in the U.S.-Mexico borderlands, see Nicole M. Guidotti-Hernández, *Unspeakable Violence: Remapping U.S. and Mexican National Imaginaries* (Durham, NC: Duke University Press, 2011).

19 So much became apparent in the case of the thousands of *desaparecidos* who have fallen and keep falling victim to state regimes (and, increasingly, drug-trafficking cartels) in Guatemala, Chile, Argentina, and elsewhere in Latin America, one of the most recent being the forty-three Ayotzinapa students who disappeared in the hands of the Mexican government's armed forces.

20 See Raúl Zurita, *Mi mejilla es el cielo estrellado*, 79–92.

21 Created in 1998 by Ricardo Dominguez, Carmin Karasic, Brett Staulbaum, and Stefan Wray, the initial mobilizations of the Electronic Disturbance Theater (EDT 1.0, distinct from the group responsible for the TBT, EDT 2.0) are structured as virtual, online sit-ins organized in solidarity with the Zapatistas in Chiapas. Ricardo Dominguez describes these interventions as follows:

> EDT recircuits agit-prop actions to mobilize micronetworks to act in solidarity with the Zapatistas in Chiapas by staging virtual sit-ins online [...] The staging of the action is html and a javascript-based tool called FloodNet, which reloads a URL several times a minute, and which slows the site down if a critical mass join the sit-in.
>
> ("Electronic Disturbance Theater" 284)

Note how Dominguez refers to the mobilizations organized by the EDT 1.0 as "acts," endowing said mobilizations with a tactical ambiguity: they are actions (interventions in the "real world" with real consequences) as much as they are parts of a narrative or play. The ambiguity is built into the very name of the art/activism collective: the Electronic Disturbance Theater.

22 "Artivists" and "artivism" are the two terms most frequently used by the members of EDT Theater 2.0/b.a.n.g. lab to refer to their role and the work they perform. Dominguez puts forward the following definition of "artivism":

> New media artivism is a «bug» in the system that seeks to constantly disturb the frameworks in reference to which art has been defined, the frameworks within which art is currently defined, the frameworks that allow us to envision what art may be like in the future; it is the canary in the coal mine, siren and fire alarm, the blind probe of that which cannot be seen yet but that must be made more and more visible.
>
> ("Error 404_Democracia no encontrada", my translation)

23 For a thorough analysis of GPS technology and its place and effects on everyday life, see Caren Kaplan, "Precision Targets: GPS and the Militarization of Everyday Life" (2013).

24 David Harvey's notion of relational space is what comes closest to defining the spatial category at work in GPS mapping and in the TBT in particular. Harvey defines relational space as follows:

The relational concept of space is most often associated with the name of Leibniz who, in a famous series of letters to Clarke (effectively a stand-in for Newton) objected vociferously to the absolute view of space and time so central to Newton's theories. His primary objection was theological. Newton made it seem as if even God was inside of absolute space and time rather than in command of spatio-temporality. By extension, the relational view of space holds there is no such thing as space or time outside of the processes that define them [...] Processes do not occur in space but define their own spatial frame. The concept of space is embedded in or internal to process.

(Harvey, *Spaces of Global Capitalism* 123)

25 "I use the term *migrant imaginaries* to encompass the world-making aspirations of Mexican border-crossers, whose mobility changed the character of both U.S. and Mexican national life over the 20th-century. The migrant in this study not only connotes one who moves within and across national boundaries; it also references a subordinate position with respect to that of the citizen" (Schmidt Camacho 5).

26 See Jacques Rancière, *The Politics of Aesthetics*, 12–13: "The distribution of the sensible," writes Rancière, reveals who can have a share in what is common to the community based on what they do and on the time and space in which this activity is performed. Having a particular 'occupation' [...] defines what is visible or not in a common space, endowed with a common language, etc.

27 A profile of Ricardo Dominguez as media artist and scholar in the *Chronicle of Higher Education* summarizes news coverage of the TBT in reference to Dominguez's raising media profile:

CNN has placed him on a list of most intriguing people; talking heads on Fox News Channel—not just Glenn Beck—have suggested that he should be thrown in jail; NPR has invited him on the air to discuss his work
(Goldstein, "Digitally Incorrect: Ricardo Dominguez's provocations: art or crimes?")

A highlight among the numerous articles and notes on the TBT was the segment Glenn Beck dedicated to it in the Fox News Channel in September 2010, where, as Ricardo Dominguez often points out, the famously controversial, zealously conservative television personality alluded to the power of poetry— and the TBT's poetics in particular—to disturb and "dissolve" the nation.

28 The authors insist on a cross-disciplinary framing of computer code in poetry, a reading that keeps in mind both the precise, functional beauty of computer code and also the function, the doing or making (the *poesis* in the strong sense of the term), of poetry. For a recent study of the place of computer code in recent Latin American literature, see Eduardo Ledesma, "The Poetics and Politics of Computer Code in Latin America: Codework, Code Art, and Live Coding," in *Revista de Estudios Hispánicos* 49.1 (March 2015): 91–120.

29 Earlier versions of the poems appeared in translations into more languages than English and Spanish, acknowledging the rich national and linguistic diversity of the migrants that cross and perish in the U.S.-Mexico borderlands.

30 For an analysis of the campaign's impact, see Colombina Schaeffer Ortúzar, "Patagonia Sin Represas: How an Environmental Campaign Transformed Power Landscapes in Chile" (2015).

31 In an incisive analogy drawn by the producers of the TBT between, on the one hand, the efforts to place water in the desert and, on the other hand, the phenomenon of "let-down" (a reflex bodily reaction experienced by

some lactating mothers in the presence of crying children), Eve Sedgwick's idea of a "privilege of unknowing" is suggestively repurposed to describe the seemingly deliberate ignorance that has grown around the subject of mass migrant deaths along the U.S.-Mexico border. They write: "Framing water-caching in terms of let-down amounts to a refusal to recount the borderlands' competing and accreting essentialisms, a U.S.-based 'privilege of unknowing' the escalating numbers of a continental humanitarian crisis" (*Sustenance: A Play for All Trans [ ] Borders*). The term is suggestive, among other reasons, to the extent that it reveals dismissive ignorance as prerogative. The act of not seeing, not knowing, not minding "that which is perceptible by feeling" is reframed as luxury, a luxury the producers of the TBT refuse to accommodate.

32 See Alejandro Portes, *Immigrant America: A Portrait* (2014), for a rich and complex picture of current immigrant to the U.S.
33 Carroll, http://post.thing.net/node/2792.
34 Continuities between the TBT, concrete poetry, and land art can be traced along the lines of the Tool's meaningful incorporation of the material support for language and also in terms of its integration, its grounding, in the landscape that envelops it. See Amy Sara Carroll's "EDT 1.0, EDT 2.0, EDT 3.0" for a more expansive elaboration of these continuities and for a thoughtful reprise of the different iterations of the EDT.

Works Cited

"Act." *OED*. Oxford English Dictionary, November 2010. Web. 1 May 2013.

Amoore, Louise, and Alexandra Hall. "Border Theatre: On the Arts of Security and Resistance." *Cultural Geographies* 17.3 (2010): 299–319.

Annerino, John. *Dead in Their Tracks: Crossing America's Desert Borderlands in the New Era*. Tucson: U of Arizona P, 2009.

Buck-Morss, Susan. "Aesthetics and Anaesthetics: Walter Benjamin's Artwork Essay Reconsidered." *October* 62 (Oct. 1992): 3–41.

Cárdenas, Micha, Amy Sara Carroll, Ricardo Dominguez, Elle Mehrmand, and Brett Stalbaum. *The Transborder Immigrant Tool/ La herramienta transfronteriza para inmigrantes*. Ann Arbor, MI: The Office of Net Assesment, the University of Michigan, 2014.

Carroll, Amy Sara. "EDT 1.0, EDT 2.0, EDT 3.0*." *Errata: Revista de Artes Visuales* 3 (Dec. 2010): 40–64. PDF.

———. "FIVE POEMS by Amy Sara Carroll." *Poets for Living Waters*. 13 June 2010. https://poetsgulfcoast.wordpress.com/2010/06/13/929. Accessed 1 May 2013.

———. "A Global Poetic/Positioning System: The Transborder Immigrant Tool." http://post.thing.net/node/2792. Accessed 2 May 2013.

Cerrutti, Marcela, and Douglas S. Massey. "Trends in Mexican Migration to the United States, 1965 to 1995." *Crossing the Border: Research from the Mexican Migration Project*. Ed. Jorge Durand and Douglas S. Massey. New York: Russell Sage Foundation, 2004. 17–44.

Certeau, Michel de. *The Practice of Everyday Life*. Berkeley: U of California P, 1984.

Critical Art Ensemble. *Digital Resistance: Explorations in Tactical Media*. New York: Autonomedia, 2001.

Dominguez, Ricardo. "Electronic Disturbance Theater." *Corpus Delecti: Performance Art of the Americas.* Ed. Coco Fusco. New York: Routledge, 2000. 284–286.

———. "Error 404_Democracia no encontrada." *Errata: Revista de Artes Visuales* 3 (Dec. 2010): 16–20. PDF.

———. Interview by Leila Nadir. "Poetry, Immigration and the FBI: The Transborder Immigrant Tool." *Hyperallergic.* Hyperallergic, 23 July 2012. https://hyperallergic.com/54678/poetry-immigration-and-the-fbi-the-transborder-immigrant-tool. Accessed 1 May 2013.

Eagleton, Terry. *The Ideology of the Aesthetic.* Cambridge, MA: Blackwell, 1990.

Electronic Disturbance Theater /b.a.n.g. Lab. *Operation Faust & Furioso: A Trans [ ] border Play on the Redistribution of the Sensible.* Ed. Amy Sara Carroll and Ricardo Dominguez. Leonardo Electronic Almanac (LEA). 21.1 (Jan 2016): 28–42.

———. *Sustenance: A Play for All Trans [ ] Borders.* New York: Printed Matter, Inc., 2010. PDF.

Goldstein, Evan R. "Digitally Incorrect: Ricardo Dominguez's provocations: Art or Crimes?." *The Chronicle of Higher Education* 3 Oct. 2010. www.chronicle.com/article/Digitally-Incorrect/124649. Accessed 1 May 2013.

Guidotti-Hernández, Nicole M. *Unspeakable Violence: Remapping U.S. and Mexican National Imaginaries.* Durham, NC: Duke UP, 2011.

Harvey, David. *Spaces of Global Capitalism.* New York: Verso, 2006.

Hernandez, Kelly Lytle. *Migra!: A History of the U.S. Border Patrol.* Berkeley: U of California P, 2010.

Jacoby, Roberto. *El deseo nace del derrumbe: acciones, conceptos, escritos.* Barcelona: Ediciones de la Central, 2011.

Kaplan, Caren, Erik Loyer, and Ezra Claytan Daniels. "Precision Targets: GPS and the Militarization of Everyday Life." *Canadian Journal of Communication* 38.3 (2013): 397–420.

Latham, Robert. "The Governance of Visibility: Bodies, Information, and the Politics of Anonymity across the US-Mexico Borderlands." *Alternatives: Global, Local, Political* 39.1 (2014): 17–36.

Ledesma, Eduardo. "The Poetics and Politics of Computer Code in Latin America: Codework, Code Art, and Live Coding." *Revista de Estudios Hispánicos* 49.1 (Mar. 2015): 91–120.

Morrison, Elise. "User-Unfriendly: Surveillance Art as Participatory Performance." *Theater* 43.3 (2013): 5–23.

Nevins, Joseph. *Operation Gatekeeper: The Rise of the 'Illegal Alien' and the Making of the U.S. Mexico Boundary.* New York: Routledge, 2002.

Ngai, Mae M. *Impossible Subjects: Illegal Aliens and the Making of Modern America.* 2004. Princeton, NJ: Princeton UP, 2014.

"Operation Gatekeeper: An Investigation into Allegations of Fraud and Misconduct (July, 1998)." *Office of the Inspector General, U.S. Department of Justice* July 1998. www.oig.justice.gov/special/9807/index.htm. Accessed 10 June 2016.

Pinder, David. "Dis-locative Arts: Mobile Media and the Politics of Global Positioning." *Continuum* 27.4 (2013): 523–541.

Portes, Alejandro. *Immigrant America: A Portrait.* Oakland, CA: U of California P, 2014.

Raley, Rita. *Tactical Media.* Minneapolis: U of Minnesota P, 2009.

Rancière, Jacques. *The Flesh of the Words: The Politics of Writing.* 1998. trans. Charlotte Mandell. Stanford, CA: Stanford UP, 2004.

———. *The Politics of Aesthetics: The Distribution of the Sensible.* 2000. trans. Gabriel Rockhill. New York: Continuum, 2004.

Richard, Nelly. "The Cultural Periphery and Postmodern Decentring." *Rethinking Borders.* Ed. John C. Welchman. Basingstoke: Macmillan, 1996. 71–84.

Sánchez, Osvaldo, and Cecilia Garza, eds. *inSITE 2000–2001: parajes fugitivos.* San Diego, CA: Installation Gallery, 2002.

Schaeffer Ortúzar, Colombina. *Patagonia Sin Represas: How an Environmental Campaign Transformed Power Landscapes in Chile.* Diss. University of Sydney, 2015. Web. 23 Sep 2017.

Schmidt Camacho, Alicia R. *Migrant Imaginaries: Latino Cultural Politics in the U.S.-Mexico Borderlands.* New York: New York UP, 2008.

Strehovec, Janez. "E-Literature, New Media Art, and E-Literary Criticism." *CLCWeb: Comparative Literature and Culture* 16.5 (Dec. 2014).

Urrea, Luis Alberto. *The Devil's Highway: A True Story.* New York: Back Bay Books, 2005.

Vukov, Tamara, and Mimi Sheller. "Border Work: Surveillant Assemblages, Virtual Fences, and Tactical Counter-Media." *Social Semiotics* 23.2 (2013): 225–241.

Walsh, James. "Remapping the Border: Geospatial Technologies and Border Activism." *Environment* and Planning D: Society and Space 31 (2013): 969–987.

Weber, Cynthia. "Design, Translation, Citizenship: Reflections on the Virtual (De)Territorialization of the US-Mexico Border." *Environment and Planning D: Society and Space* 30 (2012): 482–496.

Zurita, Raúl. *Mi mejilla es el cielo estrellado.* Saltillo: Instituto Coahuilense de Cultura: Editorial Aldus: Fondo Nacional para la Cultura y las Artes, 2004.

2 Decolonizing Youth Culture
Guatemalan Hip Hop Dissidents in Cyberspace

Esteban Loustaunau

OK, entonces al estudio yo te caigo.
Buenas chivas que escribí anoche yo te traigo.
Pa' grabarlas y subirlas al Facebook,
para el rap de Guatemala darle otro look.[1]

Shadowzito

Guate evolucionó y tira potente.
Somos un elemento maya, no somos gente.
Creen que rapeamos sólo por güeva, ¡ja!
Aquí rapeamos porque es talento maya de la nueva era.[2]

Rapsista

In present-day Guatemala, people are still experiencing the aftermath of the country's torturous modern history that includes U.S. interventions, massacres by military dictatorships, indigenous guerrilla uprisings, more than thirty years of civil war, and, most recently, a neoliberal economic shift that weakened newly instituted democratic regimes, making them unable to control impunity and drug-trafficking violence. The overthrow of Guatemalan democracy in 1954 marked the beginning of U.S. intervention and political instability that led to a dark period of military authoritarianism (Arias 38–39). Following the 1954 coup d'état, Guatemala suffered a brutal civil war that included widespread human rights violations against civilians as the government forcefully suppressed leftist guerrilla armed groups composed of ethnic Maya indigenous people and other poor Ladino peasants. Thirty years after the war had started came the promise of peace in 1996. But, finding a reconciliatory balance between the atrocities of war and the promise of a new day after the 1996 Peace Accords has been an uphill struggle for Guatemala's political and social actors. In the current postwar period, despite the signed declaration to the end civil war, impunity and violence continue to prevail across Guatemala. Nonetheless, in a country in which impunity exists to keep the powerful above the rule of law, the 2013 trial against former dictator Efraín Ríos Mont on charges of genocide and crimes against humanity demonstrated that survivors of violence have the right to continue the struggle for justice. For Nobel Peace Prize laureate Rigoberta Menchú, the promise to transform Guatemala into a more democratic and inclusive nation so far has failed in the postwar period. Menchú explains that after the signing of the Peace Accords, most political and social actors lacked the will to truly combat the deep historical causes of conflict and war that include social inequality, control of the land and of other natural resources, authoritarianism, censorship, racism, and impunity (Dada and Menjívar 1). Consequently, the unresolved problems of the past, most of which originated at the time of Spanish colonialism, continue to afflict present day Guatemalans.

In Guatemala, young people are among the social groups that continue to remain subjugated. Impoverished young Guatemalans lack basic education and work opportunities that would provide them with a fructiferous future. This is especially common among the children of men and women killed during the civil war or whose family members have had to emigrate from Guatemala in search of work in the U.S. As a result, many young people in Guatemala face social stigmatization and political exclusion (Goldín and Rosenbaum 72; Sepúlveda 264; Tierney 124). To overcome stigmatization and prejudice, young Guatemalans have engaged with hip hop[3] culture to raise their social consciousness and publicly perform their cultural creativity.[4] Today, ordinary young Guatemalans are fighting their own wars against socioeconomic oblivion and marginalization, provoked by the dynamics of late capitalism, as they transform themselves into hip hop warriors whose battles take place on the streets and walls of Guatemala as well as on the networks of cyberspace.

Living under acute uncertainty and social disconnection, many young Guatemalans see hip hop culture as a vehicle through which they can collectively overcome persecution by the police, resist forced recruitment by gangs and organized crime, combat gender discrimination, and denounce social marginalization and stigmatization. These young hip hop performers come together in musical and artistic collectives consisting of individual artists and crews (bands) working together to form horizontal networks of action. In Guatemala, hip hop collectives act horizontally, as crew members become accountable to one another through a given set of principles that emphasize collective inclusion and mutual respect. I am particularly interested in discussing two of Guatemala's most thriving hip hop organizations working today, *Asociación Guatemalteca de Artistas de Hip Hop Trasciende* and *Revolución Hip Hop*, and see how each collective is transforming the lives of ordinary young people. These two groups take children and young people off the streets by providing creative activities that include free classes and workshops on each of the four artistic elements of hip hop: "DJ-ing," the aural mixing of sound through turntablism; "MC-ing," the oral expression of rap music;

graffiti as urban visual art; and "b-boying/b-girling," break dancing performed by young men and women.

In its early origins during the 1970s, in New York's South Bronx and Harlem, disenfranchised African-American and Latino youth created hip hop through the practice of the four distinctive but complementary elements that have come to represent different manifestations of resistance against poverty, violence, and spatial exclusion (Flores 115). Since then, hip hop has continued to spread and developed in various forms across the world. Particularly, marginalized youth in the Global South (what once was referred to as the Third World) have continued to shape hip hop into a transnational countercultural movement where the global—languages and images from the Global North, including technology and the Internet—is being appropriated and resignified by the local—as represented by particular experiences of marginalization and violence in specific social and historical contexts. In contemporary Guatemala, *Trasciende* provides young people with safe spaces to perform and practice hip hop, while *Revolución Hip Hop* offers these artists opportunities to travel and participate in local and international hip hop festivals. As cultural agents committed to this alternative urban art form, the members of *Trasciende* and *Revolución Hip Hop* use the Internet and other inexpensive social networks as their primary medium to voice their social dissent and communicate their messages to people, both locally and globally (Morello 58).

To be poor and young in Guatemala today means to be subjected to dominant mischaracterizations of passivity, barbarism, and delinquency.[5] Yet, these normative categories do not represent the real-life experiences of many young people who demand access to public spaces for recognition and self-expression (Reguillo 51; García Canclini 168–169). In this new century, young Guatemalan hip hop artists, disenchanted with the false promises of late capitalism, artistically express their demands for the recognition of cultural difference and for the creation of spaces of cultural affirmation.[6] While the Guatemalan state and dominant economic classes remain in control of mainstream radio and television media, young hip hop artists are committed to working together and raising their voices as "lived experiences of people using the Internet to facilitate social change" (Friedman 2). Guatemalan hip hop artists' use of the Internet echoes Elisabeth Friedman's call to move beyond disputes of whether the Internet is a liberating instrument that extends horizontal networks across local and global levels or a technology used to reproduce the "digital divides" that increases traditional inequalities of age, race, class, and gender.[7] Instead, as Friedman suggests, the focus should be on "the reality of virtual reality," or the application of the Internet by ordinary people seeking to improve their lives and those of others (Friedman 2).

In Guatemala, hip hop culture is a dynamic and empowering force that helps transform young people into active cultural subjects by turning normative urban places into symbolic spaces of coexistence and recognition.[8] In performing one or more of the four elements of hip hop—DJ-ing, MC-ing, graffiti, and b-boying/b-girling,—young Guatemalans generate alternative ways of life that lead to higher levels of self-esteem and value (Vargas 6). The sociopolitical impact that hip hop has had in Guatemala can be measured in at least two ways: by how these young artists transform their lives, as they move from feeling abandoned to taking control of their own lives, and by how they subvert dominant meanings assigned to urban "proper places" and bodies, thereby converting them into "practiced spaces" through alternative forms of cultural creativity (De Certeau 117). As Rossana Reguillo argues, young people today configure their own cultural identities in the transversal crossings they make every day between music, speech, urban aesthetics, and technology (Reguillo 41). That is, their cultural practices simultaneously overlap and feed from each other, producing a transversal effect where social identities are formed, expressed, and shared across local, regional, and global levels (41). This explains not only the readiness with which Guatemalan youth critically challenge their marginalization through hip hop, but also helps understand the increasing relevance that the Internet plays in young people's desire to raise awareness of the social problems affecting them today. I will develop this argument by examining some of the cultural practices by young artists affiliated to the hip hop collectives *Trasciende* and *Revolución Hip Hop*.

In the Guatemalan hip hop material that I researched online, I identified three recurrent cultural inversions that hip hop artists turn into alternative spaces for dissent. In my analysis of how young Guatemalans appropriate global culture to meet their local social and cultural demands, I consider the notion of "cultural inversions" as the transformative practices through which hip hop artists use the Internet and electronic social media to deliver their collective messages and voice their resistance as they turn their particular locations and life experiences into sources of awareness, innovation, creativity, and value. These inversions include nonconformist referents of the artists' poor neighborhoods such as "la esquina" ("the corner"), "la calle" ("the street"), or "el gueto" ("the ghetto"); of Guatemala as Ixim Ulew, the symbolic locus of enunciation of Mayan cosmovision; and of women's bodies and consciousness. After introducing a brief history of hip hop in Guatemala, I will provide examples of each of these cultural inversions by artists belonging to *Trasciende* and *Revolución Hip Hop*. When hip hop artists convert fixed meanings of place from territorial property into something else that is fluid and horizontal, they begin to express other ways of thinking that lead to their own liberation.

The origins of alternative urban music in Guatemala can be traced back to the late 1990s, when young teenagers started listening to hip hop, dance, and reggae music before forming their own underground bands.[9] Even after the signing of the Peace Accords in 1996, most alternative music bands remained underground due to a lack of support by mainstream media and other cultural industries and by the threat of state repression. By 2002, the first Guatemalan hip hop collective, *La Urbe*, started organizing parties at the bar *El Tiempo*. These were small gatherings planned by a few young enthusiasts who were leaving behind the underground music scene and entering a new stage of open dialogue with various other hip hop artists.[10] The emergence of hip hop in Guatemala helped to bring to the attention of wider national and international audiences the conditions of social marginalization and political violence that many poor Guatemalans continue to endure in the postwar period, as neoliberal democratization favors the advancement of the social and economic elites and does little to combat ongoing human rights violations. Some of the original hip hop crews in Guatemala, among them Alioto Lokos, Strate Crooked, and Bacteria Sound System, spread hip hop culture throughout the capital city and into other departments around the country (MC Lovel 2). These alternative music crews had to develop their own modes of production, such as homebuilt recording studios where artists and musicians learned to depend on one another as they produced their own art works. In these early stages, it was common for young artists to come together and share with one another their limited technological equipment and access the Internet at someone's home or in cybercafés (Vargas 12).

Since the beginning stages of the movement, collective participation has been the basis of most of the production and promotion of Guatemalan hip hop. This attitude toward collaboration is also essential in understanding their reliance on Internet sites such as Facebook, YouTube, Reverbnation, SoundCloud, Veengle, Vimeo, and personal blogs. As most young people today, Guatemalan hip hop artists consider the Internet as an essential resource in their quest for producing art and disseminating it at no cost to as many people as possible. The sound principles of mutuality and reciprocity shared among these hip hop artists also enable them to remain active in more than one crew or collective. For example, several members of *Trasciende* are also involved in planning the international hip hop festivals organized each year by *Revolución Hip Hop*. Instead of *Trasciende* and *Revolución Hip Hop* being rivals, their mutual collaboration is what makes each of them better and stronger.

Today, Guatemalan hip hop is a well-established artistic movement that brings together numerous collectives and crews from around the country and also takes part in international hip hop festivals in Latin American and Europe. Known as *batallas* or battles, rap and breakdance public events gather thousands of youngsters who, through this urban art, send messages of nonviolence and cultural coexistence to the rest of society. The success of hip hop in Guatemala is due in part to the conscientious effort by the participants of this art to critically challenge traditional assumptions, stigmas, and stereotypes that link the young with idleness, rap music with violence and crime, and graffiti with gangs and vandalism. *Trasciende* and *Revolución Hip Hop* have much to do with the success of the movement. *Trasciende* is a hip hop academy that opened in 2009 and offers free classes, retreats, and workshops on urban art in Guatemala City and in schools across various departments of the country.[11] *Revolución Hip Hop* grew out of *La Urbe* collective in 2006, and now its members are responsible for organizing an annual hip hop festival that brings together the best international urban art talent to Guatemala.[12]

In recent years, *Revolución Hip Hop* has extended the Guatemala's hip hop reach by organizing an annual international hip hop festival. In 2013, it was the eighth consecutive year in which various crews from Latin America and Europe traveled to Guatemala City to compete and learn from each other about all four elements of hip hop. As with past festivals, the *VIII Festival International Revolución Hip Hop* dedicated one full day to organizing workshops, exhibitions, and battles (contests) on DJ-ing, MC-ing, graffiti, and b-boing/b-girling. Each year, the festival organizers spread the word through the use of social media (Facebook and YouTube) and the festival's official online blog. Since the first festival in 2006, more national and international sponsors, including the Red Bull's recording studio in Spain, have joined forces with *Revolución Hip Hop* to continue making this event a success. With the financial support of new sponsors, the festival organizers have made significant improvements in advertising this event through more sophisticated blogs and YouTube videos. However, this has not always been the case. In the early years of the Guatemalan hip hop movement, the first music videos, documentaries, and recorded interviews created for the website Guatemalahiphop.com lacked some of the technological sophistication with which the newer videos and blogs are made.[13] Since 2011, the quality of the material that *Trasciende* and *Revolución Hip Hop* produce online has improved significantly, as these young artists with limited financial and technological resources sought the assistance of private foundations and independent film producers in Guatemala, such as Da.Radio.com, Fundación Para Elisa, Moda Focka Films, and Zanate Mojado Films. These collaborations relate to what Friedman calls "chains of access," as they allow those who cannot go online regularly to connect with those who can (13). These chains of access are important to Guatemalan hip hop artists as they seek to attract the attention of local and global audiences in cyberspace. The results have been favorable, as the 2012 festival brought crews from Guatemala, Mexico, El Salvador, Honduras, Costa Rica, Nicaragua, Puerto Rico, Venezuela, and France (García-Gallont 1).

As I already mentioned, *Trasciende* and *Revolución Hip Hop* have improved the lives of many young men and women in Guatemala by providing them with the necessary training and public space to develop artistic expressions of recognition and self-worth. Young Guatemalans find an alternative option away from social marginalization and the dangers of street gang violence. *Trasciende* helps young people to develop their own self-esteem and human value through an emphasis on the principles of love, peace, unity, and enjoyment. These values are reinforced as more experienced artists teach beginning students the four elements of hip hop in a converted building in downtown Guatemala City. It is important to stress the relevant role that women play in this hip hop movement. In "Voces Libres," a news report on YouTube that focuses on women's participation in *Trasciende,* one learns that young Guatemalan women are active in all four elements of hip hop culture. Still, sexism prevails in Guatemalan society, as rapper Jen Soto explains how many young women feel they have to work twice as hard as the men if they want to make a name for themselves in hip hop. At the same time, the members of *Trasciende* strive to create a more unified community. This becomes clear later in the online news report, when Soto observes the constant support women receive from male students in every dance rehearsal and performance. To this end, rapper and break dancer Mr. Fer, a founding member of *Trasciende* and organizer of *Revolución Hip Hop,* adds that *Trasciende* aims to work with "the human element," regardless of gender. Aware of the patriarchal culture of machismo that persists in Guatemala, he describes how at first, many women felt uncomfortable taking break dancing classes along with men. Following a women's initiative, *Trasciende* members decided to offer hip hop classes just for women. The results have been positive, as more women have joined *Trasciende* and are raising their voices publicly through hip hop.[14] For example, through their own talent and their use of online networks, female hip hop artists Jen Soto, *Las Musas* [The Muses], and Rebecca Lane, among others, lead the alternative music scene in Guatemala today.

Members of *Trasciende* actively promote Guatemalan hip hop in cyberspace by uploading their music and performances on YouTube, Veengle, or Vimeo. For example, an early video entitled "Mini-documental Trasciende—Hip hop de Guatemala" first appeared online in 2009. In this documentary, a young dancer by the name of B-boy Denis shares what *Trasciende* means to him:

> Trasciende nos ha beneficiado en muchas partes (sic). Porque nos ha brindado el espacio donde hemos crecido como una familia. Y hemos crecido individualmente en nuestras habilidades como b-boys, verdad. También nos ha ayudado a encontrar un nuevo hogar, una nueva casa, donde podemos estar aquí todo el día y nadie nos dice nada, nadie nos discrimina (Mini-documental).[15]

For amateur artists like B-boy Denis, *Trasciende* takes over urban space and turns it into a practiced place for human growth. This take over represents a cultural inversion of public space into a reconfigured site where young men and women can freely dance and collectively recuperate a corner of the city for themselves. B-boy Denis blends the personal "I" with the collective "we" to represent the ways in which Guatemalan hip hop artists tie their personal experiences to those of their community. By saying "hemos crecido como una familia" ("we have grown together as a family"), B-boy Denis understands his individual subjectivity as being connected to the collective. His self-recognition is found in the common "we" of his hip hop crew or "familia" ("family"), moving away from other normative identity structures where he might feel "discriminado" ("discriminated"). The same happens when B-boy Denis break dances. With his performance, he comes to occupy the street, turning it into a collective practiced place now exercised by him and his crew (Villegas 71). A similar effect is happening in cyberspace, as hip hop collectives like *Trasciende* and numerous hip hop crews in Guatemala and elsewhere open their own accounts on Facebook and upload their music videos online to spread messages of hope and social justice. This becomes a cybercultural inversion by Guatemalan hip hop artists as they transgress normative discourses of exclusion and transform cyberspace into a shared, practiced place of alternative cultural production.

In the same online documentary mentioned before, Mr. Fer shares his opinion on the social meaning of this hip hop academy. According to Mr. Fer, one of the main goals of *Trasciende* is to change the image of young people in Guatemala by challenging the negative stereotypes of violence and idleness, instead underlining the fact that young people deserve their own cultural spaces. He goes on to explain that young people today are socially and economically marginalized because they represent a force of change. Mr. Fer states:

> Vos sabes que el poder económico no lo tienen los jóvenes. Entonces los jóvenes son utilizados porque son la fuerza, me entendés. Aquí canalizamos esa fuerza, de eso se trata el rollo, verdad... A lo que yo voy es que el prejuicio existe y a nosotros no nos detiene. Y lo interesante es ver como sí se rompe el prejuicio. De hecho, aquí no se le dice a la banda qué ponerse. La gente se pone lo que quiere. Lo que ve en su entorno. Igual, lo que tratamos nosotros es de no hacer prejuicio. Porque si la gente está viéndonos mal a nosotros y no nos gusta, si nosotros hacemos lo mismo con los demás, entonces ahí estamos totalmente errados, verdad (Mini-documental).[16]

As Mr. Fer explains, *Trasciende* encourages Guatemalan youth to break away from feeling subjugated to dominant forces.[17] *Trasciende* teaches young people to believe in themselves in order to release the power that remains hidden within them. In another video from 2011, a young rapper who goes by the artistic name of DJ Fender also offers his opinion on the meaning of the academy:

> La palabra "trasciende" significa trascender, verdad. Porque no-sotros consideramos que trascendimos de un punto hacia otro.... *Trasciende* para nosotros es como un trampolín para todos los jóvenes que quieran venir porque [la gente] los ve acá y ven que están haciendo algo bueno. Los ven como artistas ("Guatemala's Leap").[18]

The appeal that hip hop has on marginalized young Guatemalans opens up a path toward alternative ways of thinking and living. These young people's appropriation of hip hop culture via their postings in cyberspace and in their public urban performances unlocks what Walter Mignolo calls "decolonial thinking," that is, the dual counterpoint or "double critique" that negates the false promises of modernity and challenges the continuity of the logic of colonialism that persists today ("Epistemic Disobedience" 46). In their cultural initiatives, hip hop artists introduce online their own double critique: on the one hand, they refuse to sub-mit to the hegemonic discourses of racial, ethnic, and gender domina-tion; on the other, they release what Mignolo has described elsewhere as "knowledges that have been subalternized" and hidden from view by the dominant discourses of modernity/coloniality (*Local Histories* 67). One of the results of this double critique is the introduction of a de-location of Guatemala. According to Mignolo, de-location becomes a distance, a separation necessary to distinguish the location of enunciation of the voices of dissent from the discourse of coloniality and national hege-mony in Guatemala. In this way, hip hop artists reject dominant no-tions of Guatemala as *territory* and instead articulate another sense of Guatemala as *land* with its multiple and particular meanings regener-ated from the cultural practices of the dispossessed (270). In this way, a delocalized Guatemala symbolically becomes a contested space where young hip hop artists can create alternative cultural spaces of self-recog-nition and existence.

Delocalized spaces reveal the particular hopes and needs of margin-alized subjects such as the members of *Trasciende* and *Revolución Hip Hop*. In the present era of globalization, the young artists from *Trasci-ende* and *Revolución Hip Hop* see their access to cyberspace—especially their use of sites such as Facebook, YouTube, and SoundCloud—as a delocalizing practice or, in DJ Fender's words, as a real "spring-board" through which they manage to "transcend" oblivion and in-visibility to become agents of social change in Guatemala. The themes of gender, ethnic, and class discrimination, the need of sociopolitical awareness, and the defense of one's neighborhood tend to be the most common topics that these young artists upload in cyberspace. For fe-male hip hop artists who represent 40% of *Trasciende's* membership, their main struggle is against patriarchy, sexism, and class divisions. For impoverished rappers living in precarious neighborhoods, one of their main concerns is to reclaim their communities and way of life. Their songs demystify dominant assumption of the slums as they take pride in their local community, a main source of meaning in their lives. For members of *Trasciende* and *Revolución Hip Hop* who identified themselves as Maya, Guatemala becomes a land symbolically rooted in Maya cosmogony. All these fragmented experiences of human struggle help generate alternative meanings of space, including cyberspace, in the present time.

These other ways of thinking and of resignifying cyberspace from positions of decoloniality become evident as hip hop artists value their life experiences in poor neighborhoods of Guatemala City and recover other hidden or forgotten knowledges (Mignolo), such as the memory of Maya traditions and languages in a new century, and women's wisdom and agency. The two rap songs that appear in the epigraph at the beginning of this chapter introduce this kind of decolonial thinking. Another way to describe decolonial thinking is an alternative discourse that absorbs and displaces "hegemonic forms of knowledge into the perspective of the subaltern" (Mignolo, *Local Histories* 12). The songs included in the epigraph display a double subaltern critique, as rappers Shadowzito and Rapsista reclaim local space and Mayan legacies, respectively, and reconfigure them in a transversal cultural place shared with Facebook and the "nueva era." Shadowzito is a young rapper from *Trasciende* who has seen his career soar in recent years. Today, his music can be downloaded free of charge, either from his personal Facebook page or in Reverbnation. com, an online site that helps jumpstart the careers of independent musicians.[19] In his rap song "Esto es Guatemala" ("This is Guatemala"), Shadowzito brings together various languages, moments, and places that transform Guatemala from being a territory of dominance kept out of reach of young dissidents into a cultural practiced place that gains "*otro* look" ("*an-other* look") (my emphasis). This other look can be interpreted as a living space for other ways of being and thinking. Hip hop "absorbs" the languages and electronic networks of social media and "displaces" the hegemonic meaning of cyberspace in order to reconfigure it as a practiced place of the subaltern. In his song, Shadowzito mixes Spanish, English, and Guatemalan slang, just as he intersects his personal creative space, a recording studio, Guatemala, and cyberspace. Shadowzito manages to reshape Guatemala from territory to land by symbolically turning Guatemala into a practiced place of difference and coexistence. The title of the song "Esto es Guatemala" ("This is Guatemala") marks a cultural resignification of Guatemala, not a territorial take over as in the rhetoric of modernity, but an opening where the MC is free to move back and forth from his home in "el gueto" ("the ghetto") to the studio and cyberspace.

In the second song from the epigraph, Rapsista—a member of *Revolución Hip Hop* and one of the collaborators of the VII International Hip Hop Festival's theme song, "10 MC unidos con una sola misión" ("10 MCs United Under One Mission")—uncovers the rhetoric of modernity/coloniality that persists in the way of social discrimination against poor young Guatemalans.[20] Rapsista's lyrics defy social discrimination when he raps "Creen que rapeamos sólo por güeva" ("They think we rap because we are bored"). Here, the rapper reveals the prejudice held by the guardians of social order and good manners who think rap music is nothing but a mindless result of boredom and idleness. Rapsista refuses to be caught by the dominant social order when he raps "no somos gente" ("people are wrong about us"). This negation is his way to step outside the modern political discourse, where center, left-, and right-wing ideologies dispute the control of the people. Instead, Rapsista makes a decolonial turn and brings into light a Maya genealogy that continues to be suppressed in postwar Guatemala. This young Ladino rapper reinscribes hip hop—and all it represents to marginalized youth—in the genealogy of Maya time and space. As a result of uploading this video in YouTube and various other blogs, Rapsista and his fellow hip hop artists create a place for themselves in cyberspace that works as a medium through which audiences can unlearn the mischaracterizations of 13 Ba'k'tun as the "end of time" and, instead, relearn the meaning of this Maya cycle from the point of view of Guatemalan youth.[21] The flow of Rapsista's voice carries the memory of *Ixim Ulew*, the ancestral *tierra de maíz* ("land of corn"), that symbolically nurtures this new generation of self-claimed Maya hip hop warriors (Vargas 23). This song begins with MC Tzutu rapping in Maya-Tz'utujil, followed by MC Kastor OES3, who announces the beginning of a new era:

> 13 Ba'k'tun, inicio de una nueva era
> Con 10 MCs, lo sé, en tierra maya eterna primavera
> Para representar HH rap nacional
> Porque es mejor ser artista que un criminal
> Sin represión, más unión,
> a través de esta cultura viene la liberación.
> Revolución contra los que no nos dejan ser
> tal y como quieres ser.
> Los guerreros del hip hop no se van a detener.[22]

In his intervention, MC Kastor OES3 ties together memory, culture, and identity politics by claiming the cultural roots of *Ixim Ulew* and, at the same time, subverting the dominant narratives that attempt to silence and repress young people. The impact that this cultural inversion has on the rapper's subjectivity and the local land also carries on into cyberspace, by turning YouTube and other electronic networks into global loudspeakers for Guatemalan dissenting subaltern voices.

It is important to remember that this rap song was produced for the VII International Hip Hop Festival that took place from December 6–9, 2012 and was originally uploaded to YouTube on November 26 earlier that same year. During most of 2012, mainstream media and the global cultural industries mislead global audiences into believing that the Maya had predicted the "end of the world," as part of modernity/coloniality's narrative of continuous disregard for Maya scientific and astronomical knowledge. In defiance against this dominant narrative, MC Kastor OES3 appropriates Maya ancestral knowledge and transversally links the memory of the past with the music of the present, as he and his fellow hip hop warriors carry on their artistic revolution on the streets of Guatemala and on YouTube channels in cyberspace. This is an important step toward decolonial thinking, since without this reinscription to Maya genealogy "decolonial thinking would be nothing more than a gesture whose logic would depend on some of the various genealogies" belonging to Western civilization. (Mignolo, "Epistemic Disobedience" 47).

A final example of decolonial thinking in the Guatemalan hip hop movement comes from the cultural creativity that young female artists display in cyberspace. Since the early years of the movement, *Trasciende* and *Revolución Hip Hop* have made a point to include young women in the practice of the four elements of hip hop: DJ-ing, MC-ing, graffiti, and b-girling. After several years of training, pioneer women hip hop artists are now teaching younger girls the art of graffiti, rap, and break dance. By training together at *Trasciende*, these women have created their own spaces for reflection and resistance that serve as a harbor from the culture of machismo they confront every day at home, the street, school, and work. Out of these experiences came *Las Musas*, one of the first all-female hip hop crews in Guatemala. Formed in 2011 by three MCs, Kunti Shaw, MC Suina, MC Mai, and a beatbox, Liebre, *Las Musas* rap to raise awareness about women's rights in Guatemala. In their Facebook page, they describe their work as follows:

> Tenemos la ideología que como mujeres merecemos también ser escuchadas y debemos decir NO al silencio. Lo que nuestras letras llevan es reflexión, unidad y justicia… Nuestro propósito como Crew de Rap totalmente (sic) es motivar y dejar un mensaje alentador y positivo a las mujeres. Todas somos capaces de lograr y obtener todo lo que deseamos sin temor a ser discriminadas por la sociedad. Somos la voz de lo que muchas callan…! (*"Musas"*).[23]

The principles of reflection, unity, and justice that *Las Musas* convey in their music correspond to the main values of other crews and collectives in Guatemala's hip hop movement. These young artists establish themselves as leaders of a new era ready to break down old paradigms of apathy and discrimination. *Las Musas* and other female hip hop artists introduce a decolonial critique of gender that remembers the fragments of the past and restores women's voices against sexual abuse and gender discrimination.

In 2012, *Las Musas* collaborated with female hip hop artists Jen Soto, MC Trevi, and MC *Dinamita* in *"Unidas"* ("United"), the theme song for the Women's International Hip Hop Festival *"La otra cara del hip hop"* ("The Other Face of Hip Hop"), in which female hip hop artists and crews from Argentina, Costa Rica, El Salvador, Guatemala, Panama, Mexico, and Canada have participated. The video for this song was posted online on June 19, 2012 and was coproduced by Zanate Mojado Films, Fundación Para Elisa, Moda Focka Films, and *Trasciende*. Shot in Guatemala City, this video shows a diverse group of seventy women representing different ages, classes, ethnicities, and professions. This song makes women aware of their inner power and of the possibility to overcome any obstacle by acting together. The opening chorus mentions the many roles that women play in everyday life. Women are daughters, mothers, partners, mothers-in-law, aunts, neighbors, cousins, bosses, office employees, and cooks. This prolonged list of roles underlines the importance of diversity in the struggle for women's rights. In showing the faces of Guatemalan women of different ages, ethnicities, classes, and professions, this rap song tries to bring down barriers that often divide and prevent women from supporting each other. The video includes several shots of fragmented female bodies as a reminder of the normative objectification that women suffer. However, these powerful images invert the dominant meaning, as the fragments are turned into symbols that celebrate women's diversity and power.[24] Each of the six MCs who perform in this song raises awareness about a particular issue that affects women. The issues mentioned include domestic violence; lack of self-esteem; women's right to choose; class, ethnic, and cultural difference; disappearances; and feminicide. Despite the seriousness of the issues being addressed, the song is hopeful and upbeat. MC *Dinamita* brings her enthusiasm and energy as she sings:

> Tenemos que hacer juntas victoria colectiva
> Aprender de las otras, tener la iniciativa
> Templos infinitos de belleza espiritual
> Tenemos en la carne, todas podemos brillar
> Que todas las mujeres saquen sus poderes
> Y materialicemos todo lo que queremos
> Seamos la generación que representa la unión
> Entre las que dicen "sí," entre las que dicen "no" ("Unidas").[25]

MC *Dinamita's* celebration of women's inner beauty is another way of articulating the inner force that "Las Musas" bring out in their music. Together, these young female hip hop artists recognize the power of love, peace, unity, and enjoyment that is at the core of the hip hop movement in Guatemala.

As I have argued in this chapter, the music, blogs, websites, and videos that members of *Trasciende* and *Revolución Hip Hop* transmit in cyberspace are all cultural practices that help transform otherwise forbidden spaces into practiced places of decolonial thinking. In an era where most young people define who they are by the music they hear, the friends they share, and the ways they interact with technology and electronic social media, the Guatemalan hip hop movement's use of the Internet shows the relevance decolonial memory and cultural practice can have in the subversion of modern/colonial discourse in order to articulate alternative identities, in which the mediation of cyberspace plays a vital role. These young artists' efforts to produce quality videos on YouTube and personal pages on Facebook demonstrates the determinant role that cyberspace plays in the creation of new forms of empowerment and contestation through decolonial thinking and cultural conversion in a society that, over decades, has been beaten down by war and violence. This chapter is a contribution to the emergent field of Internet Studies in Latin America, whose process demands further and attentive observation of contestatory initiatives in cyberspace launched by marginal groups, such as the young hip hop artists in Guatemala.

Notes

1 "OK, now by the studio I'll drop / And deliver the good stuff that last night I wrote. / To record and upload 'em to Facebook, / and give Guatemalan rap another look." All translations are mine.

2 "Guate is moving on and pulling strong. / We are a Maya element, people are wrong. / They think we rap because we are bored, ha! / Here we rap because this is Maya talent of the new era."

3 In this chapter, I will spell "hip hop" without a hyphen (hip-hop) in accordance with the common use of the term by the Guatemalan urban artists I study.

4 As Matthew Gutmann points out, "cultural creativity is a far more productive concept than resistance in analyzing the inventiveness of the popular classes, because it emphasizes not only the desire of ordinary people to react to their life situations, but, more importantly, the active ways in which men and women seek to shape their lives every day" (260).

5 Since the second half of the 1990s, poorly funded public programs for children, a lack of jobs for families, persisting state repression against the poor, and a general social indifference toward the underprivileged have led to an increase in social dysfunctionality and violence in some of the most precarious neighborhoods of Guatemala City (Goldín and Rosenbaum 72).

6 Their collective frustration is due in part to the continuous history of class and ethnic divisions and to the neoliberal policies that were adopted after the civil war officially ended with the signing of the Peace Accords on December 29, 1996 and was followed by a reduction of public spending in Guatemala. Once the threat of Communism had diminished in most of the Western hemisphere, the emergence of a new era of global capitalism made way for the end of civil wars and military regimes in countries like

Guatemala. Unfortunately, in Guatemala and other Latin American countries, this geopolitical redistribution of power promoted the principles of free-market capitalism, but did little to eradicate the culture of colonialism, as this persisted in the form of authoritarianism, impunity, human rights violations, and gender, class, ethnic, and racial exclusion.

7 In 2010, the number of Guatemalans using the World Wide Web remained significantly low (Gálvez 1). According to a survey by Audience Scapes on the uses of technology among urban Guatemalans, only 36% of men and 14% of women have access to the Internet. Among young people, 77% of urban youth in Guatemala report using the Internet in a regular basis (Audience Scapes, "Urban Guatemala: Age"). The survey also shows that a majority of urban Guatemalans access the Internet from cybercafés, home, or work and use it to read email, do research, view videos on YouTube, play online games, download music, and engage in electronic social networks (Audience Scapes, "Urban Guatemala: Gender"). Yet, despite this newfound freedom, many Guatemalans, especially the young, continue to experience contempt by the state forces and the ruling elites. For politically aware young Guatemalans tired of feeling neglected or persecuted, the Internet works as a vital tool to inform and disseminate their messages of social dissent.

8 I am referring here to the distinction between place and space that Michel de Certeau proposes. For him, "place" corresponds to the normative ("proper") meaning assigned to a location, whereas "space" is best described as "practiced place." That is, the different meanings that different people might give to a particular location depending on their cultural practices and the time they spent in such place (117).

9 In an interview for Guatemalahiphop.com, once a website and now available as a YouTube channel, rapper Lovel 2, now a MC in the crew Bacteria Sound System, talks about his underground origins with the band Flowsismo. When asked on camera about his musical influences, MC Lovel 2 sees himself as a "consumidor nato de géneros y culturas musicales del mundo.... No me cierro a ningún género" ("Entrevista") ("absolute consumer of all musical genres and cultures of the world.... I don't reject any genres").

10 See the video interview of DJ Fla-K.O. for Guatemalahiphop.com from August 31, 2009.
   www.youtube.com/watch?feature=player_embedded&v=zfVBtvWSgjU.

11 *Trasciende* is committed to bringing social change, especially to the lives of young children. To reach this goal, *Trasciende* organize workshops known as "Talleres Escuelas Seguras" in public schools in and outside of the capital city. See the video "Taller Escuelas Seguras," www.youtube.com/watch?v=UgN2ZbKbwdw.

12 For the 2013 festival that took place in Guatemala City from December 5–8, *Revolución Hip Hop* created a blogspot inviting urban artists and crews from Guatemala, Latin America, and the rest of the world to send their applications directly to the festival's Gmail account.

13 Today, that website is no longer in service, and most of its interview archives have been transferred to a YouTube channel and a Facebook page by the same name.

14 As already mentioned, some of the most active female artists include Rebecca Lane, MC Jen Soto, MC Kunti, MC Suina, MC Mai, MC Maya, DJ Marcia, and graffiti artist Ivi Fix. Some of Ivi Fix's murals can be seen in the online news report "Graffiti Femenino en Guatemala," www.youtube.com/watch?v=udaoy1ZBoQk.

15 "*Trasciende* has been helpful to us in many ways. It has provided us with a physical space where we have come to grow together as a family. We have

also developed individually in our own abilities as b-boys. It has also helped us to find a new home, a new house, where we can stay all day without anyone bothering us, with no one discriminating against us."

16 "You know, economic power is not in the hands of the youth. Therefore, young people are being used because they are the force, if you know what I mean. Here we channel that force, this is what we are all about.... What I mean is that prejudice is real but it doesn't stop us. What's interesting is seeing how we are overcoming prejudice. In fact, here we don't tell anyone what to wear. People wear what they want to wear. What they see in their environment. What we try to do is not to reproduce prejudice. Because if people judge us negatively and we don't like it, if we do the same to others, then we would be doing the wrong thing."

17 To further study *Trasciende's* role in promoting nonviolence in Guatemala, see Sepúlveda.

18 "The word 'transcend' means to raise above, right. Because we believe that we have transcended from one point to another... *Trasciende* for us is like a springboard for all the young people who care to join us, because people in the street see the youth here and they see that they are doing something good. They see them as artists."

19 Launched in 2006, Reverbnation provides web promotion, digital distribution, and website hosting to over 2.7 million artists worldwide.

20 The other nine MCs who appear in this rap song are Kastor OES3, Divary Pashuli, Big Real, MC Wizard, Mr. Fer, Jen Soto, Zhekry, Kontra, and MC Tzutu, who raps in his native Maya-Tz'utujil language. This song is available in YouTube and in the blog Guateunder: www.guateunder.blogspot.com/.

21 In 2012, the organizers of the *VII Revolución Hip Hop International Festival* planned the festival as a celebration of the 13 Ba'k'tun cycle in the Maya calendar. Fla-K.O., one of the organizers, compares the dawn of a new era in the Maya calendar with the principles of hip hop that call for a new mindset and a fresh attitude. In his words, "Buscamos una revolución en la actitud y mentalidad de las personas por medio de la práctica y la difusión de los elementos principales que conforman la cultura hip hop" ("We seek a revolution in people's attitudes and minds through the practice and dissemination of the principal elements that make up hip hop culture") (García-Gallont 1).

22 "13th Baktun, beginning of a new era / With 10 MC's, I know, in Maya land of eternal spring / To represent national HH rap / Because it's better to be an artist than a criminal / Without repression, united we stand, / Through our culture, liberation will come. / Revolution against / those who do not let us be / Who we really want to be." These hip hop warriors will not be stopped."

23 "We believe that as women we also deserve to be listened to and we must say NO to silence. Our lyrics bring reflection, unity, and justice.... Our purpose as a rap crew is to motivate everyone and to leave an encouraging and positive message in all women. We are all capable of reaching and fulfilling everything that we desire without fear of being discriminated against by society. We give voice to what many women keep silent...!"

24 I thank Dona Kercher for this observation.

25 "Together we need to bring collective victory / Learn from one another, take on the initiative. / Infinite temples of spiritual beauty / We carry in our flesh, we all can shine / Let all women release their powers / And let's realize all our desires / Let's be the unifying generation / Between those who say 'yes,' and those who say 'no.'"

Works Cited

Arias, Arturo, "Politics and Society." *The Companion to Latin American Studies.* Ed. Philip Swanson. London: Arnold, 2003. 26–46.

Audience Scapes. *Urban Guatemala: Age.* The Intermedia Knowledge Center, 2010. www.intermedia.org/research-findings/audiencescapes/. Accessed 27 June 2013.

———. *Urban Guatemala: Gender.* The Intermedia Knowledge Center, 2010. www.intermedia.org/research-findings/audiencescapes/. Accessed 27 June 2013.

Dada, Carlos, and Élmer Menjívar. "Rigoberta Menchú: 'En Guatemala pospusimos la posguerra.' " *ElFaro.net,* 14 May 2012. https://elfaro.net/es/201205/noticias/8540/Rigoberta-Menchú-En-Guatemala-pospusimos-la-posguerra.htm. Accessed 5 Jan. 2014.

De Certeau, Michel. *The Practice of Everyday Life.* Trans. Steven Rendall. Berkeley: U California P, 1984. Print.

DJ Fla-K.O. "Entrevista: Primera parte." Online video clip. *YouTube.* 31 Aug. 2009. www.youtube.com/watch?v=zfVBtvWSgjU. Accessed 18 Mar. 2013.

Flores, Juan. *From Bomba to Hip-Hop: Puerto Rican Culture and Latino Identity.* New York: Columbia U P, 2000. Print.

Friedman, Elisabeth. "The Reality of Virtual Reality: The Internet and Gender Equality Advocacy in Latin America." *Latin American Politics & Society* 47.3 (2005): 1–34. www.academia.edu/1926785/The_reality_of_virtual_reality_The_internet_and_gender_equality_advocacy_in_Latin_America. Accessed 4 Jan. 2013.

Gálvez, Lucía. "El internet, un espacio dominado por los jóvenes." *Sala de Redacción* 4 (2011): 1–21. http://saladeredaccion.com/el-internet-un-espacio-dominado-por-los-jovenes-en-guatemala. Accessed 21 Feb. 2013.

García Canclini, Néstor. *Diferentes, desiguales y desconectados. Mapas de la interculturalidad.* Barcelona: Gedisa, 2004.

García-Gallont, Andrea. "Experimente la cultura del hip hop." *Siglo. 21.* 6 Dec. 2012. http://s21.gt. Accessed 6 Jan. 2014.

Goldín, Liliana, and Brenda Rosenbaum. "Everyday Violence of Exclusion: Women in Precarious Neighborhoods of Guatemala City." *Mayas in Postwar Guatemala. Harvest of Violence Revisited.* Eds. Walter E. Little and Timothy J. Smith. Tuscaloosa: U Alabama P, 2009. 67–83. Print.

"Guatemala's Leap Into The Hip Hop Scene." Online video clip. *YouTube.* 24 Oct. 2010. www.youtube.com/watch?v=YZ8leuvLk0E. Accessed 16 Mar. 2013.

Gutmann, Mathew C. *The Meanings of Macho: Being a Man in Mexico City.* Berkeley: U California P, 1996.

MC Lovel 2. "Entrevista a Lovel 2." Online video clip. *YouTube.* 22 Sept. 2009. www.youtube.com/watch?v=um6Qkixlt9o. Accessed 16 Mar. 2013.

Mignolo, Walter. "Epistemic Disobedience and the Decolonial Option. A Manifesto." *Transmodernity. Journal of Peripheral Cultural Production of the Luso-Hispanic World* 1.2 (2011): 44–66. http://escholarship.org/uc/item/62j3w283. Accessed 12 Sept. 2012.

———. *Local Histories/Global Designs. Coloniality, Subaltern Knowledges, and Border Thinking.* Princeton: Princeton UP, 2000.

"Mini documental Trasciende - Hip Hop de Guatemala." Online video clip. *You-Tube*. 8 Oct. 2010. www.youtube.com/watch?v=HBqfM0OcL-A. Accessed 16 Mar. 2013.

Morello, Henry James. "E-(re)volution: Zapatistas and the Emancipatory Internet." *A Contracorriente* 4.2 (2007): 54–76. https://acontracorriente.chass. ncsu.edu/index.php/acontracorriente/article/view/273. Accessed 27 Mar. 2013.

Musas, Las. "About" *Facebook*. 30 Sept. 2011. www.facebook.com/pg/MUSAS-339636002729740/about/?ref=page_internal. Accessed 21 Feb. 2013.

Reguillo, Rossana. "El lugar desde los márgenes: Música e identidades juveniles." *Nómadas*. 13 Oct. 2000. 40–53. www.redalyc.org/pdf/1051/105115264004. pdf. Accessed 28 Mar. 2013.

"Reportaje Trasciende—Voces Libres." Online video clip. *YouTube*. 14 Oct. 2012. www.youtube.com/watch?v=1hLmAGQVaMU. Accessed 18 Jan. 2013.

Revolución Hip Hop, "10 MC con una sola misión." Online video clip. *You-Tube*. 26 Nov. 2012. www.youtube.com/watch?v=MEREIE7ateo. Accessed 16 Mar. 2013.

Sepúlveda, Monserrat. "La filosofía de la noviolencia en Guatemala: Retirándose de la violencia a través del hip hop." *Anales de Estudios Centroamericanos* 40 (2014): 263–288. http://revistas.ucr.ac.cr/index.php/anuario/article/view/16642/16147. Accessed 20 Dec. 2016.

Shadowzito. "Esto es Guatemala." *Shadowzito The Mixtape*, Block Royal Records, 2014, *Reverbnation*. reverbnation.com/shadowzito/song/11480614-shadowzito-esto-es-guatemala.

Sin Reservas. "Graffiti femenino en Guatemala." Online video clip. *YouTube*. 17 Feb. 2012. www.youtube.com/channel/UCTWEGAebvHy_RpMg0KNuLcQ. Accessed 21 Feb. 2013.

Rapsista. Featured in Revolución Hip Hop, "10 MC con una sola misión." Online video clip. *YouTube*. 26 Nov. 2012. Web. Accessed 16 Mar. 2013.

Tierney, Nancy Leigh. *Robbed of Humanity. Lives of Guatemalan Street Children*. Saint Paul, MN: Pangaea, 1997.

"Unidas." Online video clip. *YouTube*. 19 June 2012. www.youtube.com/watch?v=z6oOrsDoeyY. Accessed 16 Mar. 2013.

Vargas, Rebeca Eunice. "Identificación nacional en el rap guatemalteco." *Revista de la Universidad de San Carlos de Guatemala*. 24 April–June 2012. 5–23. http://sitios.usac.edu.gt/revista/wp-content/uploads/2012/11/12.pdf. Accessed 21 Feb. 2013.

Villegas, Fabián. "Hip-Hop, La interpelación como emergencia y asesinato de lo real: Cromatismo, goce e improvisación en los escombros del estado de sitio." *ImaRginación: La Poética del Hip Hop como desmesura de lo político*. Bocafloja and Fabián Villegas. Mexico City: Ediciones Bajo Tierra; Sísifo Ediciones, 2008. 65–77.

3 *Narcocorridos* and Internet

Demonopolizing Mexico's Narco History in Cyberspace

Juan Carlos Ramírez-Pimienta

Despite developing in a context of antagonistic government measures, the popularity of *narcocorridos* (drug-trafficking ballads) is flourishing and continues to emerge. In Mexico, *narcocorridos* are said (mostly by state officials) to advocate for drug traffickers and hence are absent from radio and television airtime.[1] Many times, the exclusion from TV and radio is due to autoregulatory measures imposed by their own media guilds or leaderships, while other times the censorship is a result of local and state laws.[2] In what follows, I will show how the narcocorrido genre has taken to the Internet to avoid State-sponsored censorship and how, in doing so, they present a contestatory version (*vis-à-vis* that of the Mexican State) of drug trafficking and drug traffickers.

In states such as Sinaloa, Chihuahua, and Baja California, the prohibition includes live performances. In Tijuana, one *norteño* band in particular, *Los Tucanes de Tijuana* ("Tijuana Toucans"), has been forbidden from performing publicly in that city since 2009. The ban was initially implemented by then police chief Julian Leyzaola, after the band cheered drug traffickers during a live performance, presumably saying something akin to "long live the mafia" ("Arriba la maña"). Another reason for this reprimand was the airing (on November 16, 2009), by a local news agency of a YouTube video in which *Los Tucanes* were performing a new (unreleased) *corrido* that praised some very well-known local drug traffickers.[3] Although Leizazola has since moved to work in law enforcement in Ciudad Juárez, the prohibition of *Los Tucanes* in Tijuana still stands.[4]

In the cases of Chihuahua and Sinaloa, the censorship is less focalized; no *norteño* or *banda* ensemble is to sing *narcocorridos* during their concerts in the State of Sinaloa or in the city of Chihuahua. In Sinaloa, since the mid-1980s, there has been a series of initiatives to censor *narcocorridos*, all of which have been proven less than successful, as that particular state continues to be the most identified with *narcocultura* and specifically with *narcocorridos*.[5] In Mexico's imagination, the locus of enunciation for *narcocultura* is Sinaloa.[6] An important episode of the latest incarnation of *narcocorrido* censorship there took place in May 2011, when Mario López Valdez, governor of Sinaloa, instituted a prohibition making it illegal to perform *narcocorridos* live at bars, nightclubs, and concert venues. The measure, intended to inhibit the apology of crime contained in *narcocorrido* lyrics, includes the cancellation of alcohol permits to those who ignore the veto on *narcocorridos*.

The Sinaloa governor's censorship announcement was almost simultaneous to that made by Chihuahua's city mayor, Marco Quezada, whose government banned public performances of *corridos* alluding to drug trafficking. According to this measure, in order to get a permit to play in that city, a band or *narcocorrido* performer must first get clearance for the list of songs to be sung during their concerts and performances. While it is impossible to know exactly how effectively and to what extent this directive has been enforced, this procedure has failed at least once. The most publicized episode of its kind happened in March 2012, when *Los Tigres del Norte* ("The Northern Tigers"), the most famous *norteño* outfit, was admonished for performing *narcocorridos* at their concert during their city's agro fair. No authority has clarified if *Los Tigres del Norte* were required to provide a list of songs prior to their performance.[7] What transpired in national and international media is that they sang at least three *narcocorridos*: "El avión de la muerte" ("The Death Plane"), "Jefe de jefes" ("Boss of Bosses"), and "La reina del sur" ("The Queen of the South").[8] The ban on narcocorridos is rationalized as an attempt to prevent the glorifying of drug traffickers. Ironically, *Los Tigres* were publicly reprimanded for "La reina del sur," a "fake" narcocorrido; while the other two are clearly relatable to specific real life kingpins, "La reina" is a *corrido* based on a fictitious character from the namesake novel by Spanish writer Arturo Pérez-Reverte.[9]

The concert took place uneventfully, but a few days later, *Los Tigres* announced both on their Facebook page and via Twitter that the state of Chihuahua had vetoed them for singing narcocorridos. They claimed that they did not know about this prohibition and added that they lamented the decision to ban them from playing in Mexico's biggest state. Later, it was reported that the local authorities were asking Eduardo Prieto (the impresario who contracted *Los Tigres* to play in Chihuahua) to pay a fine equivalent to either fifteen hundred dollars or thirty-nine hundred dollars, depending on the source.[10]

In spite of this antagonistic context, *narcocorridos* are more popular than ever, not only in Mexico but in the U.S. as well. This popularity is made possible mainly because the process by which they are disseminated bypasses radio and TV and uses the Internet's social networks, blogs, and YouTube to thrive. This does not mean, however, that these bands are absent from TV and radio. Most *narcocorrido* ensembles also play romantic and rhythmic pieces. A typical musical production is composed of love songs as well as *narcocorridos*. In order to promote a new production, the less controversial songs are played on radio and TV, and the *narcocorridos* are left for the live presentations. It is from these concerts that the famous bands and solo acts collect their biggest revenues, since record sales have been progressively diminishing for many years.[11]

Movimiento Alterado and Hiperviolence

Sinaloan music producers Omar and Adolfo Valenzuela were fourteen years old in 1991 when their parents decided to leave their native Culiacan and move the family to Los Angeles. Following the family musical tradition (the father was a *banda* musician), the brothers joined their high school band and were still teenagers when they accompanied famous Latin musicians, icons of the caliber of Tito Puente and Celia Cruz, during their California concert tours. Soon, the Valenzuelas decided to become musical producers, creating Twiins Enterprises in the early 1990s. Since then, the brothers have produced music for pop artists such as Shakira, Paulina Rubio, Chayane, and Thalia, as well as for *grupero* artists such as Jenni Rivera, *El Recodo, Tucanes,* and many others. Even though at the beginning of their producing careers they were not associated with the *narcocorrido* genre, they played an important role in the development of *grupero* music.[12] In 2008, just prior to their massive commercial success as producers of the new wave of *narcocorridos*, they were named "the most influential and successful producers of regional Mexican music industry."[13]

The very reason behind the family move to Los Angeles was that their father did not want his sons to end up like him, playing for drug traffickers.[14] Ironically, the Valenzuela brothers are now most known as the godparents of the *Movimiento Alterado*, the hyper-graphic *narcocorrido* wave, a subgenre created and mainly disseminated on the Internet. The Valenzuelas, who are often credited with inventing *Movimiento Alterado*, have acknowledged in interviews that this was not the case. Adolfo Valenzuela told *narcocorrido* scholar Daniel Brancato that what he and his brother Omar did was christening a phenomenon that was already thriving on the web.[15] Adolfo told Brancato that, in 2007, he realized that the *corridos* being played on U.S. Hispanic radio stations sounded old and out of sync with the revolution happening on the Internet, that something was happening online that was more interesting that what the record companies were issuing. He emphasized that the new phenomenon did not have a name. Valenzuela was able to appreciate then that many youngsters were "playing" in their houses, uploading videos to YouTube, and creating a new type of *corridos*. According to Valenzuela, these new kinds of ballads had a faster tempo, different rhythms, different musical instruments, as well as different themes.[16]

The new themes certainly reflected the new developments in Mexico. On November 30, 2006, a day before taking office, Mexico's president elect Felipe Calderón announced that he would declare war on organized crime. In what has been considered by many political analysts an effort to legitimize his presidency, obtained amid myriad doubts and controversy about the election process, Calderón declared that first and foremost the Mexican State's duty was to ensure social peace and to establish a culture of legitimacy. Immediately after taking office, president Calderón sent troops out to several Mexican states.[17] Six years later, the death toll of this war has been estimated at over 100,000 among criminals, law enforcement personnel, and civilians. The number of those casualties with direct ties to the drug trade may never be known.[18] Parallel to the actual war, a monopoly on the war narrative was implemented by the Mexican government, seeking to censor any cultural production that would offer a different version of the conflict. The *narcocorrido*, or drug-trafficking ballad, was one of the first victims of stricter forms of censorship during Felipe Calderón's term. Banned from television, radio, and now in some states from live presentations, the *narcocorrido* turned to the Internet to offer divergent, constestatory versions of the war on drugs.

What is forbidden often attracts attention. The *Movimiento Alterado* has launched the career of many young artists, as well as "revived" the career of "older" performers such as Rogelio Martínez, a singer of the *grupero* genre with a trajectory spanning two decades. Martínez, who has lived in Los Angeles since his childhood, was a successful romantic *grupero* balladeer during the 1990s and the beginning of this century. He also had acted in films and soap operas in the U.S. as well as in Mexico. With the new millennium, his popularity gradually decreased until 2010, when he resurfaced on a reality show and under the auspices of the Valenzuela brothers, newly christened as RM, dressed in a military uniform, and singing hard core ballads.

Facing criticism for his new more violent musical "persona," Martínez declared that he would not stop singing romantic themes but that he would combine the two styles.[19] As stated before, this is not unusual; many *narcocorrido* performers also sing romantic themes, although the norm has usually been to start one's career by singing *narcocorridos* and subsequently become more "moderate," image-wise. Many drug balladeers started their careers singing very explicit and censorable themes, and then they went on to soften their discourse in order to have better access to massive media and to be invited to family-oriented television variety shows, such as Univision's *Don Francisco Presenta*, *El Gordo y la Flaca,* and Mexicos's *Televisa* entertainment morning show *Hoy.*[20]

In Martínez's case, his image was never a problem. During a good portion of his career, he had access to practically every entertainment TV and Radio show in the U.S. Hispanic market. In 2010, Martínez was invited to participate in the very successful Univision network dancing TV show *Mira quién baila* (Look Who is Dancing), a reality show often viewed as a medium to revitalize artistic (and sports) careers. It was during the show's airing that Martínez's popularity began to re-emerge. After finishing his participation in the competition, he tried to infuse vitality into his music career by singing *narcocorridos*. For this, he turned to the Valenzuela twins, who worked on changing his image and surprised the "Alterado" fan base by including the "new" Martínez in the fourth volume of the Alterado Movement CD series with a graphic *corrido* "Sangre de maldito" ("Blood of Dammed"):

> No se cansa de ver sangre.
> Vive al lado del peligro.
> Y cuando le jala al cuerno de chivo
> el veneno lo hace hiperactivo.[21]

Martínez is aware that his graphic new themes will most likely not be played on the radio. Felix Castillo, a reporter for *3 Grupero*, a TV show specialized in Mexican regional music, questioned him about this, and Martínez answered that he was confident that his romantic songs would be played on the radio while his graphic *corridos* would be disseminated both in his performances and via the Internet:

> Se está utilizando mucho el Internet. También yo creo que pues los *corridos* van a ser un poco difíciles de entrar dentro de lo que es la radio pero mi corte nuevo titulado 'La intrusa', que va a ser uno de los cortes que yo sé que va a empezar a sonar bastante fuerte por toda la Unión Americana y por México entero.[22]

With this reasoning, he was following the philosophy of his new producers. According to *USA Today*: "*Movimiento Alterado*'s boom began in 2009 when the Valenzuela brothers recorded songs by two bands and released them on the Internet because radio stations wouldn't play them." The article adds that "on the Internet, the songs are downloaded by the tens of thousands and *Movimiento Alterado* bands fill dirt-floor rodeo rings and swanky auditoriums across Mexico and the United States."[23]

Indeed, if a single reason of why *narcocorridos* continue to be massively disseminated had to be picked, it would likely be cyberspace, where one can find singers and the public sharing and commenting on *narcocorridos* and other aspects of narcoculture on all the different Internet platforms. The Internet provides different venues in which to challenge the official story regarding drug trafficking and the representations of its protagonists. Since these actions help to break the State's monopoly on the discourse, this treatment of *narcocultura* topics is not welcomed by the Mexican State. According to Luis Astorga, a Mexican sociologist and one of the foremost experts on drug trafficking in Latin America:

Durante varias décadas, el monopolio del sentido acerca del tráfico de drogas y los traficantes fue atribución del Estado. La academia, los medios de comunicación, la oposición política y la sociedad civil no generaron discursos distintos que le hicieran competencia. En otras palabras, el tráfico y los traficantes eran lo que el discurso oficial reproducido en los medios decía. Pero en los lugares de origen y las zonas de operación de los traficantes, las percepciones diferían. Lo distinto circulaba a través de la historia oral.

$$(160)^{24}$$

Astorga added that since the 1970s and through *corridos*, the State's discurse monopoly began to be challenged. The State recognized this and began to crack down on the media (radio and, to some degree, television) that traditionally and massively disseminated *corridos*. Astorga has documented the first official act of censorship in Sinaloa, during the governorship of Francisco Labastida in 1987. Other unofficial and/or self-imposed acts of censorship are, of course, more difficult to document, but here are some samples from the same decade, the 1980s: Jorge Hernández, leader of *Los Tigres del Norte*, has said in an interview that he would purposely lower the volume of his voice when pronouncing the word "cocaína" while singing the *corrido* "La banda del carro rojo" ("Red Car Gang") at concerts.[25] He also declared that at the beginning of the 1980s, *Los Tigres del Norte* decided to stop recording drug-trafficking *corridos* in an effort to distance themselves from the genre and recorded instead *norteño* gospel and other less controversial musical genres.[26] During most of the 1980s, they would record ballads in defense of immigrants until a return to *narcocorridos* in 1989 with their very successful production *Corridos prohibidos* ("Forbidden Corridos").[27] Also, in the mid-1980s when performing on TV shows, Francisco Avitia (nicknamed "The *corrido* king") would change the ending to a *corrido* dedicated to an early 20th-century drug trafficker by adding in a last stanza, saying that his death was not mourned by society because he was a "poisoner" and guilty of many deaths. This last portion of the *corrido* was not included in the original recording, which makes it a clear example of an exercise in self-censoring.

A very similar situation happened at the televised 2012 Latin Grammy Award ceremony. As a selling point for the show, it was advertised that for the very first time in the history of the awards a *corrido* would be performed. There was a great deal of expectation about listening to *Movimiento Alterado* alum Gerardo Ortiz perform a hard core *narcocorrido* live on international TV. Ortiz did sing one of his hits "Aquiles Afirmo," a *corrido* whose title makes a word play with the name Aquiles and the phrase "aquí les" ("here I"), as in "here I affirm to you." "Aquiles afirmo" is a somewhat cryptic *corrido* that narrates the ending of the Arellano Felix cartel rein in Tijuana and the new leadership of the

Sinaloa cartel, with their key operator known as Aquiles. In the censored version of the *corrido,* words and phrases such as cartel, attack, battles, fight to death, and fear on the blood, among others, were changed. The reaction on YouTube did not take long. Some netizens complained about censorship, blasting the Grammys organization for making Ortiz change the lyrics. Others criticized the hypocrisy of announcing in the news media that for the first time a *corrido* would be sung at the Latin Grammys. "What was the point?" they asked, "if Ortiz would not be allowed to sing the *corrido* 'como era' ('as is')" and then finished, "pinches televisiones mierda" ("damn shitty TV networks"). Other comments to the uploaded video on YouTube simply stated their disappointment that Ortiz substantially changed the song, placing the blame on him for claudicating: "Qué pasó Gera...?" ("What happened Gera...?")[28]

Narcocorridos as War Narratives in the 21st Century

Drug trafficking ballads have been around since at least the early 1930s. There has been, however, an evolution in the figure of the trafficker as a hero.[29] Nowadays, perhaps the biggest complaint about *narcocorridos* is that drug traffickers are usually panegyrized. While this is true in most of drug-trafficking ballads, the traffickers' representation is not always a blank check, and it never has been. The earliest *narcocorrido* I have documented was recorded in October 1931. The corridista of "El Pablote" ("Big Pablo") is definitely not generous in his judgment of Pablo González, a pioneer drug lord in the early 20th-century Mexican-Texas border.[30] This song portrays him as a bully who takes advantage of an outnumbered victim. It is not the purpose of this chapter to elaborate on the change of the hero/protagonist portrayal in drug-trafficking ballads, as I have discussed that evolution in other works.[31] Suffice it to say that toward the end of the 20th century, the representation of drug trafficking in *narcocorridos* began to be much less condemnatory and many times openly panegyric.

The censorship of *narcocorridos* and *narcocultura* at different levels is undeniable and very visible, but there is also censorship of the discussion of *narcocorridos* and *narcocultura* in the media.[32] Even though there is no specific law against commenting about *narcocorridos* in México's media, there was a presidential initiative (Iniciativa México), implemented during the last years of Felipe Calderón's presidency, that shaped the media's treatment of *narcocorridos* and other *narcocultura* productions. Executives of over fifty very important news media, including the two most important Mexican television networks *Televisa* and *TV Azteca*, signed the agreement for the coverage of information on violence on March 14, 2011. One of the main aspects of the agreement was to propose common editorial criteria when covering violence associated to organized crime. Among the ten points listed in the agreement, the second one required media not to become an involuntary speaker for organized crime.[33]

In Mexico, the Internet has largely escaped State censorship. It is still a place where the official narratives of drug trafficking and drug traffickers can be contested, but that does not mean that an official narrative against this counter narrative couldn't be implemented. Since the Internet is global by nature and more difficult to control, this task would be very difficult to undertake. Efforts in that direction have been implemented in the context of counterterrorism and Middle East violent extremist videos. According to Omar Ashour, counteracting this type of propaganda requires:

> International cooperation between the United Nations, governmental bodies, and serious experts on the subject matter. It also requires comprehensiveness, credibility, and wide accessibility. A comprehensive counter-narrative should be able to cover the major dimensions of the violent extremist ontology in question, namely the political, historical, socio-psychological, theological, and instrumental dimensions. It also has to be conveyed, promoted, and supported by credible messengers.

I realize there is a difference between propagandistic jihady videos, their messages and comments, and their *narcocorrido* counterparts. However, in both cases, the video's authors (and those commenting on them) want their viewers and readers to believe their messages and comments. They want to have credibility. Also, in both cases, in order to counter these messages, credible messengers are required. In the case of Mexico, the Mexican State is not considered a credible messenger. Since the very beginning of contraband *corridos*, the representation of the trafficker was linked to the defiance of monopolies; it was not only the monopoly that controls exports and imports of merchandise, but also the monopoly on the use of justified violence. The State, of course, would like to reserve all rights to the legitimate use of violence and punitive actions for itself, but often, throughout the history of the genre, *corrido* protagonists had taken justice into their own hands when they perceive that conventional justice had failed them. In a similar fashion, the State would like to monopolize the representation of the drug trafficker persona. Albeit controversial, *Narcocorridos* are instrumental in offering a counter hegemonic image of the traffickers as they present a non-state-sanctioned version of the life and deeds of the traffickers, as well as their justifications to act the way they do. However, as stated before, that does not mean that these songs are always laudatory of the drug trafficker or that what the songs say is always truthful, but they do help to fill in gaps to get a more complete historical picture.[34] Narcocorridos perform several functions. Often times, they are laudatory, but they also offer a chronicle of the war on drugs. Some narcocorridos help us understand Mexico's current violence.

In July 2010, Tom Silverman, founder of Tommy Boy Records, gave a State of the Music Industry address in the New Music Seminar in New York, where he declared that YouTube is the most important name in music, even more so than Apple's iTunes: "When people ask me what is the biggest name in music in my opinion, they want me to say Apple. I usually answer: YouTube." Silverman added that in his opinion You-Tube is "by far" the most important music platform, the "largest catalog of on-demand music on the Internet."[35] YouTube's *narcocorrido* related comments have been studied by Catherine Heau Lambert, not as counter hegemonic spaces but as spaces that permit to detonate and liberate aggressiveness (99). In her essay subtitled "Una reflexión acerca de los comentarios de los Narco-corridos en YouTube" ("A Reflexion on *Narcocorridos* Comments on YouTube"), Heau Lambert concentrates on the concept of hate speech and the discrimination and racism expressed in YouTube comments on *corridos* such as "Continuación de la Hummer" ("Hummer part two") by Tigrillo Palma and "Cien por uno" ("Hundred for one") by *Los Tucanes de Tijuana*. While it is true that many comments do express ethnic, regional, and national prejudice, many others do add to the narratives of specific *narcocorridos*, of drug trafficking and drug traffickers, and clearly challenge their official stories and representations.

One of the most successful and popular *narcocorridos* in recent years has been "Los Sanguinarios del M1" ("The Bloodthirsty Killers of M1") by Gabriel Silva:[36]

> Con cuerno de chivo y bazuka en la nuca.
> Volando cabezas al que se atraviesa.
> Somos sanguinarios, locos, bien ondeados
> nos gusta matar.
> Pa' dar levantones somos los mejores.
> Siempre en caravana, toda mi plebada,
> bien empecherados, blindados y listos
> para ejecutar.[37]

Perhaps the most representative of the Alterado movement, this *corrido* has being featured on several news articles about *Movimiento Alterado* and *narcocultura*. Not surprisingly, it has been uploaded multiple times into YouTube, all of which have been viewed widely. The most visited version has over seventeen million views and thousands of comments, many of them emphasizing the alternate historic version that *corridos* present: "Commenter 1" says "Aprendan de historia.... pero verdadera no las pendejadas que enseñan en las escuelas" [Sic].[38] In a similar vein "Commenter 2" comments about the *corridos* of the Mexican Revolution and compares them to the new *corridos*, emphatically saying:

[...] Y SI SABES DE HISTORIA DEBERIAS DE SABER QUE DON PANCHO VILLA O DOROTEO ARANGO NO ERA PRECISAMENTE UNA BLANCA NO OLVIDEMOS LAS MASACRES POR EJEMPLO LA DE ZACATECAS, NO OLVIDEMOS EL ACTUAR DE CADA QUIEN PERO SI TU ERES DE LOS QUE SE BASAN EN LO QUE DICEN LOS LIBROS DE HISTORIA DE PRIMARIA PUES TE ENTIENDO, [...]

[Sic][39]

"Commenter 3" opines about the changing roles of drug-trafficking-themed *corridos* through the decades, making emphasis on the truthful nature of these songs:

> los corridos cuenta historias verdaderas, en los años 60, 70, 80s hablar del narco eran un tabu. Nuestros padres y la gente de su generacion escuchaban a Ramon Ayala, Chalino Sanchez y otros. Nuestra generacion se escucha este tipo de corridos. PAYASO ignorante!!!!
>
> [Sic][40]

Some commenters go as far as to make the drug traffickers the good guys, blaming the (Mexican) government for the country's problems. According to "Commenter 4":

> bien sabemos todos que los del gobierno son los verdaderos delincuentes, crruptos, puercos etc. Roban y matan a los jodidos y kuando uno busca ayuda del gobierno lo rechazan por ser pobre x eso El Chapo Guzman, Mayo Zambada apoya y no mata gente inocente [...].
>
> [Sic][41]

"Commenter 5" opines about the role of the Mexican soldiers: "Lo que no saben los soldados es que no protegen a su país: defienden los intereses de los gringos y de unos cuantos políticos de mierda."[42] "Commenter 6" supports this version when he says that "Los sanguinarios andan en contra del gobierno no de nosotros" [Sic].[43] For "Commenter 7," a better Mexico would be one where the different cartels are united:

> el narco en mexico seria invencible si trabajaran juntos toodos sinaloa, michoacan tamaulipas chiuhaua, sonora, tijuana, monterrey coahuila etc. etc. y se apoyaran unos con otros para chingar al puto gobierno que chinga al pobre y le da mas al rico. Talvez un dia se aga realidad mi sueno...
>
> [Sic][44]

"Commenter 8" sums up the end of president Calderón's term. For him, it is very suspicious that some important drug trafficking lords were killed then: "Que casualidad que ya pa acabarse el sexenio estan matando a grandes. Ese Felipe no quiere dejar testigos, los esta dejando bien callados. No valla ser que los apprendan y empiezan hablar" [Sic].[45] Finally, "Commenter 9" summarizes the new presidency in no uncertain terms: "el proximo presidente peña nieto es un narco y ahi nadie dice nada, el narco tiene mas poder que el gobierno y por su puesto mas dinero si no como cren que peña gano la presidencia [...]" [Sic].[46]

There are many more comments that counteract the official narratives of drug trafficking and its protagonists. Of course, there are other commenters who support the government's perspective and criticize those who like to listen to *narcocorridos*. As of December 31, 2012, of the more than twenty-one thousands who rated the video, about 11% gave it thumbs down. In the comments themselves, the disparity is not as extreme. There are many comments critical of *Movimiento Alterado* and *narcocorridos*, but those "liking" *narcocorridos* are the overwhleming majority, and they criticize those who commented against the genre, basically asking what its critics are doing watching the YouTube video if they do not like *narcocorridos*.

It is not the purpose of this essay to suggest that what *corridos* and *narcocorridos* say about Mexico is necessarily the truth. In another venue, I have, in fact, argued just the opposite—that *corridos* are not the "pure truth."[47] They do, however, indeed offer alternative narratives to the official history and different ways of conceiving what drug trafficking and drug traffickers are and do. Simply put: the Internet allows these other voices to be collected and disseminated.

Notes

1 While *narcocorridos* are supposed to be absent from television, during the final episode of the Mexican version of the TV show *The Voice* (*La Voz Mexico*) in December 2012, *Los Tigres del Norte* ("The Northern Tigers") performed a classic *narcocorrido* "Jefe de jefes" ("Boss of bosses"), a song that is widely acknowledged as a *narcocorrido* honoring a Mexican kingpin. Perhaps only violent *narcocorridos* are to be censored, or the Mexican television giant *Televisa* was trying to test the policies of the new government (President Enrique Pena Nieto had taken office just a couple of weeks before) regarding censorship of *narcocorridos*.

2 For instance, in July 2002, the chamber of radio and television industry in Baja California instituted a voluntary ban on the playing of *narcocorridos*. On November of the same year, namesake chamber in the estate of Guanajuato adopted a similar auto regulatory measure. "Corrido Censorship: A Brief History." *Elijah Wald's Homepage*. n.d. Web. 3 Nov. 2012. www. elijahwald.com/corcensors.html.

3 "Los Tucanes Big Comeback to Tijuana." *Bordelandbeat*. 28 Nov. 2009. Web. 8 Jan. 2013. www.borderlandbeat.com/2009/11/los-tucanes-big-comeback-to-tijuana.html.

4 Victoria Infante. "Tucanes de Tijuana siguen esperando permiso para tocar en su tierra." *The Huffington Post*. 27 Sept. 2012. Web. 3 Nov. 2012.

5 Luis Astorga. "Notas críticas. Corridos de traficantes y censura."

6 *Narcocultura* permeates many aspects of Sinaloan society. See for instance: Eloy Méndez Sáinz. "De anti-lugares, o la difusión de la narco arquitectura en Culiacán."

7 *Los Tigres* alleged that they did not know about any ban in Chihuahua, although they were quoted declaring their support for a similar ban in their home state of Sinaloa. Adriana Jiménez Rivera. "Apoyan Tigres del Norte veto a *narcocorridos*." *Milenio*. 20 May 2011. Web. Accessed 28 Nov. 2012.

8 Los Tigres del Norte. "Jefe de jefes." *Jefe de jefes*. Fonovisa, 1997. C D. Los Tigres del Norte. "La Reina del Sur." *La Reina del Sur*. Fonovisa, 2002. C D. Los Tigres del Norte. "El Avión de la muerte." *Triunfo sólido*. Fonovisa, 1989. C D.

9 Arturo Pérez-Reverte. *La Reina del sur*.

10 Either twenty thousand pesos or fifty thousand pesos. Jacobo García. "Chihuahua veta a los 'Tigres del Norte' por tocar La Reina del Sur." *El Mundo*. 13 Mar. 2012. Web. 28 Nov. 2012. "Los Tigres del Norte fueron vetados en Chihuahua." *Univision*. 3 Dec. 2012. Web. 28 Nov. 2012.

11 Austin Carr. "The State of Internet Music on YouTube, Pandora, iTunes, and Facebook." *Fast Company*. 19 July 2012. Web. 28 Nov. 2012.

12 *Música grupera* or *onda grupera* is a difficult term to define. It is not really a genre but rather a music industry's label that agglutinates a number of diverse popular musical genres and groups. According to George Torres, editor of the *The Encyclopedia of Latin American Popular Music*, the *onda grupera* (literally, the group wave) is a hybrid as well as transnational phenomenon inspired by the 1960s Mexican pop ballad/rock groups that imitated English and American rock music and the Colombian *cumbia* craze that swept Mexico in the early 1960s (257).

13 M. Gonzalez. "Valenzuela Twiins join forces with DJ Flex." *Vesper*. 31 Jan. 2009. Web. Accessed 28 Nov. 2012.

14 Josh Kun. "The Twiins: Mexican Music, Made in America." *New York Times*. 14 May 2006. Web. Accessed 11 July 2013.

15 Daniel Brancato. "The Alterado Movement and the Development of Corridos and Narcocultura in Mexico."

16 Daniel Brancato. "Adolfo Valenzuela (Twiins) – Entrevista con El Llanito Pt.I." *YouTube*. 27 Dec. 2012. Web. 28 Nov. 2012. Daniel Brancato. "Adolfo Valenzuela (Twiins) – Entrevista con El Llanito Pt.II." *YouTube*. 27 Dec. 2012. Web. 28 Nov. 2012.

17 Rubén Aguilar and Jorge G. Castañeda. *El Narco: La Guerra Fallida*.

18 Daniel Hernandez. "Calderon's War on Drug Cartels: A Legacy of Blood and Tragedy." *L A Times*. L A Times, 1 Dec. 2012. Web. 28 Nov. 2012.

19 Félix Castillo. "Entrevista de Félix Castillo a Rogelio Martínez." *YouTube*. 25 Mar. 2010. Web. 28 Nov. 2012.

20 There are many examples of this. For instance, the recently deceased Jenni Rivera, who started her career singing narcocorridos where she personified the daughter of a drug lord. For more about Rivera's trajectory, see my article "Sicarias, buchonas y jefas: perfiles de la mujer en el narcocorrido."

21 Unless otherwise stated, all translations are mine. R M. *Movimiento Alterado I V*. LaDisco, 2010, C D.

> He does not get tired of seeing blood.
> He lives dangerously.
> And when he pulls the trigger of his Ak 47
> the venom makes him hyperactive.

22 ("We are using Internet a lot. I believe it will be a little hard for corridos to be played on radio but my new [romantic] song 'La intrusa' ['The Intruder']

is going to be one of the singles that I know is going to be played [on the radio] in the United States as well as in Mexico.") Félix Castillo. "Entrevista de Félix Castillo a Rogelio Martínez." *YouTube*. 25 Mar. 2010. Web. 28 Nov. 2012.

23 "Sinaloa cartel gives blessing to newest Mexican drug ballads." *UsaToday*. 21 Dec. 2011. Web. 28 Nov. 2012.

24 For several decades, the monopoly on providing meaning to drug trafficking and drug traffickers was a self-imposed task of the Mexican State. Academia, media, political opposition, and civil society did not produce any competing discourses. In other words, drug traffickers and drug trafficking were what the official discourse reproduced by the media said they were. At the traffickers' place of origin and place of operation, perceptions were different. These different perceptions circulated via oral history (160).

25 "Jorge Hernandez interview." *Elijah Wald's Homepage*. n.d. Web. 7 Nov. 2012. www.elijahwald.com/jhernan.html. Los Tigres del Norte. "La banda de carro rojo." *La banda de carro rojo*. Fama, 1975, Album.

26 "Corrido Censorship: A Brief History." *Elijah Wald's Homepage*. n.d. Web. 3 Nov. 2012. www.elijahwald.com/corcensors.html.

27 Los Tigres del Norte. *Corridos Prohibidos*. Fonovisa, 1989. C D.

28 "Gerardo Ortiz – Aqui les afirmo – Latin Grammy 2012." [Sic] *YouTube*. 15 Nov. 2012. Web. 2 Nov. 2012. www.youtube.com/watch?v=ISkjzpcyU84.

29 Juan Carlos Ramírez-Pimienta. "El corrido de narcotráfico en los años ochenta y noventa: un juicio moral suspendido" and "Del corrido de narcotráfico al narcocorrido: Orígenes y desarrollo del canto a los traficantes."

30 Juan Carlos Ramírez-Pimienta. "En torno al primer narcocorrido: arqueología del cancionero de las drogas."

31 Juan Carlos Ramírez-Pimienta. "El corrido de narcotráfico en los años ochenta y noventa: un juicio moral suspendido" and "Del corrido de narcotráfico al narcocorrido: Orígenes y desarrollo del canto a los traficantes."

32 Unfortunately, censorship and self-censorship regarding these topics are also present in academic circles. There is a perception that nothing short of a total condemnation of the phenomenon makes a scholar suspicious (or even guilty) of panegyrizing drug trafficking and drug traffickers.

33 It is unclear to what extent iniciativa Mexico was successful. With the change in presidential regime in 2012 (not only a new president but a new party in power with the return of the PRI), all that remains of the initiative is the inertia. According to Gabriela Gómez Rodríguez, most of the media are, to some extent, waiting to see what the new government rules of the game are going to be as far as control of the media.

34 Narcocorridos perform several functions. Often times, they are laudatory, but they also offer a chronicle of the war on drugs. Undoubtedly, some narcocorridos help us understand Mexico's current violence. For a more detailed account of the relationship between narcocorridos and the war on drugs, see my article "De torturaciones, balas y explosiones: Narcocultura, Movimiento Alterado e hiperrealismo en el sexenio de Felipe Calderón."

35 Austin Carr. "The State of Internet Music on YouTube, Pandora, iTunes, and Facebook." *Fast Company*. 19 July 2012. Web. 28 Nov. 2012.

36 M1 is the codename for Manuel Torres Felix, a high-ranking leader of the Sinaloa drug cartel who was killed on October 13, 2012 in a clash between army troops and cartel gunmen in the town of Oso Viejo, Sinaloa.

37   With an AK-47 and a bazooka resting on our necks.
               Taking off the heads of anyone who gets in the way.
               We're bloodthirsty, crazy, agitated, we like to kill.

                   We are the best at kidnapping.
                   Always driving in caravan, all my people.
                   Always with our bullet proof vests,
                   well-armored and ready to kill.

38 ("learn history… but the real one, not the stupidities that they teach at schools.") The English translations are mine. In order to clarify meaning I have made minor syntactical and grammatical changes. The comments in Spanish are being transcribed as they were originally written except when meaning may be compromised. "Movimiento Alterado – Sanguinarios del M1 (Prod.SaFari Films) Video Official." *YouTube*. 25 Apr. 2010. Web. 28 Nov. 2012. www.youtube.com/watch?v=7x93aqiZ51w.

39 ("If you know history you should know that don Pancho Villa or Doroteo Arango [Villa's real name] was not precisely a white [dove]. Let's not forget the massacres, for instance that of Zacatecas. Let's not forget how each person behaved, but if you are one of those that based [your beliefs] in elementary level history books then I understand.") "Movimiento Alterado – S anguinarios del M1 (Prod.SaFari Films) Video Official." *YouTube*. 25 Apr. 2010. Web. 28 Nov. 2012. www.youtube.com/watch?v=7x93aqiZ51w.

40 ("Corridos tell truthful stories. In the 1960s, 1970s, 1980s to talk about drug trafficking was taboo. Our parents and those of their generation listened to Ramón Ayala, Chalino Sánchez and others. Our generation listens to this kind of corridos [Alterados]. Ignorant clown!!!!") "Movimiento Alterado – Sanguinarios del M1 (Prod.SaFari Films) Video Official." *YouTube*. 25 Apr. 2010. Web. 28 Nov. 2012. www.youtube.com/watch?v=7x93aqiZ51w.

41 ("We know well that all those from the government are the true delinquents, corrupt, pigs etc. They steal and kill the underdogs and when we seek help from the government they reject us for being poor. That is why el Chapo Guzman and Mayo Zambada support us and do not kill innocent people.") "Movimiento Alterado – Sanguinarios del M1 (Prod.SaFari Films) Video Official." *YouTube*. 25 Apr. 2010. Web. 28 Nov. 2012. www.youtube.com/watch?v=7x93aqiZ51w.

42 ("What the army does not know is that they are not protecting their country, they defend the interests of the gringos and some shitty politicians.") "Movimiento Alterado – Sanguinarios del M1 (Prod.SaFari Films) Video Official." *YouTube*. 25 Apr. 2010. Web. 28 Nov. 2012. www.youtube.com/watch?v=7x93aqiZ51w.

43 ("Los sanguinarios are against the government not against us.") "Movimiento Alterado – Sanguinarios del M1 (Prod.SaFari Films) Video Official." *YouTube*. 25 Apr. 2010. Web. 28 Nov. 2012. www.youtube.com/watch?v=7x93aqiZ51w.

44 ("El narco in Mexico would be invincible if they [the cartels] all worked together, Sinaloa, Michoacán, Tamaulipas, Chihuahua, Sonora, Tijuana, Monterrey, Coahuila etc. If they support each other to screw the dammed government that screws the poor people and gives more to the rich ones. Maybe one day my dream will come true.") "Los Sanguinarios del M1-Movimiento Alterado – Sanguinarios del M1 (oficial video)." *YouTube*. 29 Apr. 2010. Web. 28 Nov. 2012. www.youtube.com/watch?v=MZnNkuhdhG4&feature=fvwrel.

45 ("What a coincidence that they are killing big ones. That Felipe does not want to leave any witnesses, he is leaving all quiet. If they are aprehended they may start talking.") "Movimiento Alterado – Sanguinarios del M1 (Prod.SaFari Films) Video Official." *YouTube.* 25 Apr. 2010. Web. 28 Nov. 2012. www.youtube.com/watch?v=7x93aqiZ51w.

46 ("the next president Peña Nieto is a drug trafficker and nobody says anything about it, the narco has more power than the government itself and of course more money. If not, how do you think that Peña Nieto won the presidency?") "Movimiento Alterado – Sanguinarios del M1 (Prod.SaFari Films) Video Official." *YouTube.* 25 Apr. 2010. Web. 28 Nov. 2012. www.youtube.com/watch?v=7x93aqiZ51w.

47 José Villalobos and Juan Carlos Ramírez-Pimienta. "Corridos and *la pura verdad*: Myths and Realities of the Mexican Ballad."

Works Cited

Aguilar, Rubén, and Jorge G. Castañeda. *El Narco: La Guerra Fallida.* México, D.F.: Punto de Lectura, 2009.

Ashour, Omar. "Online De-Radicalization? Countering Violent Extremist Narratives: Message, Messenger and Media Strategy." *Perspectives on Terrorism* 4.6 (2010). www.terrorismanalysts.com/pt/index.php/pot/article/view/128/261. Accessed 8 Jan. 2013.

Astorga, Luis. 2005. "Notas críticas. Corridos de traficantes y censura." *Región y sociedad.* 27.32 (2005): 145–165.

Brancato, Daniel Francis. "The Alterado Movement and the Development of Corridos and Narcocultura in Mexico." B.A. Thesis. University of Liverpool, 2011. www.openthesis.org/documents/Los-Nuevos-Terroristas-Alterado-Movement-600860.html. Accessed 3 Dec. 2012.

Gómez Rodríguez, Gabriela. "¿Acuerdo entre medios para la cobertura de la violencia? El caso de Milenio-Jalisco." Academia.edu. 28 Nov. 2012. www.academia.edu/1592724/Acuerdo_entre_medios_para_la_cobertura_de_la_violencia._El_caso_de_Milenio_Jalisco. Accessed 8 Jan. 2013.

Heau Lambert, Catherine. "Los narcocorridos: ¿incitación a la violencia o despertar de viejos demonios? (una reflexión acerca de los comentarios de narco-corridos en Youtube)." *TRACE* 57 (2010): 99–110.

Méndez Sáinz, Eloy. 2012. "De anti-lugares, o la difusión de la narco arquitectura en Culiacán." *URBS Revista de Estudios Urbanos y Ciencias Sociales* [Online] 2.2 (2012). www2.ual.es/urbs/index.php/urbs/article/view/mendez/99. Accessed 8 Jan. 2013.

Pérez-Reverte, Arturo. *La Reina Del Sur.* Madrid: Alfaguara, 2002.

Ramírez-Pimienta, Juan Carlos. *Cantar a los Narcos.* México, D.F.: Editorial Planeta, 2011.

———. "De torturaciones, balas y explosiones: Narcocultura, Movimiento Alterado e hiperrealismo en el sexenio de Felipe Calderón." *A Contracorriente: Journal of Social History and Literature in Latin America* 10.3 (Spring 2013): 302–334.

———. "Del corrido de narcotráfico al narcocorrido: Orígenes y desarrollo del canto a los traficantes". *Studies in Latin American Popular Culture* XXIII (2004): 21–41.

———. "El corrido de narcotráfico en los años ochenta y noventa: un juicio moral suspendido". *The Bilingual Review/ La Revista Bilingüe* XXIII.2 (May–August 1998): 145–156.

———. "Sicarias, buchonas y jefas: perfiles de la mujer en el narcocorrido." *The Colorado Review of Hispanic Studies* 8.9 (2010–2011). http://chamilo3. grenet.fr/stendhal/courses/NARCOARTE/document/Narcocorridos/ Perfiles_de_la_mujer_en_el_narcocorrido.pdf. Accessed 8 Jan. 2013.

Torres, George. *Encyclopedia of Latin American Popular Music.* Wesport: Greenwood, 2013.

———. Villalobos, José, and Juan Carlos Ramírez-Pimienta. "Corridos and *la pura verdad*: Myths and Realities of the Mexican Ballad." *The South Central Review* 21.3 (Fall 2004): 129–149.

4 Belén Gache's Aleatory Politics

Radikal karaoke and (Robo) Poetics Hacking Politics

Scott Weintraub

In an essay titled "The Piecemeal Bard is Deconstructed: Notes Toward a Potential Robopoetics," Christian Bök writes:

> The involvement of an author in the production of literature has henceforth become discretionary. Why hire a poet to write a poem when the poem can in fact write itself? Has not the poet already become a virtually vestigial, if not defective, component in the relay of aesthetic discourse? Are we not already predisposed to extract this vacuum tube from its motherboard in order to replace it with a much faster node? The irony here is that, while the witless machine knows much less about poetics than even the most artless amateur knows, falderal written by the mechanism invariably outclasses doggerel written by the rhymester.
>
> (10)

Bök's provocative conceptualization of a radical, futural, and posthuman poetics takes as its point of departure a book of computer-generated verse, titled *The Policeman's Beard is Half-Constructed* (1984). Written by RACTER, an algorithm developed "in compiled BASIC on a Z80 micro with 64K of RAM" ("Racter"), this flavor of "syntactically orthodox, but semantically aberrant" poetry that "can in fact write itself," according to Bök (10), depends on the logic of aleatory combinatorics, a kind of procedural methodology that has cast a long shadow on 20th- and 21st-century poetry and poetics—from John Cage to Oulipo (the *Ouvroir de littérature potentielle*) to William Burroughs to Language poetry, among many avenues of expression.[1] In the afterword to his recent book *Uncreative Writing: Managing Language in the Digital Age*, Kenneth Goldsmith glosses Bök's insightful analysis, arguing that RACTER's computer code, composed of an alphanumeric language, might be programmed and (h)activated for literary consumption by other nonhuman readers, thus

> writing a type of literature readable by other bots. And as a result of networking with each other, their feedback mechanism will create

an ever-evolving, sophisticated literary discourse, one that will not only be invisible to human eyes but bypass humans altogether.

(225)

Where Bök considers the carbon-based (human) poet—rather than the silicone (computer) one he engages in the essay on RACTER—"virtually vestigial, if not defective, component in the relay of aesthetic discourse" (Bök 10), Oulipian writer Italo Calvino had already voiced an earlier version of this argument, nearly a half century ago (1967), claiming that "[w]riters, as they have always been up to now, are already writing machines" (15).[2]

These assertions about poetry composed and read by machines provide a suggestive theoretical backdrop for an examination of a more contemporary (and thus, more technologically sophisticated) online project that creates a contestatory, virtual space in which to engage a number of important poetic and political questions. This chapter, then, explores Argentine-Spanish digital artist Belén Gache's conceptualization of aleatory *politics* in her online project *Radikal karaoke* by taking Bök's analysis as its starting point—replacing "poet" in Bök's text with "politician" and "poem" with "speech." In *Radikal karaoke*, Gache employs a fixed verbal structure and aleatory texts (generated by bots searching the Internet) to critique the creation and proliferation of linguistic clichés by political rhetors. She thereby renders politicians—and the online users who voice the empty rhetoric in Gache's online, webcam-enabled interface—zombies and "karaoke singers." In doing so, Gache hijacks or hacks a deconstructed *politics* as aleatory (robo)*poetics* with an eye to creating a user-enabled,[3] contestatory virtual space in which to critique the vacuous nature of today's political rhetoric. As we will see in examples drawn from a number of political "speeches" generated by *Radikal karaoke's* aleatory logic, the slippage from a political space to a poetic one (and vice versa) is a strong condemnation of the demagogical and parasitic character of contemporary global politics. Gache's ironic trivialization of hegemonic discourses—by appropriating them into the karaoke format—is part and parcel of her pointed (yet ludic) criticism of their virtual ventriloquism, insofar as *Radikal karaoke* mocks and challenges the ways in which politicians impose authoritarian discourses through propagandistic media saturation.

On the introductory page to *Radikal karaoke*, Gache—as in her well-known *WordToys*—provides a rigorous theorization of the underlying principles guiding her artistic exploration.[4]

Here, Gache describes the way in which *Radikal karaoke's* interface draws directly from a previous project—a *Radikal karaoke* v 1.0, if you will—titled *Manifiestos Robots* (2009), a work that she describes as:

Serie de poemas aleatorios a partir de una estructura verbal fija correspondiente al género del discurso político. Piezas sonoras

> realizadas por Belén Gache utilizando el sistema IP Poetry (desarrollado por Gustavo Romano en 2004, que realiza búsquedas en Internet a partir de palabras clave y luego las verbaliza valiéndose de fonemas pregrabados).[5]

Gache's reference to fellow experimental media artist Gustavo Romano's *IP Poetry Project* requires some further grounding. Romano defines his robopoetic apparatus—for which he was awarded a Guggenheim Foundation Fellowship in 2006—as "un sistema de software y hardware que utiliza material textual de Internet para la generación de poesía que luego será recitada en tiempo real por autómatas conectados a la red" (5).[6] The textual fragments, in general terms, are a combination of short phrases entered by users and information obtained from Internet searches, which are subsequently transmitted to the four "IP bots" who recite the larger, conglomerate text in an online interface or during a performance-installation.[7] The IP Poetry project most directly interrogates

> la creciente subjetivación de los sistemas tecnológicos, a quienes dotamos de determinadas características humanas aumentadas artificialmente (en este caso, la memoria, la capacidad de hablar, y escucharse entre sí)...saca provecho de la virtual conformación de una memoria humana colectiva a través de la red de Internet a través de una poética basada en lo maquínico y lo aleatorio.
>
> (5)[8]

Gache herself highlights the cyborg-like subjectivity of the IP bots, asking—in an essay titled "De poemas no humanos y cabezas parlantes," which accompanies the *IP Poetry Project*'s exposition booklet (from the Museo Extremeño e Iberoamericano de Arte Contemporáneo in Badajoz, España)—"¿Son máquinas con bocas humanas o es el hombre en cambio una máquina parlante?" (33).[9]

To return to Gache's concise, yet thought-provoking presentation of *Radikal karaoke*, I would like to highlight several aspects of her conceptual and technological framework, in order to flesh out the specific contestatory gestures enacted in her online project. She notes that contemporary politicians' reliance on new technologies such as teleprompters, podcasts, and social networks finds its origins in the early 20th-century embrace of then-innovative technology, such as the radio or the loudspeaker,[10] and links this kind of disembodied voice to the "non-serious" space of the carnival (as ventriloquism) and the bar scene (as karaoke). She also classifies the main function of political rhetoric as its own proliferation, connecting language (self)production and the virus in a way that recalls her own discussion of William Burroughs' *The Soft Machine* in "De poemas no humanos y cabezas parlantes":

William Burroughs asimilaba el lenguaje a un virus. En "A surreal space odyssey through the wounded galaxies", la última narración de *The Soft Machine*, Burroughs establece su propio mito de la creación: imagina el comienzo de la raza humana como un desastre biológico. Los monos se convierten en hombres debido a que se infectan con un virus que mata a la mayor parte de la especie y hace mutar al resto. Los sobrevivientes sienten la dolorosa invasión en sus cuerpos de una fuerza exterior que gradualmente produce el comportamiento humano. La humanidad se desarrolla a partir de esta enfermedad que es la enfermedad del lenguaje. La "máquina blanda" es el ser humano controlado y manipulado a partir del lenguaje.

$$(36)^{11}$$

Gache also emphasizes the radical otherness that speaks in or through humankind, since our "sociedad zombie" has (always already) been colonized by the otherness of power and market structures or perhaps by language itself. Her *Radikal karaoke,* therefore, seeks to explore the tension between "utopia and the commonplace" and "the revolutionary spirit and the scam underlying these texts."[12]

The interface employed in *Radikal karaoke* is rather uncomplicated, from the user's point of view, and offers a number of optional visual and auditory effects that respond to aesthetic and performative alterations. The "Help" instruction module—written in English, interestingly enough (whereas the aleatory speeches are in Spanish)—directs the user-operator to "Connect your microphone and when required, allows [sic] Flash to access it. Choose a speech, read and interpret what they have written for you, considering that the sound of your voice can change the image of the screen" ("Help") (Figure 4.1).

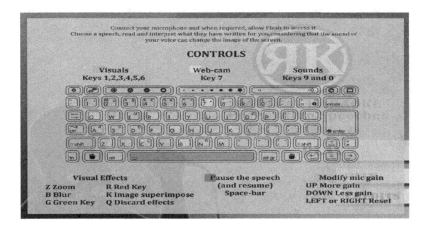

Figure 4.1 Radikal Karaoke interface.

As you can see from the image, a number of visual and audio effects are available to the user—with the most significant, I would argue, being the ability to pause and resume the quickly scrolling political discourse (for closer study, perhaps), as well as alternating between six different, prerecorded visual options and the user's live webcam, as well as between two background audio tracks, one of resounding boos and the other of roaring applause. The prerecorded visuals among which the user might choose, to suit her fancy, are as follows (Figure 4.2):

There are rather obvious thematic concerns at play in the video selections displayed above the scrolling political speeches—ranging from the collective enthusiasm shared by spectators listening to a presentation (evidently a politically charged one; Figure 4.3), to the catastrophic

Figure 4.2 Radikal Karaoke screenshot.

Figure 4.3 Radikal Karaoke screenshot.

violence of a large-scale bomb explosion (Figure 4.4), to a hypnotizing visual swirl (Figure 4.5), to a rather diverse group of virtual avatars that nevertheless "marches to the beat of the same drummer" (Figure 4.6), to a cinematic alien invasion (Figure 4.7), to a scene that evokes the construction of the Pyramids of Egypt by slaves (Figure 4.8). But, when the seventh and final visual option (the webcam) is selected, the user sees *herself* on screen, reciting the scrolling political rhetoric and

Figure 4.4 *Radikal Karaoke* screenshot.

Figure 4.5 *Radikal Karaoke* screenshot.

Figure 4.6 Radikal Karaoke screenshot.

Figure 4.7 Radikal Karaoke screenshot.

manipulating the multitude of controls to create alternative visual and auditory effects—with some very suggestive implications for the question of subversive, techno-political subjectivities in a virtual environment, as we'll see.

Upon clicking "PLAY," the user is presented with a choice of three speeches:

The first speech "Ex Africa semper aliquid novi," or "always something new from Africa," takes its title from Pliny the Elder's *Naturalis Historia* (Book 8, Section 17),[13] while the other two titles appear to be more random in nature. We might read "Mirad cómo Kate presume de su anillo" ["look at how Kate shows off her ring"] in light of the media

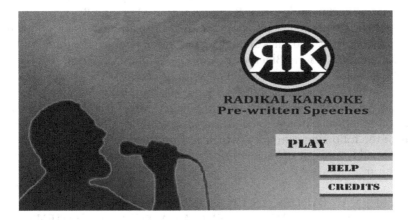

Figure 4.8 Radikal Karaoke user options.

circus that surrounded Kate Middleton's October 2010 engagement and April 29, 2011 marriage to Prince William—upon which she became Catherine, Duchess of Cambridge; "Es tiempo de escuchar a los guacamayos" ["it's time to listen to the macaws"] certainly highlights the (often mindless) linguistic mimicry of these New World parrots. Notwithstanding potential historical or openly political interpretations of the constantly changing speeches "themselves" (which would presuppose a predetermined, fixed, and non-aleatory content), *Radikal karaoke*'s ironic, (dis)embodied, and aleatory poetics pose some important questions regarding discourses of resistance and individual agency in a virtual medium—such as the potential futility of individual action in a globalized media environment (rendering us, in turn, zombies), as well as the dehumanizing effect of contemporary political discourse, to name just two examples. The speeches produced in *Radikal karaoke* are a combination of text found by bots trolling the Internet and select, fixed structures that largely preserve the contextual markers of political rhetoric, such as slight variations on an introduction like "BUENAS TARDES, ES UN HONOR ESTAR AQUÍ FRENTE A ESTA AUDIENCIA. APROVECHARE ESTA OPORTUNIDAD PARA DECIROS. TENGO UN MENSAJE PARA VOSOTROS:" ("Ex Africa...")[14] or "ELLOS PROMETIERON QUE IBAN A CUMPLIR. SISTEMATICAMENTE. NO LO HAN HECHO. CONTRA LAS FALSAS PROMESAS DE LOS OTROS. CONFRONTAMOS NUESTRAS VERDADERAS SOLUCIONES. NOSOTROS:" ("Es tiempo de escuchar...").[15] The cast of characters from *Radikal karaoke* as a whole includes myriad historical figures and pop culture references, including—but not limited to, given the generative (robo)poetics of the work—Archimedes, Chuang Tzu, Pliny the Elder, Plato, Martin Heidegger, Napoleon, Horace,

Spiderman, Paco Ventura, Friedrich Nietzsche, Justin Bieber, Selena Gomez, Pikachu, Lady Gaga, Ramoncín, Iron Man, and Britney Spears. References to technology and popular media also abound, as the political "ventriloquist" is fed lines about Twitter, music piracy, "Breaking Bad," "Watchmen," Wi-Fi, Bluetooth, Yahoo! Respuestas, blogs, TomTom GPS navigation, USB ports, PS (PlayStation) network, the Disney Channel, Web 2.0, mutant robots, tablets, 900 numbers, Windows 3.11, spam, Second Life, web hosting, and Blogger. There is a definite emphasis on humorous, ironic, vacuous, or bizarre political-sounding clichés, as in the following example—which sets up the presentation of what is presumably an issue of sociopolitical concern, only to launch into a non sequitur:

BUENAS TARDES, ES UN HONOR ESTAR AQUÍ FRENTE A TAN CALIFICADA AUDIENCIA. ANTES DE COMENZAR A EXPLICARME. QUISIERA ACLARAROS ALGO: NO HE VENIDO AQUI A CAMBIAR EL MUNDO. APROVECHARE SIN EMBARGO PARA DECIROS TRES COSAS. UNA: TENEMOS UN PROBLEMA. DOS: DEBEMOS HACER ALGO. TRES: DEBEMOS ACTUAR PRONTO.
HOY LOS SERES HUMANOS SE SIENTEN MAS SERES HUMANOS. SEGUIREMOS ALERTANDO SOBRE ESTE PELIGRO. NUESTRO PRINCIPAL ENEMIGO ES LA OMNIPOTENCIA. NUESTRO PRINCIPAL ENEMIGO ES MUCHISIMO MAS GRANDE QUE UN BLOG MEDIOCRE Y DE MALA MUERTE. NUESTRO PRINCIPAL ENEMIGO SON LOS HIDRATOS DE CARBONO. *****

("Es tiempo de escuchar a los guacamayos")[16]

As is clear from this (rather absurd) accusation against carbohydrates, *Radikal karaoke*'s robopoetic algorithm often yields sentences that are grammatically correct, yet "semantically aberrant," as Bök describes in his analysis of RACTER's poetic production (Bök 10). In this passage, however, we might locate a more specific critique: the juxtaposition of grandiose political rhetoric (regarding the immediacy of a major problem and the need to act immediately) with the daily, trivial preoccupations of contemporary (Western) societies, such as counting carbs and calories to maintain physical appearances (rather than to fight the obesity epidemic, we might say). The following examples also stand out in their potpourri of political slogans, techno-consumer products, mixed metaphors, and disconnected anaphora:

VIVAN NUESTROS REVOLUCIONARIOS COSMETICOS ANTI-AGE! VIVA LA REVOLUCION DEL WEB HOSTING!

("Ex Africa...")[17]

***** ES CIERTO QUE ATRAVERSAREMOS DIFICULTADES Y PROBLEMAS. PERO ESTAMOS JUNTOS Y ESTAMOS DIVID- IDOS. ESTAMOS INVITADOS. ESTAMOS EN EL AIRE. ESTA- MOS GUAPISIMOS. ESTAMOS INDIGNADOS. *****

("Mirad...")[18]

These misuses of language can certainly be read as critiques of the super- ficial nature of contemporary Western civilization (largely, as we'll see, with respect to globalization and multinational capitalism). But, with respect to the mixing of (ostensible) contexts in which they appear, they also recall philosopher Ludwig Wittgenstein's discussion of mishandling language in the *Philosophical Investigations* (§350–1), insofar as the Austrian philosopher shows how explanation by identity falls short in examples such as the following:

> It is as if I were to say: "You surely know what 'It is 5 o'clock here' means; so you also know what 'It's 5 o'clock on the sun' means. It means simply that it is just the same there as it is here when it is 5 o'clock."—The explanation by means of *identity* does not work here. For I know well enough that one can call 5 o'clock here and 5 o'clock there "the same time," but what I do not know is in what cases one is to speak of its being the same time here and there.
>
> (2002, 95)

Also, in §513, Wittgenstein invites us to

> [c]onsider the following form of expression: 'The number of pages in my book is equal to the root of the equation $x^3+2x-3=0$.' Or: 'I have n friends and $n^2+2n+2=0$'. Does this sentence make sense? This cannot be seen immediately. This example shews how it is that something can look like a sentence which we understand, and yet yield no sense.
>
> (2002, 119)

We might also think through *Radikal karaoke*'s nonsense statements— although it's rather taboo to move from the posthumous *Philosophical Investigations* back to the young Wittgenstein's *Tractatus*—in light of the Lewis Carroll-like examples in which Wittgenstein asserts that it makes no sense to say "'There is only one 1'" or "'2+2 at 3 o'clock equals 4'" (2001, 4.1272).

From a mathematical standpoint that certainly recalls Wittgenstein's nonsensical math (or even the infamous "fuzzy math" posited in a George W. Bush-Al Gore U.S. Presidential debate in 2000), the political rhetoric proffered by *Radikal karaoke* also clearly mocks the manipula- tion of statistics, as in the following fragments:

> TODOS LO SABEMOS: EL 80 POR CIENTO DE LAS EMPRESAS
> SE ENCUENTRAN FUERA DE LA LEY. EL 40 POR CIENTO DE
> LAS MISMAS NO PAGA NUNCA SUS IMPUESTOS. EL 20 POR
> CIENTO DE LOS MAS RICOS POSEEN EL 60 POR CIENTO
> DE LA RIQUEZA MIENTRAS EL 40 POR CIENTO DE LOS
> MAS POBRES TIENEN EL 10 POR CIENTO DE LA POBREZA.
> ***** 4 DE CADA 5 MINOS DE ENTRE 0 Y 2 ANOS DE EDAD.
> UTILIZAN EL INTERNET. 7 DE CADA 4 ESTADISTICAS SON
> ERRONEAS. *****
>
> ("Ex Africa...")[19]

> YA TODOS LO SABEMOS: EL 10 POR CIENTO DE TUS
> "AMIGOS" ONLINE NO SERA HUMANO EN 2015. POR
> OTRA PARTE, EL 80 POR CIENTO DE LOS NEGOCIOS UTIL-
> LIZARA TABLETS. EL 50 POR CIENTO DE LA POBLACION
> ACUDE AL DENTISTA MIENTRAS QUE SOLO EL 70 POR
> CIENTO ACUDE AL ODONTOLOGO.
>
> ("Mirad...")[20]

Whereas statistics are often deployed in political discourse and cam-paigns in order to create the illusion of expertise and scientific certainty in a constantly changing landscape of rhetoric, the arbitrary and non-sensical nature of these cited statistics—which, significantly, do not cite their source—certainly makes a mockery of politicians' "ventril-oquism." Thus, we might say that *Radikal karaoke*'s poetic-political output is not far from (a techno-savvy) Wittgenstein or Carroll (or even Beckett or Joyce) when it implores the karaoke politician to mime the following lines:

> ES TIEMPO DE ESCUCHAR A LOS GUACAMAYOS. EL TOM-
> TOM NOS MOSTRARA NUESTRO CAMINO. EL TOMTOM
> NOS GUIARA INDICANDONOS LA MEJOR RUTA PARA LLE-
> GAR A NUESTRO DESTINO. JUNTOS LO LOGRAREMOS.
> JUNTOS VENCEREMOS AL CICLISMO. JUNTOS VENCERE-
> MOS CON LA AYUDA DE IRON MAN. JUNTOS VENCERE-
> MOS LA DERROTA.
>
> ("Es tiempo...")[21]

In fact, the equivalence created here between political discourse and ran-domly generated poetic lines—luring the charged "JUNTOS VENCER-EMOS" into play with "CON LA AYUDA DE IRON MAN," to pick one example among many—is the site of a powerful, participatory, and contestatory space in which to critique the emptiness of today's political discourse.[22] *Radikal karaoke*, then, deconstructs politics (supposedly se-rious) as robopoetics (supposedly nonserious) in order to show the vapid nature of contemporary global politics by "hacking" the previously established (presumed) hierarchy of "politics are serious and poetry (literature) is but a trivial diversion." This logic resembles Jacques Derrida's theorization of the complex relationship between literature and politics in an interview titled "This Strange Institution Called Literature," in which the French philosopher argues that:

> [literature] gives *in principle* the power to say everything, to break free of the rules, to displace them, and thereby to institute, to invent and even to suspect the traditional difference between nature and institution, nature and conventional law, nature and history. Here we should ask juridical and political questions. The institution of literature in the West, in its relatively modern form, is linked to an authorization to say everything, and doubtless too to the coming about of the modern idea of democracy. Not that it depends on a democracy in place, but it seems inseparable to me from what calls forth a democracy, in the most open (and doubtless itself to come) sense of democracy.
>
> (37)

Gache's ironic trivialization of hegemonic discourses in *Radikal karaoke*, then, appropriates them into the poetic-karaoke format—in which one might sing or "say anything"—as part and parcel of her sharp criticism evinced through this interactive ventriloquism in cyber(literary) space. Moreover, Gache herself frames this (ludic) political project in terms of "un conjunto de poesías que se apropian de la retórica de la propaganda política a fin de interrogar los discursos hegemónicos"[23]; we might thus situate the (robo)poet as karaoke artist in this confluence of democratic and literary spaces.

Also at issue in *Radikal karaoke*'s interface is a series of profound questions regarding the embodiment of the user-virtual politician. As Gache herself suggests,

> Estas piezas sonoras están construidas a partir de una estructura verbal fija y textos aleatorios. Sólo que aquí, la voz y el cuerpo son ineludibles. Al igual que el karaoke convierte en supuesto cantante y protagonista a quien lo utiliza, mediante el uso de este dispositivo cualquiera podrá tener la ilusión de verse convertido en un líder político y arengar a las masas.[24]

The "inescapable" nature of voice and body that Gache emphasizes here reflects the strong view of embodiment taken in *Radikal karaoke*, a project that does not let the body fade into discourse, into a constellation of (vacuous political) signs. We might thus inquire as to the relationship between embodiment and the webcam-enabled interface that permits (or perhaps forces) the user to see and hear herself as a mindless drone, zombie, or karaoke singer, destined (doomed?) to mime the empty political rhetoric scrolling across the computer screen. Or, alternately, might this be an opportunity for citizens to engage in subversive tactics, virtually and corporally rejecting the formulaic discourse being "fed to them" onscreen?

In *How We Became Posthuman*, Katherine Hayles describes the performative aspects of embodiment, in a discussion that I find highly relevant to the current analysis of Gache's poetic-political project:

> Formed by technology at the same time that it creates technology, embodiment mediates between technology and discourse by creating new experiential frameworks that serve as boundary markers for the creation of corresponding discursive systems. In the feedback loop between technological innovations and discursive practices, incorporation is a crucial link.
>
> (205)

Hayles' main case study in her chapter on embodiment—in addition to the myriad theoretical and philosophical currents that she brings into conversation with each other—is William Burroughs' science fiction novel *The Ticket that Exploded*, a book that, according to Hayles, treats "technology not only as a theme but as an articulation capable of producing new kinds of subjectivities" (Hayles 217). The production of a new techno-political subjectivity in *Radikal karaoke* is strikingly similar to the portrait that Hayles draws of "the Exhibition" in Burroughs' novel:

> incorporations are transformed into inscriptions through video- and audio-recording devices; bodies understood as normative and essentialized entities are rewritten to become particularized experiences of embodiment; and embodied experience is transformed, through the inscriptions of the tape-recording, back into essentialized manifestations of "the word." The recursivities that entangle inscription with incorporation, the body with embodiment, invite us to see these polarities not as static concepts but as mutating surfaces that transform into one another....
>
> (220)

The move from incorporation to inscription—from performing bodily content to correcting and modulating its performance (200)—is precisely the kind of self-reflexive experience of "seeing oneself seeing" in *Radikal karaoke*'s deformed and deforming, pixelated webcam "reflection" on the computer screen. Do the "mutating surfaces" of screen and bodily topologies, then, leave the karaoke singer no option other than to witness the horror of her own ventriloquism of the empty poetic-political clichés, or might the recursive incorporation of the embodied self into a virtual environment permit the subversion of the hegemonic political gaze by way of the articulation of a new, contestatory avatar? In the case of the user-virtual politician, we might argue, with Hayles, that "...it is not a question of leaving the body behind but rather of extending embodied awareness in highly specific, local, and material ways that would be impossible without electronic prosthesis" (291).[25] Insofar as this extension of embodied awareness, as Hayles puts it, creates and is created by multiple, entangled feedback loops in *Radikal karaoke*—most notably, user-karaoke singer/politician and a radical politics formulated as or by way of generative poetry—its most salient contribution resides in its deconstruction and (h)activism of *politics* as aleatory (robo)*poetics*, in order to produce new virtual *and* embodied political subjectivities.

Notes

1 In *Nomadic Writings [Escrituras nómades]*, Belén Gache traces the history of this type of experimental writing procedure, beginning with the I Ching and Kabbalistic numerology, passing thorough such noteworthy (and occasionally obscure) examples as Publius Optatianus Porfyrius's Carmen XXV (dating to approximately 300 CE), Quirinus Kuhlmann's Himmlische Libes-küsse (1671), Tristan Tzara's recipes for composing Dadaist poems, André Breton's theorization of objective chance in Nadja (1928), William Burroughs' cut-up techniques, Duchamp's ready-mades, the Oulipo's use of the constraint as creative stimulus, Cage's writing-through techniques such as the mesostic poem, etc.

2 The issue of machines producing poetry certainly begs the question of a kind of literary-cultural AI (Artificial Intelligence), which is beyond the scope of the present chapter. For a suggestive exploration of a humanists' "Turing test" of sorts, see Ray Kurzweil's experiments involving the comparison of haikus "written" by a computer algorithm with those written by humans ("The Age of Intelligent Machines: 'A (Kind of) Turing Test'").

3 As we will see, however, the participatory nature of the user's intervention is quite limited in scope (perhaps even frighteningly so!)—which, I think, is consistent with the critique of contemporary politics that Gache develops in *Radikal karaoke*.

4 I would like to thank Belén Gache for permission to reproduce images from *Radikal karaoke* in this essay.

5 "A series of aleatory poems based on a fixed verbal structure, corresponding to the genre of a political speech. Sound works created by Belén Gache, using the IP Poetry system (developed by Gustavo Romano in 2004, and which carries out Internet searches based on key words, and then recites them using pre-recorded phonemes)." Translations from *Radikal karaoke* are my own.

6 "a software and hardware system that uses text from the Internet to generate poetry that is then recited in real time by automatons connected to the web" (Romano 105). The *IP Poetry Project* exhibition catalogue is bilingual; I therefore have cited the extant translations to English in this essay.

7 As Romano observes, in the context of installations of his *IP Poetry Project*—which have taken place in Portugal, Spain, the U.S., Argentina, France, Uruguay, and China—

The recitals will be performed at various public venues. Using a proximity sensor, the system detects the presence of an audience and sends a command to the robots to start reciting the poems especially created for such an event.

At that point the internet search begins. The results are sent to the automatons (IP Bots), which convert the search results into the pre-recorded sounds and images of a moving human mouth.

As new text appears on a daily basis on the web, the poems recited maintain their structure, but the varying search results ensure a poem is never recited in the same way twice. (2008, 105)

[La forma de exhibición es performática y se da mediante la intervención de diferentes espacios públicos. Utilizando un sensor de proximidad, el sistema detecta la presencia del público y envía la orden a los robots para que comiencen a recitar los poemas creados especialmente para cada evento.

Se inicia entonces el proceso de búsqueda en Internet. Los resultados encontrados son enviados a los autómatas (IP Bots) quienes convertirán esos textos encontrados en sonidos e imágenes pregrabados de una boca humana recitando.

Al aparecer diariamente nuevas páginas en la web con nuevos textos, los poemas recitados mantienen su estructura, pero los resultados de las búsquedas van variando, por lo que nunca un poema es recitado de la misma forma. (2008, 5).]

8 "the increasing subjectivity of technology, which is endowed with certain artificially enhanced human characteristics (in this case, memory, and the ability to speak and listen)" and also "uses the virtual arrangement of the collective human memory found on the internet to compose poetry that has both mechanical and random elements" (Romano 105).

9 "Are they machines with human mouths or is a man a talking machine instead?" (Gache 2008, 117).

10 Gache's assertions regarding artists' adaptation of new technological innovations recall Marshall McLuhan's insightful analysis in *Understanding Media*:

It is the poets and painters who react instantly to a new medium like radio or TV. Radio and gramophone and tape recorder gave us back the poet's voice as an important dimension of the poetic experience. Words became a kind of painting with light, again. But TV, with its deep-participation mode, caused young poets suddenly to present their poems in cafes, in public parks, anywhere. After TV, they suddenly felt the need for personal contact with their public.

(53)

11 "William Burroughs likened language to a virus. In 'A surreal space odyssey through the wounded galaxies,' the last essay in *The Soft Machine*, Burroughs formulates his own creation myth, in which he envisions the start of the human race as a biological disaster. Apes became man after being infected by a virus that kills off most of the specimens and mutates the rest. The survivors feel their bodies painfully invaded by an outside force that gradually results in human behavior. Mankind arises from this disease, which is none other than the disease of language. The 'soft machine' is the human being, controlled and manipulated by language" (Gache 2008, 120).

12 "RK trabaja con el permanente contraste entre la utopía y el lugar común; el espíritu revolucionario y el timo que subyace en estos textos."

13 Pliny the Elder's *Natural History* was an early attempt to systematize the natural world in an (Aristotelian) encyclopedic way. In the section containing the well-known—and frequently misappropriated—"Ex Africa…" quote, Pliny is discussing the promiscuous coupling of lions and lionesses, which produces "so many curious varieties of animals" (8.17).

14 "GOOD AFTERNOON, IT IS AN HONOR TO BE HERE IN FRONT OF THIS AUDIENCE. I WILL TAKE ADVANTAGE OF THIS OPPORTUNITY TO TELL YOU. I HAVE A MESSAGE FOR YOU." We might read the "all caps" text in *Radikal karaoke* in a number of ways. First, it might be for visual clarity and legibility on this "teleprompter" interface. Second, communication in "all caps" is known as "shouting" in virtual environments, which certainly fits the performative conventions of the genre of the political speech.

15 "THEY PROMISED THAT THEY WOULD COMPLY. SYSTEMATICALLY. AGAINST OTHERS' FALSE PROMISES. WE CONFRONT OUR TRUE SOLUTIONS. US:"

16 "GOOD AFTERNOON, IT IS AN HONOR TO BE HERE IN FRONT OF SUCH A QUALIFIED AUDIENCE. BEFORE I BEGIN TO EXPLAIN MYSELF. I WOULD LIKE TO MAKE SOMETHING CLEAR TO YOU: I HAVE NOT COME HERE TO CHANGE THE WORLD. NEVERTHELESS I WILL MAKE THE MOST OF IT TO TELL YOU THREE THINGS. ONE: WE HAVE A PROBLEM. TWO: WE SHOULD DO SOMETHING. THREE: WE SHOULD ACT SOON. TODAY HUMAN BEINGS FEEL MORE LIKE HUMAN BEINGS. OUR MAIN ENEMY IS OMNIPOTENCE. OUR MAIN ENEMY IS MUCH BIGGER THAN A MEDIOCRE AND SEEDY BLOG. OUR MAIN ENEMY IS CARBOHYDRATES."

17 "LONG LIVE OUR REVOLUTIONARY ANTI-AGING COSMETICS! LONG LIVE THE REVOLUTION IN WEB HOSTING!"

18 "IT IS TRUE THAT WE WILL GO THROUGH DIFFICULTIES AND PROBLEMS. BUT WE ARE TOGETHER AND WE ARE DIVIDED. WE ARE INVITED. WE ARE IN THE AIR. WE ARE GORGEOUS. WE ARE INDIGNANT."

19 "WE ALL KNOW IT: 80 PERCENT OF COMPANIES OPERATE OUTSIDE OF THE LAW. 40 PERCENT OF THEM NEVER PAY THEIR TAXES. 20 PERCENT OF THE MOST RICH POSSESS 60 PERCENT OF THE WEALTH WHILE 40 PERCENT OF THE POOREST POSSESS 10 PERCENT OF POVERTY. ***** FOUR OUT OF FIVE MINORS BETWEEN 0 AND 2 YEARS OLD. USE THE INTERNET. 7 OUT OF 4 STATISTICS ARE ERRONEOUS."

20 "WE ALL KNOW IT: 10 PERCENT OF YOUR ONLINE 'FRIENDS' WILL NOT BE HUMAN IN 2015. ON THE OTHER HAND, 80 PERCENT OF BUSINESSES USE TABLETS. 50 PERCENT OF THE POPULATION GOES TO THE DENTIST WHILE ONLY 70 PERCENT OF THE POPULATION GOES TO THE ORTHODONTIST."

21 "IT IS TIME TO LISTEN TO THE MACAWS. THE TOMTOM WILL SHOW US THE WAY. THE TOMTOM WILL GUIDE US SHOWING US THE BEST ROUTE TO ARRIVE US AT OUR DESTINATION. TOGETHER WE WILL ACHIEVE IT. TOGETHER WE WILL OVERCOME CYCLING. TOGETHER WE WILL OVERCOME WITH THE HELP OF IRON MAN. TOGETHER WE WILL OVERCOME THE DEFEAT."

22 It is worth noting that the repetition of "TOGETHER WE WILL OVERCOME" ["JUNTOS VENCEREMOS"] evokes the slogan of the Argentine left-Peronist guerrilla group the Montoneros, whose violent urban campaign of guerrilla warfare and subversion took place from approximately

the late 1960s to the mid-1970s. Certainly, we might argue here that
Radikal karaoke deconstructs the politically militant Montoneros' rallying
cry through a call for help from fictitious comic book character (and now
multimillion-dollar Hollywood franchise figure) Iron Man, to pick just one
randomly generated example from Gache's project.

23 "a group of poems that appropriate the rhetoric of political propaganda in
order to interrogate hegemonic discourses" (my emphasis).

24 "These sound pieces are composed according to a fixed verbal structure and
aleatory texts. But here, voice and body are inescapable. Just like the way
in which karaoke changes the user into a supposed singer and protagonist,
through the use of this mechanism anyone can share the excitement of seeing
herself changed into a political leader and haranguing the masses."

25 In light of this turn to the webcam as technology that mediates corporality
through an ineluctably electronic prosthesis, we must also be cognizant of
the rather insidious specter of Internet privacy issues that arise by way of
Radikal karaoke's specific interface. Immediately prior to entering the "political arena" (so to speak) making up the virtual space of Gache's interactive
project, the user is confronted with the following prompt from Adobe Flash
Player, in which she is asked to approve access to the computer's camera and
microphone in order to explore *Radikal karaoke*. We might ask, however:
what happens to the video captured by the user's webcam? Is it recorded
in some way, communicated back to the server belengache.net? Is it stored
on a remote server, through which it might be accessed at a later time by
unknown parties—or even used for other (unauthorized) purposes? While I
hardly consider myself paranoid, I would argue that this issue—insightfully
raised by my graduate students at the University of New Hampshire (in
a seminar titled "Hispanic Literatures and Cultures in the Digital Age,"
Spring 2013) and not even mentioned in *Radikal karaoke*—is certainly germane to the larger "politics" of Gache's project and might be addressed in
some way in future versions of RK.

Works Cited

Bök, Christian. "The Piecemeal Bard is Deconstructed: Notes Toward a Potential Robopoetics." *Object* 10 (2001): 10–18.

Calvino, Italo. "Cybernetics and Ghosts." *The Uses of Literature*. Trans. Patrick
Creagh. New York: Harcourt Brace Jovanovich, 1986.

Chamberlain, William. "Racter." *The UbuWeb Anthology of Conceptual Writing*. Ed. Craig Dworkin. 1984. www.ubu.com/concept/racter.html. Accessed
1 May 2015.

Derrida, Jacques. "This Strange Institution Called Literature: An Interview
with Jacques Derrida." Trans. Geoffrey Bennington and Rachel Bowlby. *Acts
of Literature*. Ed. Derek Attridge. New York: Routledge, 1992. 33–75.

Gache, Belén. *Escrituras nómades*. Gijón: Ediciones Trea, 2006.

———. "IP POETRY Y LOS ROBOTS PARLANTES: El hombre como máquina
parlante y la sociedad como máquina". *IP Poetry*. Badajoz, Extremadura:
MEIAC (Museo Extremeño e Iberoamericano de Arte Contemporáneo). *The
IP Poetry Project*. 2008. http://ip-poetry.findelmundo.com.ar. Accessed 1
May 2015.

———. "Manifiestos Robots". 2009. http://findelmundo.com.ar/belengache/
manifiestosrobot.htm. Accessed 1 May 2015.

———. *Radikal karaoke*. 2011. http://belengache.net/rk/. Accessed 1 May 2015.

Goldsmith, Kenneth. *Uncreative Writing: Managing Language in the Digital Age*. New York: Columbia University Press, 2011.

Hayles, Katherine. *How We Became Posthuman: Virtual Bodies in Cybernetics, Literature, and Informatics*. Chicago: University of Chicago Press, 1999.

Kurzweil, Ray. "The Age of Intelligent Machines: 'A (Kind of) Turing Test.'" 2002. www.kurzweilcyberart.com/poetry/rkcp_akindofturingtest.php. Accessed 1 May 2015.

McLuhan, Marshall. *Understanding Media: The Extensions of Man*. Intro. Lewis H. Lapham. Cambridge: The MIT Press, 1994 [1964].

Pliny the Elder. *The Natural History*. Eds. John Bostock and H. T. Riley. London: Taylor and Francis. Perseus Digital Library, 1855 [77–79 AD]. http://data.perseus.org/citations/urn:cts:latinLit:phi0978.phi001.perseus-eng1:8.17. Accessed 1 May 2015.

Romano, Gustavo. *The IP Poetry Project*. 2004–. http://ip-poetry.findelmundo.com.ar. Accessed 1 May 2015.

Wittgenstein, Ludwig. *Philosophical Investigations*. Trans. G. E. M. Anscombe. Malden, MA: Blackwell, 2002 [1953].

———. *Tractatus Logico-Philosophicus*. Trans. D. F. Pears and B. F. McGuinness. Intro. Bertrand Russell New York: Routledge Classics, 2001 [1922].

Part II

Blogging as Online Activism

5   On Pirates and Tourists

Ambivalent Approaches to El Blog del Narco

Emily Hind

Depending on the angle, the website El Blog del Narco (BDN) (www. blogdelnarco.com) can appear to represent a scintillating contestatory hotspot or a blandly conformist compromise. The rise and fall of BDN spans slightly more than three years, from March 2, 2010 through October 14, 2013. After the latter date, the original BDN appears to have lost its audience to competitor ElBlogdelnarco.net (www.elblogdelnarco. net), as demonstrated by metrics made available by the Internet company Alexa.[1] During its peak, BDN served as a notorious clearinghouse for news stories and images related to the violence surrounding Mexican organized crime. About six months after the blog first appeared, an interview with an anonymous founder quantified the site's popularity: three million unique visits per month (Gutierrez). Mainstream forces, including YouTube, pressured BDN to censor its often gory content, which included videos of interrogations and beheadings, as well as seemingly endless photos of dismembered and decomposing bodies. A mission statement on the blog employed a telling metaphor to describe its operative gray area: "We could be, perhaps, 'pirates,' but never peons or slaves. We are free and as such we express ourselves" ("Acerca de").[2] Perhaps "free" pirates, indeed. The success of BDN sparked numerous imitators, likely self-imagined liberated pirates in their own right, who produced a smartphone app and assorted Facebook pages, one of which borrows the "Blog del Narco" label and counts more than 220,000 "likes." The utility of the brand name to support for-profit enterprise helps to question the "contestatory" nature of BDN. In fact, in 2012, the original site stretched beyond the Internet and authorized a print spin-off, the anonymously authored, bilingual book *Muriendo por la verdad/Dying for the Truth* (2012). The possible profit motive behind the publication suggests that BDN engages not just in contestatory pirate tactics, but also in more complacent tourism. Of course, piracy can turn complacent and tourists can act out in contestatory manners, and thus pirates and tourists share unstable connotations. Both pirates and tourists can be faulted for a lack of originality. Just as some forms of piracy require expert skill, the very word "tourism" is thought to be derived from "travail," which means "suffering or work" (Merrill 14). This uncreative and even parasitical act that alternates with arduous labor remains inherent to the endeavors of "piracy" and "tourism" and therefore evinces the underlying ambiguity of the BDN project. The bulk of the present article explores the categories of pirates and tourists as a means to interpret the simultaneously naïve and rebelliously explicit blog. The refusal of BDN to parse its own content leads to my concluding section, which ventures a literary critique of two sets of images available in *Muriendo por la verdad*. Like the much commented "drug war" dialogues of the U.S. television show *The Wire*, the images of bloody terror reproduced on BDN correspond to bleak tactics of tautology and allegory.

News Pirates

For those readers unaccustomed to spotting piracy, I will begin by pointing out the various piratical manifestations on BDN. First, the site claims to give the information that other media will not transmit. An early anonymous interview quoted a founder of BDN as claiming neutrality regarding the principle that no photo or video is too horrific to post ("tratamos de publicar todo"); the blogger denied responsibility for spreading terror or promoting violence through the communication of these supposedly "unfiltered" elements (Gutierrez). In defiance of global onlookers' concern that elevated levels of impunity caused by a dysfunctional justice system drove Mexicans to "pervasive self-censorship," BDN gave the impression that the site struggled less with self-censorship and more with externally imposed controls (*Attacks* 128). For instance, in a message that wished readers a happy new year, BDN pledged to resist censors: "[...] we will try hard to impede the censorship that in the last months of 2011 they have tried to impose on us."[3] The identity of the vague "they" behind the pressure never emerged. Strangely, perhaps, BDN manages pirate status in the other direction as well: the site copied a significant portion of its stories from mainstream sources. One blogger ironically contextualized this habit: when the newsmagazine *Proceso* published complaints about plagiarism in BDN, other media sources promptly repackaged the piece, at times with incomplete attribution and at times without any attribution; plagiarist reproduction of a complaint about plagiarism reveals the labyrinthine reach of this habit (Tirzo). The same blogger used "plagiarismchecker.com" to check an additional twenty-some articles and discovered, on the one hand, that BDN had at times copied and pasted material without attribution and, on the other hand, traditional and digital media had done the same with BDN reports (Tirzo). Thus, even as the metaphor of piracy articulates some contestatory urges on BDN, the pirate act can also be seen as reflective of the status quo. The dangerous, copycat struggle of BDN to cover the violence without actually "Dying for the Truth"—as the book title predicts—scrambles a neat binary that would divide the contestatory from the official: BDN mirrored pieces published in the mainstream news media, which in turn reprinted BDN scoops, and even as the two sides possibly helped to diffuse perilous exposure to retaliation from those stories, both sides engaged in mutual accusations of either under- or over-reporting the events.

So far, I have cast BDN as a pirate (contestatory) news source about pirate (trafficking) practices of pirated (copied) news. Perhaps the most confusing aspect of these various aspects of piracy appears in the original brand that BDN managed to cultivate in the midst of anonymity. A historical perspective might expect this commercial fame, however, because the pirate endeavor implicates branding from its very origins.[4] Customized Jolly Roger flags served historical pirates' needs to warn more accurately of the precise reputation of their ship, which in turn aimed to intimidate victims and consequently minimize the attacking pirates' costs. That is, the branded pirate flags helped outlaws "to overwhelm victims without violence" (Leeson 499). Newspapers in the 18th century helped to plug specific pirates' mercilessness through "indispensable" media coverage of the flags (500). In some ways, BDN not only operates its own pirate brand but also parallels the role of 18th-century newspapers by sharing (trafficker) pirates' branding efforts at mercilessness. Participation brings contamination, and BDN ran the risk of becoming a tool for narcoviolence, rather than a "neutral" site that merely informed on it. Piracy on BDN thus presented a multidimensional contestatory activity that stretched from clever, ethically driven, well-intentioned rebellion to the perpetuation of unoriginal and antisocial acts.

And who are the pirates behind BDN? The introduction to *Muriendo por la verdad* attributes BDN to a pair of professionals, "un analista de sistemas y un joven periodista" (x).[5] The two male pronouns may intentionally mislead. After publication of the book, a resolutely anonymous "Lucy" stepped forward—though still protected by filters such as a pseudonym, vague answers, and distortion software. "Lucy" claimed to be the twenty-something journalist of the founding duo and seemed panicked for her personal safety. Data gathered from 1992 to 2011 explains this panic by ranking Mexico as ninth among the deadliest countries for journalists (*Attacks* 128). Fear among reporters only increased with the official ramp up of aggression against the narcoviolence. According to the Committee to Protect Journalists (CPJ), during the first five years of Calderón's presidency (2006–2012), the intensified drug war coincided with some forty-eight journalists and media workers being killed or disappearing (*Attacks* 112). A bloody event that spooked BDN collaborators kicks off the introduction to *Muriendo por la verdad*, which explains that a young man and woman who collaborated with BDN were found dismembered ("disemboweled" in the text's own English translation) and hung from a bridge; a message at the scene declared that the next victims would be the BDN founders (x). Days later, continues the introduction, another collaborating journalist was discovered in a menacing arrangement, with keyboards, a mouse, and other computer parts scattered near her cadaver (x). I will return to this matter of allegorical death scenes near the end of the chapter. For now, it bears mentioning that reports accessible through the public Google search engine and more specialized databases update the story on "Lucy."

In May 2013, she fled Mexico and ended up, by way of a flight from the U.S., in self-exile in Spain. Her escape, she confesses, was triggered by hearing for the last time from her programmer BDN cofounder, who contacted her with the message to "run." The unhappy story of self-exile suggests that the founders of BDN indeed engaged in contestatory acts—a self-proclaimed service to the public so controversial that it may have cost lives. Notwithstanding the self-reported derring-do of the BDN authors, the difference between BDN and more mainstream media sources may, in some ways, appear more in a naïve attitude than in substantive journalism. According to the introduction for *Muriendo por la verdad*, the BDN authors initially wanted to publicize violence in Mexico and thereby "abrir una ventana y, sin cortinas ni persianas, permitirles a los ciudadanos observar la dura realidad que los rodea" (*Muriendo* 2).[6] By contrast, the mainstream media eventually insisted on the utility of what BDN might have termed "curtains" or "blinds" by signing, in 2011, the "Agreement for the Informative Coverage of Violence" (Acuerdo para la Cobertura Informativa de la Violencia). More than 700 news outlets agreed to this initiative meant to regulate ethically the coverage of the narcoviolence ("Firman periodistas"). The media agreement attracted hearty applause from President Felipe Calderón, under whose presidency the violence escalated to unprecedented levels (Urrutia). The downside to the Acuerdo, and other gagging measures that ostensibly protect reporters by censoring gory images and cop-and-criminal vocabulary, is that to the extent that drug traffickers and law enforcers in Mexico are inextricably tangled up with one another, the lack of explicit reporting can serve the interests of manipulative *mis*information.

Just how intertwined are the licit and illicit players in Mexico? To judge from the 2013 *Forbes* list of the ten most corrupt Mexicans, certain people in Mexican politics hardly enjoy the clean record ideal for lecturing the rest of the nation on ethics. The *Forbes* writer charged with naming the most corrupt Mexicans in 2013 settled on five governors, two union leaders, one brother to a former president, one presidential cabinet member, and one presidential spokesperson (Estevez). The absence of known traffickers on this list perhaps assumes that naming organized crime bosses indulges in redundancy; however, for several years, trafficker Joaquín "El Chapo" Guzmán Loera ranked on the *Forbes* list of the most powerful people in the world (#67 in 2013) and the wealthiest (#1,153 among billionaires in 2013). Here arises yet another angle of the piracy circuits reflected on BDN: the state, in order to control these piratical groups of traffickers and its own corrupt employees, occasionally resorts to suspending the law in order to censor the media or operate undercover in search of enemy activity. Sophisticated analysis of the tenuous division between licit and illicit operators in Mexico rarely appeared on BDN.

Rather than engage with the complexities of a system of piracy that compromises nearly everyone, BDN prefers to hint at the dreamy possibility of an "outside" to the corruption. Literary critics and other observers trained in the liberal arts tend to assess the notion of an "outside" as preposterous, and correspondingly, the English-language translation on each right-hand page of *Muriendo por la verdad* at times hints at frustration with the naïveté of BDN "neutrality" and its language of "innocence." The translation does not hesitate to embellish, reorder, and at times flatly contradict the original. For instance, when totaling the bloody acts of narcoviolence in English, the text reduces an estimated "miles de veces" (thousands of times) to "scores of times" (*Muriendo* 106, 107). The unsophisticated framework of BDN emerges in its use of the word "innocent," which implies a clear division between the corrupt and the blameless, and thus insists on the nonsensical notion of an "outside" to the problem. For example, the aggressively naïve subtitle for the month of June 2010 from *Muriendo por la verdad* declares, in melodramatic style, "Masacre de inocentes" (110).[7] The implication, of course, is that other massacres related to the conflict are more deserved and thus less outrageous, a point that does not seem likely to lead to workable civic resolutions.

Occasionally, BDN gives consent to nuance. A post on May 28, 2010, for example, describes—practically blow by blow—a video recording of the interrogation and beheading of a trafficker. After reviewing this horrible procedure, the state of innocence that BDN usually claims as a heuristic for rulings of in/justice collapses from the force of empathy:

> Dicha grabación se considera extremadamente fuerte. A pesar de que siempre se trataba de delincuentes que habían matado, robado, entre otras cosas, los telesespectadores podían escuchar cómo clamaban piedad y llegaban a sentir la fragilidad de alguien que estuviera a punto de morir.
>
> (*Muriendo* 106)[8]

If the prose seems disjointed, almost incoherent in its spontaneous vocabulary and changes in verb tense, that impression accurately conveys the hasty, scattershot technique characteristic of the blog. As I mentioned, the English-language translation in the book favors assertively cleaning up the disorganization. To avoid that distortion, I rely on my own translations in the endnotes and observe that even the implicitly critical, published English-language translation accepts usage of the word "innocent."

The implication that "innocent" people, during some vaguely defined golden age of organized crime, were exempt from violence reflects nostalgia for illogical simplicity. For instance, a post dated April 27, 2010 and reproduced in *Muriendo por la verdad* copies a text that traffickers left with a returned female kidnapping victim—namely the blindfolded woman found on the cover of the book—and BDN laments with only superficial editorializing effect,

> It is well known that today the honor codes among drug traffickers are no longer all that well respected. Decades ago things were handled differently. Not even by mistake were innocent people made victims. Although they were related to a capo, women and children were respected.
>
> (74)[9]

To the contrary, historians might object that stories of women traffickers are as old as Mexican trafficking itself, and it does not require academic specialization to see that children are never wholly exempt from their elders' realities. BDN would likely engage in more productive analysis by questioning the possibility that anyone living in a corrupt system could gain value by virtue of "innocence." Given that the kidnapping victim in question was the wife of kingpin Héctor Beltrán Leyva, the example itself points out the ineffectiveness of attempting to separate strictly the compromised and the blameless. Furthermore, in the context of children's' rumored "innocence," it is interesting to note the use of the adjective "young" (joven) in the introduction to *Muriendo por la verdad*: not only the murdered BDN collaborators but also the founding journalist are labeled "young." Against this troubling implication that youth protects Mexicans from deserving a violent death, and by implicit corollary the old more likely deserve their fate, BDN reports on December 3, 2010 that authorities captured an eleven-year-old assassin who would photograph himself with his victims and post the pictures on Internet (294). The news reveals that neither age nor sex reliably indicates "innocence," in direct contradiction to the language that BDN employs.

Proof that the term "innocent" clouds the issue also surfaces when the traffickers deploy the word. For instance, a stream-of-consciousness narcocommuniqué from March 20, 2010, announces, "[...] defenderemos lo justo, [...] sabemos quién es quién, cuídense aquellos que andan mal que a los inocentes no se les molestará para nada" (42).[10] If a neat binary that would separate guilty from innocent victims proves convenient even for the narcos, then the reader really ought to question the reasoning. To the extent that BDN, the traffickers, and even some politicians agree on the convenience of the imaginary category of "innocents" and the consequently implied existence of an "outside" to the system, the contestatory potential of the website loses force. On at least one occasion when BDN does recognize a chaotic reality that defies easy binaries of inside/outside and innocent/guilty, that complexity surfaces as a dreadful specter. The introduction to *Muriendo por la verdad* worries that in a dystopic future, possibly, "nadie sabe quién está de qué lado" and that uncertainty will leave "us" with "una guerra donde nadie hace el bien, solo el mal" (14).[11] A more thoughtful analysis that avoids such drastic terms as "no one" might point out that good and evil do not always detach into perfectly disparate categories. Naturally, acknowledgment of nuance might damage BDN's brand, because ambiguity and uncertainty could make the tourists rethink the safety and relative innocence of their virtual "visit" to the scenes of narcoviolence.

Touring the News

Alongside the piratical adventures described by self-exiled "Lucy," it is also possible to think about the users and administrators of BDN as more sedate tourists. On this last point, I cite the language of initial reports on BDN that attribute the site to a university student, "working anonymously out of his bedroom somewhere in northern Mexico" (Campo-Flores). Certainly, something of the tamed nature of tourism, as it opposes the idea of pioneers and pirates, harmonizes with the bedroom endeavor of the blog, especially to the degree that home blogging ducks the dangerous reporting from the field that professional journalists undertake. In point of fact, BDN borrows the vocabulary of tourism in a single sentence that repetitively thanks all the "visitors" who have made the site one of the most "visited" in Mexico.[12] The imperiled masculinity of a geek trapped alone in the bedroom with only Internet companions to keep him company suggests an anti-macho aesthetic that contradicts the connotations of the BDN machinegun logo. Critic Hilda Chacón detects an air of hypermasculinity on the site when she surmises that the porn advertising and the health tips on the early BDN suggest a straight male and relatively young audience. Yet, the emergence of "Lucy" as a female cofounder hints that BDN attracts a more complex demographic, despite the evident aesthetic of extreme masculinity. The information available from Alexa regarding users for BDN from December 2012 through December 2013 arranges color-coded, nonnumerical graphs to show that BDN drew more than its share of women and fewer men than the general traffic of the Internet would predict; furthermore, compared to overall web users, Alexa data reveals that the BDN audience is heavily over-representative of users who visit the page from school—certainly a potential indication of curious tourist practices.

To make way for the analysis of tourism and sidestep the gender confusion regarding the unexpected twining of the obvious machismo and the concealed feminine on BDN, I want to review some positive connotations for the abstract image of the blogger as citizen-participant, typing from the bedroom or even from school rather than the office. The domestic act of home- and school-computer programmers and armchair journalists harmonizes with the academic understanding of bloggers as respectable amateurs, "in the sense of an Olympic athlete, meaning not paid by anyone to give their reports" (Lessig 44). Tourists are also, in a way, amateur scholars of the country they visit. Yet, just as debates crop up regarding professionalism among Olympians, and just as controversies arise over the contaminating influence spread by tourists, the amateur blogging front cannot guarantee that freelance actions remain on the intended "good" sides of social conflict. As one user of BDN ruefully notes on the occasion of the second anniversary, "Felicidades…y gracias por hakear mi pc solo [sic] por compartir un video."[13] A second reader asks how the first user realized that "they" hacked the computer, and yet another voice chimes in to warn: "[…] recuerda que cuando trazas una linea [sic] igual sirve tanto para mandar com [sic] para recibir."[14] Contrary to this advice, the BDN users sometimes seemed to imagine that they controlled the line of information and subsequently could watch and even threaten without risking personal harm, in the manner of an immune observer or tourist.

This immunity, if not impunity, returns to the notion of the "innocent," which if it must appear clearly agrees better with the idea of tourists than pirates. In the cited post that shuddered at the beheading of a non-innocent trafficker, BDN approached the tourist stance: entranced by the natives, but not necessarily convinced of its own voyeuristic complicity. But, to arrive at the strangely passive tour of narcoviolence, some pirate moves are required to discover the prohibited information in the first place. That is, "contestatory" action in the case of BDN strikes a balance between a defiance of mainstream forces that edges readers toward an abyss of unpleasant political information (the "pirate" push) and an opposite, non-contestatory gravitational tug (the "tourism" pull) meant to keep users alive, functional in society as it is, and coming back for more news. Neither the push of piracy nor the pull of tourism receives explicit narration on BDN, and because much of the touristic pull appeared in the advertising and user comments on the original BDN, this quality largely disappears in *Muriendo por la verdad*, making the print version a grimmer encounter with publicity for ruthless pirates and determined, yet dismayed pirate reporters. According to technology scholars, by contrast to the book *Muriendo por la verdad*, the genre of the blog can offer "a relationship, a connection" with readers and yet withhold a sustained narrative perspective of the sort offered by more traditional print media (Dean 44). The ideal of laissez-faire transmission on BDN functions somewhat less ingenuously on the Internet by way of the up-to-date sequences of "posts" by contrast to a weakly narrativized plot intimated in the book format. For example, when the original BDN announced on February 1, 2012 that the blog had successfully resisted attempts at censorship and was "returning to normality" ("Blog del Narco vuelve a la normalidad"), a reader responded, in all caps and typo-strewn boldface: "QUE SERA 'NORMALIDAD?'" [sic].[15] The impossibility of returning to an ideal of the "normal" under conditions of chaos has the Internet users playing an editorial "tour guide" role that BDN largely avoids.

In view of the difficult national economic situation already in place during BDN's peak of success, some visitors may have imagined themselves as "professional" blog users. The widespread under- and unemployment of student users may also have encouraged this serious engagement with the Internet as a "job" unto itself. The tiring (perhaps even "dry") work of touring others' gory (in police lingo, "wet") work on BDN makes sense under the tourism rubric. According to the pioneering scholar of tourism Dean MacCannell, it is work to be a tourist. MacCannell observed that tourists, driven by an urge to understand their role in modernity, visit workplaces and value authentic experience, as the latter is imagined to break with the everyday life and its routine and thereby facilitate contact with the "high life" of the modern world (6, 159).[16] Are visitors to BDN best understood as taking a break from their workaday routine and exploring the "high life" of modernity? Or are they exhausted by the "high life" of an unwelcome vacation, also known as unemployment, and thus in search of "real" work and a return to the stable workaday routine? The answers are probably lost to us, along with much of the original user comments and advertising of BDN, but it proves helpful to keep in mind the meaning of the prefix "narco," the benumbed. The narco- or soporific trance may appropriately describe the narcotized state ideal for handling the strain of working too hard and at the same time worrying about not finding enough work.

The informal economy in Mexico feeds this numbing precariousness and implicates a considerable citizen-pirate group that does not pay all its taxes. Or perhaps, rather than pirates, the informally employed onlookers in modernity might be thought of as the eternally laboring tourists of their own times—never quite settling into the stable homes and dependable careers as they had perhaps hoped for, but hardly "outside" the system, since as I have argued, such wishful innocence is likely impossible. The contestatory and implicitly optimistic ideal on BDN, or the weblog of the benumbed, aims to shake up its audience through an invigorating dose of "free" information, while also working to condition readers through the compartmentalized channels of the original (and local) exercise and diet advertising, which imparted the strength to handle the shock that comes from the news of drug violence. In the section that follows, I evaluate the force of that narco-shock by studying two sets of images from BDN, also reproduced in *Muriendo por la verdad*.

Tautology, Allegory, and Justice

If I were to devote this space to tracing the regional genealogies and vengeful motivations behind the violence depicted on BDN, I would accept the narrowed horizon that limits BDN. In order to glimpse the bigger picture, I turn to the trafficking rhetoric that BDN claims to publicize "sin filtro ni censura" (*Muriendo* 2).[17] I take inspiration from Paul Allen Anderson's article on the HBO television series *The Wire* (2002–2008). That fictionalized saga of the treacherous circuits of influence among illicit drug traffickers, surreptitious police detectives, and corrupt politicians allows *The Wire* to invent the coherent narrative framework that BDN lacks. Vaguely resonant predicaments and tableaus on *The Wire*, explored in Anderson's article, employ the tactics of tautology and allegory in ways "not necessarily antithetical" (Anderson 86). That is, in the fictional characters' inner-city, noose-like environment of "constrained agency amid institutional practices," the insight of allegory provides guidance. For example, in one early scene arranged around a game of chess, the lesson emerges that a king cannot be replaced; however, this insight never fully splits open the authority of tautology. Instead, a drug kingpin repeatedly asserts, in self-supporting logic, "The game is the game" (86, 85). Just as the fictional capo on *The Wire* establishes and defends his power through suffocating circular logic, the messages and images reproduced on BDN and *Muriendo por la verdad* stake claim to would-be peerless tautology. "Somos lo que somos," announces a narco-message reported by BDN on April 22, 2010.[18] The tautological "A is A" assertion intends to construct an incontestable reasoning system with a permanent kingpin, and this trafficking rhetoric actually supports President Calderón's, and now President Peña Nieto's, recalcitrance to think beyond prohibition, violent repression, and the lucrative whack-a-mole game of displacement that occurs when criminal activity supplies too vital an economic factor.

This one-dimensional thinking, characteristic of both the official and the extralegal perspectives, also appears in a BDN post from March 3, 2010, when a trafficker group praises media silence and adds, "[...] no hay de otra, es la única forma" (20).[19] BDN disappoints as a contestatory site to the extent that the posts do not, in the process of publicizing this news, signal toward "another way." BDN appears to agree with the tautology in trafficker messages, which thus imply even more credibly that any reasonable reader, from Calderón to the authors of BDN, would side with the gangsters' univocal reality. In another example of narcotautology that could pass for an official slogan, the eerily corporate-sounding catchphrase "Para Vivir Mejor" rounds out various threatening communiqués as the motto for one mafia group.[20] To the degree that any rational advertising plan would champion the idea of "Living Better," because "Living Worse" would not sell, the catchphrase presents a tautology. Any appetizing plan for "living" has to tout "living better." Therefore, the narcoslogan "For a Better Life" invokes, necessarily, a plan to live better, just as BDN and the Mexican government would also propose.

The flat discourse of tautology paves the way for a second tactic—that of allegory, which, in the context of BDN, falsely promises insight beyond the "A is A" logic of institutionalized corruption. Like the dull blatancy of tautology, the allegorical approach restricts complexity. A successful allegory must weave together manifest and latent levels of meaning in tight, unambiguous correspondence. The Mexican context excessively compresses this would-be imaginative technique, due to the relative secrecy of the illicit, which necessitates an extra layer of obfuscation. Sadly for the integrity of the technique on the street then, the carefully coded yet publicly presented allegory of the illicit reveals too little and thereby devolves into blank tautology. In other words, due to the illicit nature of the gruesome murders, the allegorizing "Victim as Guilt" tableaus always risk slipping into a depthless tautology: Dead is Dead. I will explore only one example of this would-be allegorical design on BDN. [Warning: Explicit description to follow.]

Pages 313–319 of *Muriendo por la verdad* record a crazed tableau of body parts. Color photographs document two freshly skinned heads arranged on the pavement below two posts, from which hang the removed, masklike, sagging faces. Each skinned skull is flanked by two severed arms, and the one palm in each set cups a severed penis with abundant pubic hair. Nearby on the asphalt, the word "METRO" appears, meticulously spelled with victims' intestines. No other crime scene in *Muriendo por la verdad* receives so many pictures, but BDN does not interpret the scene. A slant editorial comment concludes the relevant BDN post and places burden of analysis on the reader:

> Sin embargo, eso no era todo, ya que cámaras de seguridad pudieron grabar algo más terrorífico: los sicarios habían destazado y desollado a los dos hombres en el lugar donde fueron abandonados, sin temer ser sorprendidos por cualquier clase de autoridad.
>
> (312)[21]

I sympathize with the lack of analytic effort. No overriding authority exists "outside" the game to protect reporters who would publicly decode too much information. The next step, for reporters who dare, is the Op-Ed admission that drug prohibition fails miserably as public policy. Calling an end to "the game" or "the movement" would constitute the smartest contestatory interpretation of these narcoallegories. Without this journalistic interpretation, the tableaus meant to advertise the terrible forces at play, with the side of the "winner" defined by superior brutality, burn out the allegorical insight almost immediately and return the observer to the underlying tautology. "Dead is dead," or as *The Wire* would have it, "The game is the game."

In order to wrap up this review with a less disturbing image, I turn to the cover of *Muriendo por la verdad*. There, the previously mentioned blindfolded woman, Clara Elena Laborín Archuleta, wife of the infamous Beltrán Leyva, appears on the red, white, and black book design in a staged photo, along with a poster message and the tips of two machine guns. On the inside of the book, pages 76 and 77 reproduce this cover photo with the original colors and add a picture of the woman lying on the pavement where she was discovered blindfolded, with hands and feet tied, and covered by the narcomessage. This set of pictures hints an updated allegory of the blindfolded "Lady Justice" figure. Instead of holding scales, the BDN model is immobilized, and instead of remaining willingly impartial by self-imposed blindfold, Laborín Archuleta's mummy-like wrapping disempowers: the top two-thirds of her face disappear behind the postoperative-like gauze. This updated Lady Justice embodies the basic desire to live and the haplessness of knowing oneself to be a pawn who cannot opt out. This pessimism finds a more wryly humorous summary on *The Wire*, with the stinging epigraph to episode 41 ("Refugees") that comments on the drug war and larger games of corruption: "No one wins. One side just loses more slowly." Or, to return to Paul Allen Anderson's article, I repeat the citation of Richard Pryor's joking search for justice in the racist U.S. courts: "You go down there [to the criminal justice system] looking for justice; that's what you find: just us" (Anderson 86). The BDN version of the allegorical Lady Justice teeters on tautology: justice is *just us*. It seems germane to add Avital Ronell's decisive critique of the illogic of prohibition: "Clearly, it is as preposterous to be 'for' drugs as it is to take up a position 'against' drugs" (50). In other words, drugs cannot be thought "through." Similarly, no "outside" level in the allegory will come to the rescue and make sense of the mess, no matter how enticingly valid the illusions of sobriety and innocence might seem.

Coda

BDN never broadened its coverage of narcoviolence to contemplate root causes and far-reaching solutions. In order to resist these limitations and open up another manner of classifying the early material on BDN, I turn to the history of addiction that BDN ignored. My purpose is to elaborate a potential parallel between the future of contestatory websites and the troubled history of the addict. The Western imaginary first conceived of the drug addict as a pathetic figure confined to her 19th-century bedroom in passive stereotype; eventually, with the development of better drug technologies, the addict of the 20th century emerged as "younger and male," less wealthy, and more likely to be cast as a member of a minority group (Weimer 25).[22] New prohibition laws took advantage of publicity-fueled moral panics over the revisionist image of the addict and considerable policing profit emerged in punishing the "high" and keeping them low. The possible evolution of technologies for contestatory practice on the web could provoke a similar chain of moral panics and legal responses. That is, the bedroom blogging of the first stage of BDN may precede future intensified means of pirate reporting, which in turn might inspire new laws. Compared to what may come if new technologies can sidestep corporate control, BDN may ultimately represent an early, relatively feminized, and passive site of struggle. The blog perhaps anticipates the next iterations of what official interests will cast as a fearsome public menace, the foreign technological threat that will be understood to promote whatever the state and mainstream media do not see fit to allow. The question for the scholarly audience is how academics will respond to the future call to clothe, as per Avital Ronell's notion of criticism as a veil of meaning, the obscenities of the impending technologies. Will the metaphors of piracy and tourism convince, or can the reader think of something better?

Notes

1 By December 26, 2013, BDN had fallen to position 3,154 among all websites in Mexico, and the rival page had risen to 713th place, according to Alexa. The plentiful user comments on ElBlogdelnarco.net and the current absence of a chat forum on the BDN site confirm the audience migration.

2 The original language reads, "Podemos quizá, ser 'piratas,' pero jamás peones ni esclavos. Somos libres y como tal nos expresamos" ("Acerca de").

3 As per the original, "[...] trataremos hasta el cansancio de impedir la censura que en últimos meses del 2011 han intentado imponernos."

4 The degree of social threat posed by piracy is a matter for debate. One scholar observes that "piracy" as an organized and dangerous crime is, "as much a discursive creation on the part of corporate- and government-sponsored media campaigns as it is an activity undertaken by copyright infringers" (Mirghani 115). That is, it takes policing to define the activity as a threat.

5 "a programmer and a young journalist" (x).

6 "open a window and, without curtains or blinds, allow citizens to observe the harsh reality that surrounds them" (Muriendo 2).

7 "Massacre of the innocents" (110).

8 "This recording is extremely intense. In spite of, as always, dealing with delinquents who had killed and stolen, among other things, the spectators could hear how they begged for mercy and even came to feel the fragility of someone who was about to die" (106).

9 "Es bien sabido que en tiempos actuales los códigos de honor entre los narcotraficantes ya no son tan respetados. Hace décadas las cosas se arreglaban de manera diferente. Ni por error gente inocente era víctima. Aunque estuvieran relacionados con algún capo, mujeres y niños eran respetados" (74).

10 "we will defend the right thing, [...] we know who is who, watch out those who are doing bad but no one will bother the innocents" (42).

11 The translations read, "no one knows who is on which side" and "a war where no one works for good, only evil" (14).

12 "Gracias a todos esos millones de visitantes que nos han mantenido en los primeros lugares de las páginas más visitadas en México."
13 "Congratulations ... and thanks for hacking my pc just for sharing a video."
14 "[...] remember that when you draw a line it serves as much to send as it does to receive."
15 "What would normality be?"
16 Cindy Aron explores MacCannell's ideas and elaborates on the contradictions that vacations had to straddle for the early vacationers of the middle class, who could pay for a trip because they valued work, but did not want to jeopardize that work by committing fully to leisure. The solution was to tour a workplace (Aron 145).
17 "without filter or censorship" (Muriendo 2).
18 "We are what we are."
19 "[...] there is no other choice, it is the only way" (20).
20 "For a Better Life."
21 "However, that wasn't all, since security cameras managed to record something even more terrible: the assassins had cut up and skinned the two men in the place where they were left, without fear of being surprised by any type of authority" (312).
22 Weimer cites a list of academic studies in support of the idea of the threatening addict, including David T. Courtwright, *Dark Paradise*; Courtwright, Herman Joseph, and Don Des Jarlais, *Addicts Who Survived*; David F. Musto, *The American Disease*; and Mara L. Keire, "Dope Fiends and Degenerates," *Journal of Social History* 31.4 (1998): 809–822.

Works Cited

"Acerca de." El Blog del Narco. l. www.mund0narco.com/p/acerca-de.htm. Accessed 28 July 2012.

Acuerdo para la Cobertura Informativa de la Violencia. Política. *Milenio*. 24 Mar. 2011. www.milenio.com/print/cdb/doc/noticias2011/7124535617041c8e54020 57a537215. Accessed 4 Aug. 2012.

Anderson, Paul Allen. "'The Game is the Game': Tautology and Allegory in *The Wire*." In *The Wire: Race, Class, and Genre*. Eds. Liam Kennedy and Stephen Shapiro. Ann Arbor: U of Michigan P, 2012. 84–109.

Aron, Cindy S. *Working at Play: A History of Vacations in the United States*. Oxford UP, 1999.

Attacks on the Press in 2011: A Worldwide Survey by the Committee to Protect Journalists. Preface Sandra Mims Rowe. New York: CPJ, 2011.

Campo-Flores, Arian. "Hiding Behind the Web." *Newsweek* 156.15 (11 Oct. 2010). ProQuest.

Chacón, Hilda. "Cyberspace as Contestatory Civil Action at the US-Mexican Border." 2015. Typescript.

Dean, Jodi. *Blog Theory: Feedback and Capture in the Circuits of Drive*. Polity, 2010.

Estevez, Dolia. "The 10 Most Corrupt Mexicans of 2013." *Forbes*. 16 Dec. 2013. www.forbes.com/sites/doliaestevez/2013/12/16/the-10-most-corrupt-mexicans-of-2013/#35fa4c785720. Accessed 17 Dec. 2013.

"Firman periodistas Acuerdo para la Cobertura Informativa de la Violencia." 24 Mar. 2011.

Grupo Fórmula. www.radioformula.com.mx/notas.asp?Idn=163372. Accessed 8 Aug. 2012.

Gutierrez, Raul. "Leaking Secrets, Leaking Blood: Blog del Narco, the Anonymous Tracker of Mexico's Ultraviolent Drug War Interviewed by Raul Gutierrez." Special Feature. *Boing Boing.* http://boingboing.net/2010/09/14/narco.html. Accessed 6 Aug. 2012.

Leeson, Peter T. "*Pirational* choice: The Economics of Infamous Pirate Practices." *Journal of Economic Behavior & Organization* 76 (2010): 497–510.

Lessig, Lawrence. *Free Culture: How Big Media Uses Technology and the Law to Lock Down Culture and Control Creativity.* Penguin P, 2004.

MacCannell, Dean. *The Tourist: A New Theory of the Leisure Class.* 1976. Foreword Lucy R. Lippard and Epilogue by author, new. U of California P, 1999.

Merrill, Dennis. *Negotiating Paradise: U.S. Tourism and Empire in Twentieth-Century Latin America.* U of North Carolina P, 2009.

Mirghani, Suzannah. "The War on Piracy: Analyzing the Discursive Battles of Corporate and Government-Sponsored Anti-Piracy Media Campaigns." *Critical Studies in Media Communication* 28.2 (2011): 113–134. https://com327ncsu.files.wordpress.com/2013/01/mirghani_piracy.pdf. Accessed 13 May 2012.

Muriendo por la verdad: Clandestinos dentro de la violenta narcoguerra mexicana de los periodistas fugitivos de Blog del Narco/Dying for the Truth: Undercover Inside Mexico's Violent Drug War By the Fugitive Reporters of Blog del Narco. Feral House, 2012.

Pitman, Thea. "Latin American Cyberprotest: Before and After the Zapatistas." In *Latin American Cyberculture and Cyberliterature.* Eds. Claire Taylor and Thea Pitman. Liverpool UP, 2007. 86–110.

Ronell, Avital. *Crack Wars: Literature, Addiction, Mania.* Lincoln: U of Nebraska P, 1992.

Tirzo, Jorge. "El plagio, los medios y El Blog del Narco." Blog de Tirzo. Radio Nederland. 27 May 2013. http://notinarco.blogspot.com/2013/05/el-blog-del-narco-tierradelnarcocom-el_27.html. Accessed 16 Dec. 2013.

Urrutia, Alonso, David Carrizales, and Alejandra Arroyo. "Celebra Calderón en el Acuerdo para la Cobertura Informativa de la Violencia." *La Jornada* 25 Mar. 2011, 7. www.jornada.unam.mx/2011/03/25/politica/007n1pol. Accessed 8 Aug. 2012.

Weimer, Daniel. *Seeing Drugs: Modernization, Counterinsurgency, and U.S. Narcotics Control in the Third World, 1969–1976.* Kent State UP, 2011.

6 Blogging and Disability Activism in Mexico

Katia D'Artigues's "Mundo D"

Beth E. Jörgensen

In 2002, at the fifty-sixth session of the United Nations, Mexico submitted a proposal for developing an international convention to define
and promote the human rights of persons with disabilities. Mexico thus
initiated the process that led to the United Nations Convention on the
Rights of Persons with Disabilities, adopted in 2006, and they became
its first signatory nation in March 2007.[1] In 2011, the Mexican Congress
also passed a federal "Ley General de Inclusión" ("general law of inclusion") to address the inclusion of people with disabilities into all aspects of
Mexican society. While the passage of such laws lays important ground-
work for addressing the legal rights and social status of a traditionally
marginalized and discriminated group, the laws themselves do not automatically bring about the necessary changes in mentality, the refashioning
of regulations, and the creation of enforcement mechanisms that would
make their provisions a reality. A long process of education, consciousness raising, and local, state, and national legislative and legal action is required to transform centuries of stigma and discrimination into a culture
of human rights and an acceptance of bodily, intellectual, and psychosocial difference as forms of human diversity rather than radical otherness.
In light of the complexity of long-term social change, disability rights
activists in Mexico, some of whom live in a situation of disability while
others consider themselves to be able-bodied and neurotypical, continue
to characterize the experience of people living with disabilities as predominantly one of exclusion and invisibility, in spite of the recent advances in
their putative legal status. This chapter explores how the Internet and the
form of social communication and virtual community known as the weblog or blog can serve the goals of overcoming the invisibility of persons
with disabilities, changing existing paradigms surrounding the concept of
disability, and advocating for equal rights in contemporary Mexico.

The World Health Organization, as documented in their 2011 *World
Report on Disability*, estimates that roughly 15% of the adult population worldwide has one or more disabilities that create significant
difficulties in carrying out the functions of everyday life. The Mexican
population census of 2010 puts the percentage of people with disabilities in that country at 5.1%, but this is a figure that most scholars and

activists consider to be a gross underestimate based on underreporting.[2] If disability in its diverse forms is viewed as a minority identity, which some current theory asserts, it should be noted that it is the one identity category that crosses all national, ethnic, gender, age, religious, and political boundaries.[3] It is said that people with disabilities comprise the largest, poorest, and most marginalized minority sector of the human population worldwide, and, further, it is the only identity category that any one of us can enter at any time regardless of our current status.

Katia D'Artigues Beauregard is a well-established journalist in Mexico City who reports primarily on political events and issues for the daily newspaper *El Universal*, which appears in a print edition and is carried online at www.eluniversal.com.mx. She has a daily column titled *Campos Elíseos* that treats politics and a regular blog of the same name slightly modified, *C@mpos Elíseos*, that is maintained at the newspaper website. Within her blog, she has a weekly post that she calls "Mundo D," which generally appears on Fridays. In "Mundo D," in existence from January 2007 to July 2015, D'Artigues presents a theme or a current event having to do with disability in its broadest sense, and she exploits the expansive and interactive nature of the blog by including links to further information available on the Internet and by inviting and responding to comments from her readers. Like many nondisabled people who become active in the disability rights or disability studies communities, D'Artigues was motivated to start writing "Mundo D" when the reality of what it means to live in Mexico with a disability became a personal issue for her. Her first child, a son, was born with Down Syndrome in 2006, and this experience opened her intellectual, emotional, and ideological horizons to the challenges of achieving a deeper respect for human diversity, human rights, and inclusive citizenship in Mexico. An open letter to her reading public that she posted to *C@mpos Elíseos* on January 6, 2007 introduces her son Alan, then five months old, and begins to dispel myths and provide reliable information about Down Syndrome. It has been read more than 141,000 times with 256 comments posted. In an important initial gesture, D'Artigues unconditionally rejects the culture of pity that she perceived existed—and still exists—in Mexico (and in most other nations) in relation to disability, by asserting that "pity" is the least acceptable sentiment that her child could inspire in others. In a society where many people, and even those who provide services to people with disabilities, speak of the disabled Other as "poor little things," D'Artigues's firm objection to the pity/charity model of disability was an early sign that her blog would offer an alternative discourse through a new journalistic medium.[4]

The first post to the new "Mundo D" section of *C@mpos Elíseos* came some two weeks later, on January 19. It treated the broad subject of human difference, diversity, and discrimination, and it called upon readers to recognize and overcome their own discriminatory thoughts and behaviors. Just as the open letter of January 6 rejects the pity/charity model of disability, the January 19 post implicitly endorses aspects of the social model by stating that the very act discrimination in and of itself disables targeted groups. That is, society constructs disability out of difference through its privileging of the able-bodied and its processes of labeling, marginalization, and exclusion of the nonnormative Other. D'Artigues thus takes a bold step in her first two posts toward challenging the prevailing attitudes toward difference and disability in Mexico.[5] More than six years later, in researching for this chapter, I found an extensive archive of almost weekly posts to "Mundo D," and the range of topics that D'Artigues and her virtual community have addressed is impressive. My purpose is to delineate the ways in which "Mundo D," specifically, has contributed to a process of education and *sensibilización* ("consciousness raising") around disability in Mexico, has created a virtual community, and has engaged in some forms of political activism through the interactive medium of the blog. I will take examples from the first six months of "Mundo D" and from posts and comments dated December 2011 to July 2012. During the earlier time period, most of the entries sought to disseminate information about the highly diverse conditions that the term "disability" encompasses and also to raise awareness about the systemic discrimination that is practiced by institutions and by individuals in our daily lives. In the first half of 2012, with a presidential election scheduled for July 1, the topic of voting rights is prominent, and D'Artigues takes a more activist approach to the role that her blog might play in local realities and in national politics. Like others in the disability rights community, D'Artigues identifies the invisibility of people with disabilities as the most serious and persistent challenge to achieving change, and her blog is dedicated to making their reality and their status as subjects with rights visible to the larger society ("Re: De parte").

The rapid development of the Internet and the World Wide Web since the late 1980s has granted unique opportunities and new challenges to persons with disabilities and to all who aspire to live in a truly inclusive world. Early on, it was thought that cyberspace would offer an accessible venue for social interactions, knowledge production and retrieval, education, work, and commercial tasks without regard to ability or disability. People with disabilities would use the Internet to escape their historical situation of exclusion and adopt a voice and an identity free of the constraints and stigmas associated with a variety of physical, sensory, and psychosocial conditions. For many reasons, this vision of a cyberspace utopia has not been realized, but the Internet has served a highly positive role in many ways in expanding the participation of the disabled in the life of their communities.[6] The medium of the blog, specifically, has proved to be a valuable tool for persons with disabilities and disability activists. It is a public space that can be claimed and shaped by many more people than those who control the print and broadcast media. It is interactive and it allows a dialogue between bloggers and readers across both geographical distance and any number of social boundaries (Kuusisto "Roundtable"). Easily embedded links create an ever-expanding network of resources that are accessible from one base location, and over time, a blog can forge a virtual community based on affinities, shared interests, and common values (Holdom 141–142). D'Artigues's blog has realized this informative, communicative, and interactive potential in a format that reaches beyond the readership of the traditional print media.

This study of "Mundo D" comes at the question of disability and the Internet from a particular angle, because the creator of the blog does not identify as a person with a disability. That is, D'Artigues's blog is not an example of how people with disabilities might utilize the World Wide Web directly to enhance their own lives, create alternative subjectivities, engage in cyber advocacy or activism, or produce counter-discourses to mainstream concepts of disability. Launched from a site maintained by an established newspaper and created by a journalist employed by that newspaper, in some ways "Mundo D" represents a continuation of the democratizing project traditionally associated with print journalism. However, it expands that project in new directions by capturing and challenging the knowledge that constitutes Mexican society's vision of a largely hidden reality, by exploiting the expansive and interactive dimensions of the blog form in the service of new knowledge production and dissemination, and by advocating for civic engagement beyond the limits of the production and reception of the blog itself. In addition, the blog archive is a valuable resource for the disability studies researcher, who can read expressions of prevailing public attitudes and signs of social change in the wide range of individual reactions to the topics posted by D'Artigues. By giving an overview of the two key time periods that I have chosen and by addressing selected posts in some detail, I will show how "Mundo D" brings the social meanings and experiential realities of disability into a public forum and advocates for the rights of this persistently marginalized group.

In the first six months of "Mundo D," Katia D'Artigues applied her expertise as a journalist to the cause of overcoming ignorance and silence about disability by introducing as many different topics as possible and encouraging her readers to enter into a dialogue with her and with each other. The interplay of discourse produced by the author, hyperlinks to sources generated by others, contributions posted by readers, and the author's responses to some of those posts complicates the relationship between the writer and the reader and enacts the pluralistic and democratic nature of the Internet. Many of the early posts start with an anecdote or a personal story to hook the reader and then proceed to report on a specific illness or disability using a variety of data and ample hyperlinks to sources of information deemed reliable by the blogger. Underlying the structure of these posts is a desire to overcome ignorance and prejudice by appealing equally to the discourses of personal experience and those of science. Hepatitis C, obesity, blindness and low vision, ageing, attention deficit disorder, cerebral palsy, autism, and, of course, Down Syndrome, are a few of the conditions that are discussed. Other posts highlight the work of civil organizations, especially those that take an innovative, progressive approach based on inclusion and human rights, rather than those that adhere to an *asistencialista* ("assistance") approach and continue a tradition of segregated facilities. Political and legal issues are taken up as well, such as a discussion of the UN Convention or information about governmental initiatives to combat discrimination. Cultural events and art produced by people with disabilities round out the image of the complex nature of disability in Mexico as a social construction and an embodied experience.

That the subject of disability was an infrequent topic for mainstream Mexican journalism in 2007 is clearly seen in the comments that were posted to the blog in its early weeks and months, many of which express gratitude to D'Artigues for her pioneering efforts. The comments on the open letter of January 6, 2007 provide an instructive starting point. Virtually all of the readers praise D'Artigues's "courageous" embrace of her son, many identify themselves as family members of a person with a disability, and an overwhelming number of readers make reference to Alan's birth as a gift from god and a blessing to his family. The language employed by the readers often reflects common stereotypes about persons with disabilities, and specifically Down Syndrome. One is the notion that those with Down Syndrome are especially affectionate, innocent, happy, and good-natured—eternal children, harmless and pure. Besides the troubling oversimplification and the tendency to infantilize people with intellectual disabilities, there is a kind of overcompensation in the posted comments that betrays the larger society's negative view of these so-called special individuals. That is, early on some of the blog's readers reproduced the language of stereotypes and discrimination that D'Artigues's project was designed to combat. In future blogs, both D'Artigues and her readers, who soon form a virtual community with a core group of regular contributors, begin to address and combat these conventional and limiting attitudes.

For example, the fourth "Mundo D" post (February 16, 2007) reviews a theater production in Mexico City that included actors with Down Syndrome, and it provides a link to a lengthy interview with the Spaniard Pablo Pineda, the first person with Down Syndrome to graduate from a university in Spain. These topics were not in themselves particularly controversial for the readers, and yet the 122 comments that were generated during the 24-hour open period demonstrate the blog's capacity to foment dialogue. In this case, the term *angelitos* ("little angels"), which was prominent in the responses to D'Artigues open letter on January 6, appears again in numerous comments. Now, however, one

can see that the blog's regular readers have begun to think more critically about how the word is frequently used not only to express affection
but also to infantilize those with intellectual disabilities, and there is
a lively back and forth among several of them. Daniel Jiménez opened
the debate in the twenty-fourth comment of the day when he proposed
that one kind of discrimination is exemplified by those who "consideran
como eternos niños a sus hijos con síndrome de Down o aquellos que
mencionan amorosamente que son ANGELITOS, no son angelitos, son
SERES HUMANOS que como bien muestra Pablo, tienen defectos, vir-
tudes, momentos de alegría, momentos de enojo, de tristeza, el tratarlos
así también los limita" ("consider their sons and daughters with Down
Syndrome to be eternal children, or those who lovingly call them 'little
angels,' they're not little angels, they're human beings as Pablo [Pineda]
very well demonstrates, they have defects, virtues, happy moments, moments of anger, sadness, treating them that way also limits them"). The
reactions to Jiménez's remarks came quickly and from all directions.
First, one of the readers, who had earlier called his wife's special education students *angelitos*, wrote in again to acknowledge that he would do
better to refer to them simply as children. On the other hand, the next
comment, from a reader identifying herself as a mother, accused Daniel
Jiménez of not understanding what a mother would mean by calling her
children, even her grown sons, *angelitos*. Another insisted that children
with Down Syndrome are in fact literally angels sent by god to specially
privileged parents, while one more responded that all children are angels,
and so on. Ultimately, D'Artigues joined in both to moderate among
conflicting opinions and to insert her own views, taking the position
that while such words may be used as terms of endearment, they may
also become labels that limit and distort the complex reality of human
subjectivity. In particular, she challenged the very common tendency to
infantilize people with disabilities, and especially those with intellectual
or cognitive disabilities. This is just one example of how the interactive
nature of a blog can promote a virtual conversation among individuals.
It is my belief that such conversations contribute to the process of *sensibilización* that all disability activists in Mexico with whom I have spoken
identify as the most critical step toward social and cultural change.[7]

The topic of sexuality and intellectual disability, which combines two
cultural taboos, was the subject of the June 15, 2007 entry "El derecho
de todos a una vida sexual" ("the right of everyone to a sexual life").[8]
The post begins by referring to an article published earlier in the week
in *El Universal* featuring two young adults with Down Syndrome who
speak about their love for each other and their desire to have privacy
and an opportunity for physical intimacy. Their parents and teachers,
however, strictly control and supervise their time together. Tobin Siebers, in his book *Disability Theory*, asserts that persons with disabilities
have the right to privacy and to any support needed to express their

sexuality and experience sexual pleasure. He calls this the right to sexual citizenship (Siebers 136–137), and it is without question a right that is systematically and almost universally denied. D'Artigues's post shows how the testimony of people who occupy a position of marginality and exclusion can challenge mainstream social and cultural discourse, and push our thought in new directions. The medium of the blog provides a forum that makes individual responses quickly available to other readers in an interactive format that provokes agreement and disagreement with the original post and with each other. Some regular readers intervene more than once during the course of the day, creating a dialogue across both time and geographical distance. The blog is not a universally accessible public forum, as literacy, access to the Internet, and the ability to use a keyboard or voice recognition software are requirements for participation, but it can play an important role in influencing attitudes and creating a sense of community around current issues.

Katia D'Artigues maintained her commitment to "Mundo D" for the more than eight years stretching from early 2007 until mid-2015, and a small group of loyal followers continued to contribute comments, some of them on a weekly basis. The number of hits that the Friday blog received grew from an average of about 15,000 in the first six months of 2007 to more than 27,000 on some dates in 2015. The number of comments dropped off sharply however, to as few as two or three per week, whereas in 2007 there were usually between one hundred and one hundred and forty responses. The drop off in comments might be a sign that information about disabilities and disability rights was no longer such a novelty in 2015 as it was in 2007, although it evidently still attracted the interest of readers.

The blog continued its coverage of a very broad range of topics, but two items caught my attention in the period from mid-December 2011 to July 2012, because they are signs of an activism that goes beyond the already important work of educating and raising awareness about disability issues via the Internet. The December 16, 2011 post reports on the culmination of an almost three-year long project to collect funds from readers for the building of an accessible street corner in the Iztapalapa neighborhood of Mexico City. This initiative began in early 2009, when the then-mayor of Mexico City, Marcelo Ebrard, announced an initiative to build 100,000 ramps during his administration in order to create accessible corridors in high-traffic areas of the city. Funding for the program, however, would not come from the city government, but was left up to neighborhoods, businesses, civil organizations, individuals, or whomever might wish to donate. Encouraged by Federico Fleischmann, cofounder and president of the important disability rights organization Libre Acceso, in March 2009 D'Artigues and some of her regular readers decided to raise the funds for one ramp. The complete sum of money (18,750 pesos) was reached in the fall of 2011, and the corner was finally remodeled in December of that year. I mention this for two reasons. One, it was the first project undertaken through the blog and its virtual community that resulted in a material impact in the city. In some regards, the effort recalls a long history of citizens undertaking social action in the absence of governmental support of needed changes, rather than a break with existing trends. Without constituting a radical act of social transformation around disability issues, the construction of one accessible street corner nonetheless confirms that innovative uses of cyberspace can unite people and effect tangible results. The project also raised the stakes for those who had been educated and sensitized through the blog over a period of time by demanding their direct investment of time and resources. Second, the project created a focus for a series of articles over the course of almost three years that examined and critiqued the relationship between the government and the agency that it chose to administer the project, the drastic reduction in the overall goal from 100,000 to about 30,000 ramps, the high cost of public works, the many bureaucratic obstacles to achieving improvements in the city, and even the problem of malfunctioning construction equipment and unsafe working conditions. It is an example of how a blog, because it does not require resources of paper and ink and because it easily incorporates links to additional information, is able to treat a given topic in far greater depth than print or broadcast journalism.

The other item of particular interest in terms of engaging in activism via the resources of the Internet is the attention given from April through June of 2012 to the upcoming presidential election and the rights of persons with disabilities to vote and to hold public office. The right to vote is affirmed in the UN Convention, although Mexican laws and polling place regulations and accessibility are not yet set up to guarantee that right. In several posts leading up to July 1, D'Artigues addresses this issue and highlights initiatives taken by nongovernmental organizations to improve the access to voting. For example, La Pirinola—a nonprofit, nongovernmental association long involved in sponsoring cultural activities and a radio program produced by people with disabilities—started a campaign in the spring of 2012 called "Yo Elijo" ("I elect"). The dual goal was to produce a guide for poll workers about the right to vote held by persons with disabilities and to train people with disabilities to serve as process observers at polling stations.[9] In addition to publicizing these and other initiatives, D'Artigues also wrote posts that were critical of the federal elections board (IFE) for not bringing their policies and their personnel up to the standards of the Convention. The right to vote is critical for many reasons, including what it signifies for seeing oneself and for being seen as a full citizen and for having a voice that politicians must listen to, not to mention the impact on the election of any particular candidate. In a legitimate democracy, an entire sector of the population, however large or small, must not be disenfranchised from the political process in the way that persons with disabilities still commonly are. As Mexico moves away from the medical and *asistencialista* models of disability toward a human rights model, the recognition of the *capacidad jurídica* ("legal capacity") of people with disabilities is essential. It demands that society stop viewing one group of citizens as "problems" in need of special accommodations or as defective individuals in need of rehabilitation, but as subjects with equal rights that all social institutions and practices must respect and guarantee. D'Artigues's blog plays an active role in the ongoing work to achieve these goals.

Mexicans have created a disability rights movement with a significant national presence since the late 1980s.[10] Dozens of organizations of civil society now dedicate their efforts to the goals of improved conditions of life, and equal access and empowerment of people with disabilities. Government agencies such as the Consejo Nacional para Prevenir la Discriminación (CONAPRED) and Consejo Nacional de Personas con Discapacidad (CONADIS) also play an important role, although activists and some officials acknowledge that the government has historically followed the lead of the NGOs and has not been the protagonist of necessary change.[11] In this context, week by week over a period of years, "Mundo D" created an innovative, citizen-centered platform for information, a forum for dialogue, and a site for advocacy directed to bringing a marginalized group into the national consciousness and onto the national agenda for change.

Notes

1 The UN Convention is an important international document in the global movement away from a medical model of disability toward a view of persons with disabilities as equal members of society who must enjoy their full human rights and equal access to education, medical care, employment, political participation, and all other rights, services, and opportunities available in a society.

2 The inaccuracy of the 5.1% figure is shown by the fact that a large number of people who responded to the census in 2010 stated that they had a disability, but because they did not know how to classify or identify it, the disability was not properly accounted for by census takers. The consensus among nongovernmental organizations in Mexico is that between 10% and 15% of the population has a disability according to international standards of measurement, such as those used by the World Health Organization in assembling their 2011 World Health Report. CONADIS (Consejo Nacional de Personas con Discapacidad), under new leadership since the beginning of January 2013, is discussing how to carry out a specialized census targeted to identifying persons with disabilities (D'Artigues, "Mundo D," January 11, 2013).

3 There is an ongoing debate over the usefulness of identity politics and claims for minority status for persons with disabilities. Tobin Siebers theorizes disability as a minority identity in *Disability Theory* (2008), and he offers a nuanced defense of his position that identity politics remains a practical course

of action for addressing social injustices by using the theoretical power of the narratives produced by minority peoples. Minority discourse, according to Siebers, is a privileged site of cultural critique because it is produced from a liminal position *vis-à-vis* mainstream, normative society (15).

4 In my conversations in Mexico, I have been struck by the prevalence of the term "pobrecitos" used by many people, even those who are professionally involved with the disabled. The disability rights activists whom I interviewed in June 2011 all attest to the persistence of the culture of pity toward the disabled in Mexico.

5 To date, the medical model is the predominant conceptualization of disability in Mexico on the institutional level, and it largely determines government policy and medical practices. It defines a wide range of nonnormative conditions to be defects, deficits, or deficiencies in the individual that should be cured or remediated through medical intervention and rehabilitation. The religious and pity models also continue to shape the attitudes of the general public, who view persons with disabilities as divine gifts or punishments and as objects of charity. The social model, developed in Great Britain in the 1980s, distinguishes between an impairment as a condition inhering in the individual and disability, which is the condition constructed for the individual by myriad barriers (physical, sensory, social) that the ideology of ableism has created (Shakespeare 266–268).

6 Numerous studies have focused on the relationship of persons with disabilities and the Internet and other new media. Ellis and Kent (2011) detail many ways in which new media both include and exclude persons with disabilities, and they trace the history of universal design and the failure to apply its principles in a systematic fashion in the creation of most websites, including social networking sites. Goggin and Newell (2003) also explain how digital communications technologies build in disability, and they prompt the disability community to take an active role in shaping these technologies and their applications. Huang and Guo (2005) discovered through a survey that persons with disabilities in China successfully build social capital by using the Internet and that their expanded social networks and sense of satisfaction with their lives extend to their offline lives as well as their online activities.

7 In June 2011 and July 2012, a number of disability rights activists and researchers and officials of government agencies granted me interviews at their offices in Mexico City. I am grateful for the generosity of the following people: Federico Fleischmann (Libre Acceso, A.C.), Carlos Ríos Espinosa (Committee of Experts of the UN), Patricia Brogna (researcher), Marité Fernández (Consejo sobre los Derechos Humanos del Distrito Federal), Gabriela Molina (Asociación Pro Personas con Parálisis Cerebral), Rebeca Zavala (Confederación Mexicana de Organizaciones a Favor de la Persona con Discapacidad Intelectual), Alicia María Sandar González (Asociación para los Derechos de Personas con Alteraciones Motoras), and Ernesto Rosas Barrientos (Consejo Nacional para las Personas con Discapacidad).

8 In an e-mail sent to me on October 7, 2012, D'Artigues stated that sexuality and legal capacity were the two most controversial topics that she had raised on the blog ("Re: De parte").

9 More information about La Pirinola A.C. and their "Yo Elijo" campaign is available at the organization's website: http://lapirinola.org.

10 Federico Fleischmann, in his article published in 2008, dates the beginnings of the disability rights movement in Mexico to February 14, 1992, when persons with disabilities staged a demonstration in Congress (48). While in

2008 the author perceives that this sector still does not occupy the same political space as other groups such as senior citizens or indigenous peoples, he acknowledges that progress has been made in raising public awareness and in the creation of more effective networks among persons with disabilities in order to advance their cause (50).

11 In an interview (unpublished) on June 22, 2011, attorney Ernesto Rosas Barrientos of CONADIS spoke about the leading role played historically by civil associations in the face of inattention and inaction by the government. Federico Fleischmann (unpublished interview from June 20, 2012) made the same point, although both he and Carlos Ríos Espinosa (unpublished interview from June 24, 2011) warned that in recent years many NGOs have risked their independence by working too closely with the government and by not criticizing certain actions undertaken without their participation.

References

D'Artigues Beauregard, Katia. "Mundo D." *C@mpos Elíseos. El Universal*. El Universal. 6 Jan. 2007–July 2015. http://katia.mx/secciones/mundo-d. Accessed 27 Dec. 2016.

Ellis, Katie, and Mike Kent. *Disability and New Media*. New York and London: Routledge, 2011.

Fleischmann, Federico. "El papel de las organizaciones de la sociedad civil en el monitoreo de los derechos humanos de las personas con discapacidad." *Mecanismos nacionales de monitoreo de la Convención sobre los Derechos de las Personas con Discapacidad*. Mexico City: Comisión Nacional de los Derechos Humanos, 2008. 47–58.

Goggin, Gerald, and Christopher Newell. *Digital Disability: The Social Construction of Disability in New Media*. Lanham, MD: Rowman and Littlefield, 2003. Print.

Holdom, Shoshannah. "Literary E-magazines in Latin America." *Latin American Cyberculture and Cyberliterature* (2007): 140–160. Print.

Huang, Jin and Beorang Guo. "Building Social Capital: A Study of the Online Disability Community." *Disability Studies Quarterly* 25.2 (Spring 2005). http://dsq-sds.org/article/view/554/731. Accessed 15 Sept. 2011.

International Disability Rights Monitor. *Mexico, 2004 IDRM Country Report*. IDRM Publications, 2004. http://bbi.syr.edu/publications/blanck_docs/2003-2004/IDRM_Americas_2004.pdf. Accessed 27 July 2010.

Kuusisto, Stephen. "Introduction: A Roundtable on Disability Blogging." *Disability Studies Quarterly* 27.1–2 (Spring 2007). www.dsq-sds.org/issue/view/1. Accessed 10 Sept. 2011.

Shakespeare, Tom. "The Social Model of Disability." *Disability Studies Reader*. Ed. Lennard Davis. 3rd ed. New York: Routledge, 2010. 266–273.

Siebers, Tobin. *Disability Theory*. Ann Arbor: U of Michigan P, 2008.

Taylor, Claire, and Thea Pitman, editors. *Latin American Cyberculture and Cyberliterature*. Liverpool: Liverpool UP, 2007.

World Health Organization and World Bank. *World Report on Disability*. Geneva, Switzerland: WHO Press, 2011.

———. *World Report on Disability*. WHO Press, 2011. www.who.int/disabilities/world_report/2011/accessible_en.pdf. Accessed 20 July 2012.

7 *Revolución.com?*

Resemanticizing the Discourse of Revolution in Yoani Sánchez's *Generación* Y Blog[1]

Thea Pitman

> Whether by using the Internet to take part in a worldwide expression of dissent and disgust, to divert corporate agendas and militarism through the construction of freenets and new oppositional spaces and movements, or simply to encourage critical media analysis, debate and new forms of journalistic community, the new information and communication technologies are indeed revolutionary.
>
> (Kahn and Kellner 93)

The epithet "revolutionary" has often been used to characterize specifically contestatory Internet-based practices including political blogging (as evident in the Kahn and Kellner epigraph from their 2004 article, "New Media and Internet Activism: From the 'Battle of Seattle' to Blogging").[2] This choice of vocabulary is very pertinent when used carefully: it conflates what has (perhaps rather loosely) been termed a "revolution" in new information and communications technologies—on account of their newness, fast popular spread, and ability to change "the way we work"—with concrete, popular, left-wing political projects that envision change in both form of governance and social relations that are typically identified as constituting "revolutions" (see Craven 8 for a more detailed definition of the particular nature of Latin-American socialist revolutions). Blogging for social change can clearly demonstrate the synergy between both applications of the term. This chapter, however, asks how bloggers who work in the shadow of a consecrated "Revolution" relate to the "revolutionary" discourse surrounding the practice of contestatory blogging.

The boom in the use of blogging in Cuba to voice alternative opinions to those sanctioned by State-controlled media outlets is well documented and will not be detailed in any depth here (see, for example, Calvo Peña, *Buena Vista Social Blog*; see also Chapter 10 in this volume). This chapter proposes, therefore, to focus on the work of arguably the most prominent, internationally renowned of Cuban bloggers, Yoani Sánchez's *Generación Y* (2007–). This is not in order to claim that this is the first, the best, or even the most representative blog being written in contemporary Cuba, but—undoubtedly due to Sánchez's training as a philologist—because it has offered a sustained focus on the discourse of revolution. From the outset, it directly tackled the official monopolization of the discourse in Cuba after 1959. It then went on to suggest blogging and other forms of social networking as an alternative, but nonetheless revolutionary, discourse. My analysis of Sánchez's blog considers the extent to which she has been successful in proposing this alternative discourse and whether she manages to escape the centripetal force of the official discourse of revolution.

Yoani Sánchez, Blind Blogger

Sánchez started her blog in January 2007 as a way to voice her personal frustration at the slowness of political reform and the limits on freedom of expression in Cuba.[3] With it, she hoped that her individual voice would find affinities with others of her "generation," a generation that had experienced some of the years of greatest economic hardship during the Special Period in the early 1990s, as well as increasing disenchantment with the ideals of the 1959 revolution and the interpretation of those ideals by the regime in power since that point. Accordingly, the blog started by offering vignettes of all the most absurd facets of Cuban daily life, such as the scarcity of key foodstuffs, even fruits native to the tropics; the form-filling and queuing necessary to undertake even the most simple tasks; or the prohibition of ownership of new ICTs and the baroque means necessary to access the Internet.[4] Small acts of civil disobedience as survival techniques were frequently the subject of her attentions. She also commented regularly on political events on the island and on their reporting (or lack thereof) in official media outlets, and, in contrast, she offered her own reports about the cases of political prisoners and/or hunger-striking journalists, as well as those organizing peaceful protests in their support, such as the Damas de Blanco.[5] The threads of this kind of report increased in presence on her blog over time.

In the first year of its existence, the blog entries typically consisted of an image, sometimes an ironic and/or iconic photograph of contemporary Cuba taken by fellow blogger Orlando Luis Pardo Lazo or others, sometimes simply an image downloaded from the Internet illustrating the topic in hand, and a related text of some five hundred words. Given the dates of individual posts, it is clear that Sánchez was uploading a couple of entries each time she managed to get online (on average once or twice a week). Over time, her work increasingly experimented with the photo-essay format, as well as incorporated YouTube footage of events in which she was involved or videos of Sánchez offering instruction on the pragmatics of blogging. Images and videos were not simply used to illustrate her posts for aesthetic and/or ironic purposes—they also served a denunciatory function of their own, providing evidence of protesters' physical abuse at the hands of the State or the organization offline of illegal public gatherings. From early 2008 onwards, Sánchez also included increasingly prolific and complex links to other sites in her texts. Furthermore, from late 2007 onwards, the blog offered a space for readers to leave comments, and it clearly developed through this channel for dialogue with its readers.

All of this not only suggests the increasing facilities offered by blogging software and accessible to Sánchez, but also the increasing importance of the international network of like-minded people that galvanized around Sánchez. In 2008 and 2009, her blog received an average of 30,000 comments a month, with visits averaging out at ten million a month since May 2008 (Henken 217–18). Key posts were already being made available on a sister site in English by the end of 2007, and other translations of her work are also available.[6] Books of the blog have been appearing since the 2009 publication of an Italian translation, with versions now also available in Spanish, French, English, German, and Polish, and Sánchez has also gone on to publish a handbook in Spanish on blogging (*Havana Real*). Given this amount of international visibility and the strength of her network of supporters, Sánchez has not felt the need to hide her real identity online and has become increasingly emboldened in her criticism of the Castro regime.

The speed with which *Generación Y* gathered momentum can only be described as viral. According to Henken, the blog really started to take off after the addition of the reader comments facility, and it was then propelled to worldwide notoriety first by a *Reuters* news story in early October 2007 and then an unsigned article that appeared in *The Wall Street Journal* in late December 2007. As a result of this, a slew of other international news media (*El País*, *Die Zeit*, *The New York Times*, and others) picked up the story and/or started to reproduce Sánchez's blog posts directly, and its fame grew with each successive publication (Henken 219–20). It has also received a number of prestigious awards, such as the Spanish Ortega y Gasset prize for digital journalism in early 2008, while Sánchez herself was voted one of the top hundred most influential people in the world by *Time* magazine in the same year and even came to the attention of then U.S. president, Barack Obama. In early 2008, the Cuban censors managed to effectively block Sánchez's blog on the island,[7] a fact that further increased her fame internationally, and since then she has been what she terms "una bloguera a ciegas" (*Cuba libre* 14), managing to post to her blog by sending the entries via emails, texts, and phone messages to friends abroad who maintain the blog for her.[8] During this period, she could usually only access her own blog by using proxy servers.

The effects of censorship on Sánchez's blog were noticeable in the posts themselves, which in Spring 2008 were more sporadic in publication, shorter than usual, and with much less illustration. Nevertheless, one must surmise that the challenges of censorship were quickly over-come, given that her blog posts from 2009 onwards became more pro-lific and more complex in design than ever. From that point on, the question of censorship and blogging itself became a more frequent topic of the posts themselves. Many not only commented on the difficulties she encountered in terms of access to the Internet, but conveyed through their form the compromised nature of their composition. Footnotes oc-casionally attested to pragmatic issues of how a post reached the blog, and crossings-out with corrections in others signaled the problems of redaction for those posting voice messages for her.

Since the blocking of Sánchez's blog for readers in Cuba in early 2008, there has also been a noticeable nuance in terms of intended audience. As she noted in various blog posts, she continued to be read by those on the island who were in the know and who accessed the Internet using the same ruses that she did or who circulated posts via memory sticks or read them over the phone to friends in the provinces or in prison. However, since the point at which her blog switched to being maintained largely by friends living abroad, Sánchez clearly started to direct her entries at an audience that was both international as well as island-based. As a result, many entries contained information that would be self-evident to a national audience, particularly in the form of footnotes to gloss Cuban institutions, acronyms, and idiosyncratic customs. Other posts offered instructions for interested, and presumably international, read-ers (though not political parties), with regard to how to make donations in order to help Sánchez sustain herself through independent journalism, and how to provide the hardware and software necessary to help both Sánchez and other bloggers record their experiences.

Nevertheless, her national audience was still the focus of a good num-ber of posts. Particularly evident from 2009 onwards, Sánchez's blog be-came far more metatextual, focusing on blogging as a practice to achieve social change and encouraging others on the island to join the movement via posts with information on how new technology may be harnessed to circumvent censorship.[9] In line with her increased focus on blogging as a means of achieving social change, Sánchez was also attentive to changes on the world scene that were facilitated by the use of social me-dia technologies, such as the 2009 riots in Iran following the presidential elections and the uprisings of the 2011 Arab Spring.

It is clear from this brief analysis of the development of Sánchez's blog over time that she has been critical of the Castro regime. In accordance with her training as a philologist, this is particularly evident in her crit-icism of the Regime's use of language, especially its monopolization of the whole lexicon of revolutionary discourse. However, where she quickly moved toward the promotion of blogging as an alternative form of revolutionary discourse—one that had the potential, in her view, to translate into real social change rather than become fossilized at the level of discourse—her work also dialogues with the potential for the discourse of revolution to be resemanticized.

Contesting the Official Discourse of Revolution

In official Cuban discourse, the term "revolution" refers not only to the events of the overthrow of Fulgencio Batista in 1959 but, perhaps more importantly, it also refers to "living the revolution" and working "within" the framework laid out by the socialist regime in power ever since.[10] According to Sánchez, the term "revolución" and its associated lexical field—terms such as "la Patria," "el Partido," "el Máximo Líder," "verde olivo," "el hombre nuevo," "virilidad," "pionera/o," "compañera/o," together with its diametrically opposed set of terms "traición," "muerte," "gusano," "imperialismo", and so on—are almost fetishized by the State and their incantatory use is omnipresent in Cuban daily life.[11] Sánchez's standpoint with respect to the official discourse of the Cuban regime is to oppose what she sees as its unsubtle Manichaeism, its preference for obfuscation and euphemism, its bellicosity and associated *machismo*, its tendency for pomposity and overstatement, and above all, its monopolization of language itself. In the introduction written to accompany the publication of her blog in book form, Sánchez identifies as a main aim of her work the desire to challenge binary thinking "en un país donde las clasificaciones se expresan rígidas y los apelativos, contundentes" (*Cuba libre* 9).[12] She illustrates her point by listing some of the key binaries of revolutionary terminology: "Aquí solo se puede ser «revolucionario» o «contrarrevolucionario», «escritor» o «ajeno a la cultura», pertenecer al «pueblo» o a un «grupúsculo»" (*Cuba libre* 9).[13]

In the blog itself, Sánchez comments on the Government's binaristic advertising campaigns with slogans such as "Revolución o muerte" or "socialismo o muerte" (see, for example, "Cambiar el cartel" 28/06/08).[14] In other posts, she focuses on the Regime's preference for "frase[s] triunfalista[s]" and "cifra[s] engordada[s]" ("Periodismo o literatura" 08/07/08) and on its "palabrería hueca," offering her own translation of phrases such as "inviabilidad sistémica del proyecto socialista cubano" as "esto se jodió" ("La trampa de las palabras" 03/09/07—all terms given in inverted commas in Sánchez's text).[15] In other posts, she takes on the bellicosity of revolutionary discourse and its *machista* underpinnings—she identifies herself as among "los que estamos hartos del lenguaje belicista" of the Regime and as "cansada del macho enfundado en su uniforme verde olivo; del adjetivo 'viril' asociado al valor; de los pelos en el pecho determinando más que las manos en la espumadera" ("Un discurso bien macho" 01/03/09).[16] On the subject of pomposity and overstatement, Sánchez takes issue with the conceptualization of the Revolution as something eternal in the post "Los símiles, lo eterno y el poder" (01/08/07) and challenges its monopolization of the concept of utopia in entries such as "La utopía impuesta" (11/04/08).[17] In these posts, it is significant that Sánchez almost always identifies the terms of the Regime's revolutionary discourse in inverted commas to signify both its monopolization of the terms as well as to mark her own distance from them, highlighting their absurdity or caducity.

As a necessary counterbalance to so much "revolutionary" discourse, Sánchez also offers alternative suggestions. Thus, she indicates a preference for terms such as "'efímero,' 'perecedero' y 'transitorio'" over "'eterno,' 'siempre' y 'jamás'" ("Los símiles, lo eterno y el poder") and for "frases como 'prosperidad,' 'reconciliación,' 'armonía' y 'convivencia'" as opposed to the discourse of combativity and virility ("Un discurso bien macho").[18] While this antonymic methodology can become a reductive, repetitive, and Manichaean exercise in itself, Sánchez also imagines possible scenarios where revolutionary discourse is seen to be defeated by its own tautologies and intransigencies. In "Los hijos devoran a Saturno" (27/10/07), she argues that the lazy, hedonistic youth of Cuba with their MP3 players, low-slung jeans, and *reggaetón* music (a Generación Z to her Generación Y) is incapable of aspiring to the ideals of "el hombre nuevo" and will manage quite simply to outwait the "eternal" nature of the revolutionary regime (rather than directly overturn it).[19] In another post, she imagines herself as the grandmother of a child born to the current generation of Cuban youth and posits that her memories of socialism in Cuba will seem as distant a past to her grandchildren, as the memories of youth have always seemed when conveyed from grandparent to grandchild ("Nietos descrídos" 06/05/09).[20] The eternity of the Cuban Revolution thus slips semantically from permanence (in its official revolutionary interpretation) to the fixed but finished status of all memories. There is, here, the potential to interpret these vignettes as suggesting a hint of nostalgia for the Cuban Revolution proper—a Revolution that the new generations are just "not up to." Nevertheless, these vignettes also suggest a semantic bracketing of the official discourse of the Revolution in their ironic reworkings of the term "eternal" and their deliberate "pastichization" (to cannibalize Fredric Jameson's term) of the Cuban Revolution proper and its iconography, and this, for me, is the more convincing interpretation, enriched as it is by the postmodern irony of the existence of other, more conservative readings.

Proposing Social Change and Resemanticizing the Discourse of Revolution

Nevertheless, increasingly noticeable in Sánchez's work—as the Cuban blogging movement gathers strength and as she takes a lead role in promoting it—is the sense that her blogging activity is really seeking to "revolutionize" social reality, rather than simply offer an analysis or critique of the Regime and its discourse, and this entails a more complex dialogue with the discourse of the Revolution. Ironically perhaps, the prophetic, on occasion eulogistic, tone of blog posts auguring imminent social change increasingly offers parallels between Sánchez's writing and that of the "poet of the Revolution," Nicolás Guillén.

Sánchez's mockery of revolutionary discourse and in particular its use in official publications mirrors Guillén's mockery of the discourse of the bourgeoisie in *El diario que a diario* (1972), and her claiming of rights echoes those rights so proudly announced in "Tengo" (1963).[21] Indeed, Sánchez's frequent focus on the right of Cuban citizens to have access to hotels previously reserved for foreign tourists (a reform announced in Raúl Castro's liberalizing moves since 2008) echoes the assertion in "Tengo" that a black person can no longer be stopped "en la carpeta de un hotel" and denied even "una mínima pieza" (Guillén 196).[22] Sánchez also repeatedly focuses on reclaiming the right to the sea as part of the culmination of a new revolution in Cuba, reminding readers that since Cubans wanting to leave the island against the wishes of the Regime have used the sea as a route and since few Cubans have "holidays" at the beach, the sea is seen as either an almost insurmountable barrier or simply out of bounds. This echoes Guillén's poem where he associates open access to the sea(shore) with the openness of the democratic process that lay at the base of the revolutionary project and the reclamation for the nation of its natural resources that had been reserved, until then, for private use by the rich. For Sánchez, then, the sea is still in need of the reclamation of which Guillén so eloquently wrote. As a final and most compelling point of comparison in terms of poetics, even the frequent use of parentheses and other prosaic linguistic features in Sánchez's description of the leader she would like to have in "De la casa a la Nación" (07/02/08)—"No estoy esperando por un padre—omnipresente y omnipotente—sino por un Presidente, del que pueda quejarme—libremente—en público"—echo the awkward, hesitant cadence of "Tengo," where the narrator is just starting to describe the new society ushered in by the Revolution— "Tengo el gusto de ir / (es un ejemplo) / a un banco y hablar con el administrador, / no en inglés, / no en señor, / sino decirle compañero como se dice en español" (Guillén 196).[23]

Sánchez's blog, as it existed online in December 2011, made no explicit mention of Guillén's significant legacy in contemporary Cuban culture, nor did it, therefore, make any acknowledgement of her rhetorical proximity to Guillén's revolutionary poetics.[24] It did, however, make occasional references to key figures of the 1960s and 1970s musical movement, the Nueva Trova Cubana, such as Pablo Milanés, who were also responsible for putting to music key poems from Guillén's work. Thus, Guillén's influence on Sánchez might be said to be as much filtered through Milanés's musical interpretations as it is direct. What is most significant in the attention paid to the cultural producers of the Revolution such as Milanés (and more implicitly Guillén) in Sánchez's work is her awareness of the seductiveness of early Cuban revolutionary discourse. The parallels drawn between her blog and the poetry of Nicolás Guillén are not therefore proof of the fact that Sánchez does not realize how close she comes to going "full circle" in her critique of the discourse of the Revolution, but, taken in context, they reveal the hopes and aspirations of a new revolution—one not yet realized, but one that is nonetheless aware that it is, in essence, a revolutionary proposal. Sánchez's blog is not just descriptive or cathartic, as she claims it is—it proposes a methodology for achieving change to a more representative form of governance that is, in many ways, a logical renewal and continuation of Cuban revolutionary discourse.

In her blog, Sánchez works to discredit the revolutionary discourse that is clearly associated with the way that the current Regime expresses itself, seeking instead a more etymologically pure meaning for the term (see, for example, "La exclusión, la verdadera contrarrevolución" 15/07/10).[25] If the concept of revolution can be thus stripped of its "corrupting" association with the current Cuban regime, then Sánchez is happy to recycle it for her own purposes and try to express it in less dogmatic, more participatory and pluralistic terms. In a significant post entitled "Revolución.com" (13/02/09), she demonstrates her conceptualization of her activity in the same kind of revolutionary terms that many supporters of the transformatory power of new media are using across the globe and in direct contrast to the official rhetoric of revolution in Cuba where the Internet is posited as an enemy of the Revolution:

> Una verdadera **revolución.com** ocurre paralela y contraria al racionamiento que también nos quieren imponer en el mundo virtual. Esta no tiene barbudos, ni fusiles y mucho menos un líder gritando en la tribuna. Es lenta y aún focalizada, pero alcanzará a casi todos los cubanos.[26]

Sánchez's revolution uses interactive technologies such as blogging and other more fully-fledged manifestations of social networking as its modus operandi: as she notes in the same post "Sus comandantes llevan raros nombres como Gmail, Wordpress, Skype o Facebook: no crean división, sino que unen personas."[27] It relies explicitly on the creation of an online/offline network of civil society actors—Cubans living on the Caribbean island, those in the diaspora, and other sympathizers across the world—to protect those most outspoken in their demands for substantive change in Cuban politics. Sánchez identifies this network as "precaria" but unstoppable ("'Habeas data'" 12/02/08), and, even though she worries that Cubans do not have enough real practice of democratic negotiations to be qualified to handle the freedom afforded by virtual society ("Ciber-mutilados" 21/07/08), elsewhere she clearly hopes that they will succeed nonetheless and be able to weave a robust civil society of their own: "probemos hacer un resistente tejido que nos trascienda" ("La sociedad virtual" 01/04/08).[28]

In another set of related metaphors that reveal the subtle positioning of Sánchez's resemanticized revolutionary proposition, access to the Internet is described either as providing "una balsa virtual" or as creating "una isla virtual."[29] In the first case, the Internet as "balsa virtual" allows Cubans to escape the geopolitical confines of the island ("Tarde de textos y disgustos" 15/02/08), and their ability to find ways to "navegar" online is seen to compensate for the strict limitations placed on their ability to "navegar" offline (to leave Cuba on a boat).[30] In "Llévame a navegar, por el ancho mar" (21/02/09), Sánchez comments on the threat of a husband losing his job in the Cuban merchant navy as a result of his wife's blogging activities.[31] As a couple, they may manage to benefit from one or other form of escape, but not both. If, in real life, contemporary Cubans cannot embrace the Caribbean sea as part of their birthright, in the metaphorical terms of cyberspace they can do just that, thus nuancing Sánchez's recycling of Guillén's revolutionary reclamation of the sea.

These references to the Internet as "una balsa virtual" perhaps seem more appropriate a spatial conceptualization that the other frequent analogy that circulates in Sánchez's work (and more widely in contemporary Cuba) that imagines Cuban cyberspace as "una isla virtual." Nevertheless, this choice of terms is predicated on its difference from other terms such as "la blogosfera cubana," which encompasses blogs on the topic of Cuba written in exile and those written from the island itself (see Calvo Peña "Internet, comunidad y democracia"). The desire to promote the development of "una isla virtual" refers specifically to the question of direct access to the Internet for all Cubans and thus to the creation of a space online for residents of the island itself, where they can express themselves freely with a view to changing real island life if they want to. That virtual space, in contrast to the real island, is not cut-off or free-floating but part of a network of relationships and discussions that link Cubans on the island who are otherwise impeded from organizing themselves as groups on the ground, and it is also embedded within a network that links it to the rest of the world.

This is thus not a metaphor for a utopianist virtual Caribbean island, even if it does still retain an echo of Latin-American utopianist thought. Instead, it is much more grounded in online/offline dialogue. As Sánchez argues, "En ausencia de utopías a las que aferrarse, la nuestra es una generación de plantas en el suelo, vacunada de antemano contra los ensueños sociales" (*Cuba libre* 10), including those of virtual reality.[32] It is this attempt to avoid utopianism, I contend, that means that Sánchez's discourse of revolution avoids coming full circle, despite its acknowledgement of its revolutionary nature and despite the complexities of its relationship to the discourse of the Cuban Revolution.

Notes

1 An earlier publication of mine that deals in part with Yoani Sánchez's work can be found in Claire Taylor and Thea Pitman, *Latin American Identity in Online Cultural Production* (New York: Routledge, 2012).

2 Not all political blogging is contestatory, of course, and not all contestatory blogging necessarily supports the same political agenda. Some critics are even highly skeptical about the contestatory nature of blogs *per se* (see, for example, Lovink). However, a significant amount of scholarly work on blogging focuses at least some, if not all, of its attention on the areas where blogging and sociopolitical contestation coincide (see Kahn and Kellner; Atton; Tremayne; Lowenstein, and Russell and Echchaibi). For a recent and well-balanced study of blogging as a whole, see Walker Rettberg.

3 Much of the biographical information in what follows is synthesized from Sánchez's own blog posts, as well as her introduction to *Cuba libre* (9–17), Porter's introduction to Sánchez's *Havana Real* (ix–xv), and Henken's article.

4 The Castro regime considered the Internet "one of the 'myths of contemporary development' used to 'subvert our Revolution'" ("Internet: Mitos y realidades. Cuba en la Red," programme aired on *Televisión Cubana*, January 22, 2004, quoted in Uxó 12.4). Ownership of key items of technology such as PCs and accessories, as well as video recorders, photocopiers, and mobile phones, and the purchase of Internet access accounts in Cuban Pesos (though not in U.S. dollars), were prohibited in Cuba during the 2000s (Uxó 12.5), although some of these policies have been relaxed since the investiture of Raúl Castro in 2008. In 2007, Sánchez typically accessed the Internet by posing as a foreign tourist in order to access computer terminals in the lobbies of hotels. (For more on the Cuban government's policing of the Internet, see also Sullivan and Fernández, and Venegas.)

5 Trans.: "Ladies in White."

6 In 2011, sites were available in nearly twenty different languages including Italian, French, German, Russian, Japanese, and Chinese, but also Persian, Catalan, and Finnish.

7 Government censors applied a filter that slowed down the speed at which the blog loaded onto a user's browser, so as to make it virtually inaccessible (Henken 220–21). The Cuban search engine Dos por Tres also failed to return any results for "Yoani" in the period up to 2010 (Uxó 12.8).

8 Trans.: "a blind blogger." All translations are my own, unless stated otherwise.

9 See, for example, "Móvil-activismo" [Trans.: "Mobile Phone Activism"] 19/09/10 and "Móvil-activismo 2" 22/09/10. In addition to her work in the development and maintenance of the blog portal *Desde Cuba*, Sánchez has also promoted blogging by running a blogging competition (La Isla Virtual, 2008) and workshops (the Café/Academia Blogger has been in operation since Spring 2009).

10 See Kapcia for an overview of the Cuban revolutionary process (46–63) and a detailed analysis of popular mobilization and other forms of participation in Cuba in the decades following the Revolution itself (64–88).

11 Trans.: "the Fatherland"; "the Party"; "the Supreme Leader"; "olive-green"; "the new man"; "virility"; "pioneer"; "comrade"; "treason"; "death"; "worm"; "imperialism."

12 Trans.: "in a country where classifications are expressed in black-and-white terms and collective nouns are blunt tools."

13 Trans.: "Here you can only be a 'revolutionary' or a 'counterrevolutionary,' a 'writer [in support of the Regime]' or someone 'who has no culture,' a member of the 'people' or of a 'faction.'"

14 Trans.: "Revolution or death"; "socialism or death"; "Time for a New Slogan."

15 Trans.: "self-congratulatory expression[s]" ; "inflated figure[s]" ; "Journalism or Literature"; "hot air"; "systemic unviability of the Cuban socialist project"; "this is screwed"; "Verbal Trickery."

16 Trans.: "those who are fed up of the warmongering language"; "tired of the macho man dressed in his olive-green uniform; of the adjective 'virile' being associated with bravery; of hairy chests having more say than hands in sinks"; "A Really Macho Form of Expression."

17 Trans.: "Similies, Eternity and Power"; "Compulsory Utopia."

18 Trans.: "'ephemeral', 'perishable' and 'transitory'"; "'eternal', 'always', and 'never'"; "expressions like 'prosperity', 'reconciliation', 'harmony' and 'coexistence.'"

19 Trans.: "Saturn Eaten by His Children"; "the new man."

20 Trans.: "Skeptical Grandchildren."

21 Trans.: "The Daily Daily"; "I Have."

22 Trans.: "in a hotel lobby"; "a tiny room."

23 Trans.: "From the Domestic to the National"; "I'm not hoping for a father— omnipresent and omnipotent—but for a President about whom I can complain— freely— in public"; "I have the pleasure of going / (for example) / to a bank and speaking to the manager, / not in English, / not calling him Sir, / but calling him *compañero* as we do in Spanish."

24 In the published version in Spanish of Sánchez's blog, there is a post that does clearly acknowledge Guillén's work in its title, which is a quotation from "Tengo" ("abierto democrático: en fin, el mar" [Trans.: "open and democratic: in short, the sea"] 09/11/07; in *Cuba libre* 73–74). It has been impossible to establish whether this and one other contiguous post reproduced in the book have disappeared from the online blog archives by accident or as a deliberate sleight of hand intended to limit acknowledgement of Guillén's influence. The first reason seems, however, more probable than the second.

25 Trans.: "Exclusion, the Real Counter-revolution."

26 Trans.: "A real **revolution.com** is happening, running alongside and in counterpoint to the rationing that the Government also wants to impose on us in the virtual world. This revolution doesn't have men with beards or rifles and certainly not a leader shouting from a platform. It's slow and still quite patchy, but soon enough it will reach almost all Cubans."

27 Trans.: "Its leaders have strange names like Gmail, Wordpress, Skype or Facebook: they don't create social rifts but instead bring people together." Nb. The growing use of smartphones and Twitter by Sánchez and others is also significant in this context.

28 Trans.: "fragile"; "Cyber-handicapped"; "let's try to make a strong fabric that can reach out to others"; "Virtual Society."

29 Trans.: "a virtual raft"; "a virtual island."

30 Trans.: "An Afternoon of Books and Annoyances"; lit. "to navigate"; fig. "to surf the Internet." Nb. This use of the term "balsa virtual" is a relatively common metaphor to express the role that Internet access plays in the opinion of many Cubans living on the island.

31 Trans.: "Take Me Sailing on the Big Wide Sea."

32 Trans.: "In the absence of utopias to cling onto, ours is a generation with its feet firmly planted on the ground, immunized in advanced against social fantasies."

Works Cited

Atton, Chris. *An Alternative Internet: Radical Media, Politics and Creativity.* Edinburgh: Edinburgh University Press, 2004.

Calvo Peña, Beatriz, "Internet, comunidad y democracia: la blogosfera cubana teje su propia 'isla virtual.'" In *Buena Vista Social Blog: Internet y libertad de expresión en Cuba.* Ed. Beatriz Calvo Peña. Valencia: Advana Vieja, 2010. 147–79.

Craven, David. "Introduction: Revolving Definitions of the Word 'Revolution.'" In *Art and Revolution in Latin America, 1910–1990.* New Haven: Yale University Press, 2002. 1–23.

Guillén, Nicolás. *Summa poética.* Ed. Luis Íñigo Madrigal. 7th edn. Madrid: Cátedra, 1990.

Henken, Ted. "En busca de la 'Generación Y': Yoani Sánchez, la blogosfera emergente y el periodismo ciudadano de la Cuba de hoy." In *Buena Vista Social Blog: Internet y libertad de expresión en Cuba.* Ed. Beatriz Calvo Peña. Valencia: Advana Vieja, 2010. 201–42.

Jameson, Fredric. *Postmodernism, or, the Cultural Logic of Late Capitalism.* London: Verso, 1991.

Kahn, Richard, and Douglas Kellner. "New Media and Internet Activism: From the 'Battle of Seattle' to Blogging." *New Media and Society* 6.1 (2004): 87–95.

Kapcia, Antoni. *Cuba in Revolution: A History since the Fifties.* London: Reaktion, 2008.

Lovink, Geert. *Zero Comments: Blogging and Critical Internet Culture.* New York: Routledge, 2008.

Lowenstein, Antony. *The Blogging Revolution.* Carlton, Vic.: Melbourne University Press, 2008.

Russell, Adrienne, and Nabil Echchaibi. *International Blogging: Identity, Politics, and Networked Publics.* New York: Lang, 2009.

Sánchez, Yoani. *Cuba Libre: Vivir y Escribir en La Habana.* Barcelona: Mondadori, 2010.

———. *Generación Y.* 2007–. http://desdecuba.com/generaciony/. Accessed 25 Oct. 2011.

———. *Havana Real: One Woman Fights to Tell the Truth about Cuba Today.* Trans. M.J. Porter. Brooklyn: Melville House, 2011.

Sullivan, Laura, and Víctor Fernández. "Cybercuba.com(munist): Electronic Literacy, Resistance, and Postrevolutionary Cuba." In *Global Literacies and the World-Wide Web.* Ed. Gail E. Hawisher and Cynthia L. Selfe. London: Routledge, 2000. 217–50.

Tremayne, Mark, ed. *Blogging, Citizenship, and the Future of Media.* New York: Routledge, 2006.

Uxó, Carlos. "Internet Politics in Cuba." *Telecommunications Journal of Australia* 60.1 (2010): 12.1–12.16.

Venegas, Cristina. *Digital Dilemmas: The State, the Individual, and Digital Media in Cuba.* New Brunswick: Rutgers University Press, 2010.

Walker Rettberg, Jill. *Blogging.* Cambridge: Polity, 2008.

8 The Uses and Limits of Ethnic Humor and New Media in *¡Ask a Mexican!*

Amber Workman

Why do Mexicans like roses so much? Why do Mexicans get into so many bike accidents? Why is it that every Mexican I know refuses to eat chocolate? Can I demand my day laborer to work better? Why is it hard to find an educated Mexican man in New York City?

For anyone who dedicates themselves to Mexican and U.S. Latino/ Chicano cultural studies, the previous questions may seem absurd, unfounded, or entirely undeserving of serious consideration. In the U.S., Mexican immigrants now inhabit regions far beyond the states sharing a border with Mexico, making Mexican culture more present and presumably better understood throughout many parts of the country. Cultural plurality is seemingly more the norm than the exception, and the belief in cultural essentialism as *passé* as the notions of gender or racial inequalities. Yet, these and a multitude of other inquiries into Mexican, Mexican-American, and Latino cultures and their interactions with mainstream U.S. culture are the focus of Gustavo Arellano's popular newspaper column/blog *¡Ask a Mexican!*, a sort of pseudo-"advice" or educational column for the general public on understanding Mexicans in the U.S. and for U.S. Mexicans as a resource for understanding themselves and their relation to mainstream U.S. culture.

Since 2004, Arellano's column, which encourages readers to submit via the Internet any and all questions they have regarding Mexicans, has appeared in both the in-print and online versions of the OC *Weekly* (Orange County Weekly) and is syndicated in more than fifty other U.S. newspapers. The column is known for its use of satire, vulgarities, and political incorrectness in order to dispel persistent stereotypes regarding Mexicans and Mexican-Americans despite changing U.S. demographics, strategies for which the column has been both attacked and praised. The column also addresses the need for U.S. Mexicans to understand their own customs and cultural background and to embrace and defend these in the face of discrimination and anti-immigrant sentiment. As a column that encourages reader participation via the Internet, *¡Ask a Mexican!* makes extensive use of social networking and multimedia content in order to encourage readers to interact with the author and his column. In this chapter, I argue that despite the possible shortcomings of ethnic humor in *¡Ask a Mexican!*, the column plays a unique and important role in promoting dialogue and mutual understanding among U.S. mainstream society and Mexicans/Mexican-Americans, especially through the column's use of new media and social networking tools such as Twitter, Facebook, and YouTube. At the same time, the relation of Arellano's blog to the tradition of U.S. Latino journalistic chronicle writing, the emergence of cyberspace as what we might call a new "post-colonial" realm, and the increasing popularity of social networking among U.S. Latinos make this column particularly contestatory.

The Uses and Limits of Ethnic Humor

From first glance at *¡Ask a Mexican!* (www.ocweekly.com/columns/ask-a-mexican), the reader is instantly made aware of the column's humorous intent. Both the in-print and online versions of the column feature, alongside the text, a cartoon face of a dark-skinned, overweight Mexican man sporting a mustache, a large grin revealing gold tooth, and a conical shaped peasant sombrero. This image is presumably that of "The Mexican," the pseudonym with which Arellano signs his responses and to whom the readers address their inquiries. The structure of *¡Ask a Mexican!* follows a standard "advice column" format, using questions submitted by readers via Facebook, Twitter, e-mail, or YouTube. Following the salutation is the reader's question, an invented nickname signature that Arellano assigns to the reader—some examples are: "El Gringo-nator," "Grinning Gringa," "Answer my Güestion, Por Favor"—and, finally, his response. The Mexican's responses vary in length and tone, but typically fit into one or more of the following categories: a sarcastic comment, an insult, a historical explanation of some cultural phenomenon, or—if Arellano is unsure of how to answer the question or feels that it does not warrant much of his attention at all—something more creative or completely invented. The following entry from 2012, where Arellano addresses a reader's inquiry regarding artwork on lowrider cars, illustrates these features:

Dear Mexican:

Why do Mexicans with lowriders have murals on their hoods and trunks/tailgates?And how come they always have waterfalls and half-naked chicks as part of the mural?

The Crazy Filipino

Dear Chinito:

First off, *gracias* for not telling the tired lowrider joke that goes like this: "Why do Mexicans drive lowriders? So they can cruise and pick strawberries at the same time." Or "Why do Mexicans drive cars with small steering wheels? So they can drive while wearing handcuffs." All jokes aside, the use of murals on lowriders is further proof of Mexican assimilation into this country. The art, of course, comes from Mexico's proud muralist tradition, which you see in Mexican neighborhoods across America. Their placement on cars comes from kustom kulture, born in Southern California and freely mixing with Mexican traditions from the 1950s onward. Half-naked chicks? Like you have to ask! And, frankly, Mexicans cannot stand to see any flat surface unadorned, whether it's with a mural, graffiti, quinceañera pictures, Virgins of Guadalupe or the occasional college diploma. ("Why do Mexicans Paint Murals")

Typical of Arellano's column, both the inquiries and responses make use of epithets, humor, and sarcasm, as well as historical fact, in order to "educate" readers on some aspect of Mexican/Mexican-American culture. In this case, though Arellano's initial comments are humorous, he goes on to link lowrider art to the long history of the Mexican muralist tradition.

Despite the generally lighthearted tone and educational aspect of the column, critics have pointed out the shortcomings of *¡Ask a Mexican!*, such as its stereotypical logo, Arellano's inability to represent "all" Mexicans, and the use of terminology and ethnic humor. To whom or what does "The Mexican" attribute his authority to speak for "all" Mexicans? What does Arellano mean by "Mexicans" anyway? (Isn't he technically referring to "Chicanos"?) How is it possible for him to denounce *gabacho* culture in mainstream media as he does in the following response from 2012?

Dear Mexican:

It's so sad to see your wimpy answers. Your replies scream self-hatred and self-shame for your *raza*. You're pathetic! No plan or desire to fix Mexico's problems. You're a *puto* with no *huevos*. My DREAM Act would be that you Mexicans would stop groveling to gringos, and scream about fixing Mexico, like *white people* did against the Iron Curtain thing. *Only then* will your Mexican self-shaming and self-hatred of your un-macho, *puto*, groveling *raza* change to real pride, which you know you deserve, like gringos got about America.

Groveling Is Puto Stuff

Groveling? *Chulo*, this is the only column in the country that refers to *gabachos* as *gabachos* instead of the candy-ass "gringo" like your *gabacho* ass uses. No desire to fix Mexico? What's billions of dollars of remittances, then—or the Reconquista, for that matter? Or those marches of millions rallying for amnesty? That's a movement as epic as Solidarity or *glasnot* (and last I checked, a *chingo* of Eastern Bloc refugees worked from *los Estados Unidos* to liberate their homelands). Pride for America? All I hear from Know-Nothings is how horrible the United States is, yet they do nothing to improve it other than rant—they sound just like Mexicans used to until we started doing instead of crying. Self-hatred and self-shame? The only thing this Mexican is ashamed of is his *panza*—and even then, it's a *panza* more glorious in its contentment and fire than any *gabacho panza* can ever hope to attain. *Huevos* that, *pendejo*. ("How Can Mexicans Fight Gentrification?")

This question and response seems to illustrate what Agustín Gurza, a writer for the *Los Angeles Times*, claims when he writes that "Arellano has capitalized on the novelty of his syndicated column, '¡Ask a Mexican!,' in which he fields often racist questions about Mexicans with answers that are often racist themselves" ("Don't Ask This One About That Mexican"). However, according to Arellano, the column originated as a joke when his boss at the *OC Weekly* asked Arellano why he didn't "ask readers to send in questions about Mexicans and you answer them?" (*Ask a Mexican* 2). As Arellano recalls:

> Will turned to me not just because I was the only Latino on staff and trim his trees on the side, but because of my background—child of Mexican immigrants (one illegal!), recipient of a master's degree in Latin American studies, a truthful beaner—put me in a unique position to be an authority on all things Mexican.
>
> (2)

The authority of Arellano—"The Mexican"—to speak for all Mexicans or Mexican-Americans that comes both from the designation by his boss and by his status as the educated child of undocumented immigrants is reaffirmed in his byline to ¡*Ask a Mexican!*: "Dear *Gabachos*: *Bienvenidos* to ¡*Ask a Mexican!*, the world's foremost authority on America's spiciest minority! The Mexican can answer any and every question on his race, from why Mexicans stick the Virgin of Guadalupe everywhere to our obsession with tacos and green cards."

For some, it is further unclear to whom Arellano is referring when he refers to "Mexicans." The author uses the term, for instance, to refer to himself, even though he was not born or raised in Mexico, but in Anaheim, California, which, strictly speaking, does not make him Mexican, a topic that readers have also questioned. Although people of Mexican origin born in the U.S. (Chicanos, Chicanas) often refer to themselves as "Mexican" to identify themselves with and express pride in their roots (as The Mexican indicates in his response to the previous question), a careful revision of Arellano's entries since 2004 seems to show the use of the term "Mexican" where we would expect "Chicano" or "Mexican-American" would be more appropriate. The Mexican receives letters, for instance, from "Mexicans" who live in the U.S., but who are totally unaware of the culture and customs of Mexico. And when we consult one of Arellano's special glossaries he publishes in his column, Arellano notes that he often uses the word "Mexican" interchangeably in place of the word Chicano, which he defines in the following way: "Chicano: The poorer, stupider, more assimilated cousins of Mexicans. Otherwise known as Mexican-American"; "Mexicano: The greatest race of people in the world-when they're in the United States. In Mexico, they're just Mexicans" ("¡Ask a Mexican! Glossary"). Ironically, the "Mexicans" that write in with questions about "Mexicans" are supposedly more assimilated, more "Chicano," according to the glossary, since they lack this cultural knowledge. Here, Arellano seems to advocate a more fluid notion of Mexican cultural identity, one that incorporates diasporic identities and that reflects contemporary thinking that cultural/national identities are unstable and ever-changing.

Despite its potentially questionable use of terminology and ethnic humor, if we accept the idea of the blog (published online) as a contemporary form of the traditional journalistic chronicle (published in print), we might read Arellano's column as both a continuation and rupture with the tradition of chronicle writing by U.S. Latinos. This is especially true since the column does not attract only mainstream U.S. readers, but also U.S. Latinos, who perhaps—not surprisingly—seem to be the main readers of Arellano's column. While early 20th-century U.S. Latino chroniclers from the mid-19th century to the early 20th-century were mostly interested in promoting resistance to cultural and linguistic assimilation through satire,[1] Arellano's column—along with those of other writers—suggest that one role of today's U.S. Latino chroniclers is to provide a sort of public forum for discussing ethnic and racial tensions and to allow both Latinos and non-Latinos to arrive at a better understanding one another through the use of satire and ethnic humor via the Latino press.

The Uses and Possibilities of Cyberspace

Along with the potential for Arellano's blog to be inserted within a history of U.S. Latino chronicling, it seems that what should be appreciated of *¡Ask a Mexican!* is Arellano's unique and even empowering uses of cyberspace, both for himself as well as for his readers. Despite its possible shortcomings, the strength of Arellano's *¡Ask a Mexican!* column seems to lie not only in its content, but also its means of publication, advertising, circulation, and opportunities for reader interaction with the author and with each other.

Not unlike early 20th-century Latin American chroniclers, who Viviane Mahieux describes as "accessible intellectuals"—that is, intellectuals who were "easy to access," "recognizable figures" and whose writings were "cheaply and easily acquired" (Mahieux 23)—readers of the online and in-print versions of ¡*Ask a Mexican!* are made aware of Arellano's accessibility through the author's informal tone and personal availability through Facebook, Twitter, and YouTube. Both Twitter and Facebook are now popular ways for readers to "follow" and even personally contact public figures, who often post information about their daily life and thus seemingly make them more "reachable" figures to anyone.

The ¡*Ask a Mexican!* Facebook page is used to announce local events such as book signings, to include comments on daily interactions and experiences, to comment on news in the U.S. that in some way affects or involves Latinos, to post anecdotes and celebrate Latino holidays, and to invite questions and to communicate with fans. The page currently features Arellano's newest book *Taco USA: How Mexican Food Conquered America* (2012), reviews on food from local Mexican restaurants he has recently visited, links to Latino music videos, and commentary on news such as Arizona sheriff Joe Arpaio's policies on racial profiling of immigrants. These posts have attracted dozens of reader responses showing support for Arellano's opinions, with the page itself boasting over 40,000 "likes" by fans, the vast majority of them with Hispanic surnames.

With respect to Twitter, this tool can be used for "unauthorized commentary" and to provide a sense of instant thoughts. Also, "individuals with high media status (such as celebrities) use Twitter to maintain a constant online 'presence', whose informality and intimacy is geared to building a fan base..." (Couldry 41). Twitter can also be used as a means to build community, familiarity, and trust. Malcolm Gladwell, of *The New Yorker*, writes that:

> The world, we are told, is in the midst of a revolution. The new tools of social media have reinvented social activism. With Facebook and Twitter and the like, the traditional relationship between political authority and popular will has been upended, making it easier for the powerless to collaborate, coordinate, and give voice to their concerns.
>
> (par. 5)

Gustavo Arellano's personal Twitter site comments on other Twitter posts and includes information about local events of interest to Latinos. With author accessibility and off-the-wall comments made possible through Twitter and perhaps because the author uses his real name (as opposed to his Facebook page, where he always known as "The Mexican," possibly as a means to further advertise the column), people perhaps feel less inhibited to ask The Mexican anything they want. Arellano's column, his presence on Facebook and Twitter, and the sense of community that these sites seem to provide among his fans (mostly readers of Latin origin who not only comment on Arellano's posts, but also on those of other readers) are examples of how we might consider the "cyberrealm" as a "postcolonial" space capable of "destabili[zing] notions of nationhood which are so central to imperialist conceptualisations" (Taylor and Pitman, *Latin American Cyberculture* 18). By allowing for the "expression" and valorization of "diasporic identities online," Arellano's column could perhaps be said to "circumvent the traditional powers of imperialism" (18) that seek to devalue and impose limits on the expression of such identities. Social networking also permits Arellano to allow participation of readers nationally and internationally; thus, it is possible that Twitter and Facebook could be seen as sites for community building, advocacy, activism, and resistance and to even extend these beyond geographical boundaries.

¡Ask a Mexican! as Digital Advocacy

¡Ask a Mexican! already has readers who respond to others, readers who comment on the column aloud or join other readers to read and comment on it together, and readers who leave comments regarding the column (positive and negative) on the *¡Ask a Mexican!* website, on Facebook, or on the YouTube channel. Given the column's focus, its community of on- and offline readers, and its social networking community, it is not far-fetched to reason that *¡Ask a Mexican!* could also be said to serve a sort of advocacy or activist purpose. As Beth Kanter and Allison Fine note in *The Networked Nonprofit: Connecting with Social Media to Drive Change* (2010), "social media powers social networks for social change" (Kanter and Fine 9). While it is not clear if *¡Ask a Mexican!* has attained such social impact, the column does encourage readers to interact with one another and to question the reaction of others to it. Such is the case with a question/answer where Arellano even attempts to mediate between well-to-do Mexicans and Mexicans with fewer economic resources in the U.S. and between new arrivals and those who have lived in the U.S. longer. When "El Pocho" and "El Gabacho Canadian" write to The Mexican, they do so hoping resolve an issue they are having with a Mexican coworker. Their issue is that when they read the *¡Ask a Mexican!* column out loud at work, a Mexican colleague of theirs excuses himself so that he does not have to listen. Arellano's response is:

Dear Pocho y Gabacho:

Primeramente, tell your *baboso* Mexican co-worker *que se vaya a la chingada*—I'm *puro zacatecano* from the beautiful city of Jerez,

Zacatecas. Secondly, all Mexican-on-Mexican bashing stems from class conflict—bone up on your Chicano Studies, *pocho y gabacho!* Better-off Mexicans have always trashed poor Mexicans—look at the murder of Zapata, your typical telenovela plot or the battle between Mexicans north of Santa Ana's 17th Street and those living south. Similarly, loser Mexicans love nothing better than to pick on their betters. It's what one of my former professors at Chapman University, Paul Apodaca, used to call the crab theory—like crabs in a bag, loser Mexicans like to pull back those brave few who dream of a world free of Sunday-afternoon Raiders games and nightly visits to Rockin' Taco Cantina. But bringing down your race isn't exclusively a Mexican psychosis— Chris Rock once did an amazing monologue on how lower-class blacks derided their wealthier, smarter brethren for being "smarty-art niggers." Such squabbling helps keep the powerful powerful: the French pitted Hutu against Tutsi in Rwanda, Saddam Hussein did the same with Shiites and Sunni, and Cortes wrecked havoc with Tlaxcalans and Aztecs. So tell your *baboso* Mexican to stop hating you and me and turn his vitriol toward the true enemies: the Guatemalans. (Arellano, *¡Ask a Mexican!* 107)

Through sarcasm, Arellano attempts to mediate both sides.

While studies are beginning to appear on Latin American online culture such as Taylor and Pitman's pioneering *Latin American Cyberliterature and Cyberculture* (2007) and the more recent *Latin American Identity in Online Cultural Production* (2013), very few studies exist on Latino writing and new media. Yet, according to the Pew Research Center, in 2010 more U.S. Latinos used Twitter than non-Latinos, and the 2012 Pew study found that U.S. Hispanics use social networking sites more often than the general population (López et al.). This could potentially make the social networking tools associated with Arellano's *¡Ask a Mexican!* more frequented and meaningful resources for U.S. Latino users.

¡Ask a Mexican! as Didactic Column

Finally, despite its use of satire and ethnic humor, it should be pointed out that *¡Ask a Mexican!* seems to have didactic potential. The Mexican offers, in addition to insults, references to Mexican and Mexican-American history and insights gleaned from his own research into issues raised by readers' inquiries. It could also be said that his responses, tinged with a sense of humor and creativity, force readers to pay attention to these issues.

In light of anti-immigrant sentiment in the U.S. and the elimination of Mexican-American studies programs in Arizona, perhaps there is a need for this kind of column, a "neutral" space (as Arellano would call it), where all readers are welcomed to ask anything they wish regarding

Mexicans and Mexican-Americans and in this way engage in an open dialogue between two cultures.

The column's use of a Mexican (or a person who identifies as such) who assumes a position of authority and takes advantage of the press in order to defend Mexican and Mexican-American culture in a country where these are undervalued is a bold move. In the postcolonial cyberspace that is *¡Ask a Mexican!*, The Mexican has the upper hand and the final word. He is the foremost "authority on all things Mexican," he is not afraid to speak his mind or offend his readers, he redefines certain notions of cultural identity, and his column circulates widely without regard to geographical boundaries or imperialist restrictions.

Conclusions

The increasing presence of Mexican immigrants in the U.S. has encouraged questions such as those addressed by Gustavo Arellano in the controversial column *¡Ask a Mexican!* as mainstream U.S. culture must adapt to Mexican-American culture and Mexican-Americans seek to understand their own history, beliefs, and customs. In sum, *¡Ask a Mexican!* is a provocative way of promoting mutual understanding through a controversial and ambivalent ethnic humor and represents one instance of Latinos' use of the cyber realm as a contestatory space and social media for purposes of encouraging dialogue, community building, and, in some cases, even advocacy and activism.

Given the importance of social networking for U.S. Latinos and the fact that Latinos' uses of cyberspace remains largely unexplored, it seems that further study is warranted on contestatory uses of cyberspace among Latinos. The appearance and popularity of *¡Ask a Mexican!* highlights the need for better understanding of and inquiry into Latino uses of cyberspace and social networking and the connections between technology and advocacy.

Note

1 See Ignacio López Calvo, "The *Crónica* in the Spanish-Language Journalism of Los Angeles: The cases of Francisco P. Ramírez and Ricardo Flores Magón." *Journal of Spanish Language Media*, vol. 1, 2008, pp. 125–38 and Nicolás Kanellos, *Hispanic Immigrant Literature: El sueño del retorno* (U of Texas P, 2011).

Works Cited

Arellano, Gustavo. "¡Ask a Mexican! Glossary." *OC Weekly*, June 7, 2006. www.ocweekly.com/web/ask-a-mexican-glossary-6415500. Accessed 10 Apr. 2012.

———. *¡Ask a Mexican!* Scribner, 2007.

———. "How Can Mexicans Fight Gentrification?" *OC Weekly,* January 26, 2012. www.ocweekly.com/news/how-can-mexicans-fight-gentrification-6421015. Accessed 2 Dec. 2012.

———. *Taco USA: How Mexican Food Conquered America.* New York: Scribner, 2012.

———. "Why do Mexicans Paint Murals on Lowriders?" *OC Weekly,* April 19, 2012. www.ocweekly.com/2012-04-19/columns/ask-a-mexican-murals-lowriders-lotto/full. Accessed 13 May 2012.

Couldry, Nick. *Media, Society, World: Social Theory and Digital Media Practice.* Malden, MA: Polity P, 2012.

Gladwell, Malcolm. "Small Change: Why the Revolution will not be Tweeted." *New Yorker,* October 4, 2010. www.newyorker.com/reporting/2010/10/04/101004fa_fact_gladwell. Accessed 10 Feb. 2012.

Gurza, Agustín. "Don't Ask This One About That Mexican." *Los Angeles Times,* May 19, 2007. http://articles.latimes.com/2007/may/19/entertainment/et-culture19. Accessed 2 Mar. 2012.

Kanter, Beth, and Allison Fine. *The Networked Nonprofit: Connecting with Social Media to Drive Change.* San Francisco, CA: Wiley, 2010.

López, Mark Hugo, et al. "Closing the Digital Divide: Latinos and Technology Adoption." *Pew Research Center,* May 7, 2013. www.pewhispanic.org/files/2013/03/Latinos_Social_Media_and_Mobile_Tech_03-2013_final.pdf. Accessed 11 June 2013.

Mahieux, Viviane. *Urban Chroniclers in Modern Latin America: The Shared Intimacy of Everyday Life.* Austin, TX: U of Texas P, 2011.

Taylor, Claire, and Thea Pitman, editors. *Latin American Cyberculture and Cyberliterature.* Liverpool: Liverpool UP, 2007.

———. *Latin American Identity in Online Cultural Production.* New York: Routledge, 2013.

Part III

Enduring Struggles, Now Online

9 Five Hundred Years of Struggle Enter Cyberspace. Neo-Zapatism and the (Old) New Insurgency[1]

Carolina Gaínza Cortés

"Why do you keep on fighting, Demetrio?
Demetrio, frowning deeply,
absentmindedly picks up a small stone
and throws it to the bottom of the canyon.
He stares pensively over the precipice and says:
"Look at that stone; how it keeps on going..."
The Underdogs, Mariano Azuela[2]

During the peak of the protest that occurred in Turkey in 2013, which intensively used Twitter, Facebook, and other media technologies and applications to spread their demands, the prime minister, Recep Tayyip Erdoğan, accused social networks of being the worst threat to society, because anybody can divulge anything they want and those messages are disseminated like a virus through the networks. In an interview on Turkish television, he stated: "There is now a menace which is called Twitter. The best examples of lies can be found there. To me, social media is the worst menace to society" (*The Guardian* 2013). This reaction has become common from those in power, where governments, as well as economic and media powers, do not know what to do with these "viral protests" that grow and spread through innovative uses of social networks. It happened to the Chilean government with the student movement in recent years, in Spain with the *Indignados*, in the U.S. with Occupy Wall Street, with the Arab Spring, and many other examples before these.

Thus, the general question of the analysis I will present in the following pages is related to how networks created for military purposes during the Cold War period, which in the 1970s and the 1980s served mainly for the reconfiguration of capitalism and the configuration of what we all know as globalization, also became a tool for resistance, subversion, and social mobilization, even being considered a threat to political and economic powers. However, we cannot answer this question without referring to Neo-Zapatism. Thus, we are going to propose in this paper that EZLN (Ejército Zapatista de Liberación Nacional) or

Neo-Zapatism[3] was the first movement that used digital networks with the purpose of creating a focal point of resistance, both locally and globally, and, consequently, gave networks a new meaning, and they have been used and replicated by other movements after it.

From that, I propose that the networks created by Neo-Zapatism became the revolution itself. This "networked" form of struggle has been, in fact, something that characterized social movements in the last decade. Thus, of particular interest in this chapter are the uses of cyberspace by the Neo-Zapatist movement, not only because they were the first resistance movement to use networks as I have already stated, but also because of the way they appropriated networks and new technologies to serve their purposes of resistance and gave these networks new meanings for social and cultural activism. After them, many other movements have used the Internet as part of their strategy of protest and resistance, such as the big protests against globalization during the last years of the 20th century in Madrid, Seattle, Washington, Prague, and many other cities. During the first decade of the 21st century, not only the Internet, but also cell phones and other gadgets, as well as applications like Facebook and Twitter, have become an essential part of social movements, making them visible in the public sphere and allowing them to create networks of solidarity that help them by supporting their demands.

"Whoever today says 'globalization' says also 'communication,' for the emergence of this new world order would be unthinkable without telecommunications and computers that now form the electronic pathways for the circulation of money, commodities and power" (Dyer-Witheford 130). In this context, I propose that Neo-Zapatism planted a seed of transgression in appropriating and giving new meaning to digital networks, subsequently present in many other movements after them. I would even say that, to understand the current social movements mentioned before, we must turn back to Neo-Zapatism and its creative and contestatory uses of cyberspace during the 1990s. This is the main reason that we come back to EZLN after their uprising twenty years ago. The appropriation of the technologies of information and communication (TICs) was an integral part of a communicational strategy that impacted public opinion locally and internationally and that forced the Mexican government to pay greater attention to, and negotiate with, the rebellion. Within this process, the Internet began to be used as a medium for resistance, and the image of the virtual *guerrillero* who goes around cyberspace turned into a symbol of new forms of insurgency. On a different level, the use of networks has affected the constitution and forms of intervention of social movements since then. Consequently, the discussion will focus on the Neo-Zapatists' innovative use of cyberspace, which provided the basis for their identity as rebels in the era of global capitalism.

A Struggle against Capitalist Networks and New Forms of Marginalization

The fall of the Berlin Wall in 1989 and the dissolution of the Soviet Union in 1991 became the symbols of the defeat of communism and Marxist ideology by capitalism. But, these events were only the tip of the iceberg. Capitalism reinvented itself during the 1970s and the 1980s and what arose was a "reloaded" version of capitalism: a globalized version focused on the expansion of financial networks, where the uses of new technologies of information and communication[4] transformed industrial capitalism into what has been called "informational capitalism."[5]

As Harvey's works suggests, terms such as "globalization," "financial networks," and "market deregulation" were related to the reorganization of capitalism from the 1980s, after the crisis of capital accumulation and capitalist class power experienced during the 1970s. In Latin America, this process was strongly related to military dictatorships and the Washington Consensus. Particularly in Mexico, privatizations and economic restructuring after 1988 resulted in twenty-four Mexican billionaires listed on Forbes by 1994 (Harvey, *The Limits* xii). In contrast, Aguirre and Estrada propose that some regions in Mexico, such as Oaxaca and Chiapas, were marginalized, its natural resources were exploited, and the level of poverty increased. Thus, global capitalism reinforced the existence of inequalities in Mexico and in Latin America, creating new marginalized subjectivities and reinstating old marginalized populations in new forms of domination and exploitation. Therefore, scholars such as Harvey, Hardt and Negri, and Dyer-Witheford affirm that, along with informational capitalism and globalization, there was a new international division of labor.

The indigenous population from Chiapas belonged to the group of people historically marginalized from the promises of modernity. The rebels from Chiapas were well aware of the connections between globalization, neoliberalism, and capitalism, how the Mexican State was getting involved in that process, and the consequences for the indigenous population. Therefore, it is not surprising that the Neo-Zapatism rose up on January 1, 1994, the same day of the ratification of the North American Free Trade Agreement (NAFTA). Their claim was not only economic, but also, more importantly, ethical. They did not forget the land claims, economic marginalization, and exploitation, but they stressed that, in the foreground, was human dignity, freedom, democracy, and the recognition of the autonomy of the indigenous people. Therefore, it was an ethical claim about what neoliberalism in the global capitalism represents: "the adulation of money and commodity at the expense of human life" (Mignolo, *The Zapatistas's* 247).

Nevertheless, the impact that the uprising and further actions of the movement had would not have been possible without the new technologies of information and communication. They became well known around the world, mainly because of their use of the new media technologies to spread their image and their message. The rebels with a ski mask became a symbol of their struggle, especially because of the leaders' communicational strategy, where the most important figure was Marcos.[6] It would not be correct to say that Neo-Zapatism is an "Internet born" movement, because it has a history related to 500 years of struggle that started with the Spanish conquest and colonization of America, followed by centuries of struggle against domination and exploitation from the local powers and the Mexican State. However, I consider that the most innovative aspects of the Neo-Zapatist movement were their use of new media technologies and how they managed to insert their historical struggle into the local and global networks, dominated by the neoliberal Mexican State and informational capitalism.

Seeds of Transgression: Creating Connections and Solidarities around the World

Currently, all localities have been forced to interact with the flow of networks, which, as García Canclini states, even reformulates what we understand by the term local. We have also learned how to defend ourselves from their social, economic, and cultural impact, appropriating technologies, gadgets, and applications to be used in favor of old and new social demands, social movements, and those regions and people marginalized from the promises of, as McLuhan called it, the "global village." However, at the beginning of the 1990s, globalization and the Internet were new phenomena, and computers were not a mass-consumption commodity. On the contrary, they served mainly for the reinforcement of neoliberal capitalism and its global financial networks. So, how did technological networks become so important to Neo-Zapatism, impacting the subsequent collective action, not only in Latin America, but also in many movements around the world?

The EZLN appropriated TICs in a very creative way, transforming a technology that has a strong relation with power into a tool that supported their struggle by creating resistance networks. The EZLN was in fact called a "netwar" by the Pentagon (Mattelart) and "the first informational guerrilla" by the academia (Castells). In this sense, their use of the TICs is essential to understand the strategy of the movement, which explains their subsequent visibility in the public sphere and their communicational success during the 1990s. Neo-Zapatistas used cyberspace to make their identity stronger by moving their struggle and demands from the local, where Mayans were historically oppressed, to the global. By doing that, they actually change the meaning of networks, showing that globalization can serve purposes other than dominant, neoliberal economic powers. The local voices from the Mayans' in Chiapas were heard in many places, through images, declarations, blogs, books, and videos available online. The possibility of "another globalization," proclaimed by antiglobalization movements and the world social forums at the beginning of 21st century, was already present in the Neo-Zapatist movement.

Marcos, the spokesperson for EZLN, seemed to be well aware of the power of networks. Actually, the way he installed the Mayan epistemology on the World Wide Web was an act of translating the Mayan epistemology to the occidental language (Mignolo), but, paraphrasing McLuhan, he used the technology not only as a medium but as a message as well. Although the medium transmitted images, videos, and words, it actually disseminated an identity, a message, and a struggle. The medium was not only a tool used by the movement, but it actually had an effect on the governments, people, and other movements, as well as over the identity of the Mayans and the movement itself. Marcos's intervention in the level of communications says a lot about the way Neo-Zapatism managed the media, without which the indigenous demands would not have had visibility and they would have remained invisible as they had done for many centuries.

So, were new technologies the only reason for the communicational and the consequent political success of Neo-Zapatism? Of course not. Their success was based on their usage of new technologies to disseminate an image, a message, and an identity. By doing that, new technologies became a part of the identity of the Mayan Zapatist movement itself. It is in this sense that I stated that the networks became the revolution itself, because of the meaning the new technologies acquired for the movement and how they served to create a *networked movement* that impacted on the public sphere. To summarize, the last can be seen on two levels: on a communicational level, related to the transmission of an identity that at the same time shaped the identity of the movement itself, and on a physical or structural level, which relates to the organization of the movement and its forms of action and intervention.

Subcomandante Marcos was essential to the Neo-Zapatists' communicational strategy. His staging, the *pasamontañas* (ski mask),[7] his charisma, his writings, and his knowledge about, and uses of, new technologies were all factors that made the EZLN attractive in cyberspace. In fact, the *pasamontañas* became a visual sign that identified them as rebels in cyberspace, as Castells describes in his analysis: "All over the world, everybody could become a Zapatista by wearing a mask" (*The Information* 85). The language of the new media is mainly the image, and the way Neo-Zapatism managed it was crucial to promote a new mode of thinking about digital media, cultural identity, and, beyond that, a new way of political activism. Technologies were used both as a medium and as message to transmit the image of resistance, and they worked as a source of signification and identity not only for the Mayan-Zapatist movement, but also, and unexpectedly, to other resistance movements that came after Neo-Zapatism. Another important effect of the use of new technologies by the movement was that the EZLN's messages were transmitted in real time, where the Internet became a tool to distribute that message—now translated into the occidental language—to the world. The translation function that Marcos had in this context was fundamental to strategically introducing an unknown knowledge (the Mayan's), subordinated by occidental thinking, to the world audience.

Their action in cyberspace, in the form of images, language, and discourses, using different new media (blogs, online news, videos, etc.), became the most powerful weapon in the Neo-Zapatist struggle. *The New York Times'* description of the movement as "the world's first postmodern revolution" and Marcos as their "first chief" was not totally wrong. They started a new form of struggle and gave new meanings to social action in a context where the traditional ways of activism of the left were in crisis.[8] In fact, as Nick Dyer-Witheford comments, "Harry Cleaver has suggested that the success of EZLN in avoiding the normal fate of peasant revolts in Mexico—outright massacre—was partly due to their weaving of an 'electronic fabric of struggle'" (158). This "electronic fabric of struggle" consisted of establishing contacts with other networks, such as PeaceNet and Usenet, to disseminate the movement's message and demands. These networks[9] helped them to rediffuse their communiqués, news reports, and documents, and they also added additional information, analysis, and discussion. By doing that, they not only created an awareness in people unfamiliar with the indigenous situation in Chiapas, but also, and more importantly, they obtained support from many organizations and other movements, which took the indigenous demands from their local limits to put them into the global circuit.

This had many important consequences for the movement, the immediate one being the effect that this network support had after the uprising on the reaction from the Mexican government, which was forced to establish a dialog with the EZLN. In fact, following H. Cleaver's ideas about Neo-Zapatism, Dyer-Witheford suggests that "'Communicative action' then passed into 'physical action,' not only in a worldwide series of protests at Mexican embassies and government offices, but in an influx of Zapatista supporters—journalists, human rights observers, delegations—into Chiapas" (158). The connection between the peasants and the indigenous population in the local context of Mexico was strengthened by the global interconnection of these many supporters.

From then, it is possible to state that social movements acquired new features that not only disturbed political powers, but they even challenged social theory.[10] Social activism acquires a rhizomatic structure, using Deleuze and Guattari terminology, based on alliances and solidarities, established globally. In turn, networks are defined by Castells as a series of interconnected nodes. However, I think that the unstable characteristics of the networks formed by this type of political activism, which is today almost widespread around the globe, and its capacity to rapidly organize, move, and act through networks give them a viral feature that is more present in the definition of Deleuze and Guattari's rhizome than in Castells' definition of networks. Indeed, as Hardt and Negri propose, networks have "swarm intelligence." In this sense, the Neo-Zapatist network's ability to "deterritorialize" capital networks was a result of the appropriation from social activism of the "logic of networks"—by acting globally, connecting people, being flexible, and being viral. As Deleuze and Guattari propose, molecular flows—the schizo—are the ones that produce movements of deterritorialization, generating escapes or "lines of flights," that creatively challenge the limits of the social machine. After growing, these flights produce reterritorialization movements that form molar organizations:

> A molecular flow was escaping, minuscule at first, then swelling, without, however, ceasing to be unassignable. The reverse, however, is also true: molecular escapes and movements would be nothing if they do not return to the molar organization to reshuffle their segments, their binary distribution of sexes, classes, and parties.
>
> (216)

Thus, the network was not only communicational, but also affected the structure of the movement itself by transforming it into a decentralized, interconnected, flexible, and movable organization. In this process, the digital medium acquired new significance not only for the movement, but for social action in general as well: cyberspace became a place for resistance, new social relations, solidarity, and collective action.

It is in this sense that I support the idea that the network is the revolution itself, because of the interconnection feature of resistance and dissident movements that goes beyond the local. In fact, the successful impact of the discourse of Neo-Zapatism, through Marcos's words and writings, especially during the 1990s, would not have been possible without TICs. Not only did words replace weapons, as Marcos expressed in several articles collected in his "selected writings," but so too did new technologies. Using new media technologies, the EZLN raised an issue that was considered old-fashioned in the local political agenda,[11] namely the issue of the indigenous conflicts, showing that it is indeed a very contemporary problem. When the Neo-Zapatistas positioned themselves as a continuation of 500 years of struggle, they gave visibility to an indigenous population not only historically subordinated by the processes of colonization and, after that, by the national State, but also by the Marxist parties and *guerrillas*. In the context of the 1980s and 1990s, they were threatened once again by the promises of the "global village" and globalized capitalism.

Social Movements as Virus: Social and Cultural Hacking

The figure of the hacker has become popular as a social rebel who attacks government websites and those related in general with political and economic powers. Hackers have become the target of the intelligence services of the political powers and a threat to governments. However, hackers are more than that: they challenge the dominant mode of production by creating and producing software collectively and forming a community that shares not only a love for programming but also knowledge. But, what do hackers have to do with Neo-Zapatism? From what I have analyzed in the last pages, I would like to propose that Neo-Zapatists became sociocultural hackers by changing what we understood as "social movements" and giving new meaning to networks, which were initially conceived to serve war, as well as political and, later, economic purposes. In this sense, they "hacked" the networks dominated by global capitalism and planted the seed of a type of political activism that has grown over the last decades, as we have seen in some of the recent social mobilizations around the world.

In fact, what is especially remarkable from this appropriation and use of technology by Neo-Zapatism is that it was able to transform a network that was originally created to serve military purposes and, later used in favor of capital and neoliberal globalization, into a network used to resist and transmit an alternative project, coming from those historically marginalized. Their communication strategy is one of the most visible innovations in the area of social movements in the region. Their use of the TICs introduced them to global public opinion, an action that forced the Mexican government to negotiate with them. Without this support, the Mexican army would likely have, once again, defeated and silenced the Mayan people. The EZLN was the first movement to show that TICs could acquire different meanings depending on their use. Neo-Zapatism subverted the dominant uses of the networks, showing that they are also useful for social change, counter-movements, and resistance, even for those coming from an almost forgotten area of the world like Chiapas.

Of course, as Nick Dyer-Witheford poses, "For capital and its advisers, such activity is a threat" (158). The reaction from Turkey's prime minister that I mentioned at the beginning of this chapter was probably the same as Zedillo had to the EZLN uprising in 1994. And it was the same reaction as the CIA and the intelligence agencies from the U.S. had, and continue to have, in relation to "networked" movements. Terms such as "cyberwar" and "netwars" were popularized by political analysis regarding the Neo-Zapatist uprising and their subsequent uses of cyberspace, and they referred to a kind of war that was not going to be militarily won, but has to do with communications and knowledge, as authors such as Dyer-Witheford and Mattelart suggests in their works. As we learned from the Neo-Zapatist experience, the language of image and communications, united to the power of the networked style of organization, is what defines social and political activism in the digital era, where viral activity on the Internet has become a type of social activism.

Thus, Neo-Zapatism was viral in two senses. First, because it changed the signification of networks by hacking those that commonly were meant to serve global capitalism. Second, because it incorporated the logic of networks as a new way to produce social action. Its rhizomatic type of social activism allowed them to act both locally and globally, infecting global networks as a virus that spreads rapidly. This generates solidarities from other actors that supported the movement from different parts of the world. Nowadays, the viral feature is essential to characterize social movements and is challenging the mechanisms of control of the state and economic powers.

In recent years, Neo-Zapatism has faced a delicate situation because of the loss of many supporters, especially in the indigenous communities of Chiapas. However, these events cannot make us forget what Neo-Zapatism means in terms of understanding social activism in cyberspace. Particularly in Latin America, the empowerment of indigenous communities in Neo-Zapatism during the 1990s—made possible mainly because of their visibility in the new media—was pivotal in the increasing visibility that indigenous issues acquired in the region during the 1990s and, especially, the first decade of the 21st century. At the same time, the entrance of 500 years of struggle into cyberspace and the communicational strategy followed by EZLN by using digital networks changed the meaning of these networks and showed that not only can they serve the goals of capitalism but also the goals of resistance movements and their supporters. These changes of meaning, in turn, reinforced the identity of the Mayan communities and the subjects involved in the networks created. At the same time, this fact prepared the field for incoming political and social movements that actively used social networks and technological gadgets not only as a communicational strategy; more importantly, this networked type of social activism shaped what we understood as social movements.

Thus, a revolt that connected to an "old" story resulted, at the same time, in a very new story. The context of the reception of this "old" story was different, which gave new meanings to the history of the struggle of the indigenous Mayan population. In this sense, the EZLN reinvented social movements and resistance in the era of global capitalism, addressing resistance forces toward new forms of activism and social change due to their contestatory use of cyberspace.

Notes

1 Carolina Gaínza is a sociologist and M.A in Latin American Studies from the University of Chile and PhD in Hispanic Languages and Literatures from the University of Pittsburgh. Currently, she works as assistant professor at the Creative Literature Department at the Universidad Diego Portales in Chile.

2 Mariano Azuela, *The Underdogs: A Novel of the Mexican Revolution. A new rendition*. By Beth E. Jörgensen, based on the E. Munguía translation, 148.

3 We will call Neo-Zapatism the movement that rose up in 1994 and became visible during the 1990s, creating a network of supporters in Mexico and, globally, from different actors and movements from many parts of Latin America and the world. The use of new technologies, as I will argue in this chapter, were essential to this strategy. However, EZLN cannot be reduced to the uses of the Internet and networks of solidarity. EZLN represents a "new visibility" of the practices of Zapatismo from 1910, which fought for liberty and land. EZLN is related to that tradition, but it also comes from the mixture of a variety of political ideas; in Marcos's words:

> Our military instruction comes from Villa, principally from Zapata. It also comes by way of negative example from what was done by the guerrillas of the '70s. They started with a local military movement and expected that the base would slowly join in or that they would be enlightened by this guerrilla foco.
>
> (qtd. in Rabasa 580)

As we can find in the analysis of Rabasa, Aguirre, and Estrada, although EZLN derives partially from the Latin American Marxist *guerrillas* from the 1960s and 1970s, Marcos has stated that they learned to listen to the indigenous voices, and that allowed them to come up with a strategy from below, taking into account the requirements of indigenous communities and subordinating their politics to those requirements. It is also important to mention the relation they established with power, in the sense that the EZLN, as Marcos declared that the movement is not defined by revolution in terms of seizing power, an element that strongly marked the Marxist *guerrillas* in Latin America in the past. In this sense, even though they recognize the influence of these *guerrillas*, they are not strictly defined by the tradition developed by leftist movements in the subcontinent.

4 From now on, this will be abbreviated as TIC.

5 Castells proposes, in the first volume of the "Information Age," that even though the economic model of development has changed, which refers to the energy sources that generate productivity, the mode of production is still based on capitalism. In this sense, the ways to generate productivity have changed, being immaterial resources that generate value, such as information, communication, and symbols. On their part, M. Hardt and T. Negri propose in "Empire" that the mode of production has also changed because a transformation that occurred at the level of the relations of production, which affected the strategies of power, control, and forms of exploitation. This model of production, which the authors call post-Fordism, rests on immaterial production such as information, communication, and affects, which are produced collectively. For more on these topics, see: Manuel Castells, *La Era de la Información, Vol. I Economía, Sociedad y Cultura*; Michael Hardt and Antonio Negri, *Empire*; and David Harvey, *The Limits to Capital*.

6 I would like to point out that the relationship that Marcos established with the media was central to the movement to get support, locally and internationally. Walter Mignolo (2002) defines his role as translator of the Zapatist's message, by translating the Mayan epistemology to the dominant epistemology and languages by means of using the digital networks. However, Marcos's centrality to the movement has been criticized, especially by Mayans who participated in the movement at its first stages, who denounced his "caudillista" mode of leadership and the relationship that the military

insurgent leaders established with their social bases. Although an analysis like that is beyond the purposes of this chapter, I recommend reviewing the research done by Marco Estrada and published in his book *La Comunidad Armada Rebelde y el EZLN*.

7 The ski mask can also refer to those "without face" in Mayan culture, or in other words, those who have been erased from history by the hegemonic power.

8 The thesis about the lack of perspective and viability of left-wing revolutionary movements in Latin America was discussed by Jorge Castañeda in his book, *La Utopia Desarmada*, paying special attention to the Mexican case.

9 A compilation of sources that connected to the EZLN can be found in: https://webspace.utexas.edu/hcleaver/www/kczapsincyber.html.

10 For the relationship between TICs, networks, and social movements, see: Manuel Castells, *The Information Age. Vol. II: The Power of Identity*; Howard Rheingold, *Multitudes Inteligentes. La Próxima Revolución Social*; Salvador Millaleo and Pablo Cárcamo, *Medios Sociales y Acción Colectiva en Chile*; and Bruno Latour, *Reassembling the Social. An Introduction to Actor-Network Theory*.

11 See: Octavio Paz and his articles published on *Vuelta*, "Chiapas,¿Nudo Ciego o Tabla de Salvación?"; "Chiapas: Hechos, Dichos y Gestos"; "El Plato de Sangre."; "La Selva Lacandona."; and, Jorge Castañeda, *La Utopía Desarmada*.

Works Cited

Aguirre, Carlos. "A Modo de Introducción: Chiapas en Perspectiva Histórica." *Chiapas en Perspectiva Histórica*, Ed. Carlos Aguirre et al. México: Universidad Autónoma de Querétaro, 2004, pp. 7–24.

Azuela, Mariano. *The Underdogs: A Novel of the Mexican Revolution*, Translated by E. Munguía, revised with notes by Beth Jörgensen, New York: Modern Library, 2002.

Castañeda, Jorge G. *La Utopía Desarmada*. México: Editorial Joaquín Mortiz, 1993.

Castells, Manuel. *La Era de la Información. Economía, Sociedad y Cultura. Vol. I: La Sociedad Red*. México: Alianza Editorial, 1997.

———. *The Power of Identity. The Information Age. Volume II*. London: Wiley Blackwell, 2009.

Deleuze, Gilles, and Felix Guattari. *A Thousand Plateaus. Capitalism and Schizophrenia*. Minneapolis, MN: U of Minnesota P, 2009.

Dyer-Witheford, Nick. *Cyber-Marx. Cycles and Circuits of Struggle in High-Technology Capitalism*. Champaign, IL: U of Illinois P, 1999.

Estrada Saavedra, Marco. *La Comunidad Armada Rebelde y El EZLN: Un Estudio Histórico y Sociológico Sobre las Bases de Apoyo Zapatistas en las Cañadas Tojolabales de la Selva Lacandona*. México: El Colegio de México, 2007.

García Canclini, Néstor. *Culturas Híbridas. Estrategias Para Entrar y Salir de la Modernidad*. México: Paidós, 2001.

Golden, Tim. "The Voice of the Rebels Has Mexicans in His Spell." *The New York Times*, February 3, 1994. www.nytimes.com/1994/02/08/world/the-voice-of-the-rebels-has-mexicans-in-his-spell.html?pagewanted=all. Accessed 10 Dec. 2016.

Hardt, Michael, and Antonio Negri. *Imperio*. México: Paidós, 2000.

———. *Multitude. War and Democracy in the Age of Empire*. New York: Penguin Books, 2005.

Harvey, David. *A Brief History of Neoliberalism*. Oxford: Oxford U P, 2005.

———. *The Limits to Capital*. New York: Verso, 2006.

Latour, Bruno. *Reassembling the Social. An Introduction to Actor-Network Theory*. Oxford: Oxford U P, 2007.

McLuhan, Marshall. *The Gutenberg Galaxy. The Making of Typographic Man*. Toronto: U of Toronto P, 2002.

Mattelart, Armand. *Historia de la Sociedad de la Información*. México: Paidós, 2002.

Mignolo, Walter. *Local Histories/Global Designs*. Princeton: Princeton U P, 2000.

———. "The Zapatistas's Theoretical Revolution: Its Historical, Ethical, and Political Consequences." *Review Fernand Braudel Center*, 25.3, Utopian Thinking (2002): 245–275.

Millaleo, Salvador, and Pablo Cárcamo. *Medios Sociales y Acción Colectiva en Chile*. Santiago: Fundación Democracia y Desarrollo, 2013.

Paz, Octavio. "Chiapas, ¿Nudo Ciego o Tabla de Salvación?." *Vuelta*, Vol. 18, 207, February 1994, pp. C-H. http://cdn.letraslibres.com/sites/default/files/files6/files/vuelta-vol18_207_suplem_0.pdf. Accessed 10 Dec. 2016.

———. "Chiapas: Hechos, Dichos y Gestos." *Vuelta*, Vol. 18, 208, March 31, 1994, pp. 55–57. www.letraslibres.com/vuelta/chiapas-hechos-dichos-gestos. Accessed 10 Dec. 2016.

———. "El Plato de Sangre." *Vuelta*, Vol. 18, 209, April 30, 1994, p. 8. www.letraslibres.com/vuelta/el-plato-sangre. Accessed 10 Dec. 2016.

———. La Selva Lacandona. *Vuelta*, Vol. 20, 231, February 29, 1996, pp. 8–12. www.letraslibres.com/vuelta/la-selva-lacandona. Accessed 10 Dec. 2016.

Rabasa, José. "Of Zapatismo: Reflections on the Folkloric and the Impossible in a Subaltern Insurrection." *The Latin American Cultural Studies Reader*, Ed. Ana Del Sarto, Alicia Ríos, and Abril Trigo. Durham: Duke U P, 2004. 561–583.

Rheingold, Howard. *Multitudes Inteligentes. La Próxima Revolución Social*. Madrid: Gedisa, 2005.

"Social Media and Opposition to Blame for Protests, says Turkish Prime Minister." *The Guardian*, March 6, 2013. www.theguardian.com/world/2013/jun/02/turkish-protesters-control-istanbul-square. Accessed 10 Dec. 2016.

Subcomandante Marcos. *Our Word is Our Weapon. Selected Writings*. Ed. Juana Ponce de León. New York: Seven Stories P, 2001.

10 *Voces Cubanas*

Cyberactivism, Civic Engagement, and the making of *Cubanía* in Contemporary Cuba

Omar Granados

Cuba remains the most restricted country in Latin America regarding Internet freedom for its citizens. In addition to limited bandwidth and technological resources, a rigorous institutional model for access has reinforced the monopoly that the government has kept over all media, press, and cultural organizations since the 1959 revolution.[1] Internet, nonetheless, has become the most contestatory medium on the island today. Since early 2007, the work of independent Cuban-based cyberactivists has steadily consolidated as a diverse network of autonomous online projects—blogs, mostly—that expose the controversial social and political issues that the official media outlets ignore. This wave of internal criticism to Raúl Castro's government not only has included bloggers, but also a large number of politically minded artists, musicians, intellectuals, and citizen journalists who have been part of a growing cybernetwork as cyberactivists.[2] Their voices have relied on technology and the Internet's readiness as a publishing tool to document police brutality, government corruption, public health crises, the decaying state of the Cuban education system, censorship in the arts, and human and civil rights violations against citizens.

The commentary generated outside state-sponsored circuits by Cuban independent cyberactivists has been regarded by the authorities as a form of "ciberguerra" (cyber war) and a threat to national security.[3] In Cuba, it is still a crime punishable by law to disseminate uncensored information. The Penal Code restricts Cuban citizens to incur on the production, distribution, or even possession of any material that may contain unauthorized news and might be considered by the authorities as harmful to the socialist state. While the *Unión de periodistas de Cuba* (Cuba's Journalists Union) remains the only national news organization permitted by the state since 1964, Decree-Law 209 from 1996 regulates Internet access, prohibiting the hosting of public citizen content on Cuba's top domain (*.cu*). Resolution 127 from 2007, on the other hand, requires Internet providers to control access and content.[4] Cuba's long history of repression against free expression—most notably and recently the so-called *Primavera negra* (Black Spring) of March 2003, when seventy-five independent Cuban journalists were arrested and sentenced to prison—has demonstrated the extreme repercussions these practices can have for Cuban citizens.

The interest of this chapter is to delve into the contestatory character and potential of recent Cuban independent cyberactivism and to demonstrate the central role its discourse of cultural heterogeneity has played as the seed for a new civil society for Cubans. The work of Cuban-based independent cyberactivists has dismantled Raúl Castro's government positioning over the fabricated notion of *Cubanía* (that is, Cuban national identity as an intrinsic element of socialism), activating new forms of dialogue between intellectuals, artists, activists, and citizens in Cuba outside the state's discursive apparatus.[5] Cuban cyberactivism, for the most part, has subscribed to the notion of participatory democracy through networking. They have collaborated from a cultural platform toward engaging and informing citizens on their rights to free expression, and cultural and political difference as intrinsic components of Cuban national identity that have been excluded by the one-dimensional discourse of Cuban socialism.

Through the examples of the work of bloggers, artists, and civic organizations we discuss in this chapter, we focus on two main characteristics of Cuban independent cyberactivism. First, we show how its resourcing to cultural expressions (art, film, literature, music) has refashioned the discourses on freedom of expression in Cuba, making them accessible and appealing not only to those politically informed and working for a democratic transition, but also to the political apathy of younger generations born in the post-Castro era. Second, we describe how cyberactivists have used cultural expressions to confront the repression and intimidation of citizens, reconnected with Cuban exile communities, and transitioned to a status of visibility in the Cuban public sphere, where they have mobilized higher numbers of citizens, both in Cuba and abroad.

Among several Cuban-based collective initiatives that have appeared online in the last few years (many times hosted from overseas serves by foreign collaborators), the platform *Voces Cubanas* (Cuban Voices) was, since its beginning in 2009, the most culturally heterogeneous forum for civic engagement. It functioned as "a space open to all Cubans living on the island who want to have a blog," as of December 2013. *Voces Cubanas* grouped the work of over fifty independent bloggers, journalists, and artists, including Yoani Sánchez's acclaimed blog *Generación Y*.[6] Sánchez, who has been often depicted as either an isolated advocate for freedom of expression by the international media or a "cyber-mercenary" financed by the U.S. in Cuban official media, perhaps has been the most visible face of Cuban cyberactivism, but not the exclusive protagonist of a network built on its collaborative potential. In May 2014, Sánchez created *14ymedio*, the first independent online newspaper in Cuba, along with her husband journalist Reinaldo Escobar and a team of twelve editors. *14ymedio* contains news from Cuba and the world, related to national, international, economic, cultural, society, science and technology, and sports issues. It also publishes editorials and opinion articles, interviews, and reports. *14ymedio* was initially blocked by the Cuban government, but it is now accessible in Cuba. However, *Granma*, the newspaper run by the ruling Communist Party, has published several accusations of the U.S. supporting projects like *14ymedio,* whose fundamental purpose, as seen by the socialist state, is to spread misinformation and lies about Cuba.

Like Sánchez's original blog *Generación Y*, many of the blogs that were initially hosted in *Voces Cubanas* were descriptive reflections on the average life experiences of the Cuban citizen seeking to create public debate. It is important to emphasize that most members of the Cuban independent blogosphere, including those featured in *Voces Cubanas*, have been self-taught citizens, not members of an intellectual elite. Because of Cuba's high literacy levels and the education system in which this generation of bloggers was schooled, regular citizens have been able to undertake roles as bloggers, political commentators, artists, photographers, and independent journalists. The language of these blogs, therefore, has resonated with the collective frustrations of all Cubans and allowed readers and writers to share a space where Cuban cultural identity has reemerged autonomously.

Voces Cubanas featured blogs that reviewed cultural demonstrations and their repercussions by marginalized and controversial artists, such as the urban poetry troop *Omni-Zonafranca*, which since 1999 has convoked and mobilized citizens for their festival "Poesía sin fín" (Endless poetry) and has celebrated a yearly peregrination "for the good health of poetry" to the San Lázaro Sanctuary in Havana, on December 17. Another example often cited in *Voces Cubanas* was the provocative activities of punk-rock band *Porno para Ricardo* (Richard's Porn), which popularized lyrics that explicitly mocked Fidel and Raúl Castro. The work of urban graffiti artist Danilo Maldonado was also found in *Voces Cubanas*. Also known as "El Sexto" ("The Sixth One," a nickname mocking the excessive government propaganda about the "Cinco heroes," five Cuban intelligence officers who, in 1998, were imprisoned in the U.S. after being charged with spying), Maldonado was one of the most explicit and bold voices for freedom of expression in Cuba. Maldonado has been detained and jailed in several occasions by the ideological police, for which he tattooed his body with an image of the recently deceased dissident Osvaldo Payá Sardiñas as part of a public performance piece in December 2012.[7]

Voces Cubanas expanded its potential beyond the text format of the traditional blog and offered greater possibilities for citizen participation.

Among other audiovisual undertakings were *Razones ciudadanas* (Citizen Reasons), a video series of political debates and interviews anchored by independent journalist Reinaldo Escobar (which were also available on *YouTube* and *Vimeo*), and the freelance urban photography open contest "País de pixeles" ("A Country of Pixels"), where citizens submitted their own uncensored photographs of everyday life in Cuba to be published. The work of Orlando Luis Pardo Lazo, a renowned cyberactivist, blogger, fiction writer, and photographer, was also featured in *Voces Cubanas*. Pardo Lazo became a controversial figure for the Cuban government in February 2009, when his collection of short stories, *Boring Home*, was banned from the Havana International Book Fair. *Boring Home*, nonetheless, was presented independently outside the fair by Yoani Sánchez and later distributed in digital format in Cuba by Pardo Lazo and his collaborators.[8] From 2009 until 2014, Pardo Lazo coordinated and distributed *Voces* (Voices), one of Cuba's few independent online cultural magazines (also hosted by *Voces Cubanas*) that brought together exiled and Cuban-based voices.

Pardo Lazo maintained two other blogs in *Voces Cubanas*. The first one, *Lunes de post-revolución* (Post-Revolution Mondays), was an online cultural journal of what the author described as "the anachronistic entity of the Cuban Revolution, drowning in its own rhetoric."[9] A self-taught photographer, Pardo Lazo also maintained a clever interactive photo-blog project entitled *Boring Home Utopics,* which published photographs of Havana urban spaces with a given nostalgic value, as those abroad (mostly Cubans in exile) request them. "Let me know what you miss most, including Habana people, and I will cut this city in pieces of pics for you," wrote Pardo Lazo. Appearing as a hypertext to the censored stories of his book *Boring Home*, this photo blog—as Esther Whitfield has suggested—disseminated visual imagery that separated Cuba's emotional capital from the historically political significance of the Cuban Revolution.[10] The blog presented a virtual image of "home" for Cubans in exile (and on the island) that appeared as a network of relations, rather than as a geographical space bounded by the historical weight of isolation or exile.

Pardo Lazo has been no stranger to the Cuban exile community, as his columns also appeared frequently in highly credited online publications edited and maintained by Cuban exiles, such as Ernesto Hernández Busto's blog *Penúltimos días* (Penultimate Days) established in Barcelona in 2006 and the Miami-based online newspaper *Diario de Cuba*. In 2013, an immigration reform by the Cuban government loosened travel restrictions, and Pardo Lazo could travel to the U.S. to attend the event "The Revolution Recodified: Digital Culture and the Public Sphere in Cuba," celebrated in March 2013 at New York University. Pardo Lazo organized a tour of the states with the highest numbers of Cuban immigrants (Florida, New York, New Jersey) and over fifteen American universities and colleges. He spoke to radio and TV stations, solidarity groups in exile, and grassroots organizations raising awareness of Cuba's incipient civil society. Pardo Lazo, however, is just one example of the changing nature of the relation between new generations of Cuban cyberactivists and politically conscious citizens, and their counterparts in exile. New faces like Pardo Lazo and Sánchez, who on April 1, 2013 spoke to hundreds of Cuban exiles at the Freedom Tower in Miami, have provided a radical, new, and detailed understanding for conventional political bodies of action in exile of what is needed in Cuba for a peaceful transition.

Cyberactivism has enabled many Cuban citizens to collaborate with online communities internationally and nationally without the authoritarian mediation of the state. Several of the blogs found in *Voces Cubanas*, for example, were specifically directed at informing and giving voice to the public, encouraging citizens to claim their rights against the authorities. This was the case of *Juriconsulto de Cuba*, a blog by independent lawyer Laritza Diversent, which offered free legal and constitutional advice to citizens who could also exchange commentary on the blog. Ted Henken, on the other hand, described how Sánchez's "Academia blogger" (Blogger's Academy), which functioned periodically from her Havana home since December 2008, instructed hundreds of Cuban citizens on blogging and tweeting, generating over 100 *Twitter* users.[11] Since 2008, Cubans took advantage of Cuba's mobile phone companies allowing foreigners to add minutes to prepaid accounts from abroad, and Cuban citizens could ask foreign supporters and exiles to help voice their concerns via *Twitter* feeds. Cubans on the island also have been able to send SMS messages as tweets, allowing their commentary to appear on the Internet, even without a connection. Outside Cuba, supporters also have been translating news and entries from bloggers, independent journalists, and citizens writing from Cuba. This has been the case of the volunteer translation sites such as *HemosOido.com*, which functioned through crowdsourcing efforts, and *Translating Cuba*, a news site that published Cuban independent news in several languages. Both volunteer and translator, Mary Jo Porter founded both projects in Seattle.

Since 2007, the transition of power between Fidel and Raúl Castro has helped the Cuban government infuse an air of renewal to the image of the Cuban revolution abroad. The state has intensively promoted a more democratic "Cuban nation," coding *Cubanía* as state benevolence toward issues such as sexual orientation, religion, the exile community, and allowing private property and enterprise for Cuban citizens. However, any concrete form of advocacy for a transition to a truly democratic system (especially if it becomes a collective citizen initiative) is automatically casted as "anti-Cuban" or "unpatriotic" and therefore excluded from *Cubanía*.

In his well-known essay "Dissemination: Time, narrative and the margins of the modern nation," Homi K. Bhabha provides a useful critical frame to understand the political role of cyberactivists in Cuba. Bhabha denounces how essentialist definitions of "nations" are falsely elaborated from the basis of cultural traditions. Instead, the narrative of a nation, Bhabha explains, must arise from "a contested conceptual territory" of cultural interaction to prevent any political ideology from gaining total authority. "The people"—writes Bhabha—"are not simply historical events or parts of a patriotic body politic," but "the 'subjects' of a process of signification" where social visibility and collective expression may constitute the rhetoric of national affiliation (208). This explains, first, the importance of alternative dissemination networks generated through sites like *Voces Cubanas* to restore social visibility and autonomous discursive spaces for the Cuban subject. Second, it asserts the significance of the heterogeneity of the cultural discourses generated and endorsed by Cuban independent cyberactivists to reinstall a truly inclusive sense of national identity, without the mediation of the state. The validation of this cultural discourse and the possibilities of free expression created by new methods of cyberactivism (Twitter use, uncensored translation, video, and image instant uploading) have provided regular Cuban citizens with the tools to disassemble the state's discursive mechanisms over nationality.

A recurrent concern regarding the potentialities of Cuban cyberactivism has been the limited access regular citizens have to the Internet on the island. By the end of 2011, Cuba's *Oficina Nacional de Estadísticas e Información* (ONEI) (National Statistics and Information Office) had reported only 2.6 million Internet users, approximately 23% of the total population. Most of these users, however, were professionals working in state jobs who only had access to a slow, dial-up, censored government intranet. As researched by Henken, most work done by independent cyberactivists was saved and later uploaded to their sites by foreign collaborators or during visits to foreign embassies in Cuba, from countries that support pro-democracy efforts to provide free Internet access.

As to the rest of the population, Internet access is still either unavailable or obtained through illegal connections. No one can really estimate how many Cubans access the Internet on a regular basis today. Starting in 2008, new economic adjustments allowed Cubans to purchase computers from state corporations and use the Internet in tourist's hotels and cybercafés using convertible currency, but the costs were not feasible for the majority.[12] Paradoxically, home connections are not authorized (except for government officials and foreigners living permanently in Cuba), but access to the Internet is portrayed in official media as fully available to all, when government publications, radio, and television stations advertise their online versions, or *Facebook* and *Twitter* addresses. Meanwhile, state IT engineers and programmers run clandestine private businesses on the side, hacking state networks to traffic Internet "hook-ups" in the black market for 30–60 dollars a month, depending on connection speed. Information in Cuba also has circulated offline after it has been downloaded, through a flourishing underground business network using USB memory sticks and external hard drives. Among hundreds of pirated versions of Hollywood films and Miami television shows, pre-1959 censored memorabilia, Major League Baseball games, and interviews featuring Cuban defectors that are rented for profit, there is also a large amount of political material circulating clandestinely for free. Dozens of independently produced controversial films, hip hop and rap protest songs, articles from prohibited newspapers such as *El Nuevo Herald* from Miami, hacked videos of government meetings, corruption, and private parties, photographs and satirical cartoons, publications such as *Guamá* (a spoof imitation of *Granma*, the main state newspaper, created from Chile by artist Alex Lauzán), newsletters from Cuban-based human rights or religious organizations, and especially ideologically controversial books and their translations into Spanish all pass from hand to hand.

Coco Fusco, a New York conceptual artist and one of the scholars responsible for the event that brought Pardo Lazo and Sánchez to the U.S., has denoted the advantages of Cuban cyberactivism:

> Digital information is much easier to hide and to distribute than printed matter, and this has facilitated broader dissemination of oppositional culture and encouraged more attempts at transgression in recent years. Whereas dissidents and controversial artists in the 80s and 90s used impromptu performance to convey critiques that were too strong to put into forms that leave a trace, the social critics of today's Cuba use online forums and foreign media attention as protective shields.

Fusco's remarks explain why Cuban independent cyberactivists have subscribed to a nonviolent and full disclosure plan of action. A great percentage of the bloggers and artists in *Voces Cubanas*, for instance, made the jump from anonymous to public (on their blogs and in the public sphere) and embraced an identity as political dissidents and civic rights advocates, but also for sake of their physical safety. Blogger Miriam Celaya, for example, started blogging in 2008 under the pseudonym "Eva" in her blog Sin EVAsión (No Evasion) and was later a visibly recognized voice, while Claudia Cadelo displayed a copy of her identification card as the home page of her blog *Octavo Cerco* (The Eighth Frontier). As the authorities grew more frustrated with their inability to stop the dissemination of dissenting cultural and political messages, government slander to discredit the work of independent cyberactivists increased. The ideological branches of official media have ran websites such as *Cubadebate* or *La Isla Desconocida* (The Unknown Island) by official journalist Enrique Ubieta and *Cambios en Cuba* (Changing Cuba) by official commentator Manuel Henríquez Lagarde (both ferocious instigators against bloggers from *Voces Cubanas*) or *El blog de Yohandry* (Yohandry's blog) by supposed blogger "Yohandry Fontana," a copycat attempt to counteract the popularity of Sánchez's blog *Generación Y*.[13] Since late 2012, however, the Ministry of Interior has resourced to more illegal detentions, beatings, intimidation and harassment, and confiscation of technology against cyberactivists. Before Pope Benedict XVI's three-day visit to Cuba in March 2012, for instance, several cyberactivists were placed under house arrest and released after the Pope's visit had ended.[14] Another common tactic used by the state has been to use secret police agents to incite citizens to respond violently against peaceful demonstrations by activists and dissidents.

Analysts have questioned the credibility of Cuban independent cyberactivism versus more traditional forms of political dissent or its contestatory impact, based mostly on their methods of action and their somewhat limited potential to reach large numbers. Others, like Hernández Busto, have asserted that the greater majority of Cubans, albeit well informed, seek their best economic standard of living (or struggle to survive and provide the minimum necessities for their families) within the existing situation in Cuba, choosing not to join massive protests.[15] However, as will I discuss throughout the remainder of this chapter as the final part of my argument, the efforts of independent cyberactivists have begun to penetrate and reclaim urban and cultural spaces in Cuba. These efforts, which have also been framed as cultural interventions, can be compared to other recent cyberactivism experiences in Latin America and can be read as the first steps to mobilizing higher numbers of citizens beyond their computer screens.

By the end of 2013, the semi-clandestine myth created by leading figures like Sánchez or Pardo Lazo in their beginnings and through their online personas had evolved as a visible political community both for Cuban exiles (mostly in the U.S.) and Cubans on the island. As mentioned, many of the public demonstrations lead by cyberactivists had taken place intentionally at cultural forums provided by the state. The authorities insist on appropriating cultural forums to reduce the possibilities of political intervention (as it might be expressed through cultural manifestations) to a very limited sector of the population composed of artists, intellectuals, and academics. This political strategy allowed for any form of radical dissidence to be labeled as a new aesthetic trend of *Cubanía,* rather than an independent form of oppositional ideology.[16] Cyberactivists, however, made it their purpose to counteract the state's manipulation of open cultural forums by responsively challenging government officials and leaders in public and encouraging citizens to join.

In December 2008, for example, Sánchez openly confronted Mariela Castro—daughter of President Raúl Castro and director of the *Centro Nacional de Educación Sexual* (National Sex Education Center of Cuba, CENESEX)—about the falsehood of the CENESEX campaigns for LGBT rights in Cuba. The encounter happened during a conference offered by Mariela Castro at the Museum of Fine Arts, where Sánchez demanded in front of the audience that the state campaigns would also extend to freedom of press and political diversity. Months later, in February 2009, when Pardo Lazo's book *Boring Home* was banned from the Havana Book Fair, the invitation to the independent presentation of the book by Sánchez was circulated over the Internet, demanding support for the book to be published and circulated outside official spaces designated by the government. The presentation was attended by members of the international press, as well as regular visitors of the event. In a more daring public demonstration in March 2009, cyberactivists Claudia Cadelo, Ciro Díaz, and Reinaldo Escobar took center stage at the Wilfredo Lam Art Center during the 10th edition of the Havana Biennial when Cuban-American performance artist Tania Bruguera presented a piece entitled *El susurro de Taitlín* (Taitlín's whisper). Bruguera's performance was an exact reenactment of Fidel Castro's first speech after his entrance to Havana on January 1959, with the difference that open microphones were available at the podium for one minute of freedom of expression granted to anyone in the audience. Several cyberactivists and other citizens used their minute to proclaim Cuba—as Claudia Cadelo expressed—a "country where freedom of expression one day will not have to be a performance."[17]

Several mass public demonstrations have been coordinated through the blogosphere and promoted by the different blogs of *Voces Cubanas*, such as the *Marcha por la no violencia* (March for non-violence) of November 7, 2009, where over 200 citizens demonstrated peacefully along main Havana avenues and which resulted in the beating and illegal detention of Sánchez and Pardo Lazo by agents of the Cuban secret police. In June 2012, *Voces Cubanas* organized, promoted, and funded the "Festival CLIC," a three-day open fair to stimulate the use of new technologies among citizens, which was described by the official site *Cubadebate* as the first step toward developing an infrastructure for a military aggression against Cuba by the U.S.[18]

Voces Cubanas also reached out to support different independent civic initiatives such the *Union Patriótica de Cuba* (Cuban Patriotic Union, UNPACU), led by José Daniel Ferrer (one of the journalists formerly imprisoned during the *Primavera Negra* events of 2003) and *Las damas de blanco* (Ladies in White), a group created after the *Primavera Negra* by female relatives of political prisoners. *Las damas de blanco* protest the violation of human rights in Cuba by silently marching throughout Havana. Since 2010, cyberactivists from *Voces Cubanas* and other independent blogs collaborated to intensify and divulge the marches of *Las damas de blanco* and attract more supporters from the Cuban population and the international community. In numerous instances, members of *Las damas de blanco* have been violently harassed by secret police forces during their peaceful protests. Images and videos from these violations have been posted online by cyberactivists and citizens, generating even more support abroad. In 2013, Berta Soler, the leader of *Las damas de blanco* who had been detained during the 2012 visit of Pope Benedict XVI to Cuba, was able to meet with Pope Francis and U.S Vice President Joe Biden during a world tour.

On December 10, 2012, bloggers from *Voces Cubanas* collaborated with members of *Estado de SATS*—an autonomous organization founded in 2010 by physicist Antonio Rodiles to foment civic engagement—to cosponsor the "Feria de proyectos independientes" (Fair of Independent Projects) as part of a massive celebration for Human Rights Day. This event, which was promoted and coordinated online, was free and open to the public and brought together over 100 independent artists, performers, cyberactivists, and representatives from independent libraries and human rights organizations based in Cuba. Many citizens also participated in the celebration, mostly directed at informing the Cuban population.

With a prominent online presence through sites like *Facebook*, *Twitter,* and their own blog in *Voces Cubanas*, *Estado de SATS* has organized open free cultural events in Havana—such as the September 2012 panel "Literatura en libertad" (Literature in freedom) presented by Pardo Lazo—which are attended by interested citizens. The organization also has hosted public showings and discussions of censored films through their series "Cine a toda costa" (Film at any cost), where citizens can participate freely. Most events hosted by *Estado de SATS* are also recorded on video and later circulated independently through blogs and memory sticks. As philosopher Alex Jardines, cofounder of *Estado de SATS*, has explained, the project rejects the notion of *Cubanía* as an organizing and discriminatory concept for the future of Cuban society and advocates for the plurality of ideas.[19]

Estado de SATS has also been the principal organization behind "Demanda ciudadana por otra Cuba" (Citizen Demand for Another Cuba), an online campaign promoted on their blog and in coordination with *Voces Cubanas* that calls for "full respect for citizens regardless of their ideas or their political-social actions."[20] In December 2013, *Estado de SATS* also organized and promoted the "Primer Encuentro Internacional de Derechos Humanos y Pactos de la ONU" (First International Meeting on Human Rights and UN Covenants), an event convoked online featuring panels, an art exhibit with the theme "Art and Human Rights," and a concert by Cuban musicians Boris Larramendi (now a U.S. resident). The event was heavily repressed by the Cuban authorities, and dozens of activists, artists, and citizens were arrested, including Antonio Rodiles, the leader of *Estado de SATS*. The meeting, in fact, had been coordinated online as part of the national demonstrations for the Human Rights Day in 2013 to be held by different dissident groups across the county. The government had warned cyberactivists and demonstrators that "the Cuban people would respond to any attempts against socialism, whether online or in the streets,"[21] a threat that ironically resulted in the arrests of more than 130 members of *Las Damas de blanco* and dozens of members of the *UNPACU* and *Movimiento Cristiano de Liberación*, not only in Havana, but also in towns in Santiago de Cuba and Las Tunas.[22]

Cuba's transition into a more democratic system will not rest solely on the contestatory potential of social networks. However, independent cyberactivists have provided a radical reworking of conventional political bodies of action as the dialogues among art, political thought, human and civil rights activists, the exile community, and Cuban citizens are now facilitated by these cultural and social networks. Sites like *Voces Cubanas* were instrumental to the renewal of a shared feeling of empowerment and responsibility, especially for young Cubans. As blogger Miriam Celaya has expressed in her essay *"Internet, ¿vale o no vale?"* (Internet: good or not?), published in 2012 in her blog: "Nothing is more dangerous to a decrepit dictatorship than the hope reborn in a zombie people." Like Celaya, most Cuban independent cyberactivists adhere to a fearless ethical position of "no surrender," which generates in the people the type of agency necessary against the historical conflict between self-expression and self-preservation in a repressive regime like Cuba. The problem posed to political authorities by organizations like *Estado de SATS* or *Voces Cubanas* is no longer solely the impossibility to censure the free flow of information or the outmoded inoperability of the discourse of *Cubanía*, but an intense rebirth of civic action in Cuba coordinated and propelled through an expanding cybernetwork.

Notes

1 Media scholar Cristina Venegas traces Internet debates in Cuba as early as 1992. For Venegas, the conflict over Internet access centers on three issues: the state's economic and cultural development plans, the U.S. sanctions against Cuba that limit the island's capacity for access, and the limited freedom for individuals to access the Internet. For more specific data on Internet freedom on the island, see the 2012 report by *Freedom House*, which places Cuba second among 165 countries in the world with respect to government restriction to Internet access.

2 In 2011, sociologist Ted Henken reported over 1,000 blogs dedicated to Cuban issues. According to Henken, they can be roughly grouped in three major areas: foreign blogs written by the Cuban exile community, "official" blogs produced by the Cuban authorities and blogs somehow connected to state institutions (Universities, etc.), and independent blogs written from Cuba, mostly hosted in overseas servers.

3 On March 11, 2011, for instance, the state television series "Las razones de Cuba" (Cuba's Reasons) broadcasted an episode entitled "La ciberguerra" where several independent bloggers were singled out as "mercenaries."

4 See the chapter dedicated to Cuba on the 2012 report by Freedom House.

5 The strategy can be traced back to the 1990s, when the Cuban government was forced to reenter global economic systems after the fall of socialism in Eastern Europe. Notions of *Cubanía* (or what it meant to be Cuban after 1989) envisioned the political limits of the new "Cuban nation" around cultural discourses, as the government co-opted some nonconformist expressions (literature, film, visual arts) and boosted its popularity by becoming the sponsoring body of a new and more inclusive dimension of Cuban popular and lettered culture. As noted by Cuban historian Rafael Rojas, in 1992 the Cuban Constitution was rewritten specifically to reassert the State's hegemony as the gatekeeper of cultural identity (Rojas, 440–445).

6 *Voces Cubanas* began in 2004 with the online project *Consenso* (Consensus), which was established in the domain *desdecuba.com* through a server in Berlin, Germany. It was conceived as a virtual space to develop journalism by Cuban citizens and was run by an editorial board formed by independent journalists Reinaldo Escobar, Miriam Celaya, and Eugenio Leal—among others. In 2006, *Consensus* changed its name to *Contodos* (Together), with Yoani Sánchez working as the website's administrator. In April 2007, Sánchez's blog *Generación Y* emerged out of *Contodos* and gained much international visibility. By 2008, the blogger had won the *Premio Ortega y Gasset* in digital journalism awarded by the Spanish newspaper, *El país*, and had been listed 31st among *Time* magazine's 100 most influential figures. Sánchez has continued to accumulate awards and has published two books about her experience with cyberactivism. In 2013, *Generación Y* was available in over fifteen languages worldwide and received over a million hits every month.

7 Payá Sardiñas had been the leader of the *Movimiento de Liberación Cristiano* (Christian Liberation Movement) and the main force behind the 1998 "Proyecto Varela" (Varela Project). The campaign advocated for several democratic political reforms within Cuba, free elections being the main issue. It was based on article 88 of the Cuban Constitution of 1976, which allowed citizens to propose laws if 10,000 signatures by registered Cuban voters supported the proposal. The project was successful but was never given consideration by the Cuban National Assembly, and the government resolved to amend the Constitution, making permanent the socialist nature of the Cuban state. Payá Sardiñas's suspicious death in a car accident on July 2012 is still pending investigation, and the Cuban government refuses to address the circumstances of the accident with the international community.

8 Before the banning of *Boring Home*, Pardo Lazo's fiction had been consistently printed by state publishing houses, and the writer had been an influential figure of Cuban literature on the Internet. Per a personal interview with Pardo Lazo in August 2009, no official explanation was ever given to him for the banning of *Boring Home,* other than his involvement with independent cyberactivists. In 2010, the book was published by the Czech publisher Garamond, which also awarded Pardo Lazo the *Premio Novela de Gaveta Franz Kafka* given to censored authors.

9 See Pardo Lazo's online novel *Esta no es la novela de la revolución* (This is not the novel of the revolution) in his blog *Lunes de post-revolución.*

10 I am grateful to Esther Whitfield for facilitating the manuscript of her text "From Boarding Home to Boring Home: Photo-blogs and the Re-Mapping of Exile," presented at V Transatlantic Conference at Brown University, on April 2010.

11 See Henken.

12 In my recent experience in Cuba, computers are sold by state corporations for approximately $800 and about $600 in the black market. Computers and other equipment are also brought into Cuba by many visiting exiles and Cubans returning from medical missions and other state sponsored exchanges. Internet rates in authorized establishments, however, range from $8 to $12 per hour for dial-up connections. The average monthly salary of a Cuban citizen is equivalent to $20.

13 According to Hernández Busto, the *Universidad de las Ciencias Informáticas* (University of Informational Sciences, UCI), an educational complex founded in 2002 with plans to boost Cuba's economy as a software giant, instead has been the headquarters of government commentators against independent cyberactivists.

14 See Sánchez's "Reflections on Pope Benedict's Visit to Cuba" in her *Huffington Post* column.

15 My parenthesis. See Hernández Busto's analysis.

16 This was the case, for instance, with the literature of the 1990s, written by authors who still resided in Cuba, such as Pedro Juan Gutiérrez and Leonardo Padura Fuentes. Highly descriptive of the crisis of Cuban society (hunger, violence, corruption, urban ruins), these books were being sold around the world in what was known as the Cuban literary boom of the 1990s. In Cuba, however, they were pigeonholed into generic categories that became part of the new gallery of *Cubanía*. For Gutiérrez (*Trilogía sucia de la Habana*, 1998; *El Rey de la Habana*, 1999), his raw fiction was considered the Cuban contribution to Latin American dirty realism. Padura's work (*Pasado perfecto*, 1991; *Máscaras*, 1997), which revisited Cuba's censorship of artists and homosexuals during the 1970s, was casted as the rebirth of the Cuban detective thriller.

17 See the video of Bruguera's performance.

18 See the editorial "La inocenCIA imposible del Festival Clic" from June 12, 2012, on the *Cubadebate* site.

19 See Jardines's essay "La conspiración al descubierto: ¿quiénes están detrás de Estado de SATS?"

20 On June 2012, the campaign submitted a petition with 500 signatures to the Cuban National Assembly, calling on the government to ratify the *International Covenant on Civil and Political Rights* and the *International Covenant on Economic, Social and Cultural Rights*, signed by Cuban officials at the United Nations in 2008.

21 See the entry by Henríquez Lagarde "Día Internacional de los Derechos Humanos: ¿Guerra Fría o guerra de cuarta generación?" in the official blog *Cuba, isla mía*.

22 See the report by *Diario de Cuba* from December 12, 2013.

Works Cited

Celaya, Miriam. "Internet, ¿vale o no vale?" *Sin EVAsion*, June 4, 2012. www.desdecuba.com/sin_evasion/?p=2054. Accessed 17 Dec. 2013.

Cubadebate. "La inocenCIA imposible del Festival Clic". *Cubadebate*, June 20, 2012. www.cubadebate.cu/especiales/2012/06/20/editorial-la-inocencia-imposible-del-festival-clic/#. WVPt_OmP6Uk. Accessed 17 Dec. 2013.

Fusco, Coco. "Cuban Dissidence in the Age of Political Simulacra." *Emisférica*, 10.2, Summer 2013. http://hemisphericinstitute.org/hemi/en/e-misferica-102/e-102-dossier-cuban-dissidence-in-the-age-of-political-simulacra. Accessed 17 Dec. 2013.

Estado de SATS. "Demanda ciudadana por otra Cuba," June 21, 2012. www.estadodesats.com/tag/por-otra-cuba. Accessed 17 Dec. 2013.

Diario de Cuba. "Arrestos, golpizas, asaltos a viviendas: el saldo del régimen," December 12, 2013. www.diariodecuba.com/derechos-humanos/1386759276_6296.html. Accessed 17 Dec. 2013.

Freedom House. "Freedom on the net: A Global Assessment of Internet and Digital Media". *Freedom House*, 24 Sept. 2012. https://freedomhouse.org/sites/default/files/Freedom%20OnThe%20Net_Full%20Report.pdf. Accessed 17 Dec. 2013.

Hernández Busto, Ernesto. "Cyberdissidence, information and activism in today's Cuba." *Penúltimos Días*, June 27, 2012. www.penultimosdias.com/2012/11/27/cyberdissidence-information-and-activism-in-todays-cuba. Accessed 17 Dec. 2013.

Henríquez Lagarde, Manuel. "Día Internacional de los Derechos Humanos": Guerra Fría o guerra de cuarta generación?" *Cuba, Isla mía*, December 6, 2013. https://islamiacu.blogspot.com/2013/12/dia-internacional-de-los-derechos.html. Accessed 17 Dec. 2013.

Henken, Ted. "Una cartografía de la blogósfera cubana. Entre «oficialistas» y «mercenarios»"*Nueva sociedad* No 235, septiembre–octubre 2011. 90–109.

Jardines, Alexis. "La conspiración al descubierto: ¿quiénes están detrás de Estado de SATS?". *Penúltimos días*, May 29, 2012. www.penultimosdias.com/2012/05/29/la-conspiracion-al-descubierto-quienes-estan-detras-de-estado-de-sats. Accessed 17 Dec. 2013.

Pardo Lazo, Orlando Luis. "Esta no es la novela de la revolución". *Lunes de Post-revolución*, January 23, 2011. http://orlandoluispardolazo.blogspot.com/2011/01/esta-no-es-la-novela-dela-revolucion-3.html. Accessed 17 Dec. 2013.

Rojas, Rafael. *Tumbas Sin Sosiego. Revolución Disidencia y Exilio del Intelectual Cubano*. Barcelona: Anagrama, 2006.

Sánchez, Yoani. "Reflections on Pope Benedict's Visit to Cuba" *Huffington Post*, August 26, 2012. www.huffingtonpost.com/yoani-sanchez/pope-visit-cuba_b_1830931.html. Accessed 17 Dec. 2013.

"Tania Bruguera - El Susurro de Tatlin 2009. 10ma Bienal de La Habana," *Youtube*. Uploaded by latierraenmarte, September 11, 2009. www.youtube.com/watch?v=B3KOV26APlM. Accessed 17 Dec. 2013.

Venegas, Cristina. *Digital Dilemmas: The State, the Individual, and Digital Media in Cuba*. New Brunswick, NJ: Rutgers U P, 2010.

Whitfield, Esther. "From Boarding Home to Boring Home: Photo-blogs and the Re-Mapping of Exile." Paper presented at V Transatlantic Conference, Brown University, Providence RI. April 9, 2010.

11 From Wounds to Healing

Transborder *Testimonios* through Cyberspace Post-September 11, 2001

Claire Joysmith

From my particular "situated knowledge" (Haraway, 1988) vantage point—that is to say, an academic situated in Central Mexico, focusing on U.S. Latina/o and Mexican cultural and literary poetics, politics, and translation—I was deeply moved, highly disturbed, and overly intrigued by the gamut of responses and discursivities that emerged *vis-à-vis* events on and shortly after September 11, 2001.[1]

This event and its immediate ripple effects became a discursive gap, a dramatic moment of rupture, in which agency was called for in new ways for new times, which also afforded a singular opportunity to document and frame—eventually compile—polyvocal narratives that would contribute to and delve into the complexity and contestatory nature of identity politics contextualized within the specificity of a transborder wounds/healing, objective/subjective, personal/collective testimonial framework by using cyberspace as a key means of communication, expression, and exchange. The term transborder, in this particular Project, includes the aim "to shape incipient post-September 11, 2001 collectivities." I refer to it as "[encompassing] a border-transcending flux and fluidity that offers potential spaces for mobile positionings, situated knowledges, and polyvocal framed narratives" (Joysmith, 2008, 35).

In this sense, the perspectives gathered were to provide a tangible means of approaching an emergent profile of how local/global cultural experiences/products might be "negotiated" (Bhabha). Needless to say, the Internet was to play a major role in this Project.

I will briefly explore here several central issues related to this transborder monolingual, bilingual, and interlingual Project begun as a collaborative process at the UNAM in Mexico City, at the CISAN,[2] which has led to over a decade of related research and a variety of publications, the most outstanding of which are two volumes that add up to almost 1,000 book pages and the inclusion of almost 200 *Testimonio* and a webpage, in addition to a range of related meetings, conferences, readings, and sustained Internet webbing, all of which have had a decided impact across borders in *Las Americas* and beyond. In this sense, I will be necessarily addressing the role played by cyberspace in creating a transnational, or what I call a transborder, collectivity that contributed to creating, as I will refer to presently, what might be referred to tentatively as a polyvocal discourse at a time in which, as *Testimonio* contributer Gustavo Geirola expressed it, "Parece que no hay palabra ni frase, no hay discurso que pueda dar cuenta del referente" ["There seems to be no word, no phrase, no discourse that can account for its referent"] (Joysmith and Lomas, 2005, 166) or as Norma Elia Cantú wrote, "I who believe in the power of words and the way of peace cannot find the words to stop the killing" (Joysmith and Lomas, 2005, 121).

The polyphonic Testimonio tradition[3] was followed by resorting to a multivoiced textuality that brought together diverse perspectives by witnesses—through mass media and the Internet—of an event of global consequence and its aftermath. Although this Project was to produce a somewhat eclectic collectivity sharing a "commonality in singularity" (Beverley, 2004, 27) and appealing to the solidarity practices of the testimonial narrative that aspires "not only to interpret the world, but also to change it," (Beverley, 2004, xvi) it was also framed as a call to "do work that matters" (Anzaldúa, 2005, 102), a major inspiration in this Project that proved to be a long-term one.

Internet-Sent-and-Received Call for Responses

The spaces provided by the Internet as a readily available border-crossing technology *par excellence* were adopted, even as the malleability of the Testimonio genre as a framing device was adapted. The participants' access to the Internet, facing computers from varied geographical "situated knowledge" spaces, writing with a participative volition, proved vital to the Project by allowing it, for instance, to move beyond certain temporal-spatial constraints imposed on former *Testimonio* mediators. In addition, the Internet offered an immediacy lending itself to the "situation of urgency" (Beverley, 2008, 81) that characterizes *Testimonio* in providing a unique space for oral forms and written variants to be concurrently transmuted into testimonial writings sent by contributors through the Internet.[4]

The Call for Responses, sent out shortly after September 11, 2001, included questions as starting points for personal narratives.[5] The result was an unexpected number and range of poignant, precise, emotive, critical, creative, insightful, as well as sensitive and intelligently informed, personal narratives revealing a "cultural citizenship" (Rosaldo; Flores and Benmayor) concerned with crossing national boundaries—in this case, through Cyberspace—when responding to both regional and global issues of impact at the time. These testimonial writings were to lay bare the undeniable disparity between pre- and Post-September 11, 2001 paradigms, positionalities, and discursivities.

These personal narratives were originally intended to be posted for immediate distribution through the Internet, although after some time and much give and take, they were eventually accepted for paper publication, one of the reasons being copyright issues. This led to the publication of *One Wound For Another/Una herida por otra. Testimonios de Latin@s through Cyberspace (11 de septiembre de 2001–11 de marzo de 2002)*, with prologue by Elena Poniatowska. This volume elicited in turn a wide range of responses, thereby extending the Project to a follow-up stage that included a second Call sent five years later (September 11, 2006). The outcome was a second volume titled *Speaking desde las Heridas. Ciber-testimonios Transfronterizos/Transborder (September 11, 2001-March 11, 2007)*, with transborder prologue by John Beverley (U.S.), Cristina Rivera Garza (Mexico), and Maria Antònia Oliver-Rotger (Barcelona, Spain). Finally, an Internet site (www.Speakingdesdelasheridas.wordpress.com) was created to include sections of both volumes and other related material, as was the original intention, cyberspace being the main medium of our times. Ten years into Post-September 11, 2001, a third stage/Call was launched, the results of which were posted directly on the website.

The transition from the Project's original aim—focusing mainly on U.S. Latinos/as, as well as Mexicans who experienced events in the U.S. at the time—to a widened scope of participants was reflected in the range of responses from across the *Américas*, including Canada and Europe, since the Atocha bombings in Madrid (March 11, 2004) had brought Europe into the picture. The aim was to frame and cull extended transborder transcultural expressions that might articulate possibilities in remapping affiliations and cultural citizenship, as well as elicit and effect potential agency. Documented in *Speaking desde las heridas,* in several of the *Testimonios*, this material was included in the aforementioned website.

Cyber and Mass Media Witnessing

Cyber- and mass media-witnessed events on and shortly after September 11, 2001 resulted in a large number of people being globally initiated, perhaps unwittingly, into an unprecedented role. Although some became *in situ* witnesses whose experience was framed, for instance, by home or hotel windows, most contributors took part in this massive witnessing act through framing devices such as television or computer screens. This same act continued, through replay and reframing, using a diversity of techno-devices, time and again after the events themselves had taken place. In a short temporal lapse, the Internet and mass media inducted millions more into this same unwitting witnessing role. Needless to say, however, this was before social networks such as Facebook, Twitter, and others became more widely spread as of circa 2002, interestingly very shortly after September 11, 2001.

Those participants who responded to the contents of the Call for Responses and the identity politics evoked were cognizant they were acquiescing to become part of a responding collectivity and thereby participating in the specificity of the Project by means of their spontaneous testimonial written narratives sent through the Internet.

Testimonio, referred to as "the small voice of history" by Ranajit Guja (Beverley, 2004, xii, 27), has a long-standing trajectory in recovering and documenting lost or untold stories based on historical events affecting entire communities. It has come to be recognized as a spontaneous, oral narrative expression, an "affirmation of the individual self in the collective mode" (Beverley, 2004, 35) recounted by a witness "moved to narrate by the urgency of the situation" (Yúdice, 1991, 17), thereby becoming an agent within a specific region or nation-state boundary.

The immediate responses to the Internet-sent Call provided multiple instances of incipient interpretative versions and/or articulations of subjective reactions to a moment of rupture, providing an opportunity to disclose histories and narratives long under erasure in any mode of wide-reaching expression.

Transborder Narratives and Wounds

The seed of what was to grow into a long-term Project was, in fact, an unsettling yet precise personal and academic experience of discursive dislocation that I perceived to be illustrated by two major narratives that I encountered shortly after September 11, 2001, which expressed metonymically two diametrically opposed and complex discourses in visible conflict.

The first was articulated by an UNAM janitor, who gleefully expressed: "¡Se lo merecían!" ("They deserved it!"), a perspective cited in the Introduction to both volumes and which would echo throughout Latin America, indeed globally, and was reflected in several testimonial writings sent through the Internet, such as this one:

> Según encuestas recientes, después de Cuba, Argentina es el país con mayor sentimiento antiestadunidense del continente que nosotros llamamos América...
>
> Muchos—algunas de mis más queridas amigas, por ejemplo— decían cosas como ésta:
>
> —Me alegro...Por fin saben lo que es.
>
> Traduzco: ellos, los Estados Unidos
>
> (Averbach, 2008, 127–128)

[According to recent polls, Argentina, after Cuba, is the country with the greatest anti-United States sentiments in the entire continent we call *América*...

Many –some of my dearest friends, for example—said such things as: "I'm glad...At last they know what it's like.

I translate: they, the United States.]

Narratives such as these, rooted in complex historical wounds, revealed a lack of awareness that although the U.S. corporate and military power symbols were targeted, those who in fact died were mostly immigrants, documented or otherwise, many of them from Latin America. Moreover, umbrella terms commonly used (*estadunidenses, norteamericanos, "gringos"*) did not account for the active presence in the U.S. of dissenters and disenfranchised, of a multicultural, multiethnic diversity and of long-term struggles by people of color, including U.S. Latinos/as, Chicanos/as, and Mexicans living in the U.S.

The second narrative, the Bushian "[e]ither you are with us or against us" also crossed myriad borders, its ripple effect global. It unfolded into extremes, exponentially expanding the (re)production of fear, xenophobic paranoia, and (im)migrant targeting; the shifting of the semiotic territory of "terrorists" to dark-complexioned, Arab-seeming foreigners and (im)migrants (Anzaldúa, 2005, 96–97; Gómez Peña, 2008) extended to racial profiling practices applied to Latin Americans in general, as well as U.S. Latinos/as and Chicanos/as. As Gómez Peña wrote: "In 2003...a Palestinian friend told me: 'We (Arabs) are the new Mexicans, and by extension, you are all Arabs.'" (2008, 302)

Although both narratives could be seen as myopic knee-jerk reactions to previously inflicted personal and collective woundings, other voices were at the time also attempting to make themselves heard through the Internet and alternative media. The aim thus became to gather, also through the Internet, diverse voices that might articulate—by means of testimonial personal narratives[6] as potential forms of cultural healing practices—perspectives sensitive to the complexities involved and cognizant of their role in incipient/established communities. In short, the aforementioned appeal through a Call for Responses through the Internet, to participate in a bridge-building collectivity-in-the-making, was sent.

Heridas abiertas: Webbing, Healing, and Bridging

A major axis in this Project was to (ad)dress the Anzaldúan *herida abierta,* or open wound. As Chicana cultural philosopher, essayist, writer, and poet Gloria Anzaldúa[7] wrote: "The U.S.-Mexican border *es una herida abierta* where the third world grates against the first and bleeds" (Anzaldúa, 1987, 3). September 11, 2001 became a "wounding [that] opened like a gash" (Anzaldúa, 2005, 92), multiplying the *herida abierta,* expanding it beyond the specificity of the México-U.S. border.[8]

On the cusp of a moment of rupture of global consequence, Anzaldúa's "imperative to 'speak' esta herida abierta" (2005, 93) became a major motivation for this cyberspace-oriented Project, grounded in Anzaldúan iconography and theoretical framing. It seemed particularly poignant and relevant that the Anzaldúan *herida abierta* should also entail a utopic Post-September 11, 2001 wound-scar-bridge transmutation, tracing cultural healing practices bridging people, communities, and collectivities across borders. As she sustained in her *Testimonio*-essay (sent through the Internet for this Project and included in the volume *One Wound for Another*), wounds/*heridas* can be 'transshaped' (2005, 102) into *cicatrices*/scars and bridges: "We are all wounded but we can connect through the wound that's alienated us from others," since "[w]hen the wound forms a cicatrize, [sic] the scar can become a bridge linking people split apart" (2005, 102).

U.S. Latinos/as and Mexicanidades

U.S. Latinos/as—the largest so-called minority group (52 million) in the U.S.—have historically grappled with and transcended issues entailing a sense of geographic space limited by nation-state boundaries. They have also developed highly complex multiple and shifting identities, in addition to contestatory articulated discursivities. A majority has experienced numerous "borderlands" (Anzaldúa, 1987) within the U.S., whether as members of well-established communities with a historical trajectory of contested citizenship, such as Mexicans and Puerto Ricans, or as more recently arrived "economic refugees" (Anzaldúa, 1987, 11) from Mexico and other parts of Latin America. Their transnational movements have often been due to political circumstances prior to and during economic globalization, thereby making them sensitive, for instance, to the reality of other dates marked by political violence and trauma.

A key component of populations often self-identified as U.S. Latinos/as is the fact that "they have always been and continue to be constructed by themselves and others in the context of both international and U.S. historical referents" (Oboler, 1995, xiv). These constructed identities also include a sense of cultural citizenship created through historical struggles for civil and human rights. Whereas certain aspects of Latino/a cultures have been popularized for commercial purposes, both within the U.S. and transnationally, their histories still remain on the whole under erasure.

Paramount to the context of this Project, however, particularly in the second and third stages, was the Call made extensive to Latin Americans, *latinoamericanos/as*, often self-referred to in Spanish as *latinos*, differing from the term U.S. Latino/a, mostly translated in Spanish-speaking countries as *latino(a)estadunidense*, integrating a cultural referent and, often, a political one. The term *latinidades* in the U.S. has been adapted from the definition provided by the collective that produced *Telling to Live: Latina Feminist Testimonios* in providing an inclusionary scope relevant to the Project.[9] Contributors often included themselves by positioning their multiple identities in direct cultural alliance with that of *latinidades* by virtue of their lived experience in a racialized U.S.

The term *mexicanidades*, used in the plural instead of the common blanketing term mexicano/a, underscores a diversity often unacknowledged/ unaddressed discursively that refers to Mexican identities marked by race, ethnicity, and class (Joysmith, 2001, 2008). It remains to be seen, and only time can tell, whether all of the aforementioned will alter due to the effects of widespread Internet usage in Mexico, in particular, and in Latin America, in general.

Identity and Language Cartographies

As a means of documenting ways in which contributors identified as cross-border subjects—particularly since they were experientially sensitized to the full implications of self-naming and acquiesced to respond to such cues as U.S. Latinos, *latinidades, mexicanidades,* transborder—a brief self-descriptive entry was requested, zoning in mainly on genealogies and linguistic practices, appended to each testimonial piece.

The outcome might well be considered as a tentative identity cartography of participants through the Internet, offering insights into a range of genealogies, diasporic trajectories, diverse linguistic practices, a wide range of geocultural spatial mobile positionings, revealing transborder, hybrid, mestizo, mixed heritage, cross-cultural, multiple, and shifting identities, many of them in the making.[10]

Moreover, every narrative was reproduced, untranslated, unmediated, in the language it was written and sent through the Internet, whether English or Spanish, bilingual or interlingual.[11] This was intended to enhance the visibility of complex issues related to everyday realities and linguistic practices shaping the contributors' bilingual and bi-/multicultural experiences and expressions. Needless to say, the choice of language(s) to express core emotions became highly significant, the implications being not only linguistic, cultural, and social, but also political, in this sense pinpointing the "bridging" across languages as intrinsic to the Project.

"Commonality in Singularity"

A shared common belief from the outset was that perhaps through communication, catharsis, creativity—through the very act of producing *Testimonio* itself—the wounds inflicted by events on and Post-September 11, 2001 might find ways to begin some kind of healing process within the scope of the Project 's framework, implicating a "commonality in singularity" (Beverley, 2004, 27). The response to the need to "'talk' from the wound's gash" (Anzaldúa, 2005, 93) was to lead to a collectivity that "clearly shares some basic assumptions about, and affective responses to, what is happening in the world, and that has the capacity for collective action" (Beverley, 2008, 77).

Partly because the initial 2001 Call was sent to immediately available listservs that included academics, educators, activists, artists, writers, poets, journalists, and other professionals who responded to the U.S. Latino signifier, these communities have been represented more than others. Nevertheless, the immediate responses by contributors integrating this eclectic collectivity seem to indicate that they found their voices unheard and that they experienced exclusion to varying degrees in Post-September 11, 2001, within the context of local and national politics, media coverage, and violence-related events of global consequence. As Beverley points out in the "Transborder Prologue" to *Speaking desde las heridas* (in which three different voices from Mexico, the U.S., and Europe participated),[12] when referring to the collectivity in the volume:

> We are not speaking for an other, or allowing an other to speak for itself. We are speaking for ourselves. But this simply means that the question of our relation to a subaltern other has changed from an *ethical* to a *political* one. We are all in some way subaltern in the face of reactionary violence.
>
> (Beverley, 2008, 81)

Magnified Scope through the Internet

Although the Internet, as both product and reproducer of economic globalization, might be regarded as yet one more neocolonizing space within the "cultural logic of late capitalism" (Jameson 38) and even though in Cyberspace "the virtue of articulation—i.e. the power to produce connection—threatens to overwhem and finally to engulf all possibility of effective action to change the world" (Haraway, 2004, 107), it is also true that despite its "degrees of semiotic freedom," it "is hardly infinitely open" (Haraway, 2004, 311). Given, as Haraway adds, that "[w]e *are all* in chiasmatic borderlands, liminal areas where new shapes, new kinds of action and responsibility, are gestating in the world," (90) cyberspace became not merely a readily available tool but also an essential one for the testimonial framing device of this long-term Project.

In addition to this Project's contribution as a documented resource of historic value, it might well also stake a claim to an ultimately immeasurable, yet continually multipliable resonance, such as that expounded by the "butterfly effect," that is, "tiny differences [that] can be magnified by time, space, and impinging variables, into huge effects" (Fleishman, 1999, 135). In this sense, the technological analogy to the Internet can be somewhat applied. An ideal of this effect would, of course, resonate with reproduced harmony and understanding. It should be added that responses gleaned from multiple public, academic, and artistic forums, as well as publications, that span over a decade are indicators of such resonances across borders.[13] No doubt, the Internet has contributed to situated knowledge bridging of national and cultural identities, language issues, as well as local versus global spaces in this Project.

Anzaldúa writes, in her testimonial essay in *One Wound for Another*, that "the healing of our wounds results in transformation and transformation resuls in the healing of our wounds" (2005, 100), yet she is wise to caution: "[t]here is no resolution, only the process of healing" (2005, 100). She nevertheless reminds us of the ongoing responsibility and need to respond actively, individually, and collectively: "May we do work that matters" (2005, 102).

Time will perhaps be the best judge regarding the extent to which this collectivity—one that shares a "commonality in singularity" within the specificity of this ongoing transborder Project through the Internet—effects a virtual/real impact on what is known as the "Post-September 11, 2001 era," as well as the extent to which it may further appeal to agency and cultural healing practices in a "butterfly effect" perspective, through the Internet as a major flux and flow medium in our times.

Notes

1　This date is deliberately referred to in full instead of the abbreviated 9/11 and its literal translation into Spanish: S-11. It is intended mainly as a mark of due respect to other September 11 tragic and historic events (such as Chile, 1973).

2　Centro de Investigaciones Sobre América del Norte (CISAN) at the UNAM, Mexico City, in collaboration with Clara Lomas of The Colorado College, Colorado Springs, Colorado.

3　Elena Poniatowska's groundbreaking *La noche de Tlaltelolco* (1971) was from the outset a model in the multivoiced text tradition *vis-à-vis* individual responses to the same specific historic event and its immediate consequences; clearly, a major difference was that contributor *Testimonios* were sent through cyberspace and required no oral-to-written mediation.

4　The creative array of personal writings sent through Internet includes a variety of Internet-friendly forms, such as e-mail messages and personal letters, in addition to anecdotes, diaries and journals, autobiographic and confessional entries, memoirs, chronicles, journalistic writings, poetry, poetic prose, essays, short stories, mixed-genre and allegorical pieces, Testimonio collectives, an epigram, a transcript of an oral performance, as well as pictographic material and artwork. Some make use of cut-and-paste dynamics, collageing different forms into a single testimonial contribution.

5　These questions mainly zoned in on personal and observable experiential changes *vis-à-vis* a range of personal, political, professional, academic, spiritual experiences and healing practices; media impact, cultural and racial differences, development of peace politics, tolerance and compassion, creative and aesthetic challenges, reality/fiction chimeric boundaries, "us" versus "them" counter-dynamics, perspectives on migration, immigration, border restrictions, and Mexico-U.S. relations.

6　Mary Louise Pratt describes *Testimonio* as "auto-ethnography" (Beverley, 2004, xiii).

7　Her germinal *Bordelands/La Frontera. The New Mestiza* (Anzaldúa, 1987) was voted one of the 100 Best Books of the 20th century by *Hungry Mind*

Review and *Utne Reader*. According to Walter Mignolo, Anzaldúa's work has "articulated a powerful aesthetic, an alternative political hermeneutics" (Mignolo, 2000, 85).

8　Described in ways such as, to give a few poetic examples: "the magnetic field thrown off by grief"; "experimentamos muchas heridas en el momento en que la historia norteameriana se partió como las aguas en la Biblia" ["we experienced many woundings at the moment when North American history split open as did the seas in the Bible"]; "suspended in limbo in that in-between space, nepantla" (Anzaldúa, *One Wound*, 2005, 92); "Un milenio empezó con las Cruzadas/El otro con dos cifras:/9/11" [A millennium began with the Cruzades/the other with two numbers:/9/11].

9　"The national-ethnic identity categories did not encompass the actual diversity of Latinas, as they ignored difference in class backgrounds, religious traditions, sexual preferences, races, ages, cultural experiences, regional variations, and women of mixed or Native American heritage. Implicitly, we were challenging ideas about Latina identities based on nationality-ethnicity, as our group configuration attempted to reflect the complexity and multiple realities represented in our communities" (Latina Feminist Collective, 2001, 11).

10　For instance: "American of Mexican, Spanish, French and Comanche descent," "Cuban Eastern European Jewish American," "Peruana....tuve que emigrar a Estados Unidos," "Latina in the U.S.A., born in Costa Rica .... Mexican by will and by association," "Daughter of the borderlands, nacida en Nuevo Laredo, raised in Laredo, a Chicana," "half Chicana (my dad), half Jewish (my mom)...identify more as Latina in New York." These descriptions have been taken from cyber-sent-and-received *Testimonios* published mainly in *Speaking desde las heridas*.

11　"Interlinguism is a linguistic practice highly sensitive to the context of speech acts, able to shift add-mixtures of languages according to situational needs or the effects desired...[it] rejects the supposed need to maintain English and Spanish separate in exclusive codes, ... sees them as reservoirs of primary material to be molded together as needed, naturally" (Bruce-Novoa 50).

12　In *Speaking desde las heridas* (2008), Cristina Rivera-Garza (Mexico), John Beverley (U.S.), and Maria-Antònia Oliver-Rotger (Spain).

13　Such as *in situ* public—often bilingual—readings and book presentations of both volumes (in Mexico, the U.S., Canada, Brazil, and Spain) and in several transnational academic forums (LASA, NACCS). Its integration in course syllabi in Mexico and the U.S. (for instance, an international, interdisciplinary biannual video-conferenced diploma that reaches students in *Norteamérica* (Mexico, the U.S., and Canada, as well as a course on the effects of Internet on culture at the Tecnológico de Monterrey, te ITESM, in Toluca, Mexico). Additionally, both volumes were present at international book fairs (Mexico City Zocalo Annual Book Fair, Monterrey International Book Fair, Minería Book Fair in Mexico City), Cyberspace international academic forums, UNAM magazines and publications, both academic and nonacademic, among others. My essay "Nela Rio: el fluir hacia la paz transfronteriza" (2012) provides a description of several public, academic, and creative responses to the Project that have been published as an e-book. Derived from the Internet-based exchange initiated through the Project, several collaborative projects and publications have been proposed, some under way, some resulting in Internet-published items. An interesting recent (2013) and unexpected local effect has been the research project in a high school in Tepoztlán, Morelos, Mexico, for which the students were asked to read and summarize a book, locating it in a local/global context; one students chose to read the *Testimonios* in Spanish in *One Wound for Another/Una herida por otra*. My suggestion when I found out was that the results be shared on the Internet.

Works Cited

Anzaldúa, Gloria E. *Borderlands/La Frontera. The New Mestiza*. San Francisco, CA: aunt lute, 1987.

———. "Let Us Be the Healing of the Wound: The Coyolxauhqui Imperative La Sombra y el Sueño." *One Wound for Another/Una herida por otra. Testimonios de Latin@s in the U.S. through Cyberspace (11 de septiembre de 2001–11 de marzo de 2002)*. Ed. Claire Joysmith and Clara Lomas. Mexico City: Universidad Nacional Autónoma de México, Centro de Investigaciones Sobre America del Norte; The Colorado College; Whittier College, 2005. 92–103.

Averbach, Margara. "Desde la bañera." *Speaking desde las heridas. Cibertestimonios Transfronterizos/Transborder (September 11, 2001-March 11, 2007)*. Ed. Claire Joysmith. Transborder prologues by John Beverley (U.S.), Cristina Rivera Garza (Mexico) and Antònia Oliver-Rotger (Barcelona, Spain). Mexico City: Centro de Investigaciones Sobre América del Norte, CISAN, Universidad Nacional Autónoma de México, UNAM; Whittier College, California; Cátedra de Humanidades and Cátedra Alfonso Reyes, Instituto Tecnológico y de Estudios Superiores de Monterrey, Mexico, 2008. 127–131.

Beverley, John. "Prologue: The Small Voice of History." *Speaking desde las heridas. Cibertestimonios Transfronterizos/Transborder (September 11, 2001-March 11, 2007)*. Ed. Claire Joysmith. Transborder prologues by John Beverley (U.S.), Cristina Rivera Garza (Mexico) and Maria Antònia Oliver-Rotger (Barcelona, Spain). Mexico City: Centro de Investigaciones Sobre América del Norte, CISAN, Universidad Nacional Autónoma de México, UNAM; Whittier College, California; Cátedra de Humanidades, Instituto Tecnológico y de Estudios Superiores de Monterrey; Cátedra Alfonso Reyes, Instituto Tecnológico y de Estudios Superiores de Monterrey, Mexico, 2008. 77–82.

———. *Testimonio. On the Politics of Truth*. Minneapolis: U of Minnesota P, 2004.

Bhabha, Homi K. *The Location of Culture*. NewYork: Routledge, 2004.

Bruce-Novoa, Juan. *Retrospace: Collected Essays on Chicano Literature, Theory and History*. Houston, TX: Arte Público P, 1990.

Fleishman, Paul. M.D. *Karma and Chaos*. Seattle, WA: Vipassana Research Publications, 1999.

Flores, William V., and Rina Benmayor, editors. *Latino Cultural Citizenship. Claiming Identity, Space and Rights*. Boston, MA: Beacon P, 1997.

Gómez Peña, Guillermo. "Border Hysteria and the War against Difference." *Speaking desde las heridas. Cibertestimonios Transfronterizos/Transborder (September 11, 2001-March 11, 2007)*. Ed. Claire Joysmith. Transborder prologues by John Beverley (U.S.), Cristina Rivera Garza (Mexico) and Maria Antònia Oliver-Rotger (Barcelona, Spain). Mexico City: Centro de Investigaciones Sobre América del Norte, CISAN, Universidad Nacional Autónoma de México, UNAM; Whittier College, California; Cátedra de Humanidades y Cátedra Alfonso Reyes, Instituto Tecnológico y de Estudios Superiores de Monterrey, Mexico, 2008. 301–312.

Haraway, Donna. *The Haraway Reader*. New York: Routledge, 2004.

———. "Situated Knowledges." *Feminist Studies* 14.3 (Fall 1988): 575–599.

Jameson, Frederic. *Postmodernism, or the Cultural Logic of Late Capitalism*. Durham, NC: Duke UP, 1991.

Joysmith, Claire. "Crossing Ethnic and Cultural Boundaries. Translated Mexicanidades". *Raizes e rumos. Perspectivas interdisciplinares em estudos Americanos*. Nitéroi, Brazil: 7 Letras, Asociacao Brasileira de Estudos Americanos and Universidade Federal Fluminense, 2001. 427–434.

———. "Introduction: Cybertransborder Wound-Healing." *Speaking desde las heridas. Cibertestimonios Transfronterizos/Transborder (September 11, 2001-March 11, 2007)*. Ed. Claire Joysmith. Transborder prologues by John Beverley (U.S.), Cristina Rivera Garza (Mexico) and Maria Antònia Oliver-Rotger (Barcelona, Spain). Mexico City: Centro de Investigaciones Sobre América del Norte, CISAN, Universidad Nacional Autónoma de México, UNAM; Whittier College, California; Cátedra de Humanidades y Cátedra Alfonso Reyes, Instituto Tecnológico y de Estudios Superiores de Monterrey, Mexico, 2008. 15–42.

Joysmith, Claire and Clara Lomas, editors. "Introduction." *One Wound for Another. Una herida por otra. Testimonios de Latin@s in the U.S. through Cyberspace (11 de septiembre de 2001–11 de marzo 2002)*. Mexico City: Centro de Investigaciones sobre América del Norte, CISAN, Universidad Nacional Autónoma de México, UNAM; Colorado College, Colorado; Whittier College, California, 2005. 27–82.

———. "Nela Rio: el fluir hacia la paz transfronteriza." *Nela Rio. Escritura en foco: la mirada profunda*. Ed. Gabriela Etcheverry. Ottawa, ON: Qantati eBooks, 2012. 190–197.

Latina Feminist Collective. *Telling to Live: Latina Feminist Testimonios*. Durham, NC: Duke UP, 2001.

Mignolo, Walter D. *Local Histories/Global Designs: Coloniality, Subaltern Knowledges, and Border Thinking*. Princeton, NJ: Princeton UP, 2000.

Oboler, Suzanne. *Ethnic Labels, Latino Lives. Identity and the Politics of (Re) Presentation in the United States*. Minneapolis: U of Minnesota P, 1995.

Poniatowska, Elena. *La noche de Tlatelolco*. México: Era, 1971.

Rosaldo, Renato, editor. *Cultural Citizenship in Island Southeast Asia: Nation and Belonging in the Hinterlands*. Berkeley: U of California P, 2003.

Yúdice, George. "Testimonio and Postmodernism." *Latin American Perspectives. Voices of the Voiceless in Testimonial Literature*, Part I, 18.3 (Summer 1991): 15–31.

12 Cyberspace as a Tool for Political and Social Awareness

The Killings of Juárez

María R. Matz

The Internet is one of the pillars of what we know today as globalization. Its use as a relatively free and uncensored channel of communication has made information once considered private or difficult to access available to a greater number of users.[1] In the virtual world created by new technologies, the lines that rule space and time are constantly being broken and reshaped. The simulacrum of proximity results in bringing very different people together and, in certain contexts, it allows real communities to emerge. Some of these communities are reinventing civic activism and changing political processes in diverse global settings. Even more frequently, existing civic and social groups cultivate a presence in cyberspace that grows continually and extends their reach, allowing for debate, dialogue, and action to occur outside of their local limits.

Sociologist Roland Robertson describes how, in today's homogenized world, globality is customized to a local arena and, thanks to this adaptation, it is more likely to grow. Robertson refers to this process as "glocalization," and several studies have related this term to the use of the Internet in which the global impacts the local and vice versa, allowing specific individuals or, even more, social groups to post their local issues on the global cyberspace, giving them international visibility.[2]

With this virtual interplay between the global and the local in mind, I will analyze the use of the Internet as a medium for the denouncement for the killings of women and girls that began in 1993 in Ciudad Juárez, Chihuahua, Mexico and that in 2013, twenty years later, have appeared in other parts of the State of Chihuahua. These killings have been labeled as femicides, and following Diana Russell's definition of the term, it applies to "the killing of females by males *because* they are female."[3] In dealing with human rights, Rosa Linda Fregoso considers femicide to be Mexico's worst problem.

Shocked by the governmental lack of concern for these murders, the killings of Juárez have become a popular subject for cyberactivism. This chapter traces the ways in which the Internet has created a diverse community of activists working with the human rights issues of the two-decades-long epidemic killings of women. We only have to enter the words "women, Juárez, killings, femicide" in any search engine to get a quick idea of the controversy created by these murders. There are many websites and social media pages that denounce these femicides; several local and international organizations have created web pages in order to raise the awareness of the global community and to ask for funds that will help support their cause. In this vein, it might be helpful to quickly categorize the different purposes of the websites: expressions of grief, expressions of memory and memorializing, community building, fundraising, media publicity, and political influencing, among others. Nonetheless, we cannot forget that while cyberspace has contributed to the national and international awareness of these killings, the mothers and relatives still await justice for these young women and girls.

In our century, the nature of social mobilization is changing quickly; cyberactivism is a phenomenon in which many social groups are using the Internet to provide countergovernment data in what we can call glocal cyberactivism.[4] In other words, the created virtual reality awakens consciousness of the issues portrayed. Moreover, with the use of the Internet, "the mobilization of shame and in particular the framing of the Mexican state, as a *norm violating state* has yielded concrete results" (Fregoso 119). According to Fregoso, in 2003, the Spanish former judge Baltasar Garzón convened a seminar on gender violence in Spain in which he used a case of femicide in Juárez, and the documentary *Señorita Extraviada* by Lourdes Portillo was also screened (119–120).[5]

Meanwhile, the femicides started to be considered as crimes against humanity, and, as Alma Guillermoprieto wrote ten years ago in a letter to the *New Yorker*, which is available on the Internet, the kidnapping, torture, rape, and murder of women in Juárez represents:

> the most shameful human-rights scandal in Mexico's recent history: a string of brutal killings of young women which came to be called the Juarez murders, because they seemed to be confined—in the public imagination, at least—to one seedy border town.
>
> ("Letter from Mexico")

What Guillermoprieto calls a "seedy border town" has, since the beginning of the 1990s, evolved from a small border town between Mexico and the U.S. to the fourth most populated city in the whole country. A sprawling city, Juárez also includes a desert, which has become the final resting location for many of the killed women and girls.

Slowly but steadily, Ciudad Juárez has become one of the centers for Mexico's neoliberal globalization project. A key element in the growth of the city has been the NAFTA, signed by Canada, Mexico, and the U.S., which was enacted on January 1, 1994. Although *maquiladoras* [manufacturing factories] have existed in Mexico since the 1960s, the economic transformation of the area was set in motion, and "over the first six years after the onset of NAFTA, *maquiladora* employment grew

110 percent, compared with 78 percent over the previous six years" (Gruben 11).[6] Getting a job in one of the factories has allowed better opportunities for the workers; young women have been largely in high demand, as they receive a lower salary and work at a faster pace.[7]

As the Juárez population grew, the standardized killing and disappearing of young women and girls began. Hyper-sexism and strong misogyny have resulted in the failure of the Mexican federal government to seek out justice for the victims and their families. You, the reader, may use several of the many search engines available on cyberspace (Google, Yahoo, Bing, among others) and try to find an exact number of women and girls killed in Juárez. Various sites provide information; thousands of websites deal with the topic, but at the end of our search, it is clear that cyberspace is not a useful tool to get an accurate count of the victims.[8] According to the 2003 report of the *Inter-American Commission on Human Rights*, since the first murders in 1993, the number of killings grows with each year that passes. To this day, although there is no exact number, estimations of the deaths have been in the hundreds (Amnesty International, "Intolerable killings"), and "more than 100 of these murders can be classified as 'sexual homicides,' with victims having been raped, tortured, and, in many cases, mutilated. Scores of women have also disappeared without a trace" (Simmons 1).

All of these killings follow the same pattern: the victims are young (between 11 and 40 years old), students or workers at the *maquiladoras*, and have a similar physical appearance (slender physique, dark skin, shoulder-length dark hair, and "attractive" features). Again, many of these young women and girls have been kidnapped, tortured, raped, and murdered. Although some convictions have been made, the consensus in the cyberspace, as well as among the global/local community, is that to this date, the authorities have not identified or punished the real perpetrators.

The killings and disappearances are unfortunately still a common recurrence in the State of Chihuahua; just in January 23, 2013, the *Zocalo/Saltillo* online newspaper reported the disappearance of four women in five days. "Local and international non-governmental organizations (NGOs) have drawn attention to these incidents by organizing protests, conducting petition drives, and raising money for the victims' families" (Simmons 1). Moreover, in order to give global visibility to these killings, cyberspace has become a space that, for the mothers and family members of the victims, blurs the lines between public and private spheres.

In its 2003 report, the *Inter-American Commission on Human Rights* states how "family members ... received conflicting or confusing information from the authorities, and [were] treated dismissively or even disrespectfully or aggressively when they sought information about the investigations" (C.1.48). At the Federal and State level, as well as the local level of the government, the victims were blamed.[9] They were described as "loose women" that wore miniskirts, went out dancing and drinking, and were labeled as easy women or prostitutes. Government officials asserted that, as a result, these women got what they deserved (Inter-American Commission on Human Rights).[10] To counteract this statement, one recurrent strategy that we face in cyberspace is the portrayal of these women as innocent: photographs depict their innocence by showing them happy, usually smiling, and mostly wearing white.

The first person to acknowledge these murders was the Mexican activist Ester Chavez, who in 1993 had a newspaper column at the Juárez newspaper, *El Diario*, in which she started writing about the murders. In 1999, Chavez created the organization *Casa Amiga Centro de Crisis, A.C.* and in 2003 opened a shelter "where women were healed and empowered, taking on the authorities, often endangering their own lives" (Casa Amiga). In 2009, Ester Chavez passed away, but her legacy continues through the organization's website.[11] The group uses the Internet to get more attention to the victims of gender violence and to ask for donations. In the website's main page's top left corner, there is a link to the international online business PayPal, which allows payments and money transfers to be made through the Internet. Under the Paypal logo, a statement asking for donations is clearly visualized, as its background is grayish blue, while the rest of the page has a purple background.

On June 13, 2002, with the mission of finding both legal and social justice for the families of the victims, the organization *Nuestras hijas de regreso a casa* [Our Daughters On Their Way Home] established a blog.[12] On its top right side, there is a note indicating that this is the only official blog of the organization and that it was hacked in the past.[13] It is a very user-friendly site, with the main goal to communicate its mission in a clear and simple manner, as well as to facilitate access to as much information about the killings as possible. As one of the most comprehensive blogs of its kind, it lets cybercitizens know about the different activities that the association is involved in and disseminates news related to the femicides.

As a counterreaction to the incriminations made by the Mexican government that labeled the murdered women as prostitutes or "deviants," thus placing the blame on them, the title of the blog refers to the relationship between "mothers" and "daughters." Multiple civic and social groups use the concept of motherhood in their search for justice. It evolves from both the idea that there is no purer love than the maternal one from the intrinsic innocence of any child. The victims are daughters and often sisters, and their pictures haunt those who look at them in cyberspace. It is not the first time that the concept of motherhood is being used to show the innocence of the victims. One of the best examples is the Argentinean association *Madres de Plaza de Mayo* [Mothers of Plaza de Mayo], which demanded justice for their loved ones who disappeared in the hands of the military dictatorship, which ruled Argentina between

1976 and 1983. As Cynthia Bejarano states, it is through the use of technology that these mothers "[liberate] themselves and their children by becoming living altars... [as they allow] the world [to watch]...the hardships they confronted while simultaneously [the world remains] captivated by their strength as activist mothers" (421). What is new in the Juárez situation is how cyberspace has helped to show the international community that the victims are part of a larger context of human rights abuses. Moreover, in this specific blog, the mothers of Juárez present themselves as the *mater dolorosa* [mother of sorrows] who bears in her shoulders the pain for the loss of her child. Emphasizing the idea of motherhood in a State where the law and its public officials have failed their citizens, the blog allows the reader to encounter the suffering and despair of these "mothers" and gives the necessary empathy to choose the path that will support their cry for justice.

Colors and graphics are very important in the cyberspace; from a visual point of view, the blog uses the imagery of black crosses on a pink background, which symbolizes the suffering of the victims. This symbol was created in 1999 by the group *Voces sin Eco* [Voices without Echo] and was painted in public spaces to bring awareness to the lack of justice for the victims (Fregoso 229).[14] As the Mexican government ignored the situation in Juárez, civil groups such as this one looked for new ways of making their voices heard, and cyberspace has been one of the most successful tools in disseminating the information. In order to denounce not only the femicides in Juárez but also any type of violence against women, many Web pages have used the pink color or the crosses as part of their visual imagery. One example of this statement is the Web page *Arte contra la violencia de Género* [Art Against Gender Violence]:[15] where different images are presented to the cyber-reader as a tool to fight against gender violence in an international arena. These images have a very broad range, going from the already traditional pink crosses to performances inspired by dismembered female corpses.

Following this argument, whereas the traditional media has many expressive barriers,[16] cyberspace offers freedom of expression. The web page of the theatrical project *Mujeres de arena* [Women of sand] is a prime example.[17] The goal of this website is to raise awareness through the use of documentary theater. All over the world, more than 120 groups have brought this play to the stage. On a deep pink (almost purple) background that reminds us of the crosses representing the killings, the group's Web page offers the viewer the posters from different openings. According to their website, "the idea for the play was the result of watching the mothers and relatives of the victims of femicide giving talks and conferences on the subject [...] This is what the play intends to reproduce." Cyberspace allows this group to make the play available in several languages (Spanish, Italian, English, German, and French), ultimately to a global population. The text can be bought online and a percentage of the profits go to the grassroots movement *Nuestras hijas de regreso a casa* (their link is on the top right corner of the *Mujeres de arena* site).

Links redirect the viewer to a specific place that the different webmasters consider of importance, making it impossible to ignore their role in disseminating information. Among most of the groups active in cyberspace, different links to newspapers, personal blogs, videos, or even other groups' pages are the norm, but a website that they usually all share is *Amnesty International*. On its website, the group describes itself as a "Nobel Peace Prize-winning grassroots activist organization with more than 3 million supporters, activists and volunteers in more than 150 countries campaigning for human rights worldwide." Its voice is expressed via cyberspace, and we need to highlight that, when typing the word "Juárez" on its search engine, it gives us eighteen links related to human rights violations in the city and in Mexico.[18] Most of these links are related to the violence that women face in the city and/or on the lack of justice that the victims of the femicides receive from the Mexican government.

One document mentioned by scholars and social groups alike is the August 2003 *Amnesty International* report entitled "Intolerable Killings: Ten Years of Abductions and Murder of Women in Ciudad Juárez and Chihuahua." Due to its inclusion in the *Amnesty International* digital library, this report is easily accessible, allowing the public to be informed on the Mexican State's responsibilities regarding the violation of human rights related to the femicides. This organization uses the Internet as a tool to educate and mobilize the public, highlighting the places in which "justice, freedom, truth and dignity are denied" (Amnesty International).

Changing the traditional hierarchies of communication, the Internet allows for more horizontal, bidirectional interactions—especially within the context of personal blogs. An example among the hundreds of blogs that mention the killings is *Borderland Beats. Reporting on the Mexican cartel drug War*.[19] It proclaims that most of its information is "derived from open source media, unconfirmed individual sources and personal view point[s] of author[s]." One of the writers for this blog named "un vato" translated the special report, *Chihuahua un infierno para las mujeres* [Chihuahua a Hell for Women], written by Patricia Mayorga for the online newspaper *Proceso* in March 2013.[20] Beyond the translation of Mayorga's article, I would like to focus on the interaction between the readers and the translator within the comments section of the blog. All the different individuals are labeled as "Anonymous said..." It has seventy-four likes on *Facebook*, and fifty-four comments in English or Spanish appear under the translation of Mayorga's article. Given the nature of their comments, the commenters appear to be from places as diverse as Mexico and Europe and mostly male. Most of them express their disgust and shame about the situation that women still face in Mexico. Using as an example a comment posted on March 6, 2013, this reader states:

> This issue is perhaps the DARKEST cloud that hangs over the country of Mexico. Congratulations to Un Vato for reporting it - and I hope that you continue to speak out with more reports. It is essential.
> Why has this not been investigated? My thoughts are that this cancer of mens souls goes to high levels - not only within the cartels, but within the military and the Mexican Government itself. They do not speak out or investigate - because important men in power are themselves implicated.

On March 7, another reader posted:

> This is a story that needs telling, again and again and again, its absolutely unacceptable. Its not bad enough these women sometimes working long hours in bad circumstances, then have to worry about bastards roaming the streets.Good work in keeping people informed about this ... atrocity.

Keeping in mind that in cyberspace, as several scholars have pointed out, both the consumers and creators of the communication are active members of society, the prior posts are an example of the societal involvement seen throughout the reading of the blog. The authors of these posts express their opinions as a reaction to what they read and to the visual imagery (pictures and videos) included in these blogs. This glocal virtual space, in which everything seems close, allows writers and readers alike to join voices in a common cry of outrage.

Research focusing on cyberactivism has grown during the last ten years, showing how individuals or groups with a discourse that challenges the status quo have found a niche to express their voices. In this way, social networks such as *YouTube, Facebook,* or even blogs in which videos and pictures are uploaded give access to many documentaries, video clips, performances, and news clips about the killings. These expressions range from those focused on gruesome details to more sentimental ones, but all of them share the common denominator of internationally publicizing the murders of these young women and girls. As an example of the visual aspect of these blogs, in *Mujeres de Juárez* [Juarez Women], the creator asks the reader to post a comment after watching a video, and from places as far away as Italy or Argentina comments are posted,[21] all demanding action against these crimes.[22] This bidirectional type of communication is a norm in social media websites, which encourage their users to share their videos "with friends, family and the world" (YouTube).

These groups or individuals who post their materials or opinions in the virtual world pursue and expect a reaction from those who received the information. As previously mentioned, more than twenty years after the first femicides, impunity has been a constant; in many cases, due to the lack of action by the authorities, both State and Federal, most of these crimes remain unsolved. In other cases, a handful of convictions have been made based on confessions collected under torture.[23] Throughout their posts, cyberactivists brace themselves to meet the challenges they face in their quest for justice, rather than to stress the uncertainty of obtaining it.

Numerous Web pages or blogs have divergent objectives, but all of them have in common the search for justice, shedding light on the need for public awareness regarding the inabilities of the Mexican government. Moreover, during the last few years, Ciudad Juárez made it again to the news—most likely, as the result of the escalation of violence related to the drug cartels. This problem should not be ignored and needs to be denounced in the national and international media. The drug related violence is well publicized around the world, but those young women and girls who, in 2016, are still both being killed or disappearing in the State of Juárez remain voiceless. Considering the direction that the websites/blogs take in order to create change, many sites become involved in local/regional elections, other sites demand that officials make pledges to pursue investigations, and in some cases the websites allow these groups to organize protests that have brought the awareness of the killings to the global media. Thanks to the use of cyberspace and the simulacrum of proximity that it creates, the voices of the dead are alive, and the global and local communities cannot ignore their virtual presence. These voices take their denouncements to the public sphere, call for answers, and in many cases, they demand a response. Cyberspace has created a new medium of resistance—one that is filled by individual spaces, giving a uniform channel to express their request for justice. Consequently, it is becoming the center of global awareness and political action, allowing the Mexican border city of Ciudad Juárez to become a metaphor for gender-related human rights violations.

Notes

1 The Internet is less than perfectly free and uncensored, a few essays have been written about the issue of network neutrality. For more information on this topic, see Zack Stiegler. *Regulating the Web: NetWork Neutrality and the fate of the Open Internet* (Lexington Books, 2013).

2 For more information, see: Wellman's "Little Boxes, Glocalization, and Networked Individualism," Porter's *Internet Culture*, Bilic, *How Social Media Enforce Glocalization* and Slevin's *The Internet and Society*.

3 For more information on the term "femicide" see: Jill Radford and Diana E. H. Russell, *Femicide: The Politics of Woman Killing*.

4 For an outline of the early development of virtual communities, see Rheingold's *The Virtual Community.*

5 "In November 2009, the Inter-American Court of Human Rights ruled on the "cotton field" (Campo Algodonero) case that Mexico was guilty of discrimination and of failing to protect three young women murdered in 2001 in Ciudad Juárez or to ensure an effective investigation into their abduction and murder. The Court ordered a new investigation, reparations for the relatives, investigations of officials, and improved measures to prevent and investigate cases of abduction and murder of women and girls" (Amnesty International, "Annual Report: Mexico 2010").

6 During the last thirty years, these *maquila* factories owned by U.S. companies "typically import U.S. inputs, process them and ship them back to the United States" (Gruben and Kiser 22).

7 According to Andrés Villarreal and Wei-hsin Yu, in Mexico, foreign-owned and export-oriented firms employ significantly more women than nationally owned firms at the occupational level, partly due to greater employment for unskilled workers.

8 Julia Monarrez Fregoso puts the total number of girls and women known to be killed in Ciudad Juarez between 1993 and 2007 at 494.

9 For more information on the different narratives that have been employed to interpret these killings, see: Rosalinda Fregoso's "Toward a Planetary Civil Society."

10 "Según declaraciones públicas de determinadas autoridades de alto rango, las víctimas utilizaban minifaldas, salían de baile, eran fáciles o prostitutas. Hay informes acerca de que la respuesta de las autoridades pertinentes frente a los familiares de las victimas osciló entre indiferencia y hostilidad" (Inter-American Commission on Human Rights, 2003. II.A.1.C132).

11 www.casa-amiga.org.mx/.

12 http://nuestrashijasderegresoacasa.blogspot.com/.

13 The blog does not provide the specific details nor the date when the website site was hacked. It only provides the reader with the following information: *Aviso. Este es el blog oficial de Nuestras hijas de regreso a casa ya que la otra web fue hackeada* [Warning. This is the official blog of Our Daughters on Their Way Home as the other website site was hacked].

14 This group ceased to exist in 2001, giving as main reason "that journalists, NGOs and the media were profiting from the losses of the murdered women's families" (No Echo).

15 http://artecontraviolenciadegenero.org/?p=242.

16 For detailed information on this topic, see Niklas Luhmann, *The Reality of the Mass Media.*

17 http://mujeresdearenateatro.blogspot.com/.

18 www.amnestyusa.org/search/node/juarez.

19 www.borderlandbeat.com/ 2009/04/about.html.

20 www.borderlandbeat.com/2013/03/chihuahua-hell-for-women.html.

21 "POR FAVOR DEJANOS TU COMENTARIO ES MUY IMPORTANTE PARA NOSOTROS.Este video trata sobre un asesinato de una joven de Juarez, la cual nunca resolvieron su caso..." [PLEASE, LEAVE YOUR COMMENT, IT IS VERY IMPORTANT FOR US. This video presents the murder of a young woman in Juarez, it has never been solved].

22 www.youtube.com/watch?v=uSC15lrd3vM.

23 For more information, see: Teresa Rodriguez, *The daughters of Juarez* and Diana Washington Valdez, *The Killing Fields.*

Works Cited

"Annual Report: Mexico 2010." *Amnestyusa.org.* Amnesty International, 2010. www.amnesty.org/en/region/mexico/report-2010. Accessed May 2013.

"Annual Report: Mexico 2013," *Amnestyusa.org.* Amnesty International, 2013. www.amnestyusa.org/research/reports/annual-report-mexico-2013?page =show. Accessed May 2013.

Arte contra la violencia de Género, 19 abril 2011. artecontraviolenciadegenero. org/?p=242. Accessed 12 Sept. 2013.

Bejarano, Cynthia. "Transforming Motherhood and Houseskirts by Challenging Violence in Juárez, México, Argentina, and El Salvador," *Violence and the Body: Race, Gender, and the State,* Ed. Arturo J. Aldama. Indiana UP, 2003.

Bilic, Paško. *How Social Media Enforce Glocalization.* rci.mirovni-institut.si/ Docs/2010%20ASO%20text%20Bilic.pdf. Accessed 12 Sept. 2013.

Borderland Beats. Reporting on the Mexican cartel drug War, Apr. 2009. www. borderlandbeat.com/2009/04/about.html. Accessed 23 June 2013.

Ester Chavez, editor. *Casa Amiga Centro de Crisis, A.C.,* 2009. www.casa-amiga.org.mx/. Accessed 18 May 2013.

Facebook, Feb. 2004. www.facebook.com. Accessed 7 Jan. 2013.

Fregoso, Rosa Linda. "Toward a Planetary Civil Society," *Women in the U.S.-Mexico Borderlands: Structural Violence and Agency in Everyday Life,* Ed. Denise Segura and Patricia Zavella, Duke UP, 2006.

———. "'We Want Them Alive': The Politics and Culture of Human Rights." *Social Identities* 12.2 (March 2006): 109–138.

Gruben, William. "Was NAFTA behind Mexico's High Maquiladora Growth?" *Economic and Financial Review,* Third Quarter, 2001. 11–22. www. dallasfed.org/assets/documents/research/efr/2001/efr0103b.pdf. Accessed 23 Aug. 2013.

Gruben, William, and Sherry Kiser. "Nafta and Maquiladoras. Is the Growth Connected?" *Federal Reserve Bank of Dallas,* June 2001. 22–24.

Guillermoprieto, Alma. "Letter from Mexico: A Hundred Women. Why Has a Decade-long String of Murders Gone Unsolved?" *The New Yorker* 29 Sept. 2003. www.newyorker.com/archive/2003/09/29/030929fa_fact_ guillermoprieto. Accessed 9 Jan. 2013.

Inter-American Commission on Human Rights. *The Situation of the Rights of Women in Ciudad Juárez Mexico: The Right to Be Free from Violence and Discrimination.* OEA/Ser.L/V/II.117, doc. 44, 7 Mar. 2003. www.cidh.oas. org/annualrep/2002eng/chap.vi.juarez.htm. Accessed 11 May 2013.

"Intolerable Killings: 10 Years of Abductions and Murder of Women in Ciudad Juarez and Chihuahua," *Amnestyusa.org.* Amnesty International, Aug. 2003. www.amnesty.org/en/library/asset/AMR41/026/2003/en/a62f0982-d6c3-11dd-ab95-a13b602c0642/amr410262003en.pdf. Accessed 14 Jan. 2013.

Luhmann, Niklas. *The Reality of the Mass Media.* Stanford UP, 2000.

Mayorga, Patricia. "Chihuahua, un infierno para las mujeres." *Proceso,* 3 marzo 2013. www.proceso.com.mx/?p=335219. Accessed 20 Apr. 2013.

Monarrez Fragoso, Julia. "An Analysis of Feminicide in Ciudad Juárez: 1993–2007" *Strengthening Understanding of Femicide: Using Research*

to Galvanize Action and Accountability, 2008. 78–84. www.path.org/
publications/files/GVR_femicide_rpt.pdf. Accessed 20 Aug. 2013.

"Muertas de Juárez-Mariana," *Mujeres de Juárez.org* 28 May 2013. www.
mujeresdejuarez.org/muertasdejuarez-mariana. Accessed 6 June 2013.

Mujeres de Arena. n.d. mujeresdearenateatro.blogspot.com. Accessed 9 May
2013.

"muertasdejuarez-mariana." *Mujeres de Juárez.* www.mujeresdejuarez.org/
muertasdejuarez-mariana. Accessed 15 May 2013.

No Echo: Juárez Murdered Women's Group Disbands. *Women on the border* 10
July 2001. www.womenontheborder.org/Articles/no%20echo.htm. Accessed
19 Oct. 2013.

Nuestras hijas regreso a casa, 2002. nuestrashijasderegresoacasa.blogspot.com.
Accessed 18 May 2013.

Porter, David. *Internet Culture.* Routledge, 2013.

Radford, Jill y Dianna E. H. Russell, *Femicide: The Politics of Woman Killing.*
Twayne Publishers, 1992.

Reforma. "Desaparecen 4 mujeres en Ciudad Juárez.". *Zócalo/Saltillo. Newspaper* 23 Jan. 2013. www.zocalo.com.mx/seccion/articulo/desaparecen-4-
mujeres-en-ciudad-juarez-1358998372. Accessed 11 Aug. 2013.

Rheingold, H. *The Virtual Community, 2nd edition* [online version], 2000.
www.rheingold.com/vc/book. Accessed 1 Oct. 2013.

Robertson, Roland. *Globalization,* Sage, 1992.

Rodriguez, Teresa. *The Daughters of Juarez: A True Story of Serial Murder
South of the Border.* Atria Books, 2008.

Russell, Diana E.H. "The Origin and the Importance of the Term Femicide."
Dec. 2011. www.dianarussell.com/origin_of_femicide.html. Accessed 9 Aug.
2013.

Slevin, James. *The internet and Society.* Wiley, 2000.

Stiegler, Zack. *Regulating the Web: NetWork Neutrality and the Fate of the
Open Internet.* Lexington Books, 2013.

Simmons, William Paul. "Remedies for Women of Ciudad Juárez through the
Inter-American Court of Human Rights." *Journal of International Human
Rights* 4.3 (2006): 492. scholarlycommons.law.northwestern.edu/njihr/vol4/
iss3/2. Accessed 4 Sept. 2013.

Un Vato. "'Chihuahua a Hell from Women,' Transl. from Patricia Mayorga
Chihuahua, un infierno para las mujeres," *Proceso. Bordeland Beat* Apr.
2013. www.borderlandbeat.com/2013/03/chihuahua-hell-for-women.html.
Accessed 8 May 2013.

Villarreal, Andres, and Wei-hsin Yu. "Economic Globalization and Women's
Employment: The Case of Manufacturing in Mexico", *American Sociologi-
cal Review* 72 (2007): 365–389. spot.colorado.Edu/~utar/Villarreal&Yu.pdf.
Accessed 9 Aug. 2013.

Washington Valdez, Diana. *The Killing Fields: Harvest of Women.* Peace at the
Border, 2006.

YouTube, 14 Feb. 2005. www.youtube.com. Accessed 9 Aug. 2013.

Wellman, Barry."Little Boxes, Glocalization, and Networked Individualism,"
*Digital Cities II: Computational and Sociological Approaches. Digital Cities
2001.* Ed. M. Tanabe, P. van den Besselaar, and T. Ishida. Springer, 2002.

Part IV

Cyberspace and New Citizenry Representations

13 Digital *Favelas*

New Visibilities and Self-Representation

Tori Holmes

Introduction: New Visibilities

In recent years, *favelas* have gained increased social and cultural visibility in Brazil and beyond, leading to the suggestion that they have "reached a cyclical high point in their influence on Brazil's popular culture" (McCann, "The Political Evolution" 162). There have, however, been different trajectories toward this visibility, different forms of visibility, and different actors involved. While a 2006 manifesto published to mark the launch of a thematic program about the urban periphery (of which *favelas* can be considered a subcategory) on Brazil's largest television network, *TV Globo*, lauded "*o aparecimento da voz direta da periferia falando alto em todos os lugares do país*" ("the appearance of the direct voice of the periphery speaking loudly in all corners of the country") and that this periphery "*não precisa mais de intermediários*" ("no longer needs intermediaries") (Vianna 1), the increased visibility of *favelas* has not always been the result of efforts by their residents. Mainstream productions such as the 2002 film *Cidade de Deus* (*City of God*) have perpetuated both positive and negative stereotypes, which have, for example, influenced the increasing numbers engaging in *favela* tourism in Brazil (Freire-Medeiros). Films and television programs about *favelas* have also contributed to the emergence of what is known as "*favela* chic," a discourse "which stylizes and globalizes aspects of *favela* society and culture [and is] used to market commercial and cultural products" (Leu, "Brazilianism" 647), such as bars and restaurants, both in Brazil and abroad. At the same time, the role of certain mainstream television programs (such as the one announced by the previous manifesto) in affording greater visibility to aspects of life in the urban periphery beyond the clichés should not be overlooked (Souza 106).

As Vianna's manifesto highlights, however, self-representation through film, music, literature, photography, and "citizens' media" (Rodriguez) produced by *favela* and periphery residents themselves has also multiplied. The growth in the production and dissemination of such works, and their sometimes wide circulation, has much to do with increased access to digital technologies, particularly the Internet, in Brazil. Access to the Internet in urban areas of the country almost doubled from 2005 to 2010, rising from 24% to 45% (CETIC.br "TIC Domicílios 2005"; "TIC Domicílios e Usuários 2010 - Área Urbana"), and although there are disparities between the access enjoyed in different types of urban areas, levels of access in *favelas* have also risen during this period.[1] In *favelas*, these increases can be attributed largely to the spread of Internet cafés known as *lan houses* and more recently to an increase in computer ownership and home-based connectivity, thanks to falling costs, rising incomes, and access to credit. One outcome of this rise in access, which will be the focus of this chapter, has been the increased production of a whole variety of digital material by *favela* residents about their neighborhoods.

Internet content about the *favelas* of Rio de Janeiro is not a new phenomenon, of course, with well-known thematic websites and projects run by nongovernmental organizations (NGOs) and social movements having been around for almost two decades, but recent years have seen the publication and dissemination of a greater volume and diversity of content about or originating from these areas of the city. Such content has expanded on blogs, social network sites, microblogs, and other social media platforms, whether linked to the established websites mentioned before or, increasingly, produced independently by individuals and groups. It ranges from everyday uses of social network sites to texts, videos, and images that engage with, and sometimes directly contest, mainstream (often negative) narratives about *favelas*. This chapter discusses the implications of developments in Brazilian digital culture for the representation of marginalized urban areas in the country, and outlines ongoing representational challenges facing *favelas,* as well as some ways in which these are being overcome. It provides an overview of key projects producing digital content about *favelas*, from the established to the more recent, and presents data from research into blogging by residents of one *favela* in Rio de Janeiro, arguing that the contestatory nature of such content lies in explicitly positioning *favelas* as part of the city, countering dominant discourses that have long posited the opposite.

The Implications of Digital Culture for *Favela* Representation

Among Brazilian Internet users as a whole, the "intensity of the appropriation of the Internet [...] has been exceptionally high" (Fragoso 255–256), and social media platforms such as Orkut, Facebook, Twitter, YouTube, the photoblogging site Fotolog, and blogs more generally speaking are, or have been, highly popular in the country.[2] According to one market research company, 86% of Brazilian Internet users accessed social network sites in April 2010, a higher proportion than in any other country (IDG Now!). As Heather Horst (438) has observed,

"Brazilians are clearly leaders in the use and innovation around social media," although there are some variations in the practices of different social groups in this regard and overall figures for Internet use in Brazil continue to mirror socioeconomic and regional inequalities.[3]

Those persistent inequalities notwithstanding, the emergence of digital media has been identified by a leading U.S.-based Brazilianist, Bryan McCann, as one of the six trends that have most changed Brazil since the 1980s. He argues that the rise in access to digital technologies in the country has "yielded profound cultural consequences, shaking hierarchies and altering patterns of production" (McCann, *The Throes* 10). Digital culture is thus undoubtedly a compelling area of research for understanding contemporary Brazil, and I build on McCann's affirmation to propose a nuanced assessment of the effects and implications of digital culture specifically for the representation of *favelas*. This assessment recognizes that access to the Internet by *favela* residents, and its use for the creation and circulation of self-representations, has indeed challenged some hierarchies, but by no means removed them.

As Janice Perlman points out, persistent prejudices in Brazilian society continue to work against *favelas* and their residents, despite some advances: "if the word *favela* has been reappropriated by *favela* residents, it remains a term of derision in the rest of society" (*Favela* 332). Brazilian (and international) media coverage, for example, often stigmatizes *favelas* in its portrayal of them primarily as territories of violence and crime, overlooking the many other aspects of life in these areas. This representational trend both reflects and reinforces the perception by many Brazilian policymakers and non-*favela* residents, especially those living in more upmarket neighborhoods of Rio, that *favelas* are somehow not really part of the city—they are regarded as a formation "*contraposta a um determinado ideal de urbano, vivenciado por uma pequena parcela dos habitantes da cidade*" ("opposed to a specific urban ideal, which is enjoyed by only a small portion of the city's inhabitants") (Souza e Silva and Barbosa 57). However, one of the consequences of increased access to the Internet by *favela* residents, I argue, has been the emergence of more extensive and diverse content about *favelas,* which gives visibility to these territories and their residents' voices, and questions their marginalization.

That said, more research is required on the reception of such content, as a basis for making claims for concrete social and cultural transformations resulting from its publication and circulation. As Horst has highlighted in a review of the literature on new media practices in Brazil, empirical gaps in existing research on digital culture in the country, and particularly on everyday uses of the Internet, may restrict the conclusions that it is possible to draw at this stage about the overall changes effected in Brazilian society as a result of the spread of digital technologies. As she writes, "it remains unclear whose Internet we may be talking about, as well as the extent to which such participation has truly transformed the well-entrenched hierarchies in Brazil" (Horst 453). However, a shift can now be observed in empirical research on digital culture in Brazil toward objects of study that better represent the diverse (and particularly non-elite) contexts of Internet use in the country, which offer some of the missing data sought by Horst.[4] Although the consideration of what has been termed *"cultura popular digital"* ("digital popular culture") (Vianna qtd. in Bentes 59) still represents a relatively small proportion of Internet research in and on Brazil, its increasing popularity contributes to the development of a more diversified and representative narrative on digital culture, providing a broader understanding of how the Internet is being localized (Postill) in different settings and by different groups in Brazil.

Understanding *Favelas* and Their Representation by Outsiders

The discussion here, focusing on the use of the Internet for self-representation by *favela* residents, requires a consideration of broader trends in the representation of these areas. Although often erroneously perceived and portrayed as the locus of urban poverty in Rio (Valladares, *A Invenção* 151), in practice *favelas* today are highly diversified spaces, with varying demographic, socioeconomic and cultural characteristics (Valladares, *A Invenção*; Perlman, "Marginality"; McCann, "The Political Evolution"; Souza e Silva et al.). Many have intense local commerce and a dynamic housing market, as well as "their own 'middle-class' of entrepreneurs, property holders, civil servants, and NGO agents" (McCann, "The Political Evolution" 161). Reflecting a broader national trend, Rio's *favelas* have also recently seen the growth of a new Brazilian emerging middle class, known as *classe C*, or class C.[5] The increased availability of digital communication technologies in *favelas* and urban periphery areas has also contributed to reshaping the way these areas are understood.

Given this striking diversity, it has been argued that the term *favela* "encompasses such an urban variety that it no longer has a single meaning" (Jaguaribe and Hetherington 159). Nonetheless, perhaps precisely because of the tendency toward the homogenization of *favelas* in mainstream discourses, there are some common features in how *favelas* and their residents are represented by outsiders. Perlman (*Favela* 30) has suggested that "[p]erhaps the single persistent distinction between *favelas* and the rest of the city is the deeply rooted stigma that adheres to them and to those who reside in them." This stigma is largely associated with the presence in many, but by no means all, *favelas* of non-state armed groups, whether drug traffickers or militias (armed paramilitary groups). It is this (perceived) feature of *favela* life that often dominates external portrayals.

Putting forward the idea of a "territorial marginality," in which municipal, state, and federal governments have struggled to exert their authority over certain areas of Rio de Janeiro, McCann argues that "the problem of gangs in Rio's *favelas* is primarily one of territorial control and only secondarily one of drug trafficking itself" ("The Political Evolution" 162, 159). It is worth noting here that Rio's state government is currently attempting to establish a presence in certain *favelas* through its *favela* "pacification" scheme, begun in late 2008 and known by the acronym UPP (*Unidade de Polícia Pacificadora*), although recent years have seen cuts to the UPP budget and rising levels of violence in "pacified" favelas.[6] Other researchers (Machado da Silva 13) have debated the "*confinamento territorial*" ("territorial confinement") of *favela* residents, understood as the result of contiguity with drug gangs, violence suffered at the hands of the police and militias, and the distrust of residents of other areas. However, the marginality of *favela* residents themselves has been contested by Perlman, for whom they are "inextricably bound into society, albeit in a manner detrimental to their own interests. They contribute their hard work, their high hopes, and their loyalties, but do not benefit from the goods and services of the system" (*Favela* 150).

A related understanding of *favelas*, which combines Perlman's insistence on integration with the theories of territorial marginality and confinement outlined before, is that these areas are, and have long been, characterized by a "complex interplay of segregation and connection" (Hamburger 115). Although the idea of Rio de Janeiro as a "divided city" has been very influential,[7] Beatriz Jaguaribe and Kevin Hetherington (159) argue that "numerous exchanges" take place between *favelas* and other areas of the city and that "it is the ambiguity of these indistinct contact zones that allows violence and socialization to occur simultaneously." Digital culture has opened up a new contact zone for such exchanges and for the representation of the relationships between *favelas* and the city.

One existing contact zone is the mainstream media, which has been accused of all too often employing a "trope of war" in its coverage of *favela*-related stories, one that "suppresses complexity and stymies debate by encouraging a Manichean 'us' and 'them' attitude" (Leu, "The Press" 351). A further charge levelled at the media is that it tends to give differential, often preferential, treatment to violence affecting residents of middle-class areas compared to that suffered by *favela* residents (Souza e Silva and Barbosa 58; Souza e Silva 96). However, alternative perspectives on violence—as part of broader, more diverse perspectives on *favelas* in general—are increasingly being produced and circulated by organizations working in *favelas*, as well as by *favela* residents, using digital technologies.

Favela Websites: From NGOs to Hyperlocal Journalism

In Jaguaribe's discussion of a "crisis of representation" (200) affecting Rio and its *favelas*, she points to the increased participation of previously unheard actors in this arena, in the unravelling and aftermath of the Brazilian military dictatorship (1964–1985):

> The democratization of Brazilian society has brought to the forefront formerly silenced and invisible protagonists. As never before, the urban poor, the *favela* communities, and the victims of social discrimination are voicing their rights to consumption and representation.
>
> (220)

This social, cultural, and political shift has also been attributed by anthropologist James Holston to the emergence, since the 1970s, of an "insurgent urban citizenship" in Brazil,[8] in contrast to the "differentiated citizenship," which had previously been the status quo in the country ("Insurgent Citizenship"). Similarly, Brazilian academic and cultural critic Ivana Bentes has pointed to the rise of new *"sujeitos do discurso"* ("subjects of discourse") from the Brazilian urban peripheries who produce not only culture, but also a renewed discourse on racism, police violence, and poverty to rival that of academics and the media (55). The Internet has become a key site for representational practices by these actors, and the work of NGOs has also been important in "stimulat[ing] new forms of production, creation, language and mobilization" among *favela* residents (Gomes da Cunha, "Images of *Favelas*").

In recent years, there has been a particular growth in the number of web-based projects publishing content about the *favelas* or urban periphery areas in other Brazilian cities, often but not always managed and supported by NGOs of different sizes—including those set up by *favela* residents. Well-established and disseminated examples of NGO projects include *Viva Favela* (www.vivafavela.com.br), launched in 2001 by *Viva Rio* to publish content produced by a network of *favela* residents serving as local correspondents, in collaboration with professional journalists.[9] In 2010, it relaunched as *Viva Favela 2.0*, inviting contributions from a more extensive, nationwide network of users and incorporating social media such as Twitter; in 2013, it returned to a more "journalistic" approach (Santos). Other sources of content produced or facilitated by NGOs include the websites of the *Observatório de Favelas* (www.observatoriodefavelas.org.br),[10] the *Central Única das Favelas*, or *CUFA* (cufa.org.br), *Afroreggae* (www.afroreggae.org), and the *Agência de Notícias das Favelas* (www.anf.org.br). Beyond Rio, *Favela é isso aí* (www.favelaeissoai.com.br) is a site about *favelas* developed in the city of Belo Horizonte.

More recent additions include *RioOnWatch* (rioonwatch.org), set up in 2010 by NGO Catalytic Communities to publish content in Portuguese and English produced by "community organizers, residents, and international observers" (RioOnWatch), in the run-up to the 2016 Olympics. There are also local content sites relating to specific *favelas,* such as two from Rocinha: *Rocinha.org* (www.rocinha.org), run by a local NGO, and *FavelaDaRocinha.Com* (faveladarocinha.com), run by journalism students from the area. The now defunct *Wikimapa* project (see Barros, "Sociabilidade"), run by NGO *Rede Jovem*, was one of several recent digital mapping initiatives that have responded to the fact that *favelas* are often absent from maps of Rio or "coded in an uncertain or less committed strategy of representation" (Fabricius 1).

There are also examples that have grown up more organically, through the initiative of individual residents, although in practice the distinction between institutional "projects" and content creation by individuals can be less than clear-cut. The now relatively well-known *Voz das Comunidades* site (www.vozdascomunidades.com.br) and social media presence grew out of a local newspaper produced by a teenager in the Complexo do Alemão group of *favelas*, and while it maintains its focus on Alemão, it is now staffed by a larger team of young people. In a similar way, a website from the periphery of São Paulo that has attracted attention from researchers over the years (Sá; Tacca), *Capao.com.br* (capao.com. br), was originally set up by two brothers living in the area, though its interface does not appear to have undergone any technological upgrades recently.

The aforementioned is by no means an exhaustive list of projects or research into digital content about *favelas* and the urban periphery, but it gives an overview of some of the better-known initiatives. Crucially, as well as producing, curating, and publishing Internet content, many of these initiatives have also run courses and workshops to build the capacity of local residents, particularly teenagers and young adults, in the use of digital technologies for content creation. The majority of such projects now also have a presence on Facebook and other social media platforms such as Twitter, and YouTube, amplifying the potential circulation of their content.

Many of the earlier generation of local content projects relating to *favelas*, such as *Viva Favela*, were explicitly established with the aim of presenting a positive view of urban periphery communities on the Internet (Ramalho 47; Sá 126) or at least of challenging existing perceptions and representations (Gomes da Cunha, "Images of *Favelas*"). This orientation can be observed particularly in relation to the issue of violence, where the focus tends to be on how violence affects the everyday life of *favela* residents, avoiding conventional journalistic formats. For example, in a text available on its site in 2013, *Viva Favela* made explicit reference to its perspective on this prominent and challenging topic:

Com um olhar 'de dentro', estes correspondentes comunitários mostram a cultura, o comportamento, a economia, o meio ambiente, os esportes, a arte, a educação, e principalmente a criatividade das estratégias para vencer os desafios diários, e o potencial para propor e operar mudanças sociais positivas. A violência também aparece, mas pela perspectiva do morador, que raramente é ouvido pela mídia tradicional.

(n.p.)

(From an 'insider viewpoint', the community correspondents cover culture, lifestyle, the economy, the environment, sports, art, education and in particular the creativity of the strategies employed to overcome daily difficulties, as well as the potential for proposing and implementing positive social changes. Violence also appears, but it is presented according to the perspective of *favela* residents, who are rarely heard by the traditional media.)

As Cruz (88) has pointed out, therefore, negative discourses about *favelas* are so deeply rooted in Brazilian society, that *"quando o morador de favela tem oportunidade de falar de si próprio, utiliza-se de tais referências na tentativa de contrapô-los"* ("when the *favela* resident has the chance to speak for her/himself, these references are employed in an attempt to counter them"). An alternative approach can be to avoid violence precisely because this is so prevalent elsewhere, focusing instead on positive aspects of everyday life (Farias Oliveira and Dutra Ferreira).

As far as mainstream journalism is concerned, developments in social media also mean that journalists now have increased access to life in *favelas* and can, for example, consult content generated directly by residents. The UPP scheme has facilitated the access of the media to certain *favelas*, although this has not necessarily meant a change in perspective. However, following global trends toward the inclusion of hyperlocal or user-generated content in the mainstream media (Singer and Ashman 3), some initiatives of this kind have been set up in Rio. For example, *TV Globo*'s *G1* news portal and its *RJTV* local news program have established the *Parceiro do RJ* scheme (g1.globo.com/rio-de-janeiro/parceiro-rj) to involve local residents in producing content about their neighborhoods (including several *favelas*). Another relevant initiative was the *Favela Livre* blog, launched in December 2010 by *O Globo* newspaper and last updated in November 2011. However, its designation as *"Um blog que traz à tona histórias vividas por moradores oprimidos pela violência do crime organizado em favelas do Rio"* ("A blog that brings to light experiences of residents oppressed by the violence of organised crime in the *favelas* of Rio") (*Favela* Livre) suggested that negative stereotypes about *favelas* and their residents were still potentially prominent in its approach.

Other examples show how user-generated content by *favela* residents may be picked up and given greater visibility through translation or reposting on other websites. For example, in November 2009, Global Voices (globalvoicesonline.org), which describes itself as "an international community of bloggers who report on blogs and citizen media from around the world," published a post providing "A view from slum dwellers on Rio's drugs war," which included translated "eyewitness accounts" of residents, collected by *Viva Favela* correspondents, as well as photographs (Global Voices). In November 2010, the *BBC News* website published an article entitled "Rio *favela* tweets create overnight celebrity," discussing the use of Twitter by a teenage resident of the Complexo do Alemão (the originator of the *Voz das Comunidades* website mentioned before) to report on the invasion of his neighborhood by security forces in a crackdown on drug traffickers after a wave of attacks across the city (Hirsch). These examples shed some light on how the Internet opens up new possibilities for the representation of *favelas* by their residents, with the potential of achieving translocal visibility, but also suggest that the reception of such content and the way it is framed by others may still reproduce established patterns. In particular, it seems that the preference for the dramatic and spectacular, identified by Leu ("The Press" 351) in another context, remains; although both of the cases discussed before show how content generated by favela residents, rather than the mainstream media, can gain visibility and audience, it is notable that the subject matter still relates to the recurrent theme of urban violence.

Nonetheless, the continuing growth in both the volume and the diversity of this type of Internet content is indicative of the trend toward the affirmation of insider perspectives, attributable to factors such as the increasing number of university students and researchers from the *favelas* (Valladares qtd. in Rodrigues; Valladares "Educação e mobilidade"). Affirmation—in this case, an explicitly territorial affirmation (*"afirmação territorial"*) in which specific neighborhoods are referenced in song lyrics, clothing, and imagery—has been a theme of projects run by young people from Brazilian urban peripheries since the 1990s, as a response to territorial stigmatization (Ramos 242) and is one central way in which visibility is achieved. As Sá has noted about the *Capão.com* website, such territorial affirmation often means being "actively engaged in producing [one's] own idea of" one's neighborhood, one that is not necessarily "conventionally positive," but based on pride in one's origins (130). Beyond the Internet, this trend can also be clearly observed in other cultural expressions from the urban periphery, such as audiovisual production (Zanetti), so-called "marginal literature" (Peçanha do Nascimento), and *funk* music (Carvalho Lopes).

One critique of websites run by NGOs and social movements, related to the trend toward insider perspectives outlined before, has centered on the representative status of the content they produce and circulate, given the inherent diversity of *favelas* and their residents:

> The sophistication of the resources used in the construction of *favela* histories cannot prevent a questioning of whether these instruments – *favela* websites – are 'representative' of the voices of their residents. There are disagreements and criticisms about the authenticity of these representations and the legitimacy of their producers in 'speaking' in name of the residents of *favela* communities.
> (Gomes da Cunha, "The Sensitive Territory" 192)

For this reason, it is useful also to consider content created by *favela* residents outside of the scope of such projects, such as on independently maintained blogs, when considering digital representations of *favelas*. However, it is important to recognize too that connections may exist between content produced by individuals and NGO projects. For example, those creating content independently may previously have participated in NGO training programs, or their content may be picked up and reposted on NGO-run websites after its initial publication on a blog, as a result of personal connections and networks; they may also contribute to collective projects, alongside their personal content creation. The point about diversity and exceptionality is thus applicable to both types of content, even if content produced by individuals is not subject to the same pressure as projects that set out explicitly to present the collective voice of the *favelas*. Nonetheless, with the shift to increased use of social media and the encouragement of wider participation in projects, such as *Viva Favela*, institutional and personal projects are often not entirely separate realms.

Favela Blogs

My own research, carried out in 2008–2011, with fieldwork in 2009–2010, looked at the use of blogs and related Internet platforms by residents of the Complexo da Maré group of *favelas* in northern Rio. Adopting an ethnographically inspired methodology, including Internet-based observations, textual and visual analysis of content, and interviews, I focused on the work of three Maré residents engaged in independent creation and circulation of digital representations of their local area (texts, photographs, and videos) on blogs and social media platforms, as well as occasionally in print. The brief overview I provide here focuses on how bloggers responded to external or mainstream representations of *favelas* and the notable territorial affirmation of *favelas*, both in their own right and as part of the city through textual and visual references on blogs. While I found that the blog content I examined went beyond the recurrent dispute between "*a favela como campo de batalha e a afirmação da positividade da favela*" ("the *favela* as a battleground and the affirmation of the positivity of the *favela*") (Valladares qtd. in Rodrigues) and offered a more nuanced perspective, the bloggers shared with NGO projects a central concern with "[t]he question of representation" (Gomes da Cunha, "The Sensitive Territory" 189). Like those projects, they had specific motivations for producing and publishing content. Although these varied, the tone and scope of media coverage and other outsider representations was one of the most compelling.

For example, as I have discussed elsewhere (Holmes, "The Travelling Texts"), one blogger, J., living in an area of Maré affected by a conflict between rival groups of drug traffickers, became frustrated at the lack of media coverage of the disruption and suffering caused to local residents. He therefore decided to publish his own response to the conflict on various blogs and websites and to circulate it within his personal networks. This shows that despite the desire, shared with projects such as *Viva Favela*, to go beyond the dominant narrative of violence and to focus on other aspects of *favela* life, there are also times when violence is part of the story that *favela* bloggers believe needs to be told, whether because of a localized conflict or a police operation resulting in the injury or death of a local resident. Nonetheless, it is important to note that such responses to violence may take many forms, both factual and creative, and that overall, digital content produced by *favela* residents is varied. To cite only the examples I encountered in my study of blogs, it may include citizens' media, creative and literary writing, place-based activism, curation of local historical videos and photographs, and more. In other words, despite the frequent attention to media portrayals, content published by *favela* residents is not necessarily seeking to provide alternative forms of reporting on incidences of urban violence, but rather adopts a whole range of representational forms and subject matter.

The bloggers I followed also used the Internet to give visibility to aspects of everyday social and cultural life neglected in mainstream narratives (those originating both in journalism, as already discussed, or cultural production). For example, another blogger, A., told me that she liked to post information about events and activities in Maré on her literary blog "*para mostrar que dentro da favela não tem só o marginal, não tem só a violência. Também tem arte, tem cultura, tem gente que se esforça, que trabalha [...] A gente é mais um pouquinho*" ("to show that the *favela* doesn't only contain criminals, doesn't only contain violence. There is also art, culture, there are people who are making an effort, who work [...]. There's a little more to us than that") (interview, January 2010). She specifically referred to the film *City of God* as providing a portrayal of violence, which she termed "*o lado B*" ("the B side") of life in the *favela*, using a musical metaphor. In this way, rather than accepting the portrayal of violence as the "main attraction," or "A side," she reframed it as something less important, that does not necessarily fit well with the overall narrative. The "A side" of life in the *favela*, she suggested, should be local practices of solidarity and collaboration, such as *"bater a laje,"* an example of what Holston ("Autoconstruction") has termed "autoconstruction," when groups of neighbors get together in a working party to help a family in cementing the roof (*laje*) of their house for use as a leisure space or as the foundation for an additional story, with food and drink supplied by the hosts.

Nonetheless, as a third blogger, V., explained in an interview, doing justice to the different extremes of *favela* life, both the intensely positive and the intensely challenging, as well as the more straightforward practices of everyday life, requires careful negotiation. This insight not only serves as a reminder of the complexity of *favela* representation, but also points to the specific issues involved in publishing local content on the Internet, a medium that offers a potentially translocal, if not global, visibility. The careful consideration of the opportunities and constraints associated with this visibility, with an awareness (or actual targeting) of different audiences, both local and non-local, was common to the three bloggers whose work I studied. They were aware of, and sometimes explicitly catered to, potential external audiences, as well as the biases in dominant narratives, and attempted to negotiate these considerations when framing their content.

I developed the term "framing content" to refer to blog headers, footers, sidebars, and more static content on blog pages, where textual and visual resources were often used by the bloggers to make explicit reference to Maré. This "territorial embedding" of content[11] can be understood as an example of the "territorial affirmation" discussed earlier, and overall, I found that framing content was an important site for the expression of a relationship to place, as much if not more so than actual blog posts in some cases.[12] V.'s blog, for example, noted in a descriptive text on one of its pages that while the blog's current focus was everyday life in Rio as a whole, its *"lugar real,"* or "real place," was Maré. The same page also offered some factual background about Maré, avoiding more sensationalist labeling of the area as a territory of crime and violence. Similarly, for a time during my fieldwork, the sidebar of A's literary blog was customized to include two sections constructed from photographs and song lyrics, one headed *"Meu universo - Favela da Maré"* and the other *"Minha cidade maravilhosa."* These textual and visual elements explicitly affirmed the origin of the blog's content and its author, in both Maré and in the city of Rio. Biographical information supplied in the blurbs, dedications, and prefaces of print publications where A.'s writing appeared also served the same purpose, even when the actual poems or short stories did not make explicit reference to identifiable geographical places. As well as framing her work, therefore, A. explicitly framed *herself* on the Internet and in print as a student, teacher, and writer who was also an enthusiastic and passionate resident of an area of the city often associated with violence and poverty, rather than literary production.

Despite the bloggers' investment in the visibility and affirmation of Maré, they also referenced and published content about other *favelas*, *favelas* and the urban periphery collectively, and the city of Rio (as well as other places in Brazil). However, the examples from A. and V.'s blogs discussed before show how framing content was used explicitly to give visibility to and affirm belonging to Maré, at the same time as it affirmed Maré and its residents as belonging to the city. Crucially, this inclusive approach to place and to "different empirical scales of locality" (Appadurai, "The Right to Participate" 43) constituted a symbolic and contestatory remapping of urban space in Rio de Janeiro, one that explicitly claimed a "right to the city" (Lefebvre qtd. in Holston, "Insurgent Citizenship" 247–248) for its authors and others like them.

Conclusion

As this chapter has shown, the Internet has become a key site for the publication and circulation of digital representations of *favelas*. NGO-run projects producing content about *favelas*, and increasingly *favela* residents themselves, are using the Internet and social media to engage in a symbolic resignification of *favelas* and of urban space more broadly. While increased Internet access among *favela* residents has certainly led to the availability of more extensive and diverse user-generated digital representations of these areas, however, it is important to note that it is, in all likelihood, only a relatively small proportion of *favela* residents who are engaged in the activities described here. A regular routine of content creation, publication, and dissemination demands a significant amount of time and requires specific competencies and literacies, both technological and otherwise, as well as a specific kind of motivation. Furthermore, while the Internet and social media are widely used in *favelas*, the content resulting from everyday practices of Internet use is diverse—as diverse as *favela* residents themselves—and the blogs discussed here are only one variant.

While territorial stigmatization of *favelas* and their residents by outsiders is increasingly coming up against an affirmation of those territories from within, I have argued here that the growth and diversification of content about and from *favelas* on the Internet and elsewhere has not completely overturned entrenched hierarchies and inequalities in Brazil. As noted at the start of the chapter, statistics for Internet access still evidence striking inequalities between *favelas* and other Rio neighborhoods. In addition, little is known about the readership of digital content about *favelas*, nor the scale of its circulation, and I have therefore sought to provide a balanced account of the implications of digital culture for the representation of marginalized urban areas in Brazil.

Finally, some aspects of the recent contemporary sociopolitical context affecting Brazilian *favelas* and their representation have brought significant opportunities and challenges. In 2014, Rio was one of the host cities for the FIFA World Cup, and just two years later, in 2016, it hosted the Olympic Games. The city thus attracted an intensified level of global visibility and scrutiny, which had consequences for *favelas*, with the increased media coverage of the city and of *favelas* opening up a space for more balanced representations, but also leading to the proliferation of stereotypical portrayals. On a more practical level, *favelas* were directly affected by the preparations for these events, as evidenced by the UPP scheme to occupy and "pacify" certain *favelas,* which was mentioned in the chapter and is now experiencing significant difficulties. There were also forced evictions of periphery residents and the destruction of their homes near sporting venues, and along the routes of upgrades to public transport, but this was accompanied by significant protest and coverage of these both in content produced and aggregated by NGOs and social movements, as well as the international media. In this regard, digital media, with the speedy circulation and potentially wide visibility it offers, has already proved a powerful tool in activism and awareness-raising around such issues.

Notes

1 The only extensive survey of Internet use in Rio's favelas, conducted in 2003 before much of the recent expansion in access and the configuration of contemporary Brazilian digital culture, found that 11.6% of *favela* residents used the Internet, a figure close to the national average of the time (Sorj and Guedes 4–5, 9). The national figure for 2010 was 41% (CETIC. br, "TIC Domicílios e Usuários 2010 - Total Brasil"). If the same correlation has been maintained, therefore, the current level of Internet access in Rio favelas is also likely to have risen significantly since 2003. Indeed, in 2012, the Fundação Getúlio Vargas, a Brazilian research institution, released data showing that while large *favelas* in Rio had the lowest levels of digital inclusion (understood in the study as access to mobile and fixed telephony, and a computer with Internet at home) in the municipality, levels of access in those areas were still higher than the national and global averages (Quaino).
2 The Google-owned social network site Orkut, set up in 2004, was dominant in Brazil for many years and was often "seen as synonymous with social network site use" in the country (Horst 451). However, Facebook overtook Orkut in the rankings of Brazilian visitors to each platform in December 2011 (Link Estadão), and Orkut was finally shut down in 2014.
3 This point is regularly made by Cetic.br in its annual surveys of information and communication technology use in Brazil.
4 See, for example, Barros ("Games e redes sociais"; "Sociabilidade"); Scalco; Batista dos Reis; Ferraz and Lemos.
5 This new middle class is defined in economic terms (A is the highest class and E is the lowest in the Brazilian system). Its growth was most striking after 2003, but dates back to the early 1990s. In 1992, 34.96% of the Brazilian population was considered *classe* C, and by 2009 this had risen to 50.5%,

or 94.9 million people (Secretaria de Assuntos Estratégicos). A study published in 2012 by Instituto Data Popular found that 56% of *favela* residents were considered to be class C in 2011, compared to 29% in 2001 (Biller and Petroff).

6 See for example Barber.

7 *Cidade Partida* is the title of a book by journalist Zuenir Ventura published in 1994.

8 Holston was primarily referring to housing and land rights activism in periphery neighborhoods of São Paulo.

9 For more on *Viva Favela*, see Ramalho, and Lucas.

10 The *Observatório de Favelas* has also set up other related initiatives, such as the *Escola Popular de Comunicação Crítica* (*Espocc*) media school and the *Imagens do Povo* photography project (see www.espocc.org.br and www. imagensdopovo.org.br).

11 See Holmes ("The Travelling Texts") for a more in-depth discussion of "territorially embedded" content.

12 See Holmes ("Reframing") for a fuller discussion of these examples.

Works Cited

Appadurai, Arjun. "The Right to Participate in the Work of the Imagination (interview by Arjen Mulder)." *TransUrbanism.* Ed. Joke Brouwer, Philip Brookman, and Arjen Mulder. Rotterdam: NAi Publishers, 2002. 32–47.

Barber, Mariah. "Funding Shortage and Increased Violence Amounts to UPP Crisis". *RioOnWatch* 28 Apr. 2016. www.rioonwatch.org/?p=28108. Accessed 11 June 2017.

Barros, Carla. "Games e redes sociais em lan houses populares: Um olhar antropológico sobre usos coletivos e sociabilidade no 'clube local'." *Internext - Revista Eletrônica de Negócios Internacionais* 3.2 (2008): 199–216. http://internext.espm.br/index.php/internext/article/view/73. Accessed 28 Jan. 2014.

———. "Sociabilidade e 'territorialidade' no universo digital: Transitando em contextos tecnológicos de jovens nas camadas populares." *Juventudes e Gerações no Brasil Contemporâneo.* Ed. Lívia Barbosa. Porto Alegre: Sulina, 2012. 97–120.

Batista dos Reis, Juliana. "A 'periferia' na (e da) rede: Dimensões do bairro na internet." *27ª Reunião Brasileira de Antropologia.* Belém do Pará, Brazil, 2010. http://abant.org.br/conteudo/ANAIS/CD_Virtual_27_RBA/arquivos/grupos_trabalho/gt25/jbr.pdf. Accessed 30 Jan. 2013.

Bentes, Ivana. "Redes colaborativas e precariado produtivo." *Periferia* 1.1 (2007): 53–61. www.e-publicacoes.uerj.br/index.php/periferia/issue/view/262. Accessed 30 Jan. 2013.

Biller, David, and Katerina Petroff. "In Brazil's Favelas, a Middle Class Arises." *BloombergBusinessweek* 20 Dec. 2012. www.businessweek.com/articles/2012-12-20/in-brazils-favelas-a-middle-class-arises. Accessed 10 Jan. 2014.

Carvalho Lopes, Adriana. "A *favela* tem nome próprio: A (re)significação do local na linguagem do funk carioca." *Revista Brasileira de Linguistica Aplicada* 9.2 (2009): 369–390.

CETIC.br. "TIC Domicílios e Usuários 2010 - Área Urbana." *CETIC.br* 2011. www.cetic.br/usuarios/tic/2010/index.htm. Accessed 30 Jan. 2013.

————. "TIC Domicílios e Usuários 2010 - Total Brasil - Indicadores." *CETIC. br* 2011. www.cetic.br/usuarios/tic/2010-total-brasil/index.htm. Accessed 30 Jan. 2013.

————. "TIC Domicílios 2005 - Indicadores." *CETIC.br* 2006. www.cetic.br/ usuarios/tic/2005/index.htm. Accessed 30 Jan. 2013.

Cruz, Márcia Maria. "Vozes da *favela*: Representação, identidade e disputas discursivas no ciberespaço." *Stockholm Review of Latin American Studies* 2 (2007): 77–91.

Fabricius, Daniela. "Resisting Representation: The Informal Geographies of Rio de Janeiro." *Harvard Design Magazine* 28 (2008): n. pag.

Farias Oliveira, C.T., and Z.N. Dutra Ferreira. "Os movimentos sociais na rede: Produção de notícia e valorização de sujeito." *Revista PJ:BR - Jornalismo Brasileiro* 5.9 (2007). www.eca.usp.br/pjbr/arquivos/artigos9_b.htm. Accessed 30 Jan. 2013.

Favela Livre. "*Favela* Livre - O blog ligado nas comunidades." *Favela Livre: O Globo* http://oglobo.globo.com/blogs/favelalivre/default.asp. Accessed 30 Jan. 2013.

Fragoso, Suely. "WTF a Crazy Brazilian Invasion." *Proceedings of CATaC 2006- Fifth International Conference on Cultural Attitudes towards Technology and Communication*. Ed. Charles Ess, Fay Sudweeks and Herbert Hrachovec. Murdoch: Murdoch University, 2006. 255–274.

Freire-Medeiros, Bianca. "'I Went to the City of God': Gringos, Guns and the Touristic *Favela*." *Journal of Latin American Cultural Studies: Travesia* 20.1 (2011): 21–34.

Global Voices. "Brazil: A View from Slum Dwellers on Rio's Drugs War." *Global Voices* 1 Nov. 2009. http://globalvoicesonline.org/2009/11/01/brazil-a-view-from-slum-dwellers-on-rios-drugs-war. Accessed 30 Jan. 2013.

Gomes da Cunha, Olivia Maria. "Images of *Favelas*: Displacing (and Recycling) the Sites of Invisibility." *ReVista: Harvard Review of Latin America* VI (2007). http://140.247.185.227/publications/revistaonline/spring-2007/image-favelas-displacing-and-recycling-sites-invisibility. Accessed 28 Jan. 2014.

————. "The Sensitive Territory of the *Favelas*: Place, History, and Representation." *Brazil and the Americas: Convergences and Perspectives*. Ed. Peter Birle, Sergio Costa and Horst Nitschak. Madrid/Frankfurt: Vervuert/ Iberoamericana, 2008. 185–198.

Hamburger, Esther I. "Politics of Representation: Television in a São Paulo *Favela*." *Framework: The Journal of Cinema and Media* 44.1 (2003): 104–115.

Hirsch, Tim. "Rio *Favela* Tweets Create Overnight Celebrity." *BBC News* 29 Nov. 2010. www.bbc.co.uk/news/world-latin-america-11862593. Accessed 30 Jan. 2013.

Holmes, Tori. "The Travelling Texts of Local Content: Following Content Creation, Communication and Dissemination via Internet Platforms in a Brazilian *Favela*." *Hybrid Storyspaces: Redefining the Critical Enterprise in Twenty-First Century Hispanic Literature*. Ed. Debra Castillo and Christine Henseler. *Hispanic Issues Online* 9 (2012): 263–288. http://hispanicissues. umn.edu/HybridStoryspaces.html. Accessed 30 Jan. 2013.

————. "Reframing the Favela, Remapping the City: Territorial Embeddedness and (Trans) Locality in "Framing Content" on Brazilian Favela Blogs". *Journal of Latin American Cultural Studies* 25.2 (2016): 297–319.

Holston, James. "Autoconstruction in Working-Class Brazil." *Cultural Anthropology* 6.4 (1991): 447–465.

———. "Insurgent Citizenship in an Era of Global Urban Peripheries." *City & Society* 21.2 (2009): 245–267.

Horst, Heather. "Free, Social and Inclusive: Appropriation and Resistance of New Media Technologies in Brazil." *International Journal of Communication* 5 (2011): 437–462. http://ijoc.org/ojs/index.php/ijoc/article/view/699. Accessed 30 Jan. 2013.

IDG Now!. "Internauta brasileiro lidera uso de rede social em todo o mundo." *IDG Now!* 15 June 2010. http://idgnow.com.br/internet/2010/06/15/internauta-brasileiro-lidera-uso-de-rede-social-em-todo-o-mundo/. Accessed 23 Sept. 2017.

Jaguaribe, Beatriz. "Hijacked by Realism." *Public Culture* 21.2 (2009): 219–227.

Jaguaribe, Beatriz, and Kevin Hetherington. "*Favela* Tours: Indistinct and Mapless Representations of the Real in Rio de Janeiro." *Tourism Mobilities. Places to Play, Places in Play.* Ed. Mimi Sheller and John Urry. New York: Routledge, 2004. 155–166.

Leu, Lorraine. "Brazilianism, Culture and Consumption in the United Kingdom." *Bulletin of Spanish Studies* 84.4–5 (2007): 645–652.

———. "The Press and the Spectacle of Violence in Contemporary Rio de Janeiro." *Journal of Latin American Cultural Studies* 13.3 (2004): 343–355.

Link Estadão. "Facebook supera audiência do Orkut." *Link Estadão* 17 Jan. 2012. http://blogs.estadao.com.br/link/facebook-supera-audiencia-do-orkut-no-brasil. Accessed 2 Jan. 2013.

Lucas, Peter. *Viva Favela: Ten Years of Photojournalism, Human Rights and Visual Inclusion in Brazil*, 2012. http://www.vivafavela10years.net/. Accessed 23 Sept. 2017.

Machado da Silva, Luiz Antonio. "Introdução." *Vida Sob Cerco: Violência e Rotina nas Favelas do Rio de Janeiro*. Ed. Luiz A. Machado da Silva. Rio de Janeiro: Editora Nova Frontera, 2008. 13–26.

McCann, Bryan. "The Political Evolution of Rio de Janeiro's *Favelas*: Recent Works." *Latin American Research Review* 41.3 (2006): 149–163.

———. *The Throes of Democracy: Brazil since 1989*. London and New York: Zed Books, 2008.

Peçanha do Nascimento, Érica. *Vozes Marginais na Literatura*. Rio de Janeiro: Aeroplano, 2009.

Perlman, Janice. *Favela: Four Decades of Living on the Edge in Rio de Janeiro*. Oxford: Oxford U P, 2010.

———. "Marginality: From Myth to Reality in the *Favelas* of Rio de Janeiro, 1969–2002." *Urban Informality: Transnational Perspectives from the Middle East, Latin America, and South Asia*. Ed. Ananya Roy and Nezar Alsayyad. Oxford: Lexington Books, 2004. 105–146.

Postill, John. "Localizing the Internet beyond Communities and Networks." *New Media & Society* 10.3 (2008): 413–431.

Quaino, Lilian. "Metade da população brasileira está incluída no mundo digital, diz FGV." *G1*, 31 July 2012. http://g1.globo.com/tecnologia/noticia/2012/07/metade-da-populacao-brasileira-esta-incluida-no-mundo-digital-diz-fgv.html. Accessed 23 Nov. 2012.

Ramalho, Cristiane. *Notícias da Favela*. Rio de Janeiro: Aeroplano, 2007.

Ramos, Silvia. "Jovens de favelas na produção cultural brasileira dos anos 90." *"Por Que Não?" Rupturas e Continuidades da Contracultura.* Ed. Maria Isabel Mendes de Almeida and Santuza Cambraia Naves. Rio de Janeiro: 7Letras, 2007. 239–256.

RioOnWatch. "About." *RioOnWatch* n.d. http://rioonwatch.org/?page_id=8. Accessed 20 Jan. 2013.

Rodrigues, Carla. "Exotismo da *favela* dá dinheiro" [interview with Licia Valladares, originally published on *NoMínimo* on 12 Nov. 2006]. *contemporânea* 2010. http://carlarodrigues.uol.com.br/index.php/1743. Accessed 30 Jan. 2013.

Rodriguez, Clemencia. *Fissures in the Mediascape: An International Study of Citizens' Media.* Cresskill, NJ: Hampton P, 2001.

Santos, Mayra Coelho Jucá dos. Vozes Ativas das Favelas 2.0: Autorrepresentações Midiáticas numa Rede de Comunicadores Periféricos. FGV-CPDOC, Masters Dissertation, 2014.

Scalco, Lucia Mury. "Reflexões sobre a sociabilidade virtual dos jovens das classes populares." *pontourbe* 3.4 (2009). https://pontourbe.revues.org/1473. Accessed 23 Sept. 2017.

Secretaria de Assuntos Estratégicos. "45 curiosidades sobre a nova classe média." *Nova Classe Média Brasileira*, 2011. www.sae.gov.br/novaclassemedia/?page_id=58. Accessed 30 Jan. 2013.

Sorj, Bernardo, and Luís Eduardo Guedes. *Internet na Favela: Quantos, Quem, Onde, Para Quê.* Rio de Janeiro: Unesco - Editora Gramma, 2005.

Souza, Gustavo. "Políticas culturais, vídeo digital e política de representação: Fatores para o desenvolvimento do cinema de periferia brasileiro." *Fronteiras – Estudos Midiáticos* 14.2 (2012): 99–109.

Souza e Silva, Jailson de, Jorge Luiz Barbosa, Mariane de Oliveira Biteti, and Fernando Lannes Fernandes, editors. *O Que É a Favela, Afinal?* Rio de Janeiro: Observatório de Favelas, 2009.

Souza e Silva, Jailson de, and Jorge Luiz Barbosa. *Favela, Alegria e Dor na Cidade.* Rio de Janeiro: Editora Senac Rio, 2005.

Souza e Silva, Jailson de. "A violência da mídia." *Mídia e Violência - Novas Tendências na Cobertura de Criminalidade e Segurança no Brasil.* Ed. Silvia Ramos and Anabela Paiva. Rio de Janeiro: IUPERJ, 2007. 93–97.

Tacca, Fernando de. "Antropologia e imagens em rede: A periferia na internet." *La Comunicación Mediatizada: Hegemonías, Alternatividades, Soberanías.* Ed. Susana Sel. Buenos Aires: Consejo Latinoamericano de Ciencias Sociales (Clacso), 2009. 149–168. Colección Grupos de Trabajo de Clacso.

Valladares, Licia do Prado. *A Invenção da Favela: Do Mito de Origem a Favela. com.* Rio de Janeiro: Editora FGV, 2005.

———. "Educação e mobilidade social nas favelas do Rio de Janeiro: O caso dos universitários (graduandos e graduados) das favelas." *DILEMAS: Revista de Estudos de Conflito e Controle Social* 2.5–6 (2010): 153–172.

Varon Ferraz, Joana, and Ronaldo Lemos. *Pontos de Cultura e Lan Houses: Estruturas para Inovação ba Base da Pirâmide Social.* Rio de Janeiro: Escola de Direito do Rio de Janeiro da Fundação Getulio Vargas, 2011. www.estrombo.com.br/faroldigital. Accessed 30 Jan. 2013.

Vianna, Hermano. "Central da Periferia - Texto de divulgação." 16 Oct. 2006. www.overmundo.com.br/banco/central-da-periferia-texto-de-divulgacao. Accessed 30 Jan. 2013.

Viva *Favela*. "Histórico." *Viva Favela 2.0*. n.d. www.vivafavela.com.br/historico. Accessed 20 Jan. 2013.

Zanetti, Daniela. "O 'cinema de periferia' e os festivais: Práticas audiovisuais e organização discursiva." *Comunicação e Sociedade* 31.53 (2010): 191–214. www.metodista.br/revistas/revistas-ims/index.php/CSO/article/view-Article/1536. Accessed 30 Jan. 2013.

14 "Online Activist Eco-Poetry"

Techno-Cannibalism, Digital Indigeneity, and Ecological Resistance in Brazil

Eduardo Ledesma

Introduction: Poetry, Blogging, and Belo Monte

In recent decades, Brazil has experienced a growing awareness of its environmental problems, especially those involving deforestation and loss of biodiversity in the Amazon River basin. Concerns over sustainability have led to an increase in grassroots campaigns resisting controversial projects such as the Belo Monte Dam (near Xingu National Park),[1] bringing together indigenous groups, local community members, and national and international environmental organizations (such as Amazon Watch, International Rivers, Rainforest Action Network, Movimento Xingu Vivo Para Sempre) in a mobilization against the Brazilian government and energy companies. As Tracy Devine Guzmán has observed,

> Shared and increasing interest among indigenous and nonindigenous Brazilians in preventing the construction of the Belo Monte hydroelectric dam—because of the social and economic ills it will engender, the environmental destruction it will wreak, and the human rights it will violate—is surely the most significant example of our day. National and transnational opposition to the initiative articulates these issues as ultimately inseparable from one another, thus resonating with the traditional indigenous belief in the inexorable interconnectedness of all human experience, and an increasingly widespread questioning of dominant notions of progress.
>
> (*Native and National* 203)

Although these grassroots campaigns have gained some attention, in particular through the deployment of activist blogs and social media, one component that has gone largely unnoticed is the presence and potential of digital art and poetry within this framework of resistance. In this chapter, I will establish connections between the seemingly disparate phenomena of poetry and ecological movements, by exploring how some indigenous poets in Brazil are coming to terms with ecological issues and mobilizing new media to challenge the corporate and political structures responsible for environmental abuses. What I am calling here "online activist eco-poetry," whether born digital or digitized, has become a valuable tool that I propose is helping to change the dynamics of grassroots resistance (comprising indigenous and nonindigenous alliances) from its formerly localized focus to becoming a Brazil-wide and even an international effort.

In particular, I will examine how the trope of the cannibal, which has a lengthy history in Brazilian letters, has been reengaged (remediated) by poets toward new contestatory purposes.[2] To this end, I will study indigenous poet bloggers who are using the Internet to refashion popular oral poetic traditions into digital or, more accurately, "digitized" poetry—often times mobilizing these cultural productions to combat environmental abuses by government and private enterprise. Moreover, "online activist eco-poetry" represents a form of cultural resistance (through poetry) against the government's encroaching policies, as it questions official narratives that tend to privilege economic development at the cost of ecological conservation. Taking their cue from past avant-garde movements such as *Modernismo* and *Tropicália*, today's indigenous bloggers are reengaging with practices of cultural and technological cannibalism, and repurposing the trope of the cannibal as a creative and ecological force, grounding their activist poetry in an ethical and ecological vision.

In this chapter, I also argue that by turning to new media tools, indigenous environmentalist poets suggest the syncretic coexistence between seemingly incompatible binary oppositions such as nature and culture, or ecology and technology, proving the inadequacy of such dichotomies. My aim is to bring into interdisciplinary contact aspects from new media theory and from ecocriticism, to examine how indigenous bloggers draw on processes of "cannibalization" to address ecological issues.

Historical Precedents: Brazil's Cannibalism(s), Technology, and the Environment

Cannibalism has been a trope in literary discourse since Montaigne's essay "On Cannibalism" (1581). In Brazil, cannibalism or *antropofagia* as a cultural form has enjoyed several reincarnations and has been deployed to dislodge oppositions ingrained within Western colonial thought (savage versus civilized, nature versus culture). European colonizers understood the new continent as a source of natural resources ripe for pillaging, a land to be explored and exploited, both meanings contained in the Portuguese word *exploração*. Resistance to the colonizer's rapacious plunder of human and environmental resources came in many guises. *Antropofagia* as a cultural movement, for instance, is traceable to an incident of cannibalism later interpreted as an act of resistance against colonialism, which became a foundational episode in Brazilian history. When Dom Pero Fernandes Sardinha arrived to Brazil in 1556 to assume his charge as bishop-elect of Bahia, he received a most unusual welcome from the tupí-guaranís: they invited the prelate to a feast as both their guest of honor and as the main entree. Historians remain divided as to whether the episode is a true account or a colonial fabrication used to exemplify the savagery of the Amerindians (and justify their extermination).

Salacious literary and painterly exposés of New World cannibalism, common currency in the 16th century, already pointed to possible productive intersections between art and anthropophagy. Sardinha's feast served as inspiration for Oswald de Andrade's "Anthropofagic Manifesto" of 1928, which ushered in the practice of cultural cannibalism, as modern European artistic tendencies were devoured, processed, and incorporated into Brazilian art. The Brazilian works were not servile imitations but part of a creative process of hybridization that reflected (and reflected upon) the very essence of Brazil as a country suffused by syncretism, miscegenation, and heterogeneity, product of the not untroubled melding of Amerindian, European, and African cultures. In the 1920s, Brazilian modernists took from Europe what was consumable—its high culture as represented by the most radical avant-garde art and its technologies of reproduction—and "digested" it via a subversive and autochthonous process of cannibalism that incorporated Brazil's own popular culture traditions into the mix, often inverting the hierarchies of European and Amerindian values by placing the latter above the former.

Although in Brazil colonialism predates capitalism, Marxist critics have uncovered the intricate linkages between both, showing that "political control over a dependent social formation enables metropolitan capital to appropriate surplus-labour from it" (Wayne 79). Moreover, Marxist eco-criticism has shown that both colonialism and capitalism can be critiqued from an ecological perspective, given both formations' endless need to expand, consume, and engulf human and material resources, regardless of long-term environmental and human rights' costs. Thus, the trope of the cannibal, originally deployed against the colonial invader, easily morphs into a figure opposed to national, international, and transnational capitalism. While, as eco-critic Odile Cisneros observes, the cannibal can be understood as a recycler, both in "natural" and "cultural" terms, capitalist narratives of progress are instead pursuing paths of urbanization, unregulated resource extraction, and unsustainable growth. For Cisneros, eco-critical discourse can deploy the cannibal to dismantle "the age-old binaries that plague the issue of identity in Latin America, while still bringing out the radical political project that lies at the heart of the antrhopophagic project as a critique of capitalism and anthropocentric thinking" (94). As other critics have observed—Christopher Funkhouser, Augusto de Campos—the notion of cultural anthropophagy was itself an adaptation of Dadaist appropriation techniques (i.e., collage) to the Brazilian context. Thus, European art served as nourishment to fuel an artistic revolution in Brazil with ecological and anti-capitalist underpinnings.

Oswald de Andrade's somewhat elitist concept of *antropofagia* was repurposed in the 1960s by the *Tropicália* movement, which through its music engaged more directly with the hopes and aspirations of Brazil's *povo*, indeed focusing "on the quotidian desires and frustrations of 'everyday people'" (Dunn, *Brutality Garden* 3). Set against the backdrop of the military dictatorship (in power since 1964), *Tropicália* was a vehicle for artistic dissent that articulated the concerns of youth culture of all classes, fusing popular culture with the avant-garde. Singer-poets such as Tom Zé, Jorge Ben, Torquato Neto, José Carlos Capinan, Gal Costa, Gilberto Gil, and Caetano Veloso (the so-called *grupo baiano*), as well as others not based in Bahia, such as Chico Buarque, Milton Nascimento, and Antônio Carlos ("Tom") Jobim, incorporated foreign styles as disparate as Portuguese Fado, African beats, R&B, and American psychedelic rock with Brazilian bossa nova to create new sounds. Although generally upbeat, these songs often had ecological concerns at their core and represented a "juxtaposition and fusion of nature and technology, as well as of tradition and modernity, in a way that recalls the vanguardist poetics of Andrade and the pop innovations of Tropicália" (Dunn, "Jorge Mautner" 179).

Tropicália's ecological and cannibalistic sensibilities were also present in the plastic arts—in the work of Hélio Oiticica, Lygia Pape and Lygia Clark—in Concrete poetry, in architecture, in fashion, and in film, where it was enmeshed with Cinema Novo's revolutionary *estética da fome*. Tropicalists such as Oiticica had a sensibility toward the natural world, used ephemeral, recycled, and organic materials to mimic the lush tropical environment, and suffused their art with elements of ecological and political critique. Regarding *Tropicália*'s role in challenging the dictatorial regime, Dunn observes that "the tropicalists purposefully invoked stereotypical images of Brazil as a tropical paradise only to subvert them with pointed references to political violence and social misery," while reflecting the voices and tastes of popular classes, thereby becoming "an exemplary instance of cultural hybridity that dismantled binaries that maintained neat distinctions between high and low, traditional and modern, national and international cultural production" (*Brutality Garden* 3). As Roberto Schwarz, Dunn, Perrone, and other critics assert, Tropicalist songs critiqued capitalism's drive to unrestricted development and, both implicitly and explicitly, condemned the exploitation of natural resources, becoming early countercultural voices defending ecological concerns, voices that today find echoes in the blogosphere's eco-activism by indigenous and nonindigenous groups. Indeed, in recent years, former tropicalists such as Gilberto Gil have joined the protest against the endangerment of Amazonia, lending their support to the movement to stop Belo Monte and similar projects.

Thus, with each subsequent act of cultural anthropophagy, Brazilian artists—including, as we shall see, today's indigenous cyber-artists—have reinvented themselves by incorporating popular and mass culture into so-called high art, by metabolizing foreign influence into local cultural production and by assimilating previous epistemologies into new ones through processes of cultural and technological cannibalism. In fact, 1920s Brazilian modernism engaged, if somewhat superficially, with national popular culture. Appropriation of national and local models during modernism was followed by other aesthetic and technological shifts in the arts: the primacy of the written word was subsumed into the image (painting, photography, and film), poetry became increasingly visual, and film became the modern art par excellence, but samba was the modality that brought the popular and the avant-garde closest to each other. In the 1960s, Tropicalism also engulfed older media (poetry, painting, film) and brought them into performance, music, and mass communications such as television and radio.

Today's techno-cultural cannibalism is exemplified by the digital computer, which remediates—to use the term coined by Jay David Bolter and Richard Grusin—all previous media into itself, devouring older analog technologies into digital modes and bringing them even into the most difficult to reach corners of the Amazon basin. Nevertheless, several relevant questions might be asked about this latest stage of cannibalism: Have digital media users, such as indigenous bloggers, reinvented or transformed the notion of cultural cannibalism in any significant way or merely transplanted older ideas onto new media? Does the new digital cannibalism parody and appropriate texts in a way that is aggressively irreverent and contestatory to established power, as *Antropofagia* arguably did in the 1920s (in their challenge to European models) and *Tropicália* in the 1960s (in their challenge to military rule)? Does contemporary digital culture incorporate the voices of the Brazilian people, drawing on popular and mass culture in order to contest and subvert hegemonic systems? Are current ecological concerns—critical in the Brazilian context, given the rapidly disappearing rainforests and the penetration of capitalist interests into tribal lands—incorporated into the new poetic modes?

To be sure, it could be argued that a highly technological, economically expensive (from a hardware standpoint) form of online activist eco-poetry is completely compatible with capitalism, as Frederic Jameson has noted of previous styles that are performed through a somewhat de-politicized form of pastiche, typical of postmodern consumerism. Yet, these new media cultural products, I would argue, represent a "digital" anthropophagic maneuver that is loaded with political intent, as of late refocused toward environmental causes. These are the questions I will explore by examining the (undoubtedly political and politicized) work by indigenous poet-activists, in order to elucidate the connections, interconnections, links, and hyperlinks between contemporary net cultural practices and ecological activism.

Indigenous Bloggers, Online Activist Eco-Poetry, and the Belo Monte Dam

In Cisnero's eco-critical analysis of the "Manifesto Antropófago," she describes Andrade's presentation of the cannibal as one of a *bárbaro tecnizado*, a "technicized barbarian who doesn't necessarily reject technology but who only approves of those forms of technology that are not detrimental to the environment" (99). This perspective rejects the colonizer's image of the anthropophagous "primitive" ignorant of Western technology, substituting it with that of an indigenous hybrid agent who has adapted technology to a more or less "natural" environment, thereby problematizing the nature and culture divide and, indeed, striking a nonhierarchical balance between the two terms. The technicized Amerindian replaces the nature-culture distinction with an ever-shifting formation that has been dubbed "natureculture" in recent ecocriticism, blurring biological and technological boundaries.

Such boundary blurring may be politicized and technology appropriated to combat the interests of Capital's developmentalist agendas, in order to "change the political structure of society so that production to meet real needs replaces production for the accumulation of wealth" (Garrard 31). Several promising real-life instances of this trend toward indigenous technification demonstrate how the Internet might be strategically deployed toward ecological and political resistance. Admittedly, the indigenous deployment of digital forms of political resistance has been present for some time, for example, in the Mexican Zapatista movement and its reliance on cyberspace as a privileged location for launching its pro-indigenous rights message and its cyber-attacks against the Mexican government. As has been amply documented, without the political mobilization of both new and traditional media the Zapatistas would have suffered the tragic fate of many other less media-savvy indigenous uprisings. Of course, there are many other instances that fit the model, such as the activism by the U'wa people in the Colombian rainforest, whose online presence has been critical for the struggle against an oil pipeline that would cut through their ancestral lands (Landzellius 112).

The blogging resistance organized against the Belo Monte dam near the Xingu National Park (*Parque Nacional Indigena do Xingu*) has been a paradigmatic example of the socio-ecological efficacy of new media deployment by first peoples. According to environmentalist sources, the disruption to the Xingu River caused by the construction of the dam will affect biodiversity and the lives of the tribes and communities along the river. The flooding and the methane produced as a by-product of the dam's operation are also causes for grave concern. Indigenous groups hailing from diverse tribes have mobilized to stop construction using a variety of methods. In close conjunction with activist blogging, one such method has been the creation of "rainforest" or ecological poetry ("activist eco-poetry") to be deployed (read) during protests and performances, and later uploaded online—most often to blogs—to augment its exposure and eco-political efficacy. Indeed, the very multiplicity of indigenous approaches (blogs, film, poetry, performance, along with traditional activism, marches, rallies, political protests, and sit-ins) and the rapid and rhizome-like dissemination of their work—posted, reposted, and otherwise linked to by many global Internet sites—speaks volumes about both the political potential of blogging for tribal and environmental causes and the overcoming of simple distinctions such as on- and off-line modes of resistance, as these modes hybridize and continuously morph into each other.

Daniel Munduruku is an exemplary case among the indigenous poet-blogger-activists who cannibalize and deploy technology in defense of Brazil's environment. A native of Amazonia's Munduruku tribe, Daniel has been blogging for the better part of a decade, writing prose and poetry both on- and off-line, as well as maintaining a visible profile within Brazil's environmental movement. As the opening speaker at a recent environmentalist conference in Minas Gerais (*10° Congresso Nacional do Meio Ambiente,* Poços de Caldas, May 2013), Munduruku brought to the fore the negative impact of the dam projects, as well as the importance of his own tribe's resistance as part of a nationwide struggle:

> O povo Munduruku está sofrendo com a construção das barragens, seja em Belo Monte, seja em Rondônia, enfim, eles estão lutando para viver. A natureza e o ambiente que os índios vivem fazem parte da humanidade deles. Eles lutam para se manterem e lutam por um Brasil inteiro que não tem a consciência de perceber isso. A luta pelo meio ambiente é a luta de todo povo brasileiro.[3]
>
> (Balbino n.p.)

Munduruku cautiously embraces the arrival of technology, equally recognizing its potential dangers and its benefits. While concerned that media (television, radio, Internet) are bringing "noise" from the outside world to Amazonia, accelerating temporalities and mutating the rhythms of indigenous narratives based on oral culture, he also firmly believes in the need to engulf such media, "digesting" their influence and appropriating its uses by properly training the younger Amerindians:

> Acredito que seja necessário preparar os índios para trabalhar com a linguagem da média. Isto já vem sendo feito. Jovens indígenas estão trabalhando como operadores da média. Atualmente, existem rádios e emissoras de TV indígenas, como a do Parque Nacional do Xingu. Há também um trabalho muito interessante sendo realizado por uma ONG (Vídeo nas Aldeias) que capacita nossos povos no uso dos equipamentos mediáticos. São tecnologias que não conhecemos,

mas que precisamos dominar. É preciso tomar posse dessa tecnologia, produzindo coisas que sejam interessantes para a nossa cultura,
a partir do nosso ponto de vista.[4]

(Tavares n.p.)

While Amerindians' "taking possession" of media technology may re-
semble other technological appropriation practiced by marginalized
groups—for instance, the illegal accessing of Internet services in *favelas*,
facetiously known as gato.net—there is a significant difference in the cannibalistic appropriation of technology by indigenous groups for environmental purposes. Amerindians are not passive users of technology, but
reinvent and repurpose it, redirecting capitalist impulses often underlying
science and technology and imbuing them with elements of sociopolitical critique. Moreover, Munduruku's words mimic and cannibalize the
language of the dominant culture and of the colonial past—to take possession, to master, and so on—redirecting it toward a self-improvement
project that has as its goal the protection of Amazonia, thereby reconfig-
uring Western technoscience toward indigenous interests.

Sharing Munduruku's cautious faith in technology, eco-poet Graça
Graúna (from the Potiguara tribe, Rio Grande do Norte) keeps a blog
where she posts her poetry and other indigenous poets' work. The following stanza from one of Graúna's untitled poems captures its com-
bative commitment to representing indigenous struggles, environmental
and otherwise:

nos meus sonhos
meus avós têm falado.
Da cordilheira ao mar
de norte a sul,
desde o mais profundo
da nossa mãe terra
suas vozes aconselham
que expulsemos
os usurpadores
da nossa terra.
Os usurpadores
da nossa liberdade.

(n.p.)[5]

Characteristic of Graúna's postcolonial poetry, references to "mother
earth" and to the voice of the ancestors activate an ecological discourse
also mobilized by other Amazonian tribes (such as the U'wa in Colombia), defending their entitlement to the land "in terms of the continuity between past and present [...] harness[ing] the enduring momentum
of generations" (Landzellius 119). In Graúna's poetry, stewardship of

the land becomes both a right and an obligation of indigenous peoples. Moreover, the vehemence with which her poems condemn the rapacious exploitation and usurpation characteristic of the colonial and neocolonial enterprise reverses the cannibal image, presenting instead the First World's wanton exploitation of people and land as the ultimate gluttony of a devouring "civilization." Thus, the West's fear of the indigenous cannibal represents "a displacement and disavowal of the [...] consumption of human flesh that was most grievously carried out in the slave-trade but also in myriad forms of exploitation, colonialism, enforced dependency, hierarchy and [...] Christian mercy" and, perhaps worst of all, in today's transnational capitalism (Cotton 149). Martin Lefebvre also argues that the trope of the cannibal is connected by the West "both with fear of the other and the will to dominate him, and with the economics of New World colonialism and the beginnings of capitalism" (46).

Eschewing the discourse of power present in First World cannibalistic capitalism, Graúna feeds instead on a narrative favoring communal enterprise and respect toward nature. A seasoned poet affiliated to the online poetry network "Biopoética Pernambucana," Graúna explains that her poetry revolves around a sense of the collective, a notion linked to her understanding of how her individual work fits with a greater body of indigenous global poetry blogging:

> Em várias partes do mundo há milhares de povos indígenas que expressam seu amor à terra, seu desejo permanente de justiça e liberdade, seja por meio da contação de histórias, da poesia, da arte plumária, do grafismo, do barro ou dos sonhos que trazem as canções da mata e do amor à natureza.[6]
>
> (n.p.)

Both Graúna's poetry and her activism are dedicated to exposing the "civilized" cannibal exploiter and his links to global capitalism, since, "out of the image of cannibalism we may see one of capitalism emerge" (Cotton 155). Conscious of her place within the worldwide community of indigenous bloggers, poets, and artists, Graúna strengthens these networks, for instance, by providing in her blog a list of other indigenous writers from different tribes, many of whom are also protesting the wanton capitalist consumption spurring projects such as Belo Monte.[7] Moreover, even as she adopts the Internet, ancestral traditions still anchor her poetry, regardless of its medium:

> Ao escrever,
> dou conta da ancestralidade;
> do caminho de volta,
> do meu lugar no mundo.
>
> (n.p.)[8]

Graúna views her reverence for indigenous traditions as wholly compatible with her deployment of the blog format, demonstrating how the blogosphere is fundamental to maintain cohesion for networks of indigenous poets who might be globally dispersed but remain ideologically united in their resistance to unrestricted developmentalism, thus locating their "place in the world" in the act of writing and blogging, regardless of their actual physical location. As Graúna explains, online poetry networks include poets working within the Amazon and those who have become its exiles (such as Daniel Munduruku or Eliane Potiguara, both urban dwellers): "participar do ciberespaço e me emociono quando (re) encontro vozes exiladas em Blocos"[9] (n.p.).

In other cases, indigenous blogger-poets do not have their own website but post in host websites. The website "Indios Online" presents other instances of the political deployment of poetry and other arts by indigenous cyber-artists, functioning as a virtual location for cultural exchange and as a venue for tribes to share resistance strategies against the encroachment on their land.[10] Although partially funded by Brazil's Culture Ministry—and thus, arguably under the state's supervision—the indigenous bloggers retain control over the content they post in "Indios Online." The site works as a heterogeneous multi-access point where one may post poetry and prose, obtain news, link to a channel of indigenous YouTube videos, access a related Twitter account, as well as interface with multiple other networks dealing with indigenous affairs. Among the sites one can link to is a portal website called "RISADA," where environmentally minded artisanal products may be purchased from a variety of tribes (thereby providing valuable economic assistance in difficult times) and where one might also learn about each tribe's history, and oral and poetic traditions. "RISADA" exemplifies the cannibalization of marketing strategies, redirected to nonprofit communal and eco-friendly projects. "OCA DIGITAL," a free-sharing website under the creative commons license, also hosts indigenous bloggers. Curated and maintained by an NGO (Thydêwá), its content originates from seven individual access points located in seven remote indigenous communities throughout Brazil, facilitating the first experience of digital access for many Amerindians. "OCA DIGITAL" is dedicated to showcasing techno-cultural projects that reconnect poetry with the broader concept of *poesis*, understood as creations that draw on both traditional and new media arts, exemplified by works such as "vídeos, maps, mashups, soundclouds, instagrams, wallpapers, ringtones, fotografias, lifeinaday, fotografias 360°, passeio virtual"[11] (n.p.).

Although many of these projects are ecologically inspired, we should resist oversimplifying and essentializing indigenous positions as always being pro-environment, as there are isolated instances of tribes welcoming environmentally questionable development projects. Indeed, Greg Garrard argues in *Ecocriticism* (2004) that the complex relationships of indigenous tribes with technology interrogate long-held stereotypes about the "ecological Indian." Garrard traces the oversimplified construction of the ecologically minded Indian, always respectful of the natural world, to humanist antecedents, such as Montaigne's cannibal and Rousseau's noble savage. The metaphor of the primitive yet noble Indian is dangerous because "it transforms a geographical differentiation into an historical or evolutionary one, so that Indians or aborigines can be seen as being *behind* Europeans in an inevitable progression from the natural to a civilized state" (135). But, such caveats notwithstanding, the particular examples I examine reflect that Amazonian tribes today, especially those affected by large-scale projects such as Belo Monte, are actively engaged in environmental activism, even if their relationship with technology remains open and productively ambiguous.

By the same token, far from considering themselves as being *behind*, many Amazonian tribes are instead contesting techno-deterministic teleological understandings of progress, in particular with regard to development projects that disrupt traditional and eco-friendly ways of life. These challenges are made, paradoxically, through digital tools, often integrated with popular art forms such as songs and oral poetry. By embracing the latest technologies, activists ready eco-political messages for mass consumption, making them visible to global audiences and thus applying pressure to the slow-to-move political class.[12] Placing their message in poetic form, they mobilize art's possibilities toward cultural and political change.

But where is indigenous blogging occurring? Surprisingly, blogging is not just happening in urban centers, but also in places with the most limited Internet access in deep Amazonia, at special "points of access" that rely on satellite technology for connectivity. Conscious of the dangers of a technology that might, if misused, erode their cultural heritage through the invasion of hegemonic cultural values, indigenous bloggers, poets, and activists speak of using the Internet as one more communication tool that can be mobilized to defend indigenous rights, even as they remain wary of its potential threat. New media may provide a way to preserve indigenous culture (albeit in a "cannibalized" and altered form) and furnish an efficient method to disseminate indigenous ecological concerns to other Brazilians. Moreover, by creating their own blogs, Brazil's Amerindians control their own stories and images, as Anápuáka Muniz, a member of the Tupinambá tribe asserts[13]:

> Vimos que podíamos ser protagonistas da nossa história. Antes a gente precisava de intermediários, hoje temos autonomia para divulgar nossas lutas, nossa cultura, não precisamos mais dos jornais, televisões, rádios. Hoje pesquisamos o nosso passado, documentamos o nosso presente e reavaliamos como será nosso futuro.[14]
>
> (Peres 13)

Naturally, activists insist that the introduction of Web-based technology into deep-Amazonia must be judicious, guarding against an imprudent disruption of existing ways of life in isolated indigenous communities. Jerry Mander's study *In the Absence of the Sacred: The Failure of Technology and the Survival of the Indian Nations* (1995) preaches a cautionary tale about the isolating effects of technology on a Canadian Native community, where a communal way of life that emphasized human contact was supplanted by time spent alone in front of television sets. But, even if, in a worst case scenario, overexposure to consumerism and to the objectification of nature present in television and other media could lead to the degradation of the native traditional lifestyle, this is not a danger unique to indigenous populations. Preventing Amerindians from equal access to technology based on a danger that Western culture has readily chosen to accept for itself seems hypocritical at best. Although Mander makes a compelling argument for the benefits of a simple life, paternalistically denying indigenous people the choice to engage with digital technology vastly underrates their capacity to adapt, while naïvely positing that such a lack of access constitutes an advantage in the face of aggressive encroachment.

Moreover, arguments claiming that the computer itself encodes non-indigenous values—such as an encrypted scientific, Western mode of thinking—and ultimately espouses individualism over collectivism (Howe 17) do not correspond to its actual "cannibalistic" appropriation and repurposing by Amazonian indigenous peoples. There, computer use is strengthening a sense of the collective and broadening that collectivity to include many tribes, creating what some dub a "global village" and others a "new media nation" (Alia), closely linking technology to "artistic" modes of thinking, bridging the artistic and scientific divide. In fact, Amazonian tribes are disproving negative scenarios about media's influence on first peoples, having cannibalized the technologies of the "civilized" other in order to organize cultural and artistic events (such as live poetry readings, subsequently documented and posted online) with the intent to gain visibility for the "Fourth World." In so doing, they hope that through online alliances their voice will be heard beyond the national boundaries of Brazil. Significantly, media practices such as poetry blogging or filmmaking are "part of a broader project of constituting a cultural future in which their traditions and contemporary technologies are combined in ways that can give [them] new vitality" (Ginsburg 43).

Beyond the political relevance of these manifestations of ecological and indigenous-based poetry and other creative forms that are being posted online, we must recognize their potential for artistic innovation as art that engages with new digital media and draws on at least some of its particular capabilities (its rapid rhizomatic spread through reposting, the ease of self-publication, the inter-linkages between different websites). While ecological poetry posted in blogs may not be classifiable as "digital poetry", properly speaking, since it rarely uses the full capabilities of the digital medium—it does not (yet) activate kinetic script, sound, or typographical effects typically used by avant-garde digital poets—it nonetheless constitutes a popular use of poetic forms on the Internet. Although digital purists such as Katherine Hayles or Christopher Funkhouser would likely exclude print or oral poetry that has been digitized from the category of "digital poetry," other critics such as Talam Memmott, less concerned with taxonomy, are generously predisposed toward the inclusion of such mimetic cases, considering the medium in which the poem is read (the computer screen) as sufficient, defining any creative cultural practice that uses an applied technology as a form of "digital" or "digitized" art. According to Memmott, we might consider as digital poetry any object that is "mediated through digital technology and [...is] called 'poetry' by its author or by a critical reader" (293). Rita Raley has also argued, "neither software nor technique can function as a unifying or homogenizing rubric that would authorize the instantiation of digital poetry as a singular genre" (887). In the case of poems transcribed to blogs, one might indeed view them as hybrid oral-paper-digitized poetry that carry within the potential for greater "digitality," insofar as they are virally disseminated and viewed in an environment that also allows for comments, appropriations, cross-linkages with other blogs, hypertextuality, and multiple reframings.

In their do-it-yourself approach, today's environmentalist blogger-poets (indigenous and not) have much in common with the Brazilian urban youth poets of the 1970s, who Charles Perrone groups under the rubric of "poesía marginal," whose marginality was "determined from two angles: that of form, in a literal sense, of the physical making and dissemination of products, and that of content, of the texts themselves, with their constituent language and attitudes" (119). As Perrone observes, those marginal poets achieved a small and often homemade press circuit, reproducing their works through mimeographs, photocopies, and pamphlets. Today, the Internet blog has become one such place for disseminating poetry and activism, and thus its importance as a tool of social change far outweighs somewhat trivial and decidedly arbitrary, not to speak of culturally biased, questions of its literary merits. As such, indigenous poet-bloggers are not only advocating for a radical politics of ecological resistance, but they are also doing so by engaging with radical new forms, like the Modernists and Tropicalists had done before.

Concluding Remarks: A Sober Reality

In recent years, technological penetration has increased dramatically throughout Latin America, whether cell phones, computers, tablets, and Internet access. In Brazil, and in Latin America at large, technology users make new technology their own by embedding and modifying it within their social and political practices. In this chapter, I examined a strand of citizen-based activism that engages environmental causes through acts of on- and off-line poetic resistance—specifically the work of indigenous bloggers' deployment of activist eco-poetry that broaches pro-environment issues. While these forms of cyberactivism cannot be considered as "born-digital," they are attempting to operate on the realm of the digital to achieve greater diffusion for their causes.

The urgency and efforts displayed by indigenous bloggers to raise environmental awareness through poetry and other means stems directly and tangibly from growing threats to the environment, exemplified but not limited to the Belo Monte project. The work of these cyberactivists thus connects directly to the struggle waged by all the tribes inhabiting the Xingu, a struggle that has global dimensions and demands a global response, as expressed by several chiefs in an open letter to the world:

> we are here fighting for our people, for our lands, for our forests, for our rivers, for our children, and in honor of our ancestors. We are also fighting for the future of the world [...] We do not want Belo Monte.
>
> (Devine Guzmán, "Writing" 280)[15]

Moreover, the self-representations of indigenous culture on the Web has allowed for a more complex understanding of both the cannibal cultural processes and the Indian, challenging naïve beliefs of their unmediated connections to the natural and arguably replacing them with an ethical understanding of how culture and nature are inextricably imbricated with each other and with technology. Not content with lamenting the perhaps irrevocably lost "natural" world—itself a myth, since technology and culture were always already present—the approach from ecologically minded digital bloggers in Brazil, indigenous and non, goes against normative conceptions of humanity as apart from, or indeed superior to, nature. Through their engagement with digital tools, poets and bloggers—including those indigenous cyberactivists reclaiming their self-interpretations and taking control of their own ecological struggles—are thus questioning Western models of affluence and progress, thereby recycling the image of the cannibal as an ecological being who enacted a cyclical process of consuming the old and reprocessing it in new forms, imbricating the foreign other with local, autochthonous traditions. In these grassroots ecological struggles, the Internet's immense potential for resistance is only beginning to become apparent.

By way of a woeful epilogue, as I finish this chapter (December 2016), almost five years since ground was broken, the Belo Monte dam is nearly complete, despite efforts by environmental groups, several occupations of the work site, lawsuits, and growing international outrage. Recent news from tribes inhabiting areas closest to the dam report that the water nearest the construction site is no longer potable and that parts of the Xingu river are already permanently and irrevocably destroyed. The inauguration of the dam within the next couple of years and the flooding of the Xingu is practically inevitable. Thus, at least in the immediate present, corporate interest and unchecked developmentalism seem to be gaining the upper hand in Amazonia. That, however, does not render the efforts of the environmentalist poets as null. They are, in fact, providing a model for the ways in which nature and culture, technology and ecology, might find ways of coexisting in productive, nondestructive ways. Perhaps that model will be heeded, someday.

Notes

1 The dam, which would be the third largest in the world, is part of a greater project to develop the Amazon area by building large-scale hydroelectric dams (such as the Rondônia and Tucuruí dams) and roads. FUNAI (*Fundação Nacional do Índio*), a government organization responsible for the protection of indigenous rights, has voiced concerns about the dangers the dam will represent for the tribes, some of which remain "uncontacted" by the outside world. The dam project has proceeded without the proper participation or approval of indigenous groups and affected riverside communities, and with inadequate assessment of impact to the environmental and social wellbeing of the area.

2 I would like to credit here Odile Cisnero's essay "Ecocannibalism: The Greening of Antropofagia," which astutely reevaluates both Oswald de Andrade's "Manifesto da Poesia Pau-Brasil" and his "Manifesto Antropófago" in light of an eco-critical analysis. Her essay was a source of inspiration for this chapter.

3 Translation: The Munduruku people are suffering with the construction of dams, whether in Belo Monte or Rondônia, at any rate they are fighting to survive. The nature and the environment that the Indians inhabit is part of their very humanity. Their struggle to stay [in their homeland] is also a fight on behalf of all Brazilians, even if the country remains unaware of this. The battle for the environment is the struggle of all the Brazilian people.

4 Translation: I believe that it is necessary to prepare the Amerindians to work with media languages. Currently there are indigenous radio and television stations, such as the one in the Xingu National Park. There is also interesting work being done by the NGO Vídeo nas Aldeias which trains our people in the use of media technology. These are technologies we still do not know, but which we must master. It is imperative to take possession of such technologies, to produce objects that will be interesting to our culture, and from our point of view.

5 Translation:

in my dreams
my grandparents have spoken.
From the mountains to the sea,
from north to south,
from the deepest
of our mother earth
their voices advise us

to expel
the usurpers
of our land.
The usurpers
of our freedom.
See Graúna's poetry in http://ggrauna.blogspot.com/.

6 Translation: Throughout the globe there are thousands of indigenous peoples expressing their love for the Earth, their permanent desire for justice
and freedom, whether through the telling of stories, poetry, feather art,
drawing, clay or via the dreams reflected by their songs about the forest and
about their love of nature.

7 She mentions, for instance, Carlos Tiago, Tiago Hakiy, Cristino Wapichana,
Darlene Taukane, Manoel Moura, Giselda Jerá, Jeguaka Mirim, Adão Ta-
taendy, Cristino Wapichana, Eliane Potiguara, Jaime Dessano, Rosi Tapuia.

8 Translation:

When writing,
I account for ancestry;
for the return trip,
for my place in the world.
See http://ggrauna.blogspot.com/p/entrevistas.html.

9 Translation: participating in cyberspace, I am overwhelmed when I (re)en-
counter exiled voices in blogs.

10 See "Indios Online" website at www.indiosonline.net/.

11 See "Oca Digital" website at http://www.thydewa.org/projetos/oca-digital/.

12 A recent report by the Brazilian magazine *Indio* about the use of film and
new media technologies by indigenous populations states that "a naturali-
dade com que os índios interagem com equipamentos de audiovisual digitais
pode levar essa tecnologia a se disseminar mais rapidamente que os métodos
educacionais baseados na linguagem escrita" (Peres 9). There is an NGO
called "Vídeo nas Aldeias" (directed by Vincent Carelli), which is primarily
concerned with the introduction of video and new media equipment into
remote regions of Amazonia, so that the Amerindian population will not
only have an opportunity to create a video archive of their traditions, but
also to increase their visibility to the outside world and gain support for their
causes—many of them environmental issues, such as the Belo Monte dam.

13 According to *Global Voices*, a website that tracks global blogging activity and community media usage, most indigenous areas are located in
remote villages without Internet access, but "the rise of strong regional
indigenous associations such as COIAB, the Coordination of Indigenous
Associations of the Brazilian Amazon, and national level networks such
as Rede dos Povos das Florestas, led by indigenous leader Ailton Krenak,
has encouraged indigenous groups or individuals to blog to the world"
(Goldemberg n.p.).

14 Translation: We saw that we could be protagonists of our history. Before
we thought about using intermediaries, today we have autonomy to make
our struggles known, we no longer need the newspapers, television, or
radio. Today we research our past, document our present, and reevaluate
our future.

15 As stated in an open letter to the Brazilian people from tribal leaders Bet
Kamati Kayapó, Raoni Kayapó, and Yakareti Juruna, on behalf of sixty-two
indigenous leaders from the Xingu River Basin.

Works Cited

Anderson, Mark. "National Nature and Ecologies of Abjection in Brazilian Literature at the Turn of the Twentieth Century." *The Natural World in Latin American Literatures. Ecocritical Essays in twentieth-Century Writings.* Ed. Adrian Taylor Kane. New York and London: McFarloand and Co., 2010. 208–232.

Andrade, Oswald de. "Manifesto Antropófago." *Revista de Antropofagia* 1.1 (May 1928): 3, 7.

Balbino, Jessica. "'Não existem índios no Brasil', diz escritor em abertura de congreso." *Globo 1. Sul de Minas.* 22 May 2013. http://g1.globo.com/mg/sul-de-minas/noticia/2013/05/nao-existem-indios-no-brasil-disse-indigena-em-abertura-de-congresso.html. Accessed 15 Dec. 2013.

Bowers, C.A., Miguel Vasquez, and Mary Roaf. "Native People and the Challenge of Computers: Reservation Schools, Individualism, and Consumerism." *American Indian Quarterly* 24.2 (2000): 182–199.

Buell, Laurence. *Writing for an Endangered World: Literature, Culture, and Environment in the U.S. and Beyond.* Cambridge, MA: Belknap, Harvard U P, 2001.

Campos, Augusto de, et al. *Balanço da Bossa e Outras Bossas.* 2nd ed. São Paulo: Perspectiva, 1974.

Cisneros, Odile. "Ecocannibalism: The Greening of Antropofagia." *The Utopian Impulse in Latin America.* Ed. Kim Beauchesne and Alessandra Santos. New York: Palgrave Macmillan, 2011. 93–106.

Devine Guzmán, Tracy. *Native and National in Brazil: Indigeneity after Independence.* Chapel Hill: U of North Carolina P, 2013.

———. "Writing Indigenous Activism in Brazil: Belo Monte and the Acampamento Indígena Revolucionário." *A Contracorriente* [Online] 10.1 (2012): 280–309. https://acontracorriente.chass.ncsu.edu/index.php/acontracorriente/article/view/99. Accessed 15 Dec. 2013.

Dunn, Christopher. *Brutality Garden: Tropicália and the Emergence of a Brazilian Counterculture.* Chapel Hill: U of North Carolina P, 2001.

———. "Jorge Mautner and Countercultural Utopia in Brazil." *The Utopian Impulse in Latin America.* Ed. Kim Beauchesne and Alessandra Santos. New York: Palgrave, 2011. 173–185.

Dyson, Laurel Evelyn, Max Hendriks, and Stephen Grant. *Information Technology and Indigenous People.* Melbourne: Information Science Publishing, 2007.

Funkhouser, Christopher. "Cannibalistic Tendencies in Digital Poetry: Recent Observations & Personal Practices." *The Network as a Space and Medium for Collaborative Interdisciplinary Practice Proceedings.* Bergen, Norway, 2009. http://elmcip.net/critical-writing/cannibalistic-tendencies-digital-poetry-recent-observations-personal-practices. Accessed 15 Dec. 2013.

———. "Le(s) Mange Texte(s): Creative Cannibalism and Digital Poetry." *E-Poetry Proceedings.* Paris, France. 2007. www.epoetry2007.net/english/papers/funkhouseruk.pdf. Accessed 15 Dec. 2013.

Ginsburg, Faye D. "Screen Memories: Resignifying the Traditional in Indigenous Media." *Media Worlds: Anthropology on a New Terrain.* Ed. Faye D. Ginsburg, Lila Abu-Lughod, and Brian Larkin. Berkeley: U of California P, 2002, 39–57.

Goldemberg, Deborah. "Brazil: Indian Culture, Poetry and Rights on the Blogosphere." *GlobalVoices*. 5 Apr. 2009. http://globalvoicesonline.org/2009/04/05/brazil-poetry-rights-and-culture-on-the-indian-blogosphere/. Accessed 13 Dec. 2013.

Graúna, Graça. "Graça Graúna." http://ggrauna.blogspot.com. Accessed 15 Dec. 2013.

Hayles, Katherine. "Simulated Nature and Natural Simulations: Rethinking the Relation between the Beholder and the World." *Uncommon Ground: Toward Reinventing Nature*. Ed. William Cronon. New York: Norton and Co., 1995. 409–425.

Howe, Craig. "Cyberspace is No Place for Tribalism." *Wicazo Sa Review* (Fall 1998): 19–27.

Mander, Jerry. *In the Absence of the Sacred: The Failure of Technology and the Survival of the Indian Nations*. San Francisco: Sierra Club Books, 1991.

Memmott, Talan. "Beyond Taxonomy: Digital Poetics and the Problem of Reading." *New Media Poetics: Contexts, Technocontexts and Theories*. Ed. Adalaide Morris and Thomas Swiss. Cambridge, MA: MIT Press, 2006. 293–306.

Moncao, Joana. "A Poesia na luta contra Belo Monte." *Desinformémonos* 74 (Jan. 2013). http://desinformemonos.org/2011/08/a-poesia-na-luta-contra-belo-monte. Accessed 13 Jan. 2013.

Munduruku, Daniel. "Mundurukando." http://danielmunduruku.blogspot.com. Accessed 15 Dec. 2013.

Oca Digital (n.d.). http://www.thydewa.org/projetos/oca-digital/. Accessed 15 Dec. 2013.

Peres, Cristina. "Bits e maracás: A apropriação das novas tecnologias pelos indígenas." *Revista Índio* 1.2 (2011): 9–13. http://revistaindio.wordpress.com/edicoes/. Accessed 13 Jan. 2013.

Perrone, Charles. *Seven Faces: Brazilian Poetry Since Modernism*. Durham, NC: Duke UP, 1996.

Raley, Rita. "'Living Letterforms': The Ecological Turn in Contemporary Digital Poetics." *Contemporary Literature* 52.4 (2011): 883–913. Project MUSE. http://muse.jhu.edu. Accessed 15 Dec. 2013.

RISADA (Rede Indigena de Arte e Artesanato). www.risada.org/. Accessed 15 Dec. 2013.

Tavares, Marcus. "Entrevista a Daniel Munduruku: A influência da TV no universo indígena." Rio Mídia. 2 May 2007. www.direitoacomunicacao.org.br/content.php?option=com_content&task=view&id=428. Accessed 15 Dec. 2013.

Wayne, Jack. "Capitalism and Colonialism in Late Nineteenth Century Europe." *Studies in Political Economy* 5 (Spring 1981): 79–105.

15 "Yo soy": Public Protest, Private Expression

Contestatory Uses of Social Media by Contemporary Mexican Youth

Mary K. Long

During the Mexican presidential election of 2012, social media played an important role in shaping public debate. In particular, the #Yosoy132[1] student movement used a combination of YouTube, Twitter, Facebook, websites, blogs, alternative online news venues, and public rallies to contest the power of official media and to bring the issues students considered most vital to the forefront. This intervention into national politics by primarily middle- and upper-class Mexican youth began when 131 students posted a defense of the authenticity of their views to YouTube after a controversial visit by then Presidential candidate Enrique Peña Nieto to the Universidad Iberoamericana on May 11, 2012. The movement ultimately brought thousands to the streets and inspired individuals and groups across Mexico and throughout the world to create their own websites and to hold local gatherings in solidarity in the months that lead up to the elections and during the following year.[2] The #Yosoy132 movement has been compared to other recent protest movements worldwide (for example, the 15M movement in Spain or the Occupy movement in the U.S.), and during the most active phase, many observers referred to it as the "Mexican Spring."[3]

In what follows, an analysis of the uses of YouTube and other social media that lead up to and flowed from the #Yosoy132 movement, as well as the debates around the authenticity of this movement, can provide insights into the ways middle- and upper-class Mexican youth are mediating the unique responsibilities and blame assigned to them in the transition between the postrevolutionary and the neoliberal, NAFTA-centered, modernization projects of the 20th and 21st centuries. Specifically, these uses of social media constitute contestatory practices that not only question the current political order, but also reject the neoliberal obligation to consume by affirming individual and group rights to creativity and self-expression as civic acts. These themes are succinctly summarized in the poster for an event sponsored on April 2, 2013 by the group:

#SomosCiudadanosNoConsumidores
Imagina, grita, brinca, mueve, llora, informa, sueña, comunica...
#LosMediosSomosTodos; #ComunicoLuegoExisto; #TodosSo-
mosElMensaje; #LosMediosSeránSocialesOnoSerán[4]
(#Somosciudadanos)

The web of electronic texts analyzed here make up a recent chapter in
Mexico of citizens' struggle to effect change by providing alternate narratives for themselves as individuals and for their country. The tensions
represented in the Mexican context between creativity and consumerism
echo international discussion about the implications of globalization for
the rights of individuals to self-realization and also resonate within the
historically recurring discussion of the importance of Mexican youth
and their creative and intellectual projects as the agents of future national success or failure. It will be proposed in this study that a new
narrative structure is created by the intermingling of varied social media forms and that this in turn reshapes the way Mexican youth interact with not only the political structure but also with the narrative and
journalistic traditions that have existed in Mexico for processing and
creating individual and group meaning. These new narrative structures
are altering and will continue to alter the role of the public intellectual
and of cultural journalism, two forces that have traditionally been at the
center of contestatory interactions with the Mexican state.

The responsibilities assigned to young Mexicans in relation to the
public intellectual/artistic sphere in Mexico have a long history. At the
end of the armed portion of the 1910 revolution, the Mexican people
and their leaders began a quest for the optimal combination of political,
economic, and social structures that would provide all Mexican citizens access to the benefits of the "modern" world, while also preserving
ties to their complex past. In this process, intellectuals and artists—
in particular, young, educated intellectuals and artists—were assigned
a central role in defining the vision of postrevolutionary Mexico and
were urged to balance their private creative work with public service,
as educators and statesmen, and through public art projects, such as
the well-known mural campaigns. Within this scenario, public intellectuals and cultural journalism played an important role in articulating
national narratives, and the moral imperative to "hacer cosas...mover a
la gente para un cambio, para la construcción de una obra de beneficio
colectivo"[5] (Krauze 258) would shape the vision for the role of educated
youth, their transition into adulthood, and the potential of their intellectual and creative projects for the nation up through the early 1990s
in Mexico.[6]

During the neoliberal era (which, in Mexico, began to impact ordinary
people with the signing and implementation of NAFTA during the early
1990s), the imperative to work within the status quo in order to propel

Mexico "finally" into the first world of globalized consumer culture assigned an important, if decidedly less visionary, role for the young: they would become the primary new consumers behind market success. This shift reflected a general change in all of Latin America. As early as 2000, the authors of the business focused article "Tomorrow in Latin America," while predicting success for the neoliberal model in Latin America, observed with satisfaction that "the majority of experts agree that privatization already wields a profound effect on young people, who for the first time, have an almost insatiable appetite for consumer products" (Matathue 33). In 2012, twelve years into the 21st century, Mexico was still struggling with myriad social, political, and economic challenges that neither the postrevolutionary nor the neoliberal projects had been able to fully remedy. The young continued to be caught in the middle of the debate.

In 2011, the population segment between fifteen and twenty-nine years of age was closely scrutinized in the national press and in online discussions when the results of the "Panorama de la educación, 2011" carried out by the Organization for Economic Co-operation and Development (OECD) revealed that 7 million 226 thousand or 25% of Mexicans between the ages of fifteen and twenty-nine neither work nor study ("**ni** estudian, **ni** trabajan"), placing Mexico in third place for countries with the largest inactive youth population within the group of thirty-four OECD member nations[7] (Panorama).

In spite of the fact that the full report reveals significant progress in Mexico in a number of educational categories and significant nuances around issues of class and gender,[8] the press focused mainly on the size of this segment of inactive youth, which was quickly nicknamed *los ninis* (Avilés 36). Although much of the discussion in the press and online generally emphasized the government's failure to create education and work opportunities for lower- as well as middle- and upper-middle class youth, there were many who simply interpreted this demographic segment as slackers, lacking motivation and a sense of social responsibility, and the nickname *ninis* became a pejorative that often appears as a taunt in online discussion forums.

Whether they were studying or working or not, the youth of Mexico, along with their adult compatriots, were becoming expert users of the Internet. By May 2012, when the #YoSoy132 movement emerged, the Internet in general and social media in particular already reached a large number of Mexicans within the country. According to the CIA World Factbook, in 2009, Mexico ranked twelfth in the world for internet use, with just over 31 million users, and according to the study "Hábitos de los usuarios de Internet en México"[9] published in 2012 by the Mexican Internet Association (AMIPCI), that number had risen to 40.6 million by 2011. Neither data source provides a breakdown of users by age group, but as a point of general comparison, it is useful to note that the total population of Mexico in 2013 was slightly over 116 million and roughly 18% (or just over 21 million) were between the ages of fifteen and twenty-four (*World Factbook*).

Based on a survey of 2,329 people conducted in various online settings between April 23 and May 13, 2012, the AMIPCI study reported the following information that highlights the importance of social media in 2012: Mexican internet users spent an average of four hours and nine minutes per day online. The top three general uses for the Internet were receiving and sending e-mail (80%), accessing social networks (77%), and looking up information (71%), while the top three entertainment uses were social networks (86%), visiting news sites (61%), and downloading music and videos (37%). Up to 92% percent of users subscribed to an average of four social networks, and while 23% of these users had been subscribing to social networks for more than five years, 19% had taken up this activity within the last year. The top five social networks in 2012 were, in descending order, Facebook (90%), YouTube (60%), Twitter (55%), Google+ (34%), and Hi5 (25%). In addition to accessing already existing sites, 16% of users created and maintained their own websites and blogs.

Interviews conducted by the author with five Mexican youth between the ages of fifteen and twenty-five during October and December 2012 reveal further nuances of recreational social media use. Those interviewed used Facebook to communicate personal information to friends, YouTube primarily to watch already existing videos, and Twitter to comment on those videos or other trending topics, as well as to follow and comment on posts by entertainment celebrities, sports figures, news personalities, and politicians.[10] In addition, those interviewed indicated that their use habits were representative of the use habits of their peers (Moreno-Ramirez; Macias). An exploration of YouTube channels revealed that many Mexican youth also have their own YouTube channels, where in addition to sharing videos made by others, they post their own videos, which offer a wide variety of categories of performance and thought including investigative reporting, music performances, stand-up comedy, video game demonstrations, commentary on popular culture, politics, religion, and more. YouTube channels that seek to include viewers into a broader cause are often linked to Facebook sites, which further the message of the YouTube posts.[11]

This dynamic online Mexican universe has been received with ambivalence by some older Mexican intellectuals who have offered varied assessments of the Internet in relation to their analysis of the impact of neoliberalism on the intellectual sphere in general and cultural journalism in particular. For example, Roger Bartra struck a tone of great pessimism in his 1999 *La sangre y la tinta,* stating that "despues del esplendor de los años setentas,"[12] public intellectuals now live "amenazados por el espectro de la decadencia"[13] (43). Within this dark scenario, the Internet is represented as "la forma de experimentar la muerte intelectual"[14] (53). In a 2009 article that chronicles the history and supposed death of cultural journalism in Mexico, Fernando de Ita offers a more nuanced, yet still cautionary view of this communication medium. He first notes that "el Internet no es el enemigo número uno sino el mejor aliado del periodismo escrito"[15] and states that "sin duda, el gran logro de Internet es que ha democratizado la información"[16] (78). Though he recognizes that the Internet commands a strong readership among the young, since they get all the news that interests them through it, he fails to see a professional future for them there. He seems even somewhat amazed at the insatiable need for expression in the young, noting that "las carreras de comunicación siguen produciendo una cantidad industrial de licenciados en la materia,"[17] in spite of the fact that "sus fuentes de trabajo están saturados, pagan sueldo de risa y no tienen futuro, sobre todo los diarios y revistas que se hacen en los estados"[18] (77). Nevertheless, he celebrates the access that young people find to audiences and self-expression through the Internet: "Hoy mi hijo, un perfecto desconocido, tiene más de mil visitas en cada una de los performances que sube a YouTube... los jóvenes hallan en el Internet el espacio para expresarse"[19] (77). Yet, he stops short of fully embracing the new medium, and ultimately his message is one of caution:

> El medio no resuelve por sí mismo la forma y el contenido de sus materiales.... para decir algo con sentido, hay que pensarlo y luego hablarlo, escribirlo, dibujarlo, fotografiarlo, filmarlo con precisión, claridad y profundidad, y para esto no hay programa en la computadora porque aun depende del talento, la disposición, el estudio, la disciplina, la conciencia del ser humano.[20]
>
> (78)

For both Bartra and de Ita, the stakes are high, since they see the breakdown of the role of intellectuals and cultural journalism as closely tied to the overall failure of Mexico's national modernization project: "Las artes y las humanidades estarían llegando al fin de su historia a un límite en la creación de nuevas alternativas...Se ha dicho que hemos llegado a un agotamiento en la producción de estructuras significativas"[21] (Bartra 53);

> No es solo nuestro oficio el que está en quiebra. Es el entramado social de la colmena lo que está hendiendo. Doscientos años de Independencia y cien años de Revolución nos revelan que construimos un país increíblemente desigual en todos los órdenes de la convivencia civilizada...algo está podrido entre nosotros.[22]
>
> (de Ita 78)

While de Ita clearly acknowledges that the old structures no longer work and also clearly acknowledges contemporary students' impulse to seek change, in 2009 he does not express faith in the success of these impulses. Bartra and de Ita are not alone in their nostalgia for the slow, meticulous production of thought, but perhaps such nostalgia can blind us to the true social, political, and artistic significance of what is really happening with social media in Mexico. That is, even as the older intellectuals see the internet as a destructive force for politically, intellectually engaged journalism, the young are reinventing the tradition of protest narratives precisely through the medium that, ironically, is also a key vehicle of the neoliberal project whose results they are protesting.

In May 2012, youth expertise with social media combined in a powerful way with young people's "insatiable" need for expression, their pent-up frustration over being criticized and not taken seriously, and their desire to see the democratic process work, resulting in the explosion of the #YoSoy132 movement. The chain of specific events that ultimately launched the #YoSoy132 movement began on May 11, 2012.[23] The then presidential candidate for the Partido Revolucionario Institucional (PRI), Enrique Peña Nieto (who, in the end, did win the election), gave a speech to students at the University Iberoamericana ("the Ibero"), Mexico City campus as part of the forum Buen Ciudadano Ibero,[24] which had brought all four presidential candidates to the campus for separate talks.[25] After his speech, at the end of the question and answer session, a group of students raised the issue of events in 2006 known as "El caso Atenco" when, as governor of the State of Mexico, Peña Nieto ordered the use of police forces to end a popular protest. At that time, the police action ended with the death of two protestors, multiple arrests, sexual abuse of numerous women by the authorities, and accusations of violation of human rights. Though in 2009, the Mexican Supreme Court exonerated Peña Nieto of any wrong doing, in 2012 the public and specifically the young had not forgotten the events of 2006. During his speech at the Ibero, after initially seeking to avoid the question, Peña Nieto finally made a brief statement in which he justified the use of government force as necessary to restore public peace and order. This response provoked a strong reaction, and while some of the students supported Peña Nieto, a larger number both inside the auditorium and outside the building whistled and shouted slogans against him. After consulting with his advisors about the best way to avoid the protestors and after several false starts including a brief period when he stayed in the men's bathroom (which was described in mainstream online media and student-generated social media with a scornful tone as a period of time when he was "hiding" before he "fled" the University[26]), Peña Nieto was finally able to leave from a side door to go to his car, where he spoke briefly with a CNN Mexico reporter, stating that "No son genuinas todas [las expresiones], al fin y al cabo se respeta el espacio libre de la Universidad y soy total y absolutamente respetuoso"[27] (Zapata, La visita). These events were also videotaped by many students and uploaded to YouTube. However, news programs on the state-owned television networks Televisa and TV Azteca, as well as several mainstream newspapers (in particular *El sol de México*), downplayed the event and cast doubt on the authenticity of the student protest. They carried interviews or statements with several politicians who implied, or stated outright, that the protestors were not in fact students, but agitators who had been planted in the audience by the opposition.[28] Though the tactic of playing down the significance of student protests by declaring that they are in fact "planted" agitators is a standard tactic within the Mexican political landscape, on this occasion students acted quickly to affirm the authenticity of their views. On May 14, 2012, 131 students from the Universidad Iberoamericana published a YouTube video in which they showed their University student ID, gave their name, their student number, their academic major, and a statement affirming that they had not been trained for the protest.[29] The supportive response on social networks was immediate and dramatic. #YoSoy132 (as in "I am number 132") on Twitter became the slogan of support indicating solidarity with the 131 students and a shared desire for accurate, free reporting as part of the electoral process.

The movement grew quickly. By May 23, the "Primer comunicado de la Coordinadora del movimiento YoSoy132"[30] was published to the Internet, and by May 30, the movement had expanded beyond the Internet to the streets, when the first #YoSoy132 assembly attracted an estimated 7,000 students from fifty different University centers to the campus of UNAM (National Autonomous University of Mexico) (Salas Cassani). Students from both private and public universities came together for the first time, working long hours to create inclusive structures for all participants[31] and to articulate goals for resolving the concerns that united them. At the same time, the Internet facilitated the national and global spread of the movement, and #YoSoy132 groups formed across the country and created websites and Facebook pages in fifty cities around the world.[32] A number of YouTube videos emerged with activist students in other countries expressing solidarity.[33]

Initially, the three central concerns defined by the movement were: (1) the demand for democratization of mainstream media (television, newspapers), (2) the denunciation of the supposed "behind the scenes" agreements made by the state-owned media to provide biased coverage of and support for Peña Nieto, and (3) the demand for a third debate between all the presidential candidates. A number of marches and assemblies were held in Mexico City, across Mexico, and throughout the world, and a broad range of informational activities were employed to spread the message in support of truth in reporting.[34] In Mexico City, in addition to the student assemblies at UNAM and other campuses, peaceful protests were held at symbolic sites of corruption. For example, during the *Primera Fiesta de la Luz*,[35] students gathered with candle and lanterns outside the studios of Televisa in Chapultepec and projected a film on the wall of the Televisa building. The film provided a chronology of the discrepancies between the official (and incorrect) Televisa coverage of dramatic confrontations between government forces and protestors, political assassinations, disputed election results, and so forth, beginning with the 1968 student massacre up through the events of Atenco in 2006 (Igartúa). The screening and the vigil were broadcast on the Internet simultaneously by the organizers and also by many of those who attended and used their cell phones, so that multiple angles of the event were available to supporters even if they did not attend the event in person. This film screening echoed publication and speeches produced by the movement that contextualized the current protests within the history of worker, peasant, and student protests and social/political/safety issues throughout the 20th and 21st century, from the Revolution of 1910 to the student massacre in Tlalteloco in 1968, University strikes of 1988 and 1999, up through the femicides of northern Mexico and the thousands of deaths resulting from the narco-trafficking violence of recent years ("#YoSoy132. Asamblea General").

The Fiesta de la Luz film on its own (*Fiest de la luz*), the video of the crowd watching the film at the protest (*Fiesta por la luz*), and videos of student assemblies and marches both in Mexico City, the provinces, and from abroad, as well as multiple written statements, were circulated by video through YouTube (often first as live feeds and later as edited films), as texts through the #YoSoy132 website, and through articles in different online news venues. One of the major events organized prior to the election was an online dialogue with the presidential candidates (all of them attended, except for Peña Nieto, but students kept his empty chair on the air as a symbol). A unique aspect of this event was the way students used their technological know-how to set up a nationwide system that randomly allowed students to pose their questions to the candidates from different parts of the country. Subsequent to the elections, the movement continued to work for change: it reviewed the results of the election, held several marches up through inauguration day on December 1, 2012, and produced a more extensive six-point plan that focused on media, education, economics, national security, ties between politics and social movements, and a new, more inclusive national health plan.

Self-defined as a university student movement, #YoSoy132 was not tied to any particular university, and one of the central principles was the desire to maintain a nonpartisan nature: all political points of view were to be respected in a common effort to ensure freedom of speech and honest reporting (in spite of early "anti-Peña Nieto" or "anti-PRI" impulses and of later protests on inauguration day, December 1, 2013).[36] Rather than promote one party or the other, students concentrated on pooling their considerable expertise with technology and social media to create alternative sources of information. The movement quickly attracted other groups with similar goals, and also new groups formed to show the support of those outside the specific college demographic, for example Yosoy133 (younger students) and Yosoy132 académicos (professors).

Not all was smooth sailing for the movement. From the beginning, there were individuals who left the group or formed splinter groups after declaring their disappointment in the ability of the movement to set and achieve specific goals.[37] Furthermore, in addition to the traditional skepticism over authenticity of dissenting views in the Mexican political scenario, #YoSoy132 came up against one of the challenges for participatory culture that uses YouTube as a medium of distribution. Burgess and Green have observed in their book *YouTube: Online Video and Particpatory Culture* that one of the challenges for YouTube users is the difficulty in judging the authenticity of posts that predicate their legitimacy on their amateur status. In the U.S., the skewing has been most often caused by commercial media interests (for example, the early "Lonely Girl" video blogs that turned out to be a scripted entertainment industry product). In the case of #YoSoy132, it is ironic that the first post of the 131 students was done to "prove" the truth of the dissent at the Peña Nieto talk through videos of "real" students and that later "real" videos of #YoSoy132 members contradicting the standards of the movement were used to delegitimize it. For from the start of the movement, there have been continued allegations that the movement was not "spontaneous," not truly a student movement, and not unbiased, but rather a strategically constructed ruse paid for by the PRD and presidential candidate Manuel López Obrador. In June 2012, several YouTube posts of a #YoSoy132 participant discussing payments from the PRD damaged the nonpartisan credibility of the movement. Later, it was revealed that the young man who had made the video and distributed it was affiliated with the PRI, but the damage to #YoSoy132 had already been done (Poy 15).[38]

Perhaps an even more disillusioning development was the decision by several of the most prominent #YoSoy132 student spokespeople to accept employment at Televisa as part of a new political commentary program *Sin Filtro*.[39] These students spoke of "working for change from within" ("Antonio Attolini"), but most reactions seem to see their choice as "selling out."[40] The street presence of students was also greatly reduced after a large number of protestors were aggressively arrested during the protests on inauguration day December 1, 2012. By May 2013, the movement continued to lose momentum, and a much smaller group of students attended a one-year anniversary protest at the Estela de la Luz in Mexico City on May 13, 2013.

Given these ups and downs, how should #YoSoy132 be evaluated? None of the accusations questioning the authenticity of the participants in #YoSoy132 are new to the Mexican political scene, nor is the phenomenon of some of the opposition leaders taking highly paid work within the official structure.[41] While in this instance the ultimate use of state force against protestors during the inauguration day protests resulted in physical confrontation and arrests, not massacre, this is a difference of scale, not substance (though certainly an important difference). So, in spite of the rallying power of the original post of the 131 students, which lies in the straightforward, fresh use of the camera to allow the students to declare their "authenticity," and in spite of the transmission powers of the Internet to raise broader, nearly instantaneous awareness, the life cycle of this student movement to some extent follows those that have come and gone before. Though online commentary related to almost any article about #YoSoy132 includes both sharp disillusionment over the alleged behind-the-scenes manipulation by the political parties and enthusiastic defense by others who vouch for the authenticity of the motivation of participants, the overall trend in the public mind seems to be toward writing off the movement with derision and scorn like that expressed in this headline published in May 2013: "#YoSoy132, ¿dónde están ahora? ¿escondidos en algún baño?"[42] ("#YoSoy132, dónde están"), which attempts to put the movement into the same space of disgrace that Peña Nieto had occupied just a year earlier.

It would be a mistake, however, to let the difficulties listed before overshadow the significance of the movement. While certainly it is possible and even probable that some elements of the #YoSoy132 movement were more closely tied to the political party structures than the ideals of the movement wished for, there is evidence on YouTube that #YoSoy132 was preceded by an expanding waive of youth creativity, as well as intellectual and political curiosity and a will to act that emerged slightly ahead of and then continued to parallel the "official" communications of the leadership structures. Several searches of YouTube with key words like "Mexican Youth Artists," "jóvenes mexicanos," "jóvenes mexicanos literarios," and "jóvenes mexicanos músicos" lead to an interesting trip through the labyrinth of YouTube. Any word related to "youth" or "jóvenes" does bring up many videos directly related to or generated by #YoSoy132. In addition, another body of videos emerges from the sidebar of suggested videos that reveals the awakening of creative and research projects that preceded, in some cases, and expand beyond #YoSoy132, in others. One young man, Alejandro, from Northern Mexico who identified himself as the one "conocido por 10 años entre sus amigos como 'el que no habla'"[43] in September 2011 was moved to speak and posted an eloquent twelve minute "manifest" titled "Mensaje a los jóvenes mexicanos"[44] about the need for taking responsibility to create mutual understanding, charity, peaceful interaction, and kindness. This video in large part is aimed at upper-class youth and encourages them to become more engaged across the social spectrum of the country, because, as he tells them, "Somos el futuro."[45] The video directs viewers to the "Mi México Feliz" Facebook page and seeks to create its own movement in search of "el mejor México."[46] Another channel, "Airwave 182v," was created in 2007 by a young guitar player. Up until 2012, the videos are mostly posts of him playing "covers" of popular hits by international bands such as Coldplay. But, in June 2012, inspired by an early election controversy over a mistake Peña Nieto made in reference to the literary works of Carlos Fuentes, he posted his first original song (lyrics and music), an anti-Peña rock piece entitled "No qué pena Nieto."[47] In Spanish, the title links Peña Nieto's name to the idiomatic expression "qué pena" or "what a shame" ("No qué pena Nieto"). Another channel, "Tú eliges Mexico 2012," which is linked to Twitter, Facebook, and a webpage, presented a project before the election to inform young voters about the issues and the presidential candidates through interviews with experts, analysis of political discourse, and compilation and analysis of the most pertinent news items. One final example shows the transnational reach of #YoSoy132 through nonconventional channels of communication and highlights the political awareness of one of the groups most often maligned as inactive and disconnected: online video gamers. On the YouTube video game review site *Duxativa*, the Peruvian host (for whom the YouTube channel is named) sent out a "saludo" and declaration of solidarity for the "compañeros" in Mexico, before going into the screen shots of playing the video game being reviewed in that post.

Thus, #YoSoy132, rather than a beginning moment, represents an intermediate moment: it became the catalyst for uniting energies that had been building for some time. These energies exploded into the public consciousness at a crucial moment. In that moment, which stretched from May 2012 into mid-2013, #YoSoy132 did effect change on many levels. In addition to the assemblies and the stimulation of public debate around the issues of unbiased reporting, two of the concrete achievements of the group in the weeks leading up to the presidential election were its ability to influence the main television networks (Televisa and TV Azteca) to provide more extended coverage of the second presidential debate (in which all candidates participated) and the successful organization of a third presidential debate that was hosted by #YoSoy132 (though Peña Nieto chose not to participate in the third debate, since he felt that the #YoSoy132 movement was against him). As mentioned before, the third debate was broadcast live via the Google platform "Hangout en directo" and on several radio stations and was rebroadcast on the cultural television stations the following weekend. In addition, the Internet allowed for an unprecedented level of real-time communication between Mexico City and the rest of the country, which allowed for a plurality of regional voices that has the potential to chip away at Mexico City's traditional monopoly on political and intellectual debate.

Several academics offered preliminary analysis of the effects of the movement in the year after the election. Agustin Basave, Director of

Graduate Education at the Universidad Iberoamericana, considered that the movement had an impact on the election by lowering the margin of votes with which Peña Nieto and the PRI won from the 50% indicated in early polls to around 30% in the actual election. This lower margin denied the PRI the majority control of the two chambers of the Congress, and thus Basave considered that many of the reforms initiated by the new government, in particular the "Pacto por México" (an agreement signed between the government and opposition parties to move ahead on ninety-five reforms), were "de alguna manera producto de #YoSoy132"[48] (Zapata, "#YoSoy132 sigue vigente"). Jorge Rocha, an expert in the Social Sciences ("temas socials") and coordinator of the Masters in Political Science and Public Affairs (Política y Gestión Pública) at the Universidad ITESO, emphasized that the theme of democratization of the media entered the national agenda thanks to #YoSoy132 and that many of the concerns they expressed were taken into account in the 2013 "Ley de Telecomunicaciones" (Zapata, "#YoSoy132 sigue vigente"). But, perhaps the most important achievement, according to Rocha, was that

> miles de jóvenes se interesaran en la vida política del país. Es gente que quedó marcada por el movimiento y es gente que ya tiene una perspectiva crítica, distinta de la vida política frente a un escenario en el que se decía que los jóvenes eran apáticos[49].
>
> (Zapata, "#YoSoy132 sigue vigente")

In his observation about the importance of the transformative power of active participation, Rocha echoes comments made by young participants themselves as they have begun to define what they considered to be their most significant achievements. For example, Valerie Hamel, who participated in the movement through the ITAM student assembly of #YoSoy132, noted how working together had helped students from different socioeconomic backgrounds and political persuasions to come together, overcoming prejudices in their quest for "un país más democrático y más justo"[50]:

> Muchos llegamos al movimiento con prejuicios...Sin embargo, la lucha hace hermanos. Veo con emoción las fuertes amistades que se han generado entre estudiantes que se sentían antagónicos. Los prejuicios y las líneas artificiales que antes nos dividían, se han roto... La pluralidad de ideologías persiste y ...Uno de los grandes logros del movimiento ha sido el entendimiento que se ha creado entre las partes.[51]
>
> (Hamel 4)

Raúl Diego Rivera Hernández, a Mexican national and graduate student at the University of South Carolina, provided testimony of the reach of the movement outside Mexico and noted in his presentation at LASA 2013 that #YoSoy132 made him feel "reconnected" to his country. In considering the achievements of the movement, he highlighted the sheer power it exercised by opening up "nuevos canales de participación"[52] through "medios alternativos,"[53] even without a previously articulated plan for political action—which, he noted, many political theorists (and he gave as examples Slavoj Žižek and Alain Badiou) consider to be requisite for the success of political protest movements.

This young scholar's disagreement with the work of "established experts" ties into the final proposal of this study: that a new narrative structure is created by the intermingling of varied social media forms and that this in turn reshapes the way Mexican youth interact with not only the political structure but also with the narrative and journalistic traditions that have existed in Mexico for processing and creating individual and group meaning. Revolutionary movements of the 20th century in general, and in Mexico in particular, were strongly dependent on identifiable leaders and unified narratives that expressed coherent platforms. In 20th century Mexico, public intellectuals played a vital role in narrating the nation and struggled between dissent and cooperation with the state in a quest to create a balanced, just society. #YoSoy132 is part of a new revolutionary impulse seen around the world, in which leaders take backseat to the respect for the multitude and the desire to allow each voice a forum for expression. Thus, the unified narrative is not shaped by one author or even a committee; rather, the narrative emerges as these voices play across all the platform and begin to trend. The multiplicity of voices and the immediacy of their transmission leads inevitably to a different way of reading and feeling. In the process of researching this topic, the author tried to search back through the #YoSoy132 Facebook page to find the first post and requested the help of a young Facebook user. The response was "I don't know how to find that, Facebook is not about history, it is about now." For those activist scholars formed in previous eras, it is easy to fear the dangers of an ahistorical immersion in the now, in spite of growing trends in contemporary psychology to emphasize "present-ness" and "mindfulness" as productive tools on the path to greater individual peace, creativity, and enlightenment. Yet, many of these older activist scholars also recognize the failure of their previous projects to achieve the just society they had envisioned (as Bartra and de Ita do in the articles previously cited). For scholars like Fernando de Ita, used to the rules of artistic and intellectual craft in which publication came at the end of the training, not at the beginning, it can be easy to overlook the fact that the hours and hours that young people spend immersed in the medium of online activities in fact correspond to the intense training he emphasizes. The youth of Mexico have been online for years "think[ing] about it and later talk[ing] about it, writ[ing] about it... film[ing] it..." (the practices pointed to by de Ita as necessary), and it has been these hours of work that allowed them to respond to the 2012 election with the precision, clarity, and depth de Ita longed for in his lament over the death of cultural journalism. Finally, one of the key elements to the success of the contestatory power of the Internet in the #YoSoy132 movement was that the Internet brought students out of isolation in their homes and into the streets together, where they could get to know each other and overcome differences through the creative power of conversation, decision-making, and work, as noted by Hamel. What role Mexican youth will take on from here has not yet taken full form, but they are awake, creating, pushing back against the official versions of the news, politics, and, more significantly, the official version of themselves as apathetic *ninis*. They know they can do more than be consumers. They know it is possible to "do things," and on this new path toward political, civic, and artistic expression through alternative media, they will continue to redefine the role of intellectuals and journalism as the voices of many take precedent over any one individual in giving legitimacy to new views. Thus, the new narrative structures afforded by social media are and will continue to alter the role of the public intellectual and of cultural journalism, two forces that have traditionally been at the center of contestatory interactions with the Mexican state. The achievements of #YoSoy132 to create change and to introduce new themes into the public sphere point to the positive future potential of social media as a channel for civic engagement in Mexico.

Notes

1 "#Iam132"
2 One of the earliest protest events on May 23, 2012 was coordinated to start at the same time in Mexico D.F., Guadalajara, Puebla, Queréretaro, Hidalgo, and Tijuana "#YoSoy132 Time Line Photos." The #YoSoy132 International website shows International Cells in numerous countries including Spain, Germany, France, Croatia, Portugal, the U.S., Canada, Australia, and the United Kingdom.
3 See, for example, articles by Kilkenny, Miller Llana, Cave, and the Occupy Wall Street website.
4 "#WeAreCitizensNotConsumers/Imagine, shout, jump, move, cry, inform, dream, communicate.../#Weallarethemedia; #IcommunicatethereforIam; #WeAllAretheMessage/; #MediaWillBeSocialOrItWon'tExist."
5 "to do/create things...to move/inspire people for a change, for the construction of a project with collective benefits."
6 The multiple protest events of 1968 that culminated in the government massacre of students in Tlalteloco Square radically altered the relationship between intellectuals and the state (see Camp for detailed discussion), yet the postrevolutionary motivational message that inspired youth to place personal advancement second to their responsibility to Mexico (if not the government, per se) persisted for a number of decades beyond 1968, both in the educational system and society at large.

7 The thirty-four members are: Australia, Austria, Belgium, Canada, Chile, Czech Republic, Denmark, Estonia, Finland, France, Germany, Greece, Hungary, Iceland, Ireland, Israel, Italy, Japan, Korea, Luxembourg, Mexico, Netherlands, New Zealand, Norway, Poland, Portugal, Slovak Republic, Slovenia, Spain, Sweden, Switzerland, Turkey, the United Kingdom, and the U.S.

8 For example, 38% of women between the ages of fifteen and twenty-nine are not in school and are counted as "unemployed," yet many of these women are in fact maintaining the home, which, though they do not earn a wage, is not exactly the same as being unemployed and certainly does not support the image of "idle youth." A deeper analysis of this data in terms of opportunities for women falls outside this current study.

9 "Habits of Internet Users in Mexico."

10 For example, in an e-mail to the author, Sergio Macías describes the interest of Mexican youth in following celebrities on Twitter and how this leads to a culture of jokes on Twitter and YouTube: "Twitter es chistoso porque en México la gente está pendiente de lo que pasa en la vida de sus 'artistas' (personalidades de la farándula) y las tonterías que éstos escriben en sus páginas. YouTube de cierta medida está relacionado con Twitter porque lo que pasa en Twitter la gente hace videos burlándose de lo que pasa en Twitter." [Twitters is funny because in Mexico people follow closely what happened in the life of their "artists" (ShowBiz personalities) and the silly things they write on their pages. YouTube is to a certain extent related to Twitter because people create YouTube videos making fun of what happens on Twitter.] He offered as examples an interview of Ninel Conde by Adela Micha and a young man's stand-up comedy routine, where he retells Ninel Conde jokes ("Chistes de Ninel Conde"). Politicians are also a source for jokes and critical comments in Twitter and YouTube commentary in Mexico. In 2012, presidential candidate Peña Nieto's daughter caused an uproar with disparaging comments she tweeted about "el prole" (a disparaging slang use of the shortened Spanish word for "Proletariat") when defending her father from critics over a mistake he made about a book by Carlos Fuentes (Vargas).

11 See for example: "Tu eliges mexico" and "Mensaje a los jóvenes mexicanos."

12 "after the splendor of the 70s."

13 "threatened by the specter of decline."

14 "the way to experience intellectual death."

15 "the Internet is not the enemy but rather the closest ally of written journalism."

16 "without a doubt the Internet has democratized information."

17 "University communications (journalism) programs continue to produce industrial quantities of graduates."

18 "the job opportunities are saturated, salaries are laughable and there is no future, especially for newspapers and magazines in the states."

19 "Today my son, a complete nobody, gets more than a thousand hits on every one of the performances he posts to YouTube....the young find, on the Internet, a space in which to express themselves."

20 "The medium, on its own, cannot resolve (define) the form and content of its materials...in order to say something with meaning, you have to think about it and later talk about it, write about it, draw it, photograph it, film it... with precision, clarity, depth and there is no computer program that can do all this because these actions still depend on the talent, disposition, study, discipline and consciousness of a human being." The mention here of the "medium" not being sufficient echoes the phrase "the medium is the

message" coined by Marshall McLuhan, whose work is known in Mexican intellectual circles. For example, Carlos Monsiváis makes reference to him in Dias de Guardar.

21 "The Arts and Humanities are arriving at their end; to the limits of their ability to create new alternatives...It has been said we have exhausted the production of signifying (important) structures."

22 "It's not only our profession that is bankrupt. It is the social framework of the hive that is being split apart. Two hundred years of Independence and 100 of Revolution show us that we have built an incredibly unequal country in all the levels of civilized coexistence...something is rotten among us."

23 This overview of the events leading up to the #YoSoy132 movement have been compiled from a number of online news sources (Cave, Hamel, Igartúa, Kilkenny, Miller Llana, #YoSoy132media.org) and from the English and Spanish Wikipedia entries for the movement. The evolution of the Wikipedia entries and the difference between the English and the Spanish versions served as an interesting barometer of the rise and "fall" of the movement throughout the first year, as well as of the international understanding of #YoSoy132. A deeper discussion of the ways the Wikipedia entries presented a changing interpretation of the contestory power of the movement would be an interesting project, but one that is outside the scope of this current study.

24 "Good Ibero Citizen."

25 The Buen Ciudadano project was created by alumni and the administration of the Universidad Iberoamericana to stimulate an internet conversation about how students, professors, workers, and alumni of the "Ibero" defined what it meant to be a "good citizen" and then, as a community, to create questions for the presidential candidates and then to invite them to campus for a dialogue ("Se celebró"). Peña Nieto initially turned down the invitation but then changed his mind late in the campaign.

26 For example "Por la puerta de atrás y escondido, el candidato del PRI a la Presidencia de la República, Enrique Peña Nieto, salió de las instalaciones de la Universidad Iberoamericana. Durante diez minutos permaneció refugiado en el baño ubicado en el edificio de Radio Ibero para que se calmaran los furibundos estudiantes que afuera lo esperaban con gritos de: cobarde y asesino" [The presidential candidate for the PRI, Enrique Peña Nieto, left the building of the University Iberoamericana hidden and through the back door. Before that he took refuge for 10 minutes in the bathroom located in the Radio Ibero building so that the furious students who were waiting for him outside shouting "coward and assassin" could calm down] (Cervantes) or "Twitter: Peña Nieto se esconde en el baño de la Ibero" [Twitter: Peña Nieto hides in the bathroom at the Ibero] (Tovar).

27 "Not all [the expressions of protest] are genuine, nevertheless, the free space of the University is respected and I am totally and absolutely respectful."

28 For example, Senator Arturo Escobar y Vega, representative of the Partido Verde Ecologista de México, stated in an interview on Cadena Tres what he presented to be his own eyewitness observations: "Hay un grupo ahí de de, no quiero decir jóvenes oiga, por que ya estaban mayorcitos, cálculo de 30 a 35 años para arriba, incitando, era un grupo minoritario, no pasaban de 20 personas... y estoy convencido que aquellos que abanderaron... no son estudiantes de la Ibero" [There is a group there of, I don't want to say young people because they were kind of old already, I calculate about 30–35 years old and older, protesting and it was a minority of those present, no more than 20 people and I am convinced that those who were protesting... are not students at the Ibero]

("Yuriria platicó"). It's important to note that the interviewer, Yuriria, points out that such claims need to be backed up with proof.

29 The original YouTube post can be seen at "131 Alumnos de la Ibero responden," uploaded by Recreo.

It was first posted May 14, 2012 and viewed for this chapter April 20, 2013, June 10, 2013, July 28, 2013, and December 13, 2016. At the last viewing by the author, this post had over 1,236,260 hits. This video can freeze up, but there are a number of reposts where the original video can be viewed. Each has several thousand hits, for example see the post "131 alumnos de la ibero responden (no son acarreados ni porros)" posted by Alfonso Ramirez.

30 "First Communication from the YoSoy132 movement Coordinators."

31 "Después del diálogo derivado de la primera reunión interuniversitaria del movimiento 'Yo soy 132,' en donde convergieron una gran diversidad de ideas, comienzan a surgir acuerdos, a perfilarse posturas políticas y a definirse las acciones que siguen. Estudiantes de universidades públicas y privadas, así como miembros de organizaciones civiles y movimientos sociales que han comenzado a participar en el diálogo convocado por los jóvenes, pone de manifiesto que al interior del movimiento existe muchas y muy variadas corrientes y posturas políticas" [After the dialogue derived from the first interuniversity meeting for the movement "Yo Soy 132," where many diverse ideas converged, agreements and political positions are forming and the next steps are being defined. University students from public and private institutions, as well as members of civic organizations and social movements have begun to participate in the dialogue begun by the young which demonstrates that within in the movement there are many different currents and political positions] (Salas Cassani).

32 A search of Facebook provides over fifty pages and groups sites from Mexico and around the world.

33 See videos through links on the www.yosoy132media.org website.

34 See Hamel for detailed list and description of activities.

35 "the First Festival of Light."

36 See "Quiénes somos."

37 See, for example, Pérex de Acha.

38 Some of the videos are: "Obrador detras del movimento #yo soy 132 (La verdad nos hará libres)"; Response from the accused "Saúl Alvídrez :Revelación Detras de #YoSoy132 Cómo Urdió Manuel Cossío PRI (Parte 1)."

39 Unfiltered.

40 See Contreras and "Comunicado."

41 During its seventy years in power during the 20th century, one of the most successful strategies of the PRI for controlling intellectual dissenters was to pull them into the system through ambassadorships or directorships of cultural centers. Prestigious literary prizes were another tactic for calming dissent while seeming to reward intellectual independence. In "Informe confidencial sobre la posibilidad de un mínimo equivalente mexicano del poema Howl (el aullido) de Allen Ginsberg," which is part of Días de guarder the collection of chronicles that Carlos Monsivais published in the year following the 1968 student massacre, he laments the stultification of his generation by their self-imposed imperative to work within the system "que se justificaron ante sí mismos diciendo que todo lo hacían porque la única manera de transformar las cosas es estar adentro para influir....." [those who justified themselves saying that everything they did was because the only way to change things was to be inside in order to have influence] (292). The language here is strikingly similar to the statements made by the ex-#YoSoy132 members who joined Televisa. For example, Antonio Attonlini stated: "Lo

mismo que decía afuera, lo voy a decir adentro…¿Por qué queremos estar ahí? ¡Porque es una lupototota! Va a magnificar al discurso; Televisa hoy por hoy controla el 70% del mercdo…" [I will say the same thing from the inside as I did from the outside…Why do we want to be there? Because it is a huge magnifying glass. It will magnify the discourse. Televisa today controls 70% of the market…] ("Antonio Attolini promote").

42 "#YoSoy132, Where are they now? Hiding in some bathroom?"

43 "known among his friends as 'the one who doesn't speak.'"

44 "Message to the Youth of Mexico."

45 "We are the future."

46 "the best Mexico."

47 "No what a shame Nieto."

48 "in some way a product of #YoSoy132."

49 "Thousands of students became interested in the political life of the country. These are people who were marked by the movement and who already have a critical perspective, a different one about political life in contrast to a scenario in which it was said that the young were apathetic."

50 "a more democratic and just country."

51 "Many of us came to the movement with prejudices…Nevertheless, fighting together creates brotherly/sisterly unity. I am moved by the strong friendships that have formed between students who felt themselves to be antagonists. The prejudices and artificial lines that divided us before have been broken…the plurality of ideologies persists and…one of the greatest achievements of the movement has been the understanding that has been created among the different players."

52 "new channels for participation."

53 "alternative media."

Works Cited

"131 Alumnos de la Ibero responden." *YouTube*, uploaded by Recreo, 14 May 2012. www.youtube.com/watch?v=P7XbocXsFkI. Accessed 13 Dec. 2016.

"131 alumnos de la ibero responden (no son acarreados ni porros)." *You-Tube*, uploaded by Alfonso Ramírez, 14 May 2012. www.youtube.com/watch?v=aYyu1M815-0. Accessed 13 July 2013.

"Antonio Attolini promete criticar a Televisa desde adentro." *ADNpolítico*, 25 Oct. 2012. www.adnpolitico.com/ciudadanos/2012/10/25/antonio-attolini-promete-criticar-a-televisa-desde-adentro. Accessed 8 July 2013.

Avilés, Karina. "OCDE: *ninis*, 7 millones 226 mil mexicanos de entre 15 y 29 años." *La Jornada*, 13 Sept. 2011, p. 36. www.jornada.unam.mx/2011/09/13/sociedad/036n1soc. Accessed 9 Apr. 2013.

Bartra, Roger. *La sangre y la tinta*. Oceano, 1999.

Burgess, Jean, and Joshua Green. *YouTube: Online Video and Participatory Culture*. Polity P, 2009.

Camb, Roderic A. *Intellectuals and the State in Twentieth-Century Mexico*. U of Texas P, 1985.

Cave, Damien. "In Protests and Online, a Youth Movement Seeks to Sway Mexico's Election." *The Lede Blogs/New York Times*, 11 June 2012. www.thelede.blogs.nytimes.com/2012/06/11/in-protests-and-online-the-yosoy132-movement-seeks-to-sway-mexicos-election/?_r=0. Accessed 10 Dec. 2013.

Cervantes, Jesus. "Huye EPN de la Ibero tras repudio de universitarios." *Proceso*, 11 May 2012. www.proceso.com.mx/?p=307119. Accessed 10 Dec. 2013.

"Chistes de Ninel Conde." *YouTube*, uploaded by CHAPARROUWW, 21 Aug. 2011. www.youtube.com/watch?v=SpRpCkcHnGs. Accessed 13 July 2013.

"Comunicado del #YoSoy132-ITAM con respecto a Antonio Attolini y el programa Sin Filtros." *Yosoy132media.org*, 25 Oct. 2012. www.yosoy132media.org/sin-categoria/comunicado-del-yosoy132-itam-con-respecto-a-antonio-attolini-y-el-programa-sin-filtros/#sthash.X1txIMxX.dpuf. Accessed 13 July 2013. www.publimetro.com.mx/mx/noticias/2012/10/25/comunicado-yosoy132-itam-programa-filtros.html accessed 25 Sept. 2017

Contreras, José. "Yo Soy 132: una estrella más." *Crónica.com.mx*, 10 Feb. 2013. www.cronica.com.mx/notas/2012/701417.html. Accessed 8 July 2013.

de Ita, Fernando. "La extinctión de un oficio." *Revista de la Universidad de Mexico*. Nueva época núm 70 diciembre 2009, 74–78.

"Estrategia maquiavélica, disturbios del 1 de diciembre: #Yosoy132." *Aristegui Noticias*, 4 Dec. 2012. http://aristeguinoticias.com/0412/mexico/estrategia-maquiavelica-disturbios-del-1-de-diciembre-yosoy132/. Accessed 19 Dec. 2013.

"Fiesta de la Luz." *YouTube*, 13 June 2012. www.youtube.com/watch?v=hYtm zuyGgqc. Accessed 13 July 2013.

"Fiesta por la Luz de la Verdad." *YouTube*, 13 June 2012. www.youtube.com/watch?v=XGIwXF8BqyM. Accessed 13 July 2013.

"Habitos de los usuarios de Internet en México 2012." *AMIPICI*. www.amipci.org.mx/?P=editomultimediafile&Multimedia=115&Type=1. Accessed 9 Apr. 2013.

Hamel, Valeria. "YoSoy132: Un mosaico de biografías." *Animal Político*, 24 Sept. 2012. www.animalpolitico.com/blogueros-blog-invitado/2012/09/24/yosoy132-un-mosaico-de-biografias/#axzz2aAshebBW. Accessed 13 July 2013.

Igartúa, Santiago. "Con 'fiesta de luz' protesta #YoSoy132 contra Televisa y EPN." *Proceso*, 13 June 2012. www.proceso.com.mx/?p=310864. Accessed 25 July 2013.

Kilkenny, Allison. "Student Movement Dubbed the 'Mexican Spring.'" *The Nation*, 29 May 2012. www.thenation.com/blog/168099/student-movement-dubbed-mexican-spring#. Accessed 7 Dec. 2013.

Krauze, Enrique. *Caudillos culturals en la Revolucion Mexicana*. Siglos XXI, 1976.

Macías, Sergio. "Chistes." Message to the author. 26 Oct. 2012. E-mail.

Matathue, I., and M. Salzman. "Mañana en América Latina." *Latin Trade* 8.1 (2000): 33–40.

"Mensaje a los jóvenes mexicanos." *YouTube*, uploaded by Miméxicofeliz. www.youtube.com/watch?v=RlcCq_cvigU. Accessed 13 Dec. 2013.

McLuhan, Marshall. *Understanding Media: The Extensions of Man*. McGraw Hill, 1964.

Micha, Adela. "Ninel Conde Desbanqué a Pepito - Entrevista Adela Micha se ríe de Chistes." *YouTube*, 4 Sept. 2011. www.youtube.com/watch?v=IW13uQ RkCco. Accessed 16 Dec. 2013.

Miller Llana, Sara. "The 'Mexican spring': A new student movement stirs in Mexico." *The Christian Science Monitor*, 31 May 2012. www.csmonitor.com/World/Americas/2012/0531/The-Mexican-spring-A-new-student-movement-stirs-in-Mexico. Accessed 7 Dec. 2013.

Monsivais, Carlos. *Días de guardar.* Ediciones Era, 1970.
Moreno-Ramírez, Francisco, and Hiram Moreno-Ramírez. Personal interview. 28 Dec. 2012.
Nilan, Pam, and Carles Feixa, editors. *Global Youth? Hybrid Identities, Plural Worlds.* Routledge, 2006.
"No qué pena Nieto." *YouTube,* uploaded by Airwave 182v, 2 June 2012. www. youtube.com/watch?v=lpF2FW_HrfM&list=TLncJNdm549jU. Accessed 15 Dec. 2013.
"Obrador detras del movimiento #yo soy 132 (La verdad nos hará libres)" *YouTube,* uploaded by Zatarra Films, 18 June 2012. www.youtube.com/ watch?v=C3Vj41uy9KU. Accessed 17 Dec. 2013.
OccupyWallSt. "#TodosSomos132: Solidarity with the Mexican Spring," 25 May 2012. http://occupywallst.org/article/mexico-yosoy132/. Accessed 7 Dec. 2013.
"Panorama de educación, 2011 Nota de País: México." *OECD,* www.oecd.org/ mexico/48667648.pdf. Accessed 13 July 2013.
Pérez de Acha, Gisela. "La democracia de #YoSoy132." *Animal Político,* 19 Sept. 2012. www.animalpolitico.com/blogueros-blog-invitado/2012/09/19/ la-democracia-de-yosoy132/#axzz2aAshebBW. Accessed 7 July 2013.
Poy, Laura, et al. "Intentan de ligar a #YoSoy132 con López Obrador, 'una campaña de descrédito.'" *La Jornada,* 20 June 2012, p. 15. www.jornada.unam. mx/2012/06/20/index.php?section=politica&article=015n2pol. Accessed 8 July 2013.
"Primer comunicado de Coordinadora del Movimiento 'YoSoy132.'" *Terra-México,* 30 mayo 2012. http://noticias.terra.com.mx/mexico/yosoy132/ primer-comunicado-de-coordinadora-del-movimiento-yosoy132, e6b13370a9f97310VgnVCM20000099cceb0aRCRD.html. Accessed 13 July 2013.
"Quienes somos." *YoSoy132Media.* www.yosoy132media.org. Accessed 13 July 2013.
Salas Cassani, Marcela. "Yo soy 132: mosaico de pensamientos." *Desinforme-monos.org,* 3 June 2012. http://desinformemonos.org/2012/06/yo-soy-132-mosaico-de-posturas-y-pensamientos. Accessed 8 July 2013.
"Saúl Alvídrez: Revelación Detras de #YoSoy132 Cómo Urdió Manuel Cossío PRI (Parte 1)" *YouTube,* uploaded by ForoPolitica, 20 July 2012. www. youtube.com/watch?v=p3NOsA8JKhI. Accessed 13 July 2013.
"Se celebró el foro 'Buen ciudadano Ibero.'" *Universia-México,* 16 Feb. 2012. http://noticias.universia.net.mx/en-portada/noticia/2012/02/16/912534/ celebro-foro-buen-ciudadano-ibero.html. Accessed 7 July 2013.
"#Somos ciudadanos, no consumidores." *Yosoymedia.org,* 28 Mar. 2013. www.yosoy132media.org/2013/03/. Accessed 30 Apr. 2013.
Tovar, Carlos. "Twitter: Peña Nieto se esconde en el baño de la Ibero." *Notigab,* 11 May 2012. www.notigape.com/?id=2669. Accessed 17 Dec. 2013.
"Tú eliges Mexico 2012." *YouTube,* uploaded 26 Jan. 2012. www.youtube. com/watch?v=TogsU5U9tDw. Accessed 13 July 2013.
Vargas, Rosa Elvira. "Hija de Peña Nieto causa ira en Twitter al renviar mensaje que insulta a críticos." *La Jornada,* 6 de diciembre 2011, p. 13. www.jornada. unam.mx/2011/12/06/politica/013n1pol. Accessed 13 July 2013.
The World Fact Book. Central Intelligence Agency. www.cia.gov/library/publi-cations/the-world-factbook/geos/mx.html. Accessed 14 July 2013.

"#YoSoy132. Asamblea General 30 de mayo del 2012." *YouTube*, uploaded by Comisión Registro, 3 June 2012. www.youtube.com/watch?v=Okn-AongWlUI. Accessed 13 July 2013.

#YoSoy132media official website. www.yosoy132media.org/. Accessed 13 July 2013.

#YoSoy132 International Website. yosoy132internacional.wikispaces.com/. Accessed 13 July 2013.

"#YoSoy132 Time Line Photos." *YoSoy132media Facebook*. www.facebook.com/photo.php?fbid=441131162564684&set=a.436984236312710.106068.436916642986136&type=1. Accessed 13 July 2013.

#YoSoy132media Facebook, n.d. www.facebook.com/yosoy132media. Accessed 13 July 2013.

"#YoSoy132, ¿dónde están ahora? ¿escondidos en algún baño?" *Terra-México*, 13 May 2013. noticias.terra.com.mx. Accessed 8 July 2013.

"YoSoy132 regresa a la estela de luz por su primer aniversario." *Terra-México*, 11 May 2013. noticias.terra.com.mx/videos/yosoy132-regresa-a-la-estela-de-luz-por-su-primer-aniversario, 471872.html. Accessed 13 July 2013.

"Yuriria platicó con Arturo Escobar, coordinador del PVE, acerca de lo ocurrido en la Ibero con EPN." *Cadena3*, 11 May 2012. www.youtube.com/watch?v=nV3-8PkbilA. Accessed 17 Dec. 2013.

Zapapta, Belen. "La visita de Peña Nieto motivo de abucheos de estudiantes en la Ibero." *CNN Mexico*, 11 May 2012. http://mexico.cnn.com/nacional/2012/05/11/la-visita-de-pena-nieto-divide-a-estudiantes-en-universidad-iberoamericana. Accessed 17 Dec. 2013.

Zapata, Belen. "#YoSoy132 ¿sigue vigente en la agenda nacional?" *CNN Mexico*, 10 May 2013. http://mexico.cnn.com/nacional/2013/05/10/el-legado-del-movimiento. Accessed 9 July 2013.

16 Interactive Projects from Colombia
Rethinking the Geopolitics of Territory

Claire Taylor

This chapter provides a comparative analysis of three recent interactive digital works by Colombian cultural producers of the mid-2000s: Juan Ospina González's *Juegos de Guerra Colombianos: Tácticas de Guerra Irregular* (2004); the joint-authored work, *Quiasma: Oráculo y Paisaje* (2004) by Clemencia Echeverri, Bárbara Santos, Santiago Ortiz, and Andrés Burbano; and Martha Patricia Niño's *Demo Scape V 0.5* (2005). It focuses on how all three of these works strive to provide alternative representations of the Colombian terrain and to provide spaces for reflection on Colombia's contemporary sociopolitical conflicts. In their different ways, each work attempts to make use of digital technologies and online space to provide a contestatory stance on Colombia's troubled recent history and enable, to varying extents, audience/user participation in the creation of alternative, resistant narratives.

Juan Ospina González is a Colombian-born web designer and web artist who studied in Bogotá and subsequently moved to the Netherlands. He is founder member, along with Juan Obando and Juan Ríos, of the countercultural art group, Bazuco Media Corporation, established in 2005 in Bogotá. Ospina González's art works range from offline art, including paintings and drawings, such as his *Guerras de dependencia* series of illustrations created for the 200th anniversary of Colombian independence and included in the *Our Business is None of Your Art* exhibition of 2010. His online works include his several "web toys," including *Flipbook!*, an interactive web toy that allows users to create their own frame-by-frame animations and publish them online, and *Sketch Star*, an animation toy aimed at creators of interactive games. He has also created interactive installations involving both on- and offline participation, including the installation for the *Ritratto di una Collezione* exhibition in Mantova, Italy, involving touch screens, projects and physical art works, and a physical installation adaptation of his animation toy *Flipbook!*, originally presented in the Centre Pompidou, Paris.

The particular work under analysis in this chapter—his *Juegos de guerra colombianos (Colombian War Games)*—is one of Ospina González's most overtly political pieces to date and one that is closely embedded in representations of physical place. It was exhibited as part of the *net art Colombia: es feo y no le gusta el cursor* (*Colombia net. art: It is Ugly and it Doesn't Like the Cursor*) exhibition of 2006–2007 and is an online work comprising several interactive narratives that each take a variant on the computer game genre. In this work, Ospina González mobilizes a range of different gaming formats, from pre-digital formats such as backgammon and Battle Ships to more recent digital technologies such as arcade games, and creates gameworlds in which the user/player takes on a particular avatar within the complex armed conflict plaguing contemporary Colombia. This contemporary armed conflict has parallels with an earlier period of widespread violent conflict in Colombia known as La Violencia (1948–1960s), which pitted Liberals against Conservatives and traces its roots also to the rise of rebel groups in isolated regions of the Colombian territory in the 1960s; the conflict escalated massively in the 1980s and 1990s following the emergence of illegal drug cultivation and the rise of paramilitary groups. It is this complex, fraught sociopolitical situation that forms the backdrop to Ospina González's work, as with the other two works analyzed in this chapter.

Here, Ospina González's shares impulses with the work of other Hispanic online cultural producers who have remobilized pre-digital gaming formats for contestatory purposes; examples can be seen in Coco Fusco and Ricardo Dominguez's *Turista Fronterizo* (*Border Tourist*), which reworks the board game format established by *Monopoly* and *Turismo Nacional* (*National Tourism*) into an interactive, critical commentary on the socioeconomic inequalities of the U.S.-Mexico border region, or in Spanish artist Cristina Buendía's *No-pasatiempo* (2004) (*Not a Pass-time*), which creates a digital version of the classic join-the-dots game to critique domestic violence. His work also shares concerns with the now-growing body of what has variously been described as "political game-art" (Wilson 269), "experimental game projects" (Crogan 88), "Games with an Agenda," "Serious Games," "Persuasive Games," or "Social Change Games" (Jahn-Sudmann 9), terms coined to describe gaming works that are "explicitly arranged as a critical, interceding practice in order to call attention to social problems in the 'real world'" (Jahn-Sudmann ibid). Here, Ospina González's concerns are never purely ludic; in fact, as my analysis that follows will show, Ospina González is less interested in the creation of a slick, sophisticated interface—in which the bond between player and avatar is seamless and in which violence is fetishized—and more in calling our attention to the internal contradictions of the gameworld and to the violence with which we are forced to become complicit. The paratextual features and the gameworlds in themselves all situate the viewer/user in the context of Colombia's contested terrain and bloody internal war. As will be analyzed in the following, the graffiti aesthetic in the presentation of text, the collage-effect graphics, and the use of post-digital sound function together to resignify the conventions of the computer game genre and to force the viewer/player to take a critical standpoint during gameplay.

This ironic, critical stance *vis-à-vis* the gameworld we are about to go into is evident even before we enter the games proper. As has frequently been noted in computer gaming research, paratextual features are integral to the experience of play and in locating the viewer/player in the gameworld (Jones 14), and *Juegos de guerra colombianos* is no exception. A variety of features in the opening page, employing a limited palette of white, black, and red, immediately alert us to the critical stance we are encouraged to take. To the top left of the screen, a black-and-white image depicts three male figures in a line drawing. The figure to the left represents a guerrilla, wearing a camouflage jacket, holding a machine gun, and with his face masked by a scarf. The middle figure wears a suit and glasses and stands with his arms crossing his body, the index finger of each hand pointing at the man to either side of him. Clearly a politician, this figure, although unnamed, represents Álvaro Uribe, President of Colombia for two consecutive terms from 2002 to 2010 and incumbent at the time of making of this work. The figure to the right of him appears to represent a member of the paramilitary forces, dressed also in camouflage, carrying a machine gun, and wearing a balaclava. This image thus presents for us—in a shorthand, reductive fashion—Colombia's contemporary conflict: Uribe as torn between two opposing forces and whose crossed arms indicate his conflicted loyalties. Splashes of red over his suit (otherwise depicted in black and white) indicate his implication in the bloody conflict that is tearing the nation apart; as a synecdoche for the Colombian government, Uribe's blood-soaked clothes here stand for the role that the Colombian ruling parties have in the decades-long conflict. Of course, the reality is much more complex, since there are many more than simply two sides to the conflict raging in Colombia; Ospina-González's image is deliberately reductive, and, as we explore this work, we see him constantly presenting two-dimensional characters that are then undercut.

Part of the undercutting of this reductive image comes in the textual detail given on the page surrounding the image. Above the heads of the two armed figures, words are scrawled in red font, but are indecipherable at the resolution at which the page is rendered; even if we change the resolution or the view of our browser, the image remains the same and the text unreadable. Similarly, cutting across the middle of the screen, directly below the title of the work, appears a strip of text in red font that is illegible at the preset resolution. It is only by playing around on the interface that we discover a hidden "zoom" function, located in the title of the work that runs across the center of the page. Right-clicking on this allows us to zoom in, and the text across the middle of the screen becomes legible, informing us "Si lees esto es porque has hecho zoom in" ("If you can read this it's because you have zoomed in"); in effect, the text has failed to inform us of anything. Over the heads of the two armed figures in the image, the text "izquierda" ("left") and "derecha" ("right") becomes visible; these two terms combine both a reference to basic computer game commands and an implicit reference to Colombia's political situation, with the polarization between left- and right-wing. What Ospina González is hinting here is that these two reductive terms—Colombia as being pulled two ways, in a battle between left- and right-wing forces—is no more informative than the other text.

If this is the hidden interactive feature of this page, a more overt interactive feature is located toward the top left of the screen. An image of a spray can, alongside an exclamation mark, is located in a comment balloon in red font, with the commands "graffiti control/grabar graffiti/limpiar/limpiar todo" ("save graffiti/clear/clear all"). This function of the opening screen permits the viewer/user to alter the appearance of the homepage itself; by using the mouse, we can position the spray can over the screen and scrawl our own messages, color over what is already there, and add our own images. Ospina González's tactic here thus explicitly invokes the countercultural tactic known as "digital graffiti" or "cybergraffiti." Involving hacking into a website's source code to change the homepage or leave a statement in the form of a slogan or an image, cybergraffiti involves partial defacement of a Web page, leaving all other information intact and so constitutes a "critical intervention in the hegemonic status quo," aiming for visibility as well as functioning as an "artistic expression of dissent" (Vegh). Ospina González's insertion of a graffiti function into his work, thus, means that he is actively inviting us to deface this image, to overwrite the reductive image of Uribe/the Colombian state as simply torn between two sides and to forge our own narratives over the top.

Indeed, this graffiti aesthetic is given further significance by another feature of the homepage whereby, before we can take up the spray can for ourselves, a preloaded statement is sprayed across the screen: words—in red, scrawling font—slowly appear across the screen, eventually spelling out "que mierda esto" ("this is shit").

The words appear in the margins of the "official" text that is displayed on the homepage, this official text being composed of the titles and brief descriptions of the seven individual games that make up this work. Here, therefore, right from the outset, Ospina González is encouraging us to critique, rather than play along with, the gameworlds he has created for us: whereas the titles and their descriptions encourage us to play (along with) the game, Ospina González's graffiti here warns us against this easy option. The *mierda* ("shit") refers to the works themselves and what they represent and puts the viewer/player on guard, deliberately *not* facilitating the easy insertion of the player into the game world, as would be the case with standard computer games.

If the opening page to *Juegos de guerra colombianos* thus presented us with an uneasy combination of two-dimensional or reductive images

Figure 16.1 Ospina González, *Juegos de guerra colombianos* (2004).

that are then problematized by other of the paratextual features, so, too, the main content via the seven links presents the viewer with a series of troubling, Manichean scenarios that are undercut by their deliberate presentation as two-dimensional. In each of the game narratives, we are figured as a member of one of the armed groups—either guerrilla or paramilitary—and forced into taking an active role in acting out violent scenarios between the two sides. Yet, at the same time, the way in which these game narratives are presented encourages us to start questioning the game world in which we find ourselves.

Crucially, the avatars within the games are deliberately two-dimensional cutouts, presented in collage format. Rendered in thick lines, using strong colors and little shading, each figure also has a jagged white outline clearly visible, as if cut from a piece of paper or cardboard. Similarly, when animated, the avatars are deliberately jerky; when moving across the screen, they do not walk smoothly, in a lifelike fashion, but are either animated crudely, their legs jerking forward or backward, or simply do not walk at all, but enter the screen in a statuesque fashion. These are emphatically not slick, lifelike figures employing the latest in computer animation to generate fluidity of movement and interpellate us into the game; instead, the figures are deliberately awkward, flat, and two-dimensional.

Ospina González's avatars thus overtly recycle commonplaces of the Colombian conflict: the use of deliberately cutout figures, jerky movements, and lack of realistic animation all point to these avatars representing commonplaces with which we are not encouraged to empathize. Similarly, instructions are given to the player in crude comment balloons that appear next to the avatar; like the avatar, the comment balloons are rough-hewn, with a jagged white space around them. There is, thus, a deliberate use here of awkward, collage-effect images; far from a slick computer game drawing us into a seamless gameworld and encouraging us to consume the violence fetishistically, Ospina González's avatars and backdrops are cutouts, deliberately awkward and jarring. At the same time, the sound accompanying these instructions is intentionally disconcerting; set on a loop, the sound is tinny and composed of fragments of metallic rasping sounds and screeching. In contradistinction to the standard voice-overs or diegetic sounds that would usually introduce us to a video game, Ospina González's sounds here are fragments of post-digital sound, representing the detritus of the digital age.

Such, thus, is the opening interface that guides us into the gameworld, and this sense of unease continues when we load the game proper. Of the seven games we can play, games 1, 2, 3, 4, and 5 take the same format: an adapted version of the Battleships board game, although inflected differently each time with a different narrative. The final two games, meanwhile, follow an arcade game format, where we use the cursors to move our avatar and the space bar to shoot. Crucially, before we can play each game, we are required to write ourselves into the conflict, by way of a red text box running across the foot of the screen, commanding us in uppercase letters: "ESCRIBE ACA EL NOMBRE DE TU ORGANIZACION" ("WRITE THE NAME OF YOUR ORGANIZATION HERE"). Only if we fill this out will the game load; it is significant that Ospina González forces us to acknowledge our own presence in the gameworld/conflict, before he allows us to play. Again, this feature forces us to take a step back and question our motives in playing the game and disrupts any immediate, easy identification with the avatar.

As we play, specific reference is made to the particularities of the Colombian conflict that inflect these game narratives. For instance, the second of these game narratives, entitled "Pesca Milagrosa" ("Miraculous Catch"), borrows from the popular term employed to describe the growing trend in Colombia for the indiscriminate and mass kidnapping of random victims from the late 1990s onward. Its original meaning coming from the Biblical tale—Jesus's miracle in filling the fishing nets of Simon in the Sea of Galilee, narrated in the Gospel of Saint Luke—the term has been corrupted in contemporary Colombian use to refer to tactics in which an armed group sets up a roadblock, stops every vehicle, and abducts those with the means to pay a ransom. According to Fernando Estrada Gallego, the *pesca milagrosa* (miraculous catch) has become one of the foremost metaphors of Colombia's conflict today and is an "estratagema discursiva que produce los efectos cognitivos de dejar "fuera de foco" referentes no deseados" ("discursive strategy that

creates the cognitive effect of leaving unwanted referents 'out of focus'")
(Estrada Gallego 27).

Ospina González's choice of title for this game is thus a highly charged
one, making reference as it does to this controversial practice, and the
game instructions specifically command us to "encuentra la carretera
aledaña y crea un retén para recaudar fondos para la revolución" ("find
the road to the village and set up a roadblock to generate funds for the
revolution") (2004). It is worth noting that Ospina González's version
explicitly interpellates us as a member of the guerrilla here, with the
specific reference to generating funds for the revolution; the game narrative is thus deliberately slanted to present the *pesca milagrosa* as a practice of the leftist rebel groups within Colombia. The reality, however, is
somewhat more complex; as Mauricio Rubio notes, the final phase of
kidnapping in Colombia that is represented by the *pesca milagrosa* was
the phase in which "se suman los grupos paramilitares al conjunto de
actores armados que recurren al plagio para financiarse" ("the paramilitary groups joined other armed groups in using kidnapping as a means
of finance") (25). Ospina González's rendering of the *pesca milagrosa*
here as an (exclusively) guerrilla activity is thus ambiguous. On the one
hand, the fact that the entire scenario is represented as a deliberate cutout and our avatar, if successful in creating a roadblock, appears with
a clumsy fishing rod are warnings that we should not take the gameworld at face value; in effect, Ospina González overtly oversimplifies
the practice of the *pesca milagrosa*, which involves tools far removed
from a mere fishing rod. Yet, on the other hand, the representation of
this practice as one exclusively undertaken by the guerrilla within the
gameworld is troubling and risks reinforcing the Manichean stereotypes
that depict the leftist guerrilla as the main perpetrators of this practice.
Ospina González thus plays with this highly charged "estragema discursiva" that Estrada Gallego had identified, yet rather than attempt
to demonstrate a more complex reality behind it, he instead critiques it
through deliberately presenting it as reductive and so refusing the player
any easy identification with its rhetoric.

Throughout this and the other six games that comprise *Juegos de
guerra colombianos*, the viewer/player is subject to an increasing unease
while playing. At various points in the games, we are encouraged to
"matarlos a todos" ("kill everyone"), to "dele chumbimba" ("fill them
with bullets"), and to take "venganza [...] en esta misión" ("vengeance [...]
in this mission"), yet the way in which the avatars are presented means
that identification with them is thwarted, and we become increasingly
disturbed by the violent rhetoric of the game commands. Here, Ospina
González's overall strategy is to disrupt any possibility for empathy with
the avatars (that is, with the violent actors in Colombia's contemporary
conflict) and so attempt to block us from identifying with the revolutionary or paramilitary rhetoric. Ultimately, Ospina González's aim is to

encourage us to take a step back, to refuse to play (along with) the game. That said, there is no other option to create an alternative scenario; our only way of contesting the logic of these Manichean gameworlds is by deliberately attempting to lose the game, since we cannot select an alternative response that enables us to construct a different, positive scenario. Ospina González's work, then, is bitingly ironic, but ultimately offers us no alternatives to construct our own, oppositional narratives.

In contrast to Ospina González's critical yet highly sardonic take on the Colombian conflict, the next work under analysis in this chapter, the joint-authored *Quiasma: oráculo y paisaje*, (*Chiasm: Oracle and Landscape*) takes a different tack entirely in terms of its aesthetics, portrayal of characters, and approach. Aesthetically, whereas Ospina González's work was clearly informed by popular culture, combining elements such as graffiti, computer gaming, and board game conventions in a visual format that spoke to popular cultural conventions, *Quiasma*'s interface is much sparser and draws on mathematical schemes of visualization. Regarding character, where Ospina González's work presented us with deliberately two-dimensional cutouts, refusing to create lifelike avatars, the source materials for *Quiasma* predominantly feature real human beings, captured in photographs, sound files, and video files taken in the field. Finally, in terms of approach, Ospina González's attempt to undermine revolutionary and paramilitary rhetoric by the use of irony is here contrasted to *Quiasma*'s highly serious tone in its attempt to bring to light hidden or disavowed interconnections in Colombia's complex sociopolitical makeup.

The project was developed by the members of *grupo Quiasma*, comprising four Colombian artists: Santiago Ortiz, Andrés Burbano, Clemencia Echeverri, and Bárbara Santos. Ortiz is a scholar and artist whose works explore the intersections between art, science, and artificial life, and he has in particular focused on the visualization of data, including his *Hipercontrol^3* (2007), a data navigation machine, *Atlas of Electromagnetic Space* (2008), a visualization of the radio spectrum, and *GNOM* (2005), a project creating digital and physical interfaces for visualization, navigation, and experimentation with genetic networks and which borrows from the *Quiasma* interface analyzed in this chapter. Andrés Burbano is a researcher and artist whose works include *Typovideo* (2001), an online ASCII video-streaming system that explored the relationship between communication, image, and technology; *Telegrama* (2006), a mobile phone-based artwork; and *Two Cycles/Dos ciclas* (2008–2010), a system for performances in the urban environment employing bicycles, laptop computers, and a mobile wireless network. Clemencia Echeverri is a scholar and artist who has worked particularly in video and sound installations, such as her *Cal y canto* (2002), a video installation narrating the hectic life of Bogotá and mixing images of poverty, street children, congestion, and public protest; *Treno* (2007), a video installation conveying a dialogue between the two banks of the Cauca river; and *Voz: resonancias de la prisión* (*Voice: Resonances of the Prison*), a video and sound installation at the Museo Nacional de Colombia, which was formerly one of Colombia's largest prisons and which captures images of the site along with fragments of testimonies from male and female prisoners. Bárbara Santos works with video art and multimedia art in a variety of roles, including directing, camera work, and montage; her recent works include the short film *Video turquesa* (2010) (*Turquoise Video*) that she codirected along with Guillermo Santos and Mateo Pizarro, her work as camerawoman on the 2008 documentary film *Son de gaita* (*Sound of the Bagpipe*) directed by Pablo Burgos, and her video installation *Video Pantalla* (*Video Screen*) of 2011.

The project on which these four artists collaborated and which is under analysis here combines the visualization of relations between terms via digital technologies, the representation of Colombia's contemporary society, and an attempt to rethink geography. The work consists of two interfaces, through which the user can access over 200 content files making up the work; these files are made up of still images, short videos, sound files, and texts, and the interfaces are accessed via an interactive DVD, as well as also being downloadable from the project website. The content material was created by the four artists and is, for the most part, based on real-life journeys made by the various artists throughout different regions of Colombia.

This is a work that, thus, very clearly knits together the attempt to present content through digital visualization techniques with the specificities of the Colombian terrain. In the description of the project, the four artists set out their aim as to generate:

un mapa de acceso propio, donde fue necesario repensar la geografía, dadas sus disímiles características y sus atomizadas zonas de riesgo. El proyecto Quiasma se inicia ante la sensación y progresiva condición de encierro que impone el conflicto colombiano y su excesiva mediatización. (Echeverri *et al*) [a map with its own access points, in which it was necessary to re-think geography, given its varied characteristics and its atomized danger zones. The Chiasm project started in response to the progressive feeling and condition of being trapped that is created by the Colombian conflict and its excessive mediatisation]

Here, the emphasis on "repensar la geografía" ("rethinking geography") is fundamental to the workings of *Quiasma*, since it attempts, as will be discussed in the following, alternative presentations of the Colombian national terrain by creative and multiple relinkings and visualizations. Significantly, its attempt to counter the "excessive mediatization" of the Colombian conflict can be read as a reference to the excessive reporting of *acts* of violence in the media, with a disregard for the *systemic* violence underpinning it. *Quiasma*'s attempt to uncover precisely this systemic violence will be enacted through the constant and multiple interrelations that the work sets in motion, interrelations that enable us to glimpse the structural violence so often disavowed.

This attempt at rethinking geography by creating a "cartografía de tensión territorial y emocional" ("cartography of territorial and emotional tension") or a "mapa narrativo relacional" ("relational narrative map") (Echeverri et al. ibid) is enabled through the two different interfaces with which the user can access the content material: *Oráculo* and *Paisaje*. The *Oráculo* (*Oracle*) interface comprises a black screen, over which the key terms are arranged in a circle; each individual term is an interactive link and, as we move our mouse over it, a number of colored lines show up, emanating out from the term we have selected and connecting up with other terms around the circle.

Here, the interface is in effect visualizing the interrelatedness of whichever term we have selected with other terms around the screen, and the bolder the line appears, the stronger the link between the terms. Some terms generate only one connecting line (such as the term "viejito" ("old man"), which links only to "representación de desplazados" ("representation of displaced peoples")), while others, such as the term "Álvaro Uribe Presidente de Colombia" ("Álvaro Uribe President of Colombia") have well over a dozen. Clicking on the button to the top right of the screen entitled "Ver todas las relaciones" ("View all relations") draws all the relationships for us; these are etched slowly across the circle, until we end up with a complex web/texture crisscrossing the entirety of the circle. On clicking on each individual term, the content file associated with each term opens in a pop-up window that appears over the circle, partially obscuring it.

The second interface, *Paisaje* (*Landscape*), provides us with access to the same content files, but with their interrelations visualized in a different way: although starting with a very similar black background and terms written in a circle in white font, a different interface is launched once we click on any of the terms. Here, the interface is a graphic representation of the relations between these content files rendered as a landscape in which hills and valleys are marked out in lines and the terms of the content files appear along ground level. As with the first interface, interrelations between the individual terms are again marked out in lines, but these rise upwards from each term in an arc and connect at multiple points beyond the limits of the screen. Navigating this interface proves a disorientating and dizzying experience, since movement of the mouse does not allow us to position the cursor over a particular point of the screen, but instead controls the velocity of the interface; once we move the cursor above the midway point in the screen, the content in front of us starts to zoom left or right, and moving the cursor further up accelerates the rate at which the terms speed past.

As we navigate through these two challenging, visually complex interfaces, meaning and shape is given to the content as much through the interrelations that are drawn as in the content files themselves. The content files themselves cover many of the traditional festivals, rituals, and celebrations of distinct regions of Colombia, ranging from the *Festival de la Cultura Wayuu* (*Festival of Wayuu Culture*) in La Guajira (files "Mirada" ["Glance"] and "Movimiento" ["Movement"], for instance) to the *Fiesta del gallo* (*Cockrell Festival*) in Chocó (files "Niños cantando vallenato" ["Children singing vallenato"] and "Ritmo" ["Rhythm"], for instance) and the *Carnaval de Blancos y Negros* (*Black and White Carnival*) in Pasto (files "Noche roja" ["Red night"] and "Orquesta" ["Orchestra"], for instance), while others simply depict the more mundane features of everyday life, such as street vendors, open-air markets, and the preparation of food. Many of the images are strikingly beautiful, such as the still photographs of "Bandarines" ("Bunting") capturing street decorations backlit against clear blue sky, while others are of grainy quality and depict violent acts, such as "Borrachos" ("Drunks"), a short video that captures men brawling and urinating in the street. This display of interconnectedness among different individuals in Colombian society aims to make overt the structural connections between these many and varied elements and so draw to our attention the underlying structural or, to borrow Žižek's term, "systemic" violence. As Žižek has forcefully argued, this systemic violence is "inherent in the social conditions of global capitalism which involve the 'automatic' creation of excluded and dispensable individuals" (12). Thus, in *Quiasma*—in contrast to Ospina González's tactic, which was, in essence, to lay bare the reductiveness of standard rhetoric about the conflict by overemphasizing the violent actors and making them two-dimensional—here the tactic is the opposite: the authors of *Quiasma* want us to focus not on the *violent actors* but on the *structural violence*, on the violence of the neoliberal system wreaking its work on Colombia.

Indeed, meaning is created in *Quiasma* just as much through the individual content of these files as through the narratives that we trace as we click on them and explore the many interrelations that appear. The file "Agonía" ("Agony"), for instance, consists of a video file depicting the suffering of a cockerel in the *Fiesta del gallo* (*Cockrell Festival*), via a close-up, in a long take, of the cockerel's head, its eyes shut, beak open, and barely breathing. In itself, then, "Agonía" appears to represent animal suffering in this particular festival, but, when we trace the various lines that arc from it to other terms, it takes on a more explicitly politicized meaning. The line linking "Agonía" to the file "referencia a desplazados" ("Reference to displaced peoples"), for instance, encourages us to make connections between these two terms and construct a narrative of the suffering of the estimated 3 million internally displaced peoples in Colombia at the time of making of *Quiasma*.[1] One of the most prominent issues in Colombia's contemporary society is the massive forced internal displacement that has been generated by the decades-long conflict escalated in the 2000s, making Colombia the country with the largest population of internally displaced peoples in Latin America and the second-largest population of internally displaced peoples worldwide, after Sudan (Carrillo 527). Here, our understanding of "agonía" thus is no longer that of animal welfare but a crucial issue of human suffering, which is directly linked to political instability, state policy, and the violence perpetrated by the many actors in Colombia's internal conflict.[2]

Similarly, other terms that are more explicitly politicized then encourage a rereading of potentially apolitical ones. The term "Alvaro Uribe Presidente de Colombia," for instance, opens up a short sound file that consists simply of a burst of applause; we do not hear Uribe speaking, nor any other commentary to make sense of this file. In itself, the sound file does not therefore signify, but when tracing the link to the term "hueco" ("hollow"), we are encouraged to interpret this as illustrating the emptiness of Uribe's political rhetoric. Similarly, following the line traced from Uribe to "Botas negras" ("Black boots") encourages us to establish further connections; this latter file, depicting a man's feet, clad in large black boots, treading down the earth around the head of a clearly suffering cockerel in preparation for the *Fiesta del gallo*, takes on a new meaning when linked to Uribe. Here, via the interlinking, we are encouraged to view the black boots as a visual metaphor for Uribe's presidency, implying that his famous "mano dura" ("firm hand")—excessive focus on security issues and strengthening of the armed forces to the detriment of social justice, in the eyes of some—is represented here visually by the harsh, thick boots crushing the earth. Conversely, we could also read the interconnection as implying how overt displays of masculine power, such as those displayed in the cockerel rite, subtend Colombia's patriarchal ruling order, as embodied by Uribe.

In these and the many other interconnections we trace while we navigate the two interfaces of *Quiasma*, we are constantly in the process of elaborating new narratives and discovering illuminating interconnections. In this way, user participation becomes central to *Quiasma* since, rather than there being a preset narrative and a teleological order in the presentation of materials, there are multiple entryways and exits, allowing the users to create their own narrative. Here, *Quiasma* makes use of the potentials of digital technologies that have been frequently noted by hypertext theorists to enable nonlinear readings and offer greater user participation (Landow 38–40 & 64–68). Indeed, the artists themselves have affirmed that their aim was precisely to "reunir un material diverso, fragmentado, lleno de interrogantes" ("bring together material that is diverse, fragmented and full of questions") with the interfaces attempting to make the user to "disponga sus propios límites imaginativos y de localización personal frente a lo que ve y recorre" ("employ his/her own imaginative limits and personal localization when faced with what s/he sees and travels through"), thus "invitando a crear nuevas formas de interrelación de relatos" ("inviting him/her to create new forms of interrelation between the stories") (Echeverri et al.). In this way, *Quiasma* attempts to provide us with new ways of comprehending Colombia's contemporary society, encouraging the user to explore multiple interconnections, construct alternative narratives, and so bring to light potentially hidden connections.

The final digital artwork to be considered in this chapter, Martha Patricia Niño's *Demo Scape V 0.5* is a web-based work combining a variety of interactive features, including clickable maps, feeds from Google, forms, questionnaires, images, and static text. Niño is a Colombian creative multimedia artist and scholar, and her works to date combine both web-based pieces and site-specific installations, including *Recorridos del cartucho (Travels Around El Cartucho)* (2003) an interactive system that provides personal testimonies of the district Santa Inés del Cartucho in Bogotá, historically one of the most troubled areas of Bogotá; *Hack-able Curator* (2007), a ludic curating program, based on an algorithm, that searches for images on Flickr; and *Relational Border Map* (2007), a web-based work that imaginatively combines a series of terms that provide links to external sites and constantly retraces new connections across the screen.[3] The particular work under analysis in this chapter, *Demo Scape V 0.5*, shares with *Quiasma* a desire to provide alternative visualizations of power relations within Colombia, although Niño undertakes this not through alternative mathematical mappings, but via a resemanticization of the map of Colombia itself.

The title of *Demo Scape V 0.5* is a neologism and plays simultaneously on political terminology, cartographic representations, and new media technologies. The first half of the neologism is drawn from the term "democracy," while the second half refers firstly to cartographic representations, where the suffix "scape," derived from the term "landscape" (which itself derives from the Dutch term *landschap*), is now commonly appended to words to indicate "view" or "mapping" (in terms such as "seascape," "cityscape," "mindscape," and so forth). The "scape" thus indicates visualization and mapping, a feature that we see coming to the fore in the work itself. At the same time, the term "scape" also clearly makes reference to the early web browser, Netscape, first released by Netscape Communications Corporation in 1994 and popular throughout the mid-1990s, and thus to struggles for control of media content.[4]

Niño's title thus obviously references democracy, but at the same time references mapping and new media technologies themselves. It is of no surprise, then, that these key terms invoked by her title—political regimes, the visualization of data through maps, monopolistic and corporate practices in the use of new media technologies—are then subjected to an extended critique throughout the work itself. The work is divided into five main sections, of which two in particular—"Funciones" ("Functions") and "Mapa" ("Map")—are analyzed in this chapter.[5]

The first of these, "Functions," sets out the purported features of a mock software package—the *Demo Scape v 0.5* of the title of this work. Short sections of text promote the functions of this spoof software in the left and right side of the screen, while the center of the screen is taken up with a large image: a map of Colombia, marked out in green phosphor font and set at an oblique angle. This font is one of Niño's preferred fonts and appears in other of her works: visually striking against a black background, it apes green phosphor screen-display font, typical of the iconic IBM 5151 monochrome monitors of the 1980s, which has now become a visual metaphor for computer-generated code. This particular font, then, brings into question the use of new media technologies, in particular questioning who has control over the data and what lies behind the surface of what we see.

In addition to the font, the orientation and makeup of the map itself give further indications of the fact that this map will be a potentially resistant one. The fact that the map is set at an oblique angle indicates that Niño's work will attempt to reposition or rethink the conventional cartographical contours of the Colombian nation and is also a signpost forward to what we later see enacted in the "Maps" section of this work (see as follows). As we move our mouse over the map to particular *departamentos* (administrative regions) of Colombia, URLs in white text appear, traversing the borders of the map; these links are to external sites containing information about Colombia, focusing particularly on issues relating to democracy, conflict, and social justice.

The sites to which these *departamentos* link range from NGOs, anti-war organizations, and think tanks to conference reports. For example, the two links that appear when moving the mouse over Norte de Santander, a region located in the north of the country and bordering Venezuela, lead firstly to a page on *Why-war.com*—a student organization set up post-9/11 to promote peace and nonviolence—that draws together a list of fifty-one articles that have been tagged with reference to Colombia. These

Figure 16.2 Martha Patricia Niño, *Demo Scape V 0.5.* (2005).

include those that specifically discuss aspects of Colombia's contemporary situation in detail—such as an Agence France Presse article of 2002 detailing attempts by the U.S. to request Colombia sign a waiver granting immunity for its troops before the International Criminal Court—and others that mention Colombia more briefly in relation to conflicts elsewhere in the globe, such as David S. Broder's article for the *Washington Post* in 2002, which discussed worsening relations between the U.S. and Europe and which mentioned U.S. troops in Colombia in passing.

The second of the links, meanwhile, loads a page on the Council on Foreign Relations (CFR) website; the page contains a report based on a session held at a conference in 2000, and the content of this particular link thus reflects official or quasi-official U.S. government approaches to policy in Colombia.[6] Viewed together, these two links force the user to bring together potentially conflicting viewpoints; the first draws together many articles openly hostile to U.S. foreign policy; the second represents a limited range of views that, essentially, focus on how best to implement U.S. foreign policy rather than challenge it. At the same time, as we read these very different articles, we see a common thread emerging that is mentioned in almost all links: Plan Colombia, and its effects on the country and the wider region.

Plan Colombia, the multibillion dollar package of U.S. aid for Colombia initiated in 1999 and approved by U.S. Congress in 2000, focused on a supply-side approach to combating coca production in Colombia, running to over five billion dollars by some estimates.[7] Given the complexities of the sociopolitical conflict within Colombia and also its strained relationship with the U.S., it is thus of no surprise that Plan Colombia has attracted widespread condemnation from NGOs, human rights associations, scholars, and the general public. Criticisms range from the impact the plan has had on the natural environment due to large-scale fumigation undertaken by private defense contractors (Erler 84; Dion and Russler 405), the overly militaristic nature of the scheme (Tate 54; Mugge 311), and the detrimental effects on human rights, due to the excessive prioritization of military aspects (Elhaway 395; Hylton 109).

The contents of these links in Norte de Santander, thus, bring up one of the most controversial issues in the recent history of U.S.-Colombia relations. As we peruse the various links and read the articles within them, as with the links from other regions in the map, our attention is drawn to the power relations that are mapped out, both by the content of what we read and also, significantly, by the technique by which Niño presents them. For, as we move our mouse over these links, the text of the links itself quite literally traverses the boundaries of the map; rather than fitting within the contours of the Colombian nation, these links traverse it, lying partially within and partially beyond the map. Niño's resistant map thus visualizes how the boundaries of the nation are being traversed in contemporary global politics; her tactic here is thus to resemanticize the map and resemanticize the very notion of the (hyper-) link itself, since the link in Niño's map functions, quite literally, as a linking mechanism, illustrating the hidden links between Colombian state policy and U.S. (state or corporate) interests. In this section of the work, then, Niño constantly draws our attention to what lies beneath or beyond the map, to the conflicts that are not rendered on conventional mappings of the nation, and to the power relations that go beyond the boundaries of the map.

The resemanticized map we find in "Functions" subsequently finds its counterpart in another cartographic representation in the "Map" section of this work. Here, we access once again a map of Colombia, again set at an oblique angle. Dozens of dots, in the same green phosphor font used elsewhere in this work, constantly quiver and move around the map. To the left of the map, in lieu of an explanatory key, we are provided with two sets of statistics; the first indicating the "población desplazada interna" ("internally displaced population") and the second indicating this figure as a percentage of the "población mundial desplazada" ("worldwide displaced population"). The figures that accompany these texts are not static, but instead constantly fluctuating, giving the impression of real-time data feeding into the statistics of the map. In the light of these statistics, we are thus encouraged to read the quivering and constantly mobile dots on the map as representing the flows of displaced peoples to and from the hot spots in the country. It is worthy of note that neither the fluctuating statistics nor the dots themselves remain still long enough for us to read them clearly. The statistics fluctuate so quickly that we cannot discern a concrete figure at any one point in time, with the percentage of the total population of displaced peoples worldwide varying somewhere between 12% and 13%. Here, the effect created by these statistics that never remain still is that the immensity of the situation is difficult to grasp and the population is constantly under threat of a shifting, never-ending process of forced internal migration. The ephemeral nature of the statistics here thus represents the ever-shifting boundaries of Manuel Castells's Fourth World under transnational capitalism, in which "multiple black holes of social exclusion" are generated through the uneven geography of social/territorial exclusion (169).

The dots, similarly, never settle and traverse Colombia's terrain, tracing paths in particular from some of Colombia's most troubled rural regions to its increasingly populous urban centers; they thus trace out the routes of internally displaced peoples (IDPs), which, as statistics have shown, predominantly involve the movement of poor rural peoples displaced from the countryside by violence to urban or peri-urban centers (Muggah 205–206). Other dots, meanwhile, go beyond the borders of the map, across the 640 km-long border that Colombia shares with Ecuador (although again, the country is not explicitly marked out as such on the map) and represent those who are forced into exile to escape the violence of the country, with Ecuador being one of the main destinations of Colombia's refugees.[8] Among these dozens of moving dots, three remain fixed, located in and near Cundinamarca, a central region that houses the country's capital; although not labelled, these dots presumably represent Bogotá, one of the main destinations for displaced peoples within Colombia.[9]

This map, thus, displays one of the most prominent issues in Colombia's contemporary conflict, which was also featured in *Quiasma*: the massive forced internal displacement that has been generated by the decades-long conflict. Internal displacement is directly linked to the country's sociopolitical situation, and yet, it is often sidelined in official government policy, with internally displaced peoples lacking visibility within national debates, creating an "official invisibility" (Villaveces-Izquierdo). Niño's alternative mapping practices in this work thus has direct relevance to the specifics of Colombia's contemporary sociopolitical situation. Her revision of mapping norms—the setting of the map at an oblique angle that refuses the primacy of the North-South axis, the resemanticization of cartographical terms, and the fast-moving data—all function to contest conventional mapping functions, but also, specifically, to contest the (lack of) representation of IDPs in Colombian national debates.

Niño's *Demo Scape v0.5*, then, presents us with a sustained critical approach to existing representations of the Colombian terrain and attempts, via a series of alternative mapping projects, to make visible the effects of that country's sustained conflicts. Niño's techniques of employing links and symbols that traverse the boundaries of the maps point toward the international dimensions of the conflict and, in particular, the role of the U.S. in shaping Colombia's national policies. The work combines a wealth of hard-hitting facts and harrowing stories conveyed in the many links it contains, with an attempt to visualize these facts and their interrelations through alternative, resemanticized maps.

In summary, the three works analyzed in this chapter have each, in their different ways, attempted to engage with the complexities of Colombia's contemporary internal conflict, awaken the viewer/user to the harsh realities of the conflict, and provide alternative forms of visualization. *Juegos de guerra colombianos* attempts to do this through a deliberately Manichean, ironic interface that does not allow the viewer/player to identify with the revolutionary or paramilitary avatars depicted, but instead take a step back and question the validity of their rhetoric. *Quiasma*, by contrast, attempts to do this by providing interfaces that allow for alternative visualizations of the Colombian national territory and offer multiple interconnections that illuminate the underlying structures of Colombia's society. *Demo Scape V 0.5*, meanwhile, creates alternative cartographies and employs hyperlinking to encourage the user to explore the human rights issues of Colombia's contemporary conflict and grasp how this conflict crosses national boundaries. All three works strive to engage the viewer/user, although the level of open-endedness varies from Ospina González's tightly scripted computer game narratives, right through to *Quiasma*'s attempt to allow users to generate their own narratives as they negotiate the multiple pathways and interconnections through the material. In each case, via very different tactics, each work has attempted to make alternative uses of online space and digital technologies more broadly in order to foment contestatory narratives that interrogate Colombia's contemporary sociopolitical setup.

Notes

1 The figure of three million internally displaced peoples relates to figures for the early 2000s, the time of making of *Quiasma* (figures cited in Villaveces-Izquierdo), although the figure has risen since then; Ibáñez and Moya cite Acción Social's estimates of more than 4.5 million people by August 2009.

2 Indeed, it is worth noting that the individual file "Referencia a desplazados" in itself turns a national festival into a politicized issue; the image in the file is in fact a photograph of a pile of dummies on the side of the road, in preparation for the Colombian tradition of *año viejo* in which effigies of the past year are burned in celebration of a better year to come. The position of the dummies alongside the road visually recalls, however, displaced peoples forced out of their homes and making a living on the roadside.

3 For a detailed analysis of *Relational Border Map*, see Taylor and Pitman (2012), chapter four, "'Civilisation and Barbarism: New Frontiers and Barbarous Borders Online."

4 For more on the broader context of the Browser Wars, which led to the demise of Netscape, see Chiaravutthi.

5 For a complete analysis of the other sections of this work, see my chapter "Questioning Democracy and Re-encoding the Map of Colombia: Martha Patricia Niño's *Demo Scape V 0.5*" in Taylor (2014).

6 Established in 1921, with its headquarters in New York and Washington DC, the CFR was highly influential on U.S. foreign policy, particularly during the Second World War and the first two decades of the Cold War era when it was at the height of its power, and has been the subject of critique from some parts for its the excessive influence it exerts on U.S. policy (see McMahon 445).

7 In a 2008 article, Dion and Russler estimated that the U.S. had provided well over four billion dollars (Dion and Russler 400) under the auspices of Plan Colombia, while in 2009 Tate gave the figure of more than 5.4 billion U.S. dollars (Tate 54).

8 Since the mid-1990s, hundreds of thousands of Colombians have fled across the borders to the neighboring countries of Ecuador, Panama, and Venezuela. Statistics cited in Riaño Alcalá give approximately 260,000 Colombians living in refuge-like situations in neighboring countries such as Ecuador and beyond (Riaño Alcalá 5). Formal applications for refugee status by Colombians in Ecuador totaled 27,851 between 2000 and September 2004 (figures cited in Moreano Urigüen), although actual figures of refugees are much higher.

9 Bogotá is the city with the largest displaced population in the country, followed by Santa Marta and Medellín; see table in Carrillo (532), for the full list of Colombian cities with IDP populations.

Works Cited

Buendía, Cristina. *No-pasatiempo*, 2004. http://2-red.net/nopasatiempo/. Accessed 27 Mar. 2013.

Carrillo, Angela Consuelo. "Internal Displacement in Colombia: Humanitarian, Economic and Social Consequences in Urban Settings and Current Challenges", *International Review of the Red Cross*, 91 (2009): 527–546.

Castells, Manuel. *End of Millennium*. 2nd ed. Oxford: Blackwell, 2010.

Chiaravutthi, Yingyot. "Firms' Strategies and Network Externalities: Empirical Evidence from the Browser War", *Journal of High Technology Management Research*, 17 (2006): 27–42.

Crogan, Patrick. "Playing Through: the Future of Alternative and Critical Game Projects", *Worlds in Play: International Perspectives on Computer Games Research*. Ed. Suzanne de Castell and Jennifer Jenson. New York: Peter Lang, 2007. 87–100.

Dion, Michelle L. and Catherine Russler. "Eradication Efforts, the State, Displacement and Poverty: Explaining Coca Cultivation in Colombia during Plan Colombia", *Journal of Latin American Studies*, 40 (2008): 399–421.

Echeverri, Clemencia, Bárbara Santos, Santiago Ortiz and Andrés Burbano. *Quiasma: Oráculo y Paisaje*. 2004. http://moebio.com/santiago/quiasma. Accessed 8 Jan. 2013.

Elhawary, Samir. "Security for Whom? Stabilisation and Civilian Protection in Colombia", *Disasters*, 34: 3 (2010): 388–405.

Erler, Carolyn. "Targeting 'Plan Colombia': A Critical Analysis of Ideological and Political Visual Narratives by the Beehive Collective and the Drug Enforcement Administration Museum', *Studies in Art Education*, 50:1 (2008): 83–97.

Estrada Gallego, Fernando. *Las Metáforas de una Guerra Perpetua: Estudios Sobre Pragmática del Discurso en el Conflicto Armado Colombiano*. Medellín: Fondo Editorial Universidad EAFIT, 2004.

Fusco, Coco and Ricardo Dominguez. *Turista Fronterizo*. 2005. www.thing.net/~cocofusco/StartPage.html. Accessed 27 Mar. 2013.

Hylton, Forrest. "Plan Colombia: The Measure of Success", *Brown Journal of World Affairs*, 17:1 (2010): 99–115.

Jahn-Sudmann, Andreas. "Innovation NOT Opposition: the Logic of Distinction of Independent Games", *Eludamos: Journal for Computer Game Culture*, 2 (2008): 5–10.

Ibañez, Ana María and Andrés Moya. "Vulnerability of Victims of Civil Conflicts: Empirical Evidence from the Displaced Population in Colombia", *World Development*, 38.4 (2009): 647–63.

Jones, Steven Edward. *The Meaning of Video Games: Gaming and Textual Studies*. New York: Routledge, 2008.

Landow, George P. *Hypertext 2.0: The Convergence of Contemporary Critical Theory and Technology*. 2nd ed. Baltimore: Johns Hopkins U P, 1997.

McMahon, Robert J. "A Question of Influence: the Council on Foreign Relations and American Foreign Policy. Review of *The Wise Men of Foreign Affairs: The History of the Council on Foreign Relations* by Robert D. Schulzinger", *Reviews in American History*, 13.3 (1985): 445–450.

Muggah, H. C. R. "Conflict-Induced Displacement and Involuntary Resettlement in Colombia: Putting Cernea's IRLR Model to the Test", *Disasters*, 24.3 (2000): 198–216.

Mugge, Zachary. "Plan Colombia: the Environmental Effects and Social Costs of the United States" Failing War on Drugs' *Colorado Journal of International Environmental Law and Policy*, 15:2 (2004): 309–340.

Niño, Martha Patricia. *Demo Scape V 0.5*. 2005. www.martha-patricia.net. Accessed 4 July 2012.

Ospina González, Juan. *Juegos de Guerra Colombiana: Tácticas de Guerra Irregular*, 2004. www.piterwilson.com/games. Accessed 27 Mar. 2013.

Riaño Alcalá, Pilar. "Journeys and Landscapes of Forced Migration: Memorializing Fear Among Refugees and Internally Displaced Colombians", *Social Anthropology/Anthropologie Sociale* 16.1 (2008): 11–18.

Rubio, Mauricio. "Del rapto a la pesca milagrosa: breve historia del secuestro en Colombia", *Documentos CEDE* (2003). http://economia.uniandes. edu.co/investigaciones_y_publicaciones/CEDE/Publicaciones/documentos_ cede/2003/del_rapto_a_la_pesca_milagrosa_breve_historia_del_secuestro_ en_colombia. Accessed 27 Mar. 2013.

Tate, Winifred. "U.S. Human Rights Activism and Plan Colombia", *Colombia Internacional*, 69 (2009): 50–69.

Taylor, Claire. *Place and Politics in Latin American Digital Culture: Location and Latin American Net Art*. New York: Routledge, 2014.

Taylor, Claire and Thea Pitman. *Latin American Identity in Online Cultural Production*. New York: Routledge, 2012.

Vegh, Sandor. "Classifying Forms of Online Activism: The Case of Cyberprotests against the World Bank" *Cyberactivism: Online Activism in Theory and Practice*. Ed. McCaughey and Ayers. New York: Routledge, 2003. 71–95.

Villaveces-Izquierdo. "Internal Diaspora and State Imagination: Colombia's Failure to Envision a Nation". *Categories and Contexts: Anthropological and Historical Studies in Critical Demography*. Ed. Simon Szreter, Hania Sholkamy and A. Dharmalingam. Oxford: OUP, 2004. 173–184.

Wilson, Laetitia J. "Encountering the Unexpected: Play Perversion in the Political Art-game and Game-art", in *Proceedings of the 2006 International Conference on Game Research and Development*. Perth, 2006. 269–274.

Žižek, Slavoj. *Violence*. London: Profile Books, 2009.

List of Contributors

Hilda Chacón is Professor of Latin American literature and culture in Nazareth College, Rochester, NY. Her first career was as a journalist, and she has experience in media writing, as well as in radio and TV production. She has researched and published about uses of cyberspace in Latin America, political cartoons in cyberspace, US-Mexico cultural exchanges in the global era, and gender issues in postwar Central America. She is currently a board member of the Northeast Modern Language Association, NeMLA (2017) and President of Feministas Unidas (FemUn)—a cross-disciplinary network of Hispanic cultures feminist scholars and an MLA-allied organization. She is currently completing the edited volume, *Online Activism in Latin America* (Routledge).

Sergio Delgado Moya is Associate Professor of Romance Languages and Literatures at Harvard University. He is the author of *Delirious Consumption: Aesthetics and Consumer Capitalism in Mexico and Brazil*, University of Texas Press (2017) and coeditor, with Tom Cummins and José Falconi, of *Conceptual Stumblings, a Volume on Experimental Art in Chile* (forthcoming 2018). His articles, reviews, and short-form essays are published in *Frieze*; *Film Criticism*; *Revista Hispánica Moderna*; *Revista de Estudios Hispánicos*, *Review: Literature and Art of the Americas*; and *HemiPress*, with forthcoming contributions to *Cuadernos de Literatura*; *Handbook of International Futurism* (ed. Günter Berghaus); and *Online Activism in Latin América* (Routledge, 2018, ed. Hilda Chacón). A book-length study tentatively titled "The Logic of Sensationalism: Approaches to Violence in Art and Literature of the Americas" is forthcoming in 2019. He earned a PhD in Spanish and Portuguese Languages and Cultures from Princeton University, Princeton, and a B.A. in Philosophy and in Spanish Language and Literature (Highest Honors) from the University of California at Berkeley. He was born in Tijuana, Mexico and raised in the Californias.

Carolina Gaínza Cortés obtained a PhD in Hispanic Languages and Literatures at the University of Pittsburgh; she has a major in Sociology and a master's degree in Latin American Studies from the University of Chile. She is currently assistant professor at the School of Creative Literature (Escuela de Literatura Creativa), Universidad Diego Portales (Santiago, Chile). She is also the main editor of the prestigious academic journals *Revista Laboratorio* (revistalaboratorio.udp.cl) and *Laboratorio de Escrituras* (www.laboratoriodeescrituras.cl). Her foremost research interests are related to digital humanities, digital cultures, and digital literature in Latin America; she has also researched and published on cultural studies, postproduction, posthumanism, and networks and subjectivities in the digital era. She is currently pursuing research on digital culture in Chile with a focus on music, cinema, and literature.

Omar Granados is an Associate Professor of Spanish and Latin American Studies at the University of Wisconsin La Crosse. He studied at the University of Havana and later received a PhD in Latin American Literatures and Cultures from Emory University in Atlanta. He is the author of numerous articles, translations, and chapters in edited collections and academic journals such as *La Habana elegante, Cuban Counterpoints, Letral,* and *Hispania.* He is currently working on a book entitled *After Fidel: The Cultural Work of Mourning in Post-Socialist Cuba,* which examines the rise of post-dictatorial narratives in Cuba through the study of trauma in films and novels from Cuba and the Cuban diaspora produced during the Raúl Castro period (2005–2015). At the University of Wisconsin La Crosse, Dr. Granados serves as the Director of the Institute for Latin American and Latino Studies. He generally teaches courses on Latin American cultural studies and Latin American and Latino film and literature, memory, and migration studies.

Emily Hind is an Associate Professor with the University of Florida and has published two books of interviews with Mexican writers, as well as a book of criticism on the *Mexican Woman Intellectual from Sor Juana to Poniatowska.* She was a Fulbright scholar in Mexico in 2015, and her essay on Rosario Castellanos won the Feministas Unidas essay prize. Hind has published more than twenty articles on Mexican literature and film in academic journals, and nearly as many chapters in books of collected criticism. She is hard at work on *Dude Lit,* a book about the performative aspect of Mexican men writers' literary labors.

Tori Holmes is Lecturer in Brazilian Studies at Queen's University Belfast, Northern Ireland. Her main research interests are in digital culture and the texts and practices of urban representation in Brazil, particularly relating to the *favelas* of Rio de Janeiro. She has worked on blogging by *favela* residents, and her current research focuses on web documentaries relating to urban change in Rio de Janeiro. Dr. Holmes has broader interests in digital ethnography, and ethical and methodological issues in interdisciplinary research on digital culture. She is a member of the Digital Latin American Cultures Network and one of the founders of REBRAC (European Network of Brazilianists working in Cultural Analysis).

Beth E. Jörgensen is Professor of Spanish at the University of Rochester, where she teaches contemporary Spanish-American literature and culture and courses in disability studies. Her research has specialized in Mexican literature, particularly the work of women writers and the genre of the chronicle, as well as representations of disability in fiction, poetry, and life writing. She is coeditor with Susan Antebi (University of Toronto) of the collection of essays *Libre Acceso: Latin American Literature and Film through Disability Studies* (SUNY Press, 2016) and the author of *The Writing of Elena Poniatowska: Engaging Dialogues* (U Texas P, 1994) and *Documents in Crisis: Nonfiction Literatures in 20th-Century Mexico* (SUNY Press, 2011). With Ignacio Corona (Ohio State University), she co-edited *The Contemporary Mexican Chronicle: Theoretical Perspectives on the Liminal Genre* (SUNY Press, 2002).

Claire Joysmith has worked at the Universidad Nacional Autónoma de México (UNAM) for over three decades. Her academic and creative work focuses on transcultural and transborder expressions, as well as translation, testimonio, poetry, self-narrative, and gender. Her critical essays, translations, and poetry have been published in volumes and magazines such as *Signs; 20th anniversary edition of Gloria Anzaldúa's "Borderlands/La Frontera"; Chicana Feminisms. A Reader; Forum for Inter-American Research* (Germany); *Debate feminist; Diálogo; Blanco Móvil; Voices Without Borders* I and II (U.S. National Best Book Award for Fiction & Literature, 2009), among others. She is the editor of *Las formas de nuestras voces. Mexicana and Chicana Writers in México* (1995) (UNAM '96 Award winner); *One Wound for Another/Una herida por otra. Testimonios de Latin@s through Cyberspace (11 de septiembre de 2001–11 de marzo de 2002) (2005); Speaking desde las heridas. Cibertestimonios transfronterizos/ Transborder (September 11, 2001–March 11, 2007) (2008); Cantar de espejos. Poesía testimonial Chicana de mujeres* (2012 & 2nd ed. 2014); *Nepantla: liminalidad y transición* (2016), among others. She is the recipient of the Sor Juana Inés de la Cruz Award, UNAM.

Eduardo Ledesma is an Assistant Professor of Spanish at the University of Illinois at Urbana-Champaign, where he teaches Hispanic and Lusophone literature, film, and new media. After a first career as a

Structural Engineer, he received his PhD in Romance Languages and Literatures from Harvard University in 2012. He is the author of *Radical Poetry: Aesthetics, Politics, Technology, and the Ibero-American Avant-Gardes, 1900–2015* (SUNY, 2016). His articles on film, new media, and digital literature have appeared in the *Studies in Spanish and Latin American Cinemas, Arizona Journal of Hispanic Cultural Studies, Revista Iberoamericana, Revista Hispánica Moderna*, and the *Revista de Estudios Hispánicos*, among other venues. He is currently completing a book titled *Cinemas of Marginality: Experimental, Avant-Garde and Documentary Film in Ibero-America* (under contract SUNY).

Mary K. Long (PhD, Princeton University) is Senior Instructor and Director of the Spanish for the Professions major in the Department of Spanish and Portuguese at the University of Colorado, Boulder. She pursues research rooted in a focus on the role of artists and writers in the nation-building projects of the Mexican post-revolutionary period. She has published on the intertwining issues of cosmopolitan vs. national identity, the chronicle and Mexico City, and sexuality and performance in the work of Salvador Novo. Her current research examines the tensions between "official" and "marginal" voices and genres in the quest for Mexican national self-expression up to the present, most recently with a focus on the tensions between creativity and consumerism in Mexican youth culture. She has also published on topics related to cross-cultural communication and cultural sustainability in the global setting. Long is the author of numerous articles and book chapters and is the editor or coeditor of three volumes: *Mexico Reading the United States* (Vanderbilt UP, 2009); *Teaching Gender through Latin American, Latino and Iberian Texts and Cultures* (Sense Publishing, 2015); and *Language for Specific Purposes: Trends in Curriculum Development* (Georgetown UP, 2017).

Esteban Loustaunau is Associate Professor of Spanish at Assumption College in Worcester, Massachusetts. His published work focuses on contemporary Latin American literature, film, and music as these intersect with issues related to migration, youth culture, subalternity, and Internet Studies. His current research project examines the possibilities and limitations of literary journalism, music and documentary film to represent acts of defiance and recognition by people who have had to confront social, political and economic expulsions in the forms of dispossession, displacement and violence in Central America's Northern Triangle, Mexico and the U.S.-Mexico border. Combining teaching with community activism, he has developed workshops and programs to empower Mexican immigrant families in the Midwest and, most recently, Central American unaccompanied refugee minors in New England. He is co-editor of the volume *Telling Migrant*

Stories: Latin American Diaspora in Documentary Film, a collection of critical essays and interviews with contemporary documentary filmmakers that addresses multiple ways in which Latin American immigrants to the United States and Europe imagine their fluid and at times contradictory notions of identity, memory, and belonging.

María R. Matz is an Associate Professor of Latin American Studies and Culture in the department of World Languages and Cultures at UMass Lowell. From an interdisciplinary approach, her current research and scholarship reflects an interest in transnational literatures and human rights, feminist theatre and performance in the Americas, and film studies. Among her publications are the book *Definiendo a la mujer: Cristina Escofet y su teatro* (Puerto Rico: Penelope Academic Press, 2012) and a coedited bilingual (English and Spanish) volume *How the Films of Pedro Almodóvar Draw upon and Influence Spanish Society* (New York: Edwin Mellen Press, 2012), as well as several publications in peer-reviewed journals and edited volumes.

Thea Pitman is Senior Lecturer in Latin American Studies at the University of Leeds. Her research focuses on the subject of Latin Americans online and, more broadly, digital, cultural production. This work is published in both article form as well as in the coedited anthology *Latin American Cyberculture and Cyberliterature* (Liverpool University Press, 2007; with Claire Taylor) and the coauthored monograph *Latin American Identity in Online Cultural Production* (Routledge 2013; also with Claire Taylor). She also has chapters on digital cultural production in the *Cambridge Companion to Latina/o Literature* (2016) and the *Cambridge Companion to Latin American Poetry* (forthcoming, 2017). Her current research focuses on issues of race and gender in digital cultural production, with a particular interest in (*mestiza/o*) cyborg subjectivities and the "indigenization" of new media by Latin American indigenous groups. Together with Claire Taylor (Liverpool) and Tori Holmes (Queen's University Belfast), she maintains the Digital Latin American Cultures Network blog (https://latamcyber.wordpress.com/), Facebook page (www.facebook.com/dlacnet/), and Twitter account (@latamcyber).

Juan Carlos Ramírez Pimienta is a Professor in the Department of Spanish and Portuguese at San Diego State University-Imperial Valley. His current research focuses on Mexican and Chicano popular culture, especially Popular Poetics and Border cultural and literary studies. Dr. Ramírez Pimienta is the author of the books *Cantar a los narcos: voces y versos del narcocorrido* (Editorial Planeta, 2011) and *De El Periquillo al pericazo: Ensayos sobre literatura y cultura mexicana* (Universidad Autónoma de Ciudad Juárez, 2006). He has coedited with Salvador Fernández the book *El norte y su frontera en la* *narrativa policiaca mexicana* (Plaza y Valdés / Occidental College, 2005) and with María Socorro Tabuenca Córdoba, *Camelia la texana y otras mujeres de la narcocultura* (Universidad Autónoma de Sinaloa, 2016). His research and opinions on topics related to narcoculture are often featured in national and international media outlets such as *El Universal, Milenio, The New York Times, Le Monde,* and *the BBC.*

Claire Taylor is Professor of Hispanic Studies at the University of Liverpool. She is a specialist in Latin American literature and culture, and has published widely on a range of writers, artists, and genres from across the region. Her particular geographical areas of interest are Colombia, Argentina, and Chile, although she also worked on literature, art, and culture from other regions. Within Latin American Cultural Studies, she takes a particular interest in the varied literary and cultural genres being developed online by Latin(o) Americans, especially hypertext novels, e-poetry, and net art. She has published numerous articles and book chapters on these topics and is the co-author of the recent volume *Latin American Identity in Online Cultural Production* (New York: Routledge, 2012) and author of the recent monograph *Place and Politics in Latin America Digital Culture: Location and Latin American Net Art* (New York: Routledge, 2014). She recently held an Arts and Humanities Research Council Follow-On Funding grant for a project on Latin(o) American Digital Art, which included a series of impact and engagement events and a book entitled *Cities in Dialogue* (LUP, 2016).

Scott Weintraub (PhD Emory University, 2006) is an Associate Professor of Hispanic Studies at the University of New Hampshire. He is the author of two books on experimental Chilean poet Juan Luis Martínez: *La última broma de Juan Luis Martínez: 'No sólo ser otro sino escribir la obra de otro'* (Santiago: Cuarto Propio, 2014) and *Juan Luis Martínez's Philosophical Poetics* (Lewisburg, PA: Bucknell University Press, 2014). He has published articles in numerous journals in the United States, Canada, Latin America, and Europe, and has edited an e-book on Chilean poet Vicente Huidobro (with Luis Correa-Díaz; Minneapolis: The University of Minnesota Press Hispanic Issues OnLine, 2010), as well as an e-book on digital poetry in Latin America (with Luis Correa-Díaz; Bogotá: Ediciones Universidad Central, 2016). Professor Weintraub has also edited special issues of and dossiers in several academic journals in the United States, Chile, and Norway, about such topics as the problematic relationship between literature and philosophy in Spain and Latin America, the literary and scientific figure of the membrane, avant-garde poetry, and electronic literature in Latin America, Spain, and Portugal.

Amber Workman has taught Spanish classes at Arizona State University and the University of California, Santa Barbara, where she was also Interdisciplinary Humanities Research Fellow. She received her PhD in Hispanic Languages and Literatures from the University of California, Santa Barbara in 2012. Her research interests center on Mexican contemporary cultural studies. In 2010, she founded the peer-reviewed journal *Textos Híbridos. Revista de estudios sobre la crónica latinoamericana* and continues to serve as the journal's Editor-in-Chief. She is currently working on a book on representations of reading and readership in contemporary Mexican film, literature, and popular culture. Her newest project is an online research institute dedicated to producing scholarly works of a collaborative nature. The project also serves as a public scholarship initiative that aims to share resources with the general public.

Index

Printed in the United States
by Baker & Taylor Publisher Services